TYSON

Also by Peter Heller

IN THIS CORNER . . .!

TYSON

IN AND OUT
OF THE RING

PETER HELLER

 Robson Books

This updated Robson paperback edition first published 1996
First published in Great Britain in hardback 1989 by Robson Books
Ltd, Bolsover House, 5-6 Clipstone Street, London W1P 8LE

Copyright © 1989, 1996 Peter Heller

The right of Peter Heller to be identified as author of this work has been
asserted by him in accordance with the Copyright, Designs and Patents
Act 1988

British Library Cataloguing in Publication Data
A catalogue record for this title is available from the British Library

ISBN 0 86051 982 1 (pbk)

Printed in Great Britain by St Edmundsbury Press, Bury St Edmunds,
Suffolk.

Contents

*For my parents, to commemorate their
milestones in 1995:
My dad, Milton, 80 years old – Oct 3, 1995
My mom, Phyllis, 75 years old – July 20, 1995*

Acknowledgements

NO WORK OF contemporary non-fiction can be properly completed without the insights, help and cooperation of many people with particular pieces of knowledge or information they are willing to share. Because many insiders have shared such knowledge with me but prefer to remain anonymous, I will respect their wishes. I offer posthumous thanks to my dear friend of twenty years, Jim Jacobs, who shared much of his knowledge of boxing with me, as well as many behind-the-scenes insights into the management of fighters in general, and Mike Tyson in particular. I also thank the late Cus D'Amato for the time he gave me during the final dozen years of his life.

Others who shared their knowledge and information with me include Camille Ewald; Jay Bright; Kevin Rooney; Jeff Levine; Michael Marton; John Halpin; Harry Markson; Mickey Duff; Bill Cayton; Steve Lott; Ted Atlas; Bob Stewart; Reuben Givens; Loraine Miller; Butch Lewis; Richard Stickles; Joe Bruno; Nat Loubet; Teddy Brenner; Steve Dunleavy; Holly Robinson; Tony D'Amato; Fred Chetti; Lee Bordick; Wallace Matthews; Tim Layden; Ernie Butler; Joe Mahoney; Paul Grondahl; Phil Paul, and Lee Pollock. In addition, I would like to thank Mike Tyson for the time he periodically allowed me to spend with him in Catskill from 1986–88.

Thanks are also due to my editor in Great Britain, Liz Rose, who did a wonderful job under extreme deadline pressure; to my friend and partner, Judd Maze, for allowing me to use him as a sounding board during the completion of this manuscript in 1988 and 1989, and who often kept me on the right track; to my colleagues at ABC News, Pat Roddy and John Snyder, who tolerated me during the writing of this book, and to my friend of more than twenty years, Edgar Rodriguez, who facilitated the transporting of manuscript material between New York and London. In addition, my appreciation goes to the Turnberry Isle Yacht and Country Club in North Miami, Florida, who provided wonderful ambiance during the preparation of a portion of this manuscript.

Although much of what is contained in this book was derived from first-hand interviews and research, the following sources

were of great help in filling the gaps, and use of them as research
sources is hereby acknowledged: for information on Don King:
Thomas Hauser's book, *The Black Lights*, (1986, McGraw-
Hill); 'Don King's Boxing Monopoly', by Jack Newfield (*Vil-
lage Voice,* September 13, 1983); Ed Schuyler's profile for the
Associated Press on February 17, 1989; Bill Brubaker's 'The
Fight Came' (pt. 2) *Washington Post,* February 20, 1989; 'Don
King's Tight Grip on Boxing' by Glen Macnow, (*Philadelphia
Inquirer,* June 26, 1988); *Mean Business: The Selling of Shawn
O'Sullivan*, by Stephen Brunt (published 1987, in Canada, by
Viking Penguin (Canada) Ltd). For information on Bill Cayton:
the Gannett-Westchester Newspapers profile by Bill Varner on
May 10, 1988. For information on Cus D'Amato: *Victory Over
Myself,* by Floyd Patterson and Milton Gross (published 1962
by Bernard Geis Associates); 'Fury, Fear, Philosophy', by
Norman Mailer, in the September 1988 issue of *Spin* magazine;
'Hail, Hail, The Gang's All Here', by Robert Boyle, (pub-
lished in *Sports Illustrated* magazine, February 20, 1961); *Floyd
Patterson, Heavyweight King* by Jack Newcombe, (published
1961, by Bartholomew House). For information on Ruth Roper
and Robin Givens: *Jet* magazine for June 22, 1988, and January
4, 1988; 'Robin and Marryin', in the August 8, 1988, issue of
US magazine; 'Tyson Turmoil', in the November, 1988, issue of
Vanity Fair magazine; 'The Lady And The Champ', in the July,
1988, issue of *Life* magazine, and 'The Woman And Tyson', by
Mitch Gelman and Jonathan Mandell, in the October 5, 1988,
edition of *Newsday.* For information on Jim Jacobs, the June,
1988, issue of *Handball* magazine; 'Really The Greatest', by
Robert Boyle, in the March 7, 1966, issue of *Sports Illustrated*
magazine; 'The Ring Leader', by Joshua Hammer, in the April,
1986, issue of *Manhattan, Inc.* magazine. For information on
the IBC, *Jim Norris And The Decline of Boxing*, by Barney
Nagler, (published 1964 by Bobbs-Merrill). For information
on the WBA, WBC, and IBF, 'Time To Clean Up Boxing
Again,' and 'Fighting the Rulers of the WBA', by Pat Putnam,
published in 1981 in *Sports Illustrated*; 'The Alphabet War,' in
the December 1988, issue of *Ring* magazine; 'The Fight Game'
(pt. 1) by Bill Brubaker, in the February 19, 1989 issue of *The
Washington Post,* as well as Tom Hauser's *The Black Lights*.
For information on Donald Trump, 'Flashy Symbol of An
Acquisitive Age', by Otto Friedrich and Jeanne McDowell in
the January 16, 1989, issue of *Time* magazine; 'The People's
Billionaire', by Glenn Plaskin in the February 26, 1989, issue of

the *New York Daily News*; 'The Billionaires', in the September 12, 1988, issue of *Forbes* magazine; 'The Art of the Steal', by Rick Hornung, in the August 9,1988, issue of *Village Voice*. In addition, the *New York Daily News*, including stories by Mike Katz and Bill Gallo; the *New York Times*, including stories by Phil Berger and Dave Anderson; *New York Newsday*, including stories by Mark Dionno and Michael Marley,were used as sources of corroboration from 1985 to 1989, as well as the magazines *Sports Illustrated*, *People*, and *Time* during that same period. Quotes from columns and articles by Michael Katz in the *New York Daily News*; Wallace Matthews, now writing for the *New York Post*, and Mark Kriegel; Greg Logan in *Newsday* and articles in *TV Guide*; John Saraceno in *USA Today*; Dave Anderson and James Sterngold in the *New York Times*; Mike Lupica in the now-defunct *National Sports Daily*; and columns by Pete Hamill and Jack Newfield were in the preparation of the final three chapters added to this new edition.

Peter Heller
New York City

Boxing is entertainment, so to be successful a fighter must not only win but he must win in an exciting manner. He must throw punches with bad intentions.

– CUS D'AMATO
teacher/mentor of Mike Tyson

1

Comeback!

Mike Tyson was back! Iron...Mike...Tyson. His more than four years of exile from the ring – three of them spent in prison on a rape conviction – were over. Unlike Muhammad Ali a generation earlier, Tyson's years of absence from boxing were not spent as a martyr to principle. Ali had chosen to sacrifice his boxing career during his prime in the late 1960s by refusing induction into the US Army because he did not believe in, nor wish to fight in, the Vietnam war. Tyson, on the other hand, was a victim of himself – his own arrogance, his constant flaunting of the rules and laws of society, his own belief that he was, indeed, not subject to those rules and laws. Finally, it had all caught up with him and in the early weeks of 1992, a jury of his peers had unanimously found him guilty of forcing himself sexually on a teenage beauty pageant contestant, Desiree Washington, in Indianapolis, Indiana.

Tyson went to prison in March 1992. He emerged three years to the day later, in March 1995. Tattooed on one arm was a portrait of Mao Tse Tung, on the other, a portrait of Wimbledon Champion Arthur Ashe. Both tattoos had been done in prison. He said he had read and learned while incarcerated, having been profoundly influenced by the writings of both Mao and Ashe. Tyson also announced that he had converted to Islam while in prison. Now, he said, he was returning to Don King, who would be his promoter, and that John Horne and Rory Holloway, two cronies from his pre-prison days, would be his co-managers. Of course, everyone knew they were King's men. They understood little, if anything, about managing a fighter. Not that the public really cared, any more than they did when Tyson named Jay Bright, a young man with little experience, as his trainer. Bright's qualification for the job – loyalty to Tyson. As youngsters, they had lived together in the Catskill, New York, home of Tyson's mentor, Cus D'Amato. Bright liked the theatre, and he wanted to be an actor. He never really worked much, never developed a career of any sort, spending a good deal of his time helping the elderly Camille Ewald, Tyson's surrogate 'mother', who owned the house. He had never trained any fighters. Now, he suddenly found himself the trainer of Mike Tyson.

After a period of readjusting to freedom, Tyson began preparing for the one thing he knew – boxing, and his eventual return to the ring. While he was gone, the title had become fragmented once again and in four years various Heavyweight Champions, both legitimate and pretenders, had come and gone – Evander Holyfield, Riddick Bowe, George Foreman, Lennox Lewis, Michael Bentt, Tommy Morrison, Michael Moorer and the rest. As Tyson prepared to resume his career, four men were recognized as heavyweight champion by the various sanctioning organizations – Oliver McCall, Bruce Seldon, Bowe and Foreman. The IBF title was vacant. King put a deal together, said to be worth $150 million, with the MGM Grand Hotel in Las Vegas and the Showtime cable TV network. What it boiled down to was this: Tyson would fight a series of undistinguished and overmatched opponents for the first years of his comeback. Who they were didn't matter, because Tyson would be the selling point of the fights. The vacant IBF title would be filled during that time by a fighter with ties to King. McCall, the WBC Champion, was a King fighter, and Seldon, the WBA Champion, also had strong ties to King. So, in 1996, when the plan called for Tyson to step up and regain his titles, King would have all the sacrificial lambs in place, and Tyson would win back the titles one by one and once again unify the crown. Foreman would probably not be in the picture. A Foreman fight would be a tremendous revenue producer, but Foreman swore never to fight Tyson if King was involved; moreover, King was opposed to Tyson facing Foreman, because the promoter was fearful of the potential damage the ageing Foreman could do to his meal ticket if he caught the short, crouching Tyson with his still-powerful uppercuts. As for Bowe, a big money showdown loomed somewhere in the near future with him, but not the immediate future, not while there were easy title pickings out there like McCall, Seldon, or even Axel Schultz. Jose Sulaiman, the WBC President who was always anxious to please King, had smoothed the way by automatically ranking Tyson No.1 in the world even though he hadn't fought in more than four years! It pays to have friends in high places. It also pays to pay friends in high places.

Somewhat unexpectedly, a new opponent for Tyson emerged on September 2, 1995. On that night in Wembley Stadium, the British ring hero, Frank Bruno, outpointed WBC Champion Oliver McCall over 12 rounds to capture the Heavyweight Championship in the twilight of his career. After three previous unsuccessful tries, including a KO loss to Tyson in 1989, Bruno

was, at last, a champion and a future rematch with Tyson would
be a big money earner.

Tyson had trained for his comeback in utter secrecy. Only his inner
circle had seen him in the ring. His sessions were off-limits to
reporters and spectators. For one thing, everyone knew there was
bound to be a layer of rust that Tyson had to shake off from the
years of inactivity, and that was best done in private. Secondly,
keeping Tyson under wraps would add an air of mystery, inject an
element of the unknown, whet the public's appetite to see Tyson's
first fight, or to pay between $40 and $50 on home pay-per-view
TV for the privilege of watching the comeback.

And so, on Saturday night, August 19, 1995, the celebrities,
the high rollers, the beautiful people gathered in Las Vegas. Five
months after his release from prison, this was the night of Mike
Tyson's comeback fight. Also gathered on the street outside the
MGM Grand Hotel were a group of women representing the
National Organization of Women. They were protesting Tyson's
appearance, carrying signs on a picket line that read 'Rape Is Not
A Sport' and 'Women Are Not Punching Bags'. Inside, gathering
at ringside as fight time approached, was a Who's Who of the
famous – Madonna, Tom Jones, Jim Carey, NBAA star Shaquille
O'Neal, Denzel Washington, Pamela Sue Anderson, Donald
Trump and Marla Maples, Neil Diamond, Francis Ford Coppola,
James Caan, Kareem Abdul-Jabbar – the list was endless. The
place was packed, a sellout of 17,000 on hand, with a top ticket
price of $1,500 for ringside, and the cheapest seats going for $200
face value. Of course, several thousands of the expensive seats
were giveaways to the casino high rollers and the celebs.

Tyson's fight was a ten-round non-title bout, but he, of course,
was the main attraction, even though there was a WBA Heavyweight title bout in which Bruce Seldon, looking uninspired,
pounded game but outmatched Joe Hipp and TKO'd him in ten
rounds. Ordinarily, that would have been the main event. But on
this night, the bout was just an appetizer for the main course.

Tyson's opponent was very carefully chosen. His name was
Peter McNeeley. Until he was picked to fight Tyson, even most
people who follow boxing hadn't heard of him. But he was well
qualified to be King's choice as Tyson's comeback opponent. He
was white, he was Irish and at 6' 2" and 224 pounds, he was
physically imposing. Moreover, he had a glossy record: 36 wins
against just one defeat, with 30 of his victories by KO (20 of these
in the first round) – never mind that all his opponents were

unknown, most of them with terrible, losing records. McNeeley was colourful, he could talk and he would be a dream at press conferences. He had attended Bridgewater State College, where he majored in political science, and he came from the town of Medfield, Massachusetts, outside the Irish stronghold of Boston. His main qualification for being Tyson's first opponent, however, was that everyone knew he would present no danger at all to the former champ, regardless of how rusty Tyson might be.

McNeeley was from a three-generation fighting family. His grandfather had been a boxer, as had his father. And there was an interesting irony. His father, Tom McNeeley, had fought Floyd Patterson for the World Heavyweight Championship eight years before Peter was born. During that fight, in Toronto on December 5, 1961, McNeeley, who did manage to knock Patterson down once, was himself knocked down eight times and KO'd in the fourth round. McNeeley senior, a 10-to-1 underdog 34 years earlier, was not a legitimate contender. But Patterson's manager, Cus D'Amato, was hand-picking Patterson's opponents very carefully, so Tom McNeeley got the nod and his brief moment in the sun. Now, for similar reasons, his equally outmatched son was getting a similar opportunity in the spotlight, and ironically it was against another fighter developed by Cus D'Amato.

Peter McNeeley was a 17-to-1 underdog at the Las Vegas books. But he was getting his chance, and a pretty decent payday. He was guaranteed $540,000. That was peanuts in comparison to what Tyson was said to be earning – $25 million! Twenty-five million dollars for a fight against an unknown opponent that most fans and reporters knew would not last more than a couple of rounds. On the other hand, McNeeley had no reason to complain. He was getting the opportunity to pull off an upset and thrust himself into the centre of the heavyweight picture. And while his $540,000 purse was less than 3 per cent of Tyson's, it was quite an improvement over his previous fight. In that one, just a few months earlier, McNeeley was paid $500. A Las Vegas newspaper polled 38 members of the media for their view on the fight. Twenty-two said Tyson would stop McNeeley in the first round. All of them predicted Tyson would win by KO at some point.

Now, the sun was setting in the Nevada desert. The lights in the arena dimmed, and spotlights began to swirl around the ring. The moment had arrived, the moment many had been awaiting for more than four years. Iron Mike Tyson was about to return to the ring to begin his second reign as the world's most dominant heavyweight fighter...

2

Little Fairy Boy

People who are born round don't die square.

LIVING ON THE edge, running the streets. That was what the young boy loved best. Even now, years later, it's where he loves to return to, where he feels free, where the sense of danger is a natural high, yet where he feels safe, because he knows the streets are his turf. He is a product of the streets, a creature of the streets, not the tree-lined suburban streets of lawns and private homes, not the neatly-paved streets of terraced houses and apartment buildings of the middle class, but the mean streets, the city streets of Brooklyn.

Mike Tyson was born to these streets. They were what he knew from the day he drew his first breath of life, June 30, 1966. It is always hotter on the city streets than in the country, and it always seems to be hotter in the ghetto streets than elsewhere in the city. It was already hot, July hot, when Lorna Tyson brought home Michael, her second son, to their tenement apartment in Bedford-Stuyvesant. In the streets, children ran free, ran wild, in and out of the water gushing all day from the fire hydrants, the only way to stay cool where there were no swimming pools, and no air conditioners to cool tenement apartments. His father, Jimmy Kirkpatrick, was a strapping black man 42 years of age, over 200 pounds, a construction worker. Jimmy, too, was wild, liked to run free; he never got around to marrying Lorna, so Lorna's maiden name, Tyson, was the one entered on Michael's birth certificate. There were two other children, Rodney, five years older than Mike, and, in between the two boys, sister Denise.

When Mike was just two years old, the family fell apart. Jimmy developed a heart condition and was hospitalized; when he came out he could no longer work. Unable to support his family, he felt strangled, smothered, boxed in. He needed to be free, so he left. The streets of Bedford-Stuyvesant are not a good place, especially for a family floundering without its breadwinner, its man, its father. For Lorna, with three children and no means of support, there was only one answer. Welfare. Public Assistance. That is how the Tysons survived. It was a comedown, for Lorna Tyson had education, but the burden of seeing to it that she and her children survived was a full-time job where they lived, so she couldn't work.

Things got worse, and around the time Mike was nearing his tenth birthday, Lorna was forced to move her brood further into the depths, to the section of Brooklyn known as Brownsville. Watts – Chicago's South Side – Houston's Fifth Ward – Fort Apache – the Bronx: some of America's most notorious addresses. Brownsville ranked right up there with the worst of them. In any jungle the strong prey on the weak. Mike Tyson was one of the weak ones. Small for his age then, he was an easy victim for the predators of this urban jungle. He spoke softly, with a lisp, so they called him 'fairy boy'. He was there to be beaten up. Even the girls beat him. If he had some money, they took it from him. If he was wearing a jacket someone wanted, it was gone in a flash, and all he could do was to run home and cry. Lorna cared about Mike, and she hurt for him. It tore her up inside when he came home in tears, but there was nothing she could do out on the streets of Brownsville to shelter him from the hurt, the humiliation, the taunting – 'Fairy boy, gimme that dollar. . . Fairy boy, run home and cry to yo' momma befo' I kick yo' ass.' But even at home he found no refuge. When Lorna was not there, Rodney took his turn beating up his baby brother.

In the winter, they slept with their clothes on. There was no heat, and no hot water. And sleep was uneasy, because they had to be always on the alert for smoke. Maybe someone would start a fire in another apartment to try to keep warm. Or maybe someone would set the building on fire on purpose. After all, if you got burned out, then the city had to take care of you, send you and your family somewhere to sleep that was warm, give you food, maybe find you a better place to live.

The family moved from Herzl Street to Amboy Street, and Brownsville continued to nurture Mike Tyson. His playground was the inside of abandoned tenements, or the empty lots strewn with rubble, broken bottles, discarded refrigerators, rusting, burned-out car hulks, bricks from the apartment buildings that had once stood on those lots. He saw things that no ten year-old should see. Junkies dead from overdosing. People beaten with baseball bats or shot with guns. Yet, shielded by his mother as best she could, his sister his primary playmate, he remained gentle, and therefore a victim, in the midst of all this violence, violence that his mother abhorred, that she hoped against hope she could keep him from succumbing to. What are the odds that a young boy could rise from a cesspool like this to become the richest, the strongest, the most exalted athlete in the world? 100,000-to-1? 500,000-to-1? A million-to-one?

Without friends, he turned to animals, and began to keep a pigeon coop. When his pigeons flew, the young boy watched them in the sky, marvelling at their freedom, their ability to soar above the filth and danger and rubble. He loved those birds more than anything; indeed, he would continue to raise and fly pigeons even when he became Heavyweight Champion of the World. He kept his makeshift coop on the roof of an abandoned building. Accustomed to staying out all night, sleeping sometimes in deserted tenements, now he sometimes stayed with his birds. These were his babies, just as he was Lorna's, and he loved them the same way. He stroked them, cared for them when they were sick.

Then, one day it happened: the turning point. Perhaps Mike Tyson would have gone on to become Heavyweight Champion of the World ten years later had it not occurred. Who knows? There have been several turning points in his life, without which, by his own admission, he would probably have ended up in jail instead of winning the most coveted individual title in sport. For young Mike Tyson, the little 'fairy boy' of Brownsville, this was certainly the first of those decisive moments. A teenager, the kind of anonymous punk that the neighbourhood breeds so well, approached him at his pigeon coop. He didn't want the birds, had no interest in them. He was just out for some fun at the expense of someone weaker, smaller and helpless. He grabbed one of the pigeons. Mike pleaded with him to give it back, to let it go, but the older boy just laughed, and taunted him with the bird. Then, suddenly, the boy took the pigeon's head and twisted it around until its neck snapped and the head was torn off. He tossed the lifeless body at Mike's feet and watched as its legs and wings twitched, even with its head gone. In an instant, without thinking, just reacting, Mike pounced on the bigger boy. For the first time in his life, he fought back. Someone had unknowingly crossed over the line, and from that moment on there would never be any return for Mike Tyson to the meek little kid he had been. Fighting was new to him, he didn't know what to do, but his instincts, his blind rage, the surge of revulsion at what this boy had done, his fear, his pent-up emotions, all spilled over, and he attacked like a cornered animal, gouging, pulling, kicking, punching. He would admit, many years later, that he loved the feeling, that he still relished the memory of it. It was the first time he emerged triumphant by using his fists.

As Mike's reputation in the streets spread, he was no longer regarded as the lisping, effeminate little 'fairy boy'. He gained a new respect, he could sense it, and it gave him a feeling of acceptance, of self-worth as judged by the law of the streets. Suddenly, as he began to run with a gang called the Jolly Stompers, the streets were his turf. Bristol Park. . .Pitkin Avenue. . .Rockaway Avenue. . .Herzl Street. . .Lincoln Terrace Park. . . . all of it, all of Brownsville, was now his territory. He was a gladiator, a warrior; the prey had now become the predator, getting his thrills from making others his victims. He got a natural high, taking from others. He was eleven years old, and rapidly becoming a cunning street criminal. His sister recalls that he became one of the best pickpockets in Brooklyn, able to remove a wallet, or a wristwatch, so deftly as to go completely undetected. Sometimes it was a less sophisticated theft just snatching a necklace or a gold chain from someone's neck, and running.

In Public School 396, he was so poor that teachers sometimes gave him shoes, and when they wore out, he had to put cardboard inside them to cover the holes. However, with the money from his crimes, he could now buy his own shoes, and have cash in his pocket. Never mind that he caused his mother grief and anguish over whether he would kill someone – or wind up dead in the gutter himself. Then Mike and his gang graduated to holding up stores. There were small neighbourhood markets, and the storefront cheque-cashing service where they could lie in wait for those newly-flush with cash. Mike was still only eleven, too small to handle a gun, so he was the bagman, loading up their spoils and then running. Sometimes the police would come, and the gang would scatter, Mike running, his heart pumping with fear and exhilaration as the adrenalin raced through his veins, using his turf, his streets, as a familiar sanctuary, ducking into the burned-out shell of a windowless, deserted building, darting up the stairs into an abandoned apartment, scattering the rats and vermin as he hid, safe from the police, who prudently refrained from risking their lives in vacant tenements at twilight. He would sit quietly and wait, feeling his heart pounding inside his chest, enjoying the sexual charge of doing wrong, of being chased, and of escaping. Later in life, he would tell interviewers that though he did bad things, in his heart he was good, implying, somehow, through some convoluted reasoning, that his behaviour should be excused, because inside he was pure. But neighbours remember that he was 'a bad-ass kid'. When he wasn't with his gang, he'd commit his crimes solo. In the opinion of one young woman who grew up with him in Brooklyn, 'That boy is a devil. You can see the devil in his eyes. He always was bad. I don't care how much money he makes, he'll always be a devil, he'll always be evil.'

Escape from the police was not possible every time, and Mike began to get caught. However, there are more street criminals, more youthful offenders and juvenile delinquents than there are places to house them, and the system is too overloaded to deal effectively with all the under-age recidivists who plague the sidewalks. When Mike was caught, he would be sent to various juvenile detention centres in Brooklyn, only to escape or be released, sent home to his mother who asked him, 'Why? *Why*?' And then, to return to his now familiar way of life, a life he had learned to love. He knew he would be caught again, knew that if he lived long enough it was only a matter of time before he ended up in a prison cell, but he liked what he was doing too much to stop.

He would wait by bus stops, and as the buses began to pull away from the curb, reach in through the open windows and pull chains off women's throats. He would offer to help women loaded down with groceries to carry their bags, then hand them back and grab their purses. He and his gang of Jolly Stompers would roll drunks at night, take their money, and pull the rings from their fingers and the watches from their wrists. Tyson blames no one else for his behaviour. 'I wasn't sucked in by anyone else. I wanted to be sucked in,' he has said.

Now he was nearly 12 years old, getting bigger, and now he could handle a gun. A pistol replaced his fists; a pistol was much more of a status symbol in Brownsville, and putting a pistol in a shopkeeper's face was even more of a kick. Now he was playing for higher stakes. But higher stakes carry higher risks, and the next time he was caught he finished up in the Spofford Detention Center in the Bronx, and escape from Spofford was tougher than Mike anticipated, and so there he stayed.

Muhammad Ali was then the Heavyweight Champion of the World, and one day he came to visit the kids in Spofford. Mike Tyson saw Ali in the flesh that day for the first time.

Like everyone else, he knew the legend from television, the magazines, but here he was, larger than life, close enough for Mike to reach out and touch, being mobbed by the screaming kids, giving out autographs, talking to them about being good, doing right, leading good lives when they left there. Mike saw the way people responded to him, looked up to him, listened to him. He saw the smiling faces of the guards, the counsellors as they looked at Ali, and he said to himself, 'That's what I want to be, I want to be champ of the world some day.' And then, Ali was gone, and Mike returned to reality.

By now, his past had caught up with him. Barely twelve years old, he already had a rap sheet that might have belonged to a much older offender. Lorna could not handle him, hard as she tried, and he was becoming increasingly dangerous. It was decided that it would be best for all concerned if Mike was removed from the streets of Brownsville for a good while. He was sentenced to be incarcerated at the Tryon School for Boys in the mountains of upstate Johnstown, New York, nearly two hundred miles from the hollow tenement skeletons and cracked pavements of his beloved Brooklyn streets.

3

The Discoverer

There are very few new things in this world, very few. That's why people that are young, if they're smart, try to profit from the experience of an older guy so they won't have to go through all the pain and suffering. But a certain amount of pain and suffering is good, because it makes a person think they've learned.

– Cus D'Amato

THE FORMAL STRUCTURE at Tryon was a new experience for Mike, and one he didn't take to very well. To all intents and purposes Tryon was a prison, although it was not called so because those sent there were not adults in the eyes of the law. There were three so-called 'open' cottages, where the boys had privileges and discipline was relatively relaxed. Then there was Elmwood, the confined cottage, where the kids who made trouble, the kids who needed a tight rein, were sent. Before long, Mike Tyson would be headed for Elmwood.

During his first weeks at Tryon, he began to lash out. He had little confidence in himself, and he was on new, unfamiliar ground, where instinct told him he had to establish himself. As the psychological counsellors put it, Mike began 'acting out'. First it was fights with the other boys, then it escalated to threatening a teacher – anything to make himself look good in the eyes of his peers.

One theory is that kids who act out like this are asking to be disciplined, asking for some order to be imposed on their lives and on their inner turmoil. Perhaps this is what Mike Tyson was crying out for. But there may have been another reason why he wanted to be sent to the disciplinary cottage. He had heard that one of the head counsellors at Elmwood had been a fighter, and a pretty good one at that. His name was Bobby Stewart. Five years earlier, in 1974, Stewart had won the US National Golden Gloves Light-Heavyweight Championship by defeating Michael Dokes. (Dokes would later go on to win the WBA Heavyweight Championship of the World.) Bobby Stewart turned pro, had a modest career of a dozen fights or so, most of them in small towns like Latham, New York, and then quit and went to work for the Tryon School, not far from his home in upstate New York. Mike Tyson remembered that day that Muhammad Ali came to Spofford in the Bronx, remembered how he'd thought how great it would be if he could be a champion some day, too. Maybe a guy like Bobby Stewart held the key, could show him, teach him. He wanted to meet Stewart, he told one of his counsellors.

By accident, by design, or by a fortuitous mixture of both, he got that chance before long. One day he beat up another kid, and went into a rage. It took several guards to subdue him. Bob Stewart recalls the first time he saw Tyson, two of the biggest guards at Tryon were escorting him over to Elmwood, the 'bad cottage'. It happened to be during Stewart's shift. Tyson was placed in a 'secure room' with people assigned to watch him. 'Be careful of this kid', one of the guards who had brought Tyson over said. 'He's trouble. He beats the kids up, he'll attack anybody.'

Immediately, Tyson told those assigned to watch him that he wanted to talk to Bobby Stewart, but Stewart decided to let him cool down for a while and then see what happened. The next day, Tyson's overseers reported to Stewart. For a complete animal, such as they had been warned he was, he had been amazingly well behaved; he had not caused any trouble. So Stewart ordered that Tyson be shifted from his secure room into the general living area of Elmwood, though he was still kept isolated from the other boys. Tyson kept asking to speak to Stewart. Another day passed. All three shifts reported back to Stewart that Tyson had been well behaved, had done every-thing they'd asked, had caused no trouble. Stewart was satisfied – to a point. He decided to bypass the standard procedure in his first encounter with Tyson. To establish his dominance, to test Tyson's motives, he would skip the psychologically-approved, kid-gloves approach. Instead, he went up to Tyson's window and startled the boy by banging on it and shouting, 'I'm Stewart. What the fuck do you want?' Tyson responded, 'I want to talk to you. I want to be a fighter.' 'So do the rest of these assholes around here,' Stewart screamed back, 'but they can't even clean up their own act. You keep your act straight, and maybe in a week or two we'll see what happens.'

From that day on, Tyson was a model inmate. Stewart was astonished by the radical change in his behaviour, considering the reports he'd received about the boy's constant flare-ups prior to coming to Elmwood. Finally, Stewart told him, 'I'll work with you, teach you to box, if you behave yourself in school. Don't fool with the teachers, don't mess with the other

students. I want you to try. I don't care if you flunk every subject, but you pay attention and you try.'

Stewart still had a lesson to teach Tyson. The first time he
boxed with the youngster, he wanted to make a point, to give
the young bully a taste of his own medicine. With the other boys
watching, 'He tried to humiliate me so the other kids would see
I was nothing,' Tyson recalled. 'He hit me in the body and I
went down. My air stopped. I thought I was dead.' Stewart had
made his point. There would be no need to repeat it.

Stewart began to work with him in the afternoons, teaching him some moves, footwork, and began to win the boy's
confidence. Tyson had come from an environment where the
only white people he had interacted with were those he was
in conflict with: school authorities, police, court officers and
judges, detention-home officials. He mistrusted them. He was
withdrawn, sullen, branded by the school authorities as having a violent personality. Stewart could sense that Mike was
embarrassed because he could not read or write. Here was
this boy in a man's body, 5'8", 190 pounds, yet mentally still
a child. Stewart could nevertheless sense there was a spark
there, an intelligence, that just needed to be nurtured. He
went to another kid at Elmwood and asked him for a favour.
This boy, also black, was pretty clever. Stewart asked him to
work with Mike, to help him with his reading skills.

One day, Stewart went to the school psychiatrist to read
Tyson's file. He saw that Mike was classified as 'borderline
retarded'. Mike was very slow mentally, the psychiatrist told
him. 'He's not very slow at all,' Stewart said. 'How did they
determine he's borderline retarded?' 'We tested him, reading
and writing test,' was the response. Stewart exploded. 'He can't
read and write! How can you determine he's retarded if he
can't read and write?' He stormed out.

Stewart continued his work with Mike in his own way, and the
results quickly became apparent. After about a month, he got
a call from Tyson's teacher. 'Whatever happened to this kid?'
the teacher asked. 'He has no more problems, he's trying hard,
his behaviour has completely changed.' In three months, Tyson
had improved his reading abilities by three grade levels.

Physically, as well as mentally, Tyson continued to grow over
those final months of 1979. He was up over 200 pounds, all
solid muscle packed on a frame still just 5'8" tall. The first
time Stewart put him on a weight bench, Mike bench-pressed
250 pounds ten times, something most men can't do once in a

lifetime. Stewart spoke by phone periodically to Lorna Tyson in Brooklyn. 'Mrs Tyson,' he would tell her, 'this kid is changing himself.' She would just laugh, only half believing him. 'She sounded like a nice woman,' Stewart would later recall. 'She did care about the kid. She tried to keep him in line. According to records, she was a registered nurse, had gone to school. But when the old man took off, she couldn't raise the kids and work, so she went on welfare.'

1979 turned to 1980. Mike Tyson was 13½ years old. By now, Stewart had realized that Tyson's interest in boxing was not a passing phase. He saw real talent emerging, talent that he had neither the time nor the skills to continue developing. He'd seen a dramatic change in the boy over the months. 'The thing that impressed me the most,' Stewart recalls, 'was not the physical part, but his ability to . . . give up all the bullshit . . . he'd done for thirteen years to devote himself to something else. The physical stuff impressed me, but the mental stuff shocked the shit out of me.' Stewart brought Tyson down to Matt Baranski's gym in Albany and showed him to Baranski. Later, Baranski would work as Tyson's cut-man from the outset of his pro career all the way through his heavyweight title matches. Both Baranski and Stewart knew there was one person who could assess this burgeoning phenomenon: the legendary – and controversial – boxing manager, Cus D'Amato, who was then, at the age of 72, living in semi-retirement in the little town of Catskill, New York, where he ran a gym for amateur kids to train. Stewart knew about the programme he ran for the kids, knew that some of them actually lived in the big white Victorian house overlooking the Hudson River that Cus shared with Camille Ewald. If you seriously wanted to learn and you toed the line, you could live with Cus, go to school in town, learn how to box.

It was a Monday when Stewart phoned D'Amato in Catskill and asked him for the favour. 'Cus, I've got a kid up here I'd like you to look at. He's pretty good.'

That night, Stewart sat Tyson down and told him where they were going the next evening. 'Mike,' he said, 'Cus is the guy who made Floyd Patterson the Heavyweight Champ of the World. When I was a fighter I was able to fight on international teams. I travelled all over the United States, I went to South America, to Canada, all for free, man, because I was a fighter. Mike, you can do the same if you want to. Maybe you can better yourself through boxing. You're good, you've got talent.' Tyson listened, a little dubious about the whole thing, yet at the same time excited. Maybe he could really become a fighter. Maybe he could.

Stewart knew that the boy was good – at least, that he had potential. But Tyson would have to make an impression on D'Amato that first night they went to Catskill. There were a few moves he knew would impress Cus if Mike was able to perform them the next night, a few tricks, smart manoeuvres in the ring that a veteran fighter would know, moves that D'Amato was sure to notice in a 13-year-old kid. Some of the moves, such as how to slip out of a corner a certain way, were techniques Stewart knew Cus taught, so they were sure to catch the eye of the old man. He spent the evening showing them to Mike, then making him repeat them over and over until it was time for lights out, and for Stewart to head home.

All was quiet that night until about 3:30 in the morning, when the silence was broken by noises coming from Tyson's room. A couple of counsellors headed down the hall to see what was the matter. From inside the room came grunting, snorting sounds. When they opened the door, the counsellors found Mike in the pitch dark, shadow-boxing, rehearsing, practising the moves Bobby Stewart had shown him hours earlier. Mike Tyson was ready to impress Cus D'Amato.

On Tuesday evening, a March night in 1980, Stewart and Tyson made their fateful drive from Johnstown to Catskill, a journey of about 75 miles. They stopped at the house to pick up Cus, and Tyson had never seen anything quite like it. 'What am I gonna do here?' he asked Stewart, 'Sweep the floors?' 'No, Mike. You can live here if you want to,' said Stewart. 'If you behave yourself.'

They went over to the small gym above the police station that was the Catskill Boxing Club. With D'Amato was his young trainer, Teddy Atlas, and the one professional fighter under his wing, Kevin Rooney, both of whom lived in the house that had become a sort of fighters' dormitory. The three men were immediately sceptical of Tyson's age: how could those 210 pounds of rippling muscle compressed into that stocky frame belong to a 13-year-old? In any case, it was one thing for a young fighter to show off his physique, to look good hitting the bag or shadow-boxing; Mike Tyson had to be tested under fire. If he passed the test, Atlas knew that it would be a long time before D'Amato would put him in a ring again to box, that first a long teaching and conditioning process would have to take place. But a new fighter must first be tested mentally, in the ring, much as a young bull is tested on the farm to see if he has what it takes to fight on a Sunday afternoon in the Plaza de Toros in Madrid. Both must demonstrate that they at least have the potential in their character not to falter later on, when hundreds or thousands are watching, and the moment of truth arrives.

D'Amato decided that Tyson should box with Stewart, who at 27 was still in his physical prime. His active ring career had ended recently enough for him still to be able to perform at a professional level, yet he was mature enough to know that his job was to allow Tyson to show what he was capable of without egotistically trying to outdo this raw, green kid in order to make himself look good. At about 180 pounds, Stewart was outweighed by Tyson by some 30 pounds. But his vast experience as a national amateur champion and in the professional ring, as well as the fact that he was facing a kid literally half his age, should easily overcome the weight advantage Tyson possessed.

When the bell rang, Tyson came at Stewart very aggressively. Certainly he was trying to impress his select audience, but it was immediately apparent that there was a resolve, a determination in this young boy that was somewhat unique. And then there was the power – the power that in a few years would intimidate opponents before they even entered the ring to face him. It was obvious that first night. Tyson fired shots to Stewart's ribs. He was too experienced to show it, but later Stewart told them it felt as though his ribs were breaking. And there was a quickness, a cat-like speed of reflex that was also unusual in an untrained, unschooled fighter. Tyson refused to take a backwards step. He kept coming forward with such a raw power, such grit and determination, that Stewart was forced to do something they all thought the ring generalship would make unnecessary – he was compelled for his own preservation to open with force on Tyson to keep the young fighter off him. One of the shots Stewart fired in aggressive defence caught Tyson flush on the nose and he began to bleed. By the second round, the nose was bleeding very badly, and Tyson's face was smeared red. Yet still he kept coming, punching, absorbing blows, coming, coming, unrelenting, until the bell rang.

Atlas wiped the blood from Tyson's face in the corner and said that was it, he'd seen enough. 'One more round,' Tyson said. 'No, that's all, I don't have to see any more,' replied

Atlas. Tyson appealed to Stewart: 'No, no, we always box three rounds.' D'Amato glanced over at Stewart in a manner which said, 'Holy Christ, look at this kid.' Tyson had, indeed, impressed.

Cus and Atlas recognized that a good part of the tenacity, the persistence, the strength of mind that Tyson had demonstrated was bravado, put on by the youngster because he was in strange surroundings, and knew well that he was on display, being tested. Inside he might not have felt as confident as he looked. Most likely he didn't, but he nevertheless forced himself past his doubts and insecurities and made himself perform this way. And this was of vital importance in a fighter if he were to transcend the level of the ordinary. Untrained eyes would simply have seen a brave, tough kid. But D'Amato and his disciples, Atlas and Rooney, understood the psychology of what they had just witnessed. 'I figured,' says Atlas, 'that he could mature that, nurture that, and with that ability – not just his physical attributes, but that mental ability – he would do what we wanted him to do.'

Bobby Stewart, breathing heavily, climbed out of the ring. He walked over to D'Amato and said, 'Well, Cus, what do you think? Is he a pretty good kid?' He was totally unprepared for D'Amato's reply. 'Pretty good kid?' he said incredulously. 'That's the Heavyweight Champion of the World. If he wants it, and can avoid outside distractions, Bobby, you're looking at the future Heavyweight Champion of the World.'

'I had told Mike,' Stewart reminisced, 'I'll bring you down three or four times. Maybe if Cus likes you he'll take an interest in you.' Now, when he heard D'Amato's words, he was so stunned he felt like crying. 'When we were going out, I said, "You know what – he said you're going to be a champ," and Mike hugged me. It was a really nice deal.'

In the weeks that followed, Tyson and Stewart returned frequently to Catskill, where D'Amato or Atlas would work with the youngster, showing him moves or combinations that Stewart would then make him practise over and over until they returned to the gym for the next lesson. Tyson picked things up so naturally that even Stewart was impressed by the way he could adapt and incorporate each new move and rapidly make himself look like an experienced fighter.

When Tyson was allowed weekend furloughs away from Tryon, he spent them in Catskill with D'Amato and Atlas. It was arranged that Tyson, still a ward of the state, would be released in D'Amato's custody. He would live in Camille Ewald's home with Cus, Atlas, Rooney and the other boys, he would go to school in Catskill, and he would learn under the supervision of the master to be a lethally efficient machine in the boxing ring. The school term began in September. In order to settle him in to his new home, new surroundings, with new people, he was released a few months early from Tryon, and moved to Catskill in the summer of 1980.

With his knowledgeable boxing eye and his compassion for a sullen youngster who needed a break, Bobby Stewart had discovered the fighter the world would come to know as one of the greatest Heavyweight Champions and the richest, the highest-paid athlete in history. And yet, the discoverer would become a footnote, the first of several people who would be swept away and forgotten when they had outlived their usefulness to Team Tyson. There were rumours that, in gratitude, Tyson's people had set Stewart up in an automobile livery business, but he just chuckles when asked about these reports. No one set him up in any business. After leaving the Tryon School, he went to work as a chauffeur for a doctor. He does not own the car he chauffeurs. It belongs to his employer. The only recognition he got for bringing Mike Tyson to Cus D'Amato was an afterthought. A year after D'Amato died, when Tyson won the title, Kevin Rooney (by then Tyson's trainer) asked Stewart if he had been taken care of. Taken care of? Stewart didn't know what he was talking about. Rooney was angry. He went to Tyson's manager, Jim Jacobs, and confronted him about the matter. Jacobs summoned Stewart to his New York office and handed him a cheque for $10,000. He told him Cus had wanted him to have it, but he was not to tell anyone. It wasn't even given tax free. Stewart ended up with $7,800. 'When Cus passed on, they sort of forgot me, I guess. Believe me, I'm not crying or anything like that,' says Stewart. 'It just irks me, their playing games over stuff like that. . . . I wish they didn't give me nothing, to be honest with you. It belittled me in my own mind. Money can ruin people. I liked the kid, I did it because I liked doing it. I really cared about the kid.'

4

Cus

All idealism is falsehood in the face of necessity.

– Friedrich Nietzsche

WHEN MIKE TYSON arrived in Catskill to live with and learn from Cus D'Amato, it is certain that the 13-year-old unschooled youngster had only a vague notion of who this man was. After all, D'Amato had fought his battles and made his mark long before Michael Tyson came on the scene. D'Amato had come to Catskill (population: 5,000) in the 1960s, with the aim of establishing a gym in the small town located some thirty miles from the state capital of Albany. Situated on the west bank of the Hudson River, Catskill is connected to the town of Hudson, NY, on the east side of the river, by the Rip Van Winkle Bridge.

D'Amato's idea was to run an amateur club where he would train local youngsters, take in some young fighters to live in his house, boys who had trouble of one kind or another, and the house and gym would also serve as a camp for professional fighters who made the pilgrimage to Catskill to seek the old master's advice. Economically depressed and located in Greene County, the poorest in New York State, the town needed a recreational outlet for its boys, especially one run by a man with the knowledge and experience of Cus D'Amato. His proposal that the town give him the small hall above the police station and fire company no. 5 on Main Street was accepted, and thus was established the Catskill Boxing Club, which nearly two decades later would spawn the young phenomenon dubbed by TV commentator Randy Gordon 'Catskill Thunder' – Mike Tyson.

If D'Amato had a special warmth, an empathy, for troubled youngsters, his own background might well explain it. He was born on January 17, 1908 in the Classen Point section of the Bronx. His given name was Constantine, but he soon became just Cus on the streets. When Cus was five years old, his mother died. In later years, he would say, 'I don't remember my mother, and I was fortunate because I was self-reliant at a very young age. I was not confused by the ideas, the thoughts of mothers and fathers who, well-meaning though they may be, mess up the minds of their children.'

It was a rough, tough neighbourhood, and the five D'Amato brothers found out quickly they had to be tough to survive. Brother Tony had a reputation for being able to take on four or five cops by himself in the street, and lay them out. Later, when Tony owned a bar, he was closing up one night, alone, when two hulking bruisers entered. When Tony informed them he was closing, they told him they were going to drink for a while, so he was staying open whether he liked it or not. Tony went to the door, but instead of fleeing as they had expected him to, he locked it so they couldn't get out, and then beat the living daylights out of them both. When the police arrived, the two were laid out on the floor of the bar, barely conscious. Tony's wife says things like that happened 'quite often' in those days. All Tony says is, 'I didn't let nobody step on me.'

In 1925, Cus's oldest brother, Jerry, got tough with a cop on the street. Jerry was drunk. When the cop poked him a little too hard, perhaps, with his nightstick to move him along, Jerry responded by striking back and grabbing the nightstick. An altercation followed; when it was over, Jerry D'Amato lay dead, shot by the cop. Cus was then 17 years old.

At the same time that Babe Ruth was slugging home runs on the other side of the Bronx in the brand-new Yankee Stadium, the young Cus D'Amato was learning valuable lessons about fear and cowardice, toughness and courage and survival on the streets, lessons he would later incorporate in the unique philosophy of life and boxing which he imparted to his fighters. One lesson that became familiar to his disciples was that the fear of something is usually worse than the reality, a lesson he expounded using an example from his own life. He would describe how a guy from another neighbourhood who had a reputation as one of the best knife fighters on the streets of the Bronx, was swaggering around Cus's own patch and intimidating his pals. One day the hoodlum challenged each of them to a knife fight. Everyone was afraid and no one would accept the challenge. Once his dominance was established, he began insulting and humiliating them until he'd had his fill, and then left. Word of this reached Cus that evening; he was so angered that he sought out the antagonist and challenged him to a fist fight. The reply was no; instead, D'Amato was offered the opportunity to avenge the honour of his friends in a knife fight. The foolhardy Cus accepted. It was agreed the two would meet at an abandoned building at seven the next morning, alone. There would be no witnesses in case one of them ended up dead. On his way home, Cus couldn't help but think it was most likely to be him. Fear gripped him as it never had before. He hadn't the slightest idea how to wield a knife in a fight, yet here he was about to face an expert. When he was finally able to control his fear, he thought up an idea that would at least give him a chance. Maybe he didn't know about knife fighting, but he did know about boxing, about using his fists. He found an ice pick, carved the handle down so it would fit in his closed palm, with the blade extending out between his middle and ring fingers. He then practised as if he were boxing, only now, at the end of his fist, was a deadly blade as he jabbed the air.

In the few hours that remained until dawn, he tried unsuccessfully to sleep. He then headed for the empty warehouse where the fight was to take place, getting there early on purpose to check out the surroundings, and prepare himself for his adversary. He taped the ice pick inside his fist, made sure the blade protruded far enough, and wrapped a jacket around his forearm for protection. Then, he waited. When the fear built up too much and threatened to overwhelm him, he danced around, practising his technique. He learned that motion relieves tension. The minutes passed. Seven o'clock came and went, and the knife fighter had still not appeared. D'Amato felt relieved, but then checked himself. If he began to wind down and his opponent suddenly materialized, he knew his resolve to fight might be weakened. Finally, when more than an hour had passed, Cus realized that fear must have got the better of the knife fighter. He wasn't going to appear. Cus went home, a hero to his friends. The knife fighter never showed himself again. Cus knew he had won a victory, not only over his adversary, but over himself. He had faced his fear and refused to allow it to get the better of him.

Another time, when he was a young boy, long before the challenge of the knife fight, he found himself alone, in a deserted lot at nightfall. It was common knowledge among the kids that a monster roamed this lot, and no one ever went there at night, especially alone. But it was late and Cus had to get home, and the lot was a short cut. He forced himself to carry on although he was afraid. When he had gone too far to turn back, he saw it: a shadow looming, large and menacing, against the night sky ahead. There was nothing for it but to go forward, to see if he could somehow slip past this horrible thing unnoticed, or maybe outrun it to the safety of the tenements a short distance away. As he kept walking, it got larger and more terrifying, as the stories his friends had told him about this monster raced through his head. Then, suddenly, he saw what it was. A tree. A large, dead tree, standing in the middle of the lot, its branches moving in the wind. That was the monster he had seen against the sky. What his imagination had conjured up was far more horrible than the reality. Cus never forgot those lessons about fear and imagination, courage and reality. He would teach them over and over to the fighters he would eventually train.

As a young man, Cus 'wasn't the type that wanted to work', according to his brother, Tony. 'My father used to support him.' By the time he was 31, other than an occasional job, his one major achievement had been running a fusion political club in his neighbourhood and carrying the heavily Democratic district for Fiorelle LaGuardia in his successful mayoral campaign. Jerry D'Amato had done some boxing, as had another brother, Nick, and so Cus started to learn a little about the sport.

In 1939, along with two friends who eventually dropped out, Cus opened a gym, the Gramercy, at 116 East 14th Street in Manhattan, and began to handle some fighters, interrupted by a spell in the Army during World War II. Nick and Tony (when he could get time away from his bars) helped Cus, who started to build a stable of good fighters that included Jimmy Anest, a deaf mute, Johnny Brown, Joe Juliano and Artie Diamond.

In 1945, when he returned from the Army, he met the only woman in his life: Camille Ewald, a Ukranian girl who had grown up in western Canada before moving to New York. They began a relationship that only ended forty years later, with D'Amato's death. When the stories about Mike Tyson began to emerge in newspapers and magazines in the mid 1980s, Camille's name came to public attention for the first time, because she ran the big Victorian house in Catskill where the young fighters lived, and Tyson would refer to her as his 'mother' or his 'white mother'. She was described as the sister of the wife of D'Amato's brother Rocco, although Rocco actually married her sister long after Cus and Camille began their relationship. Though they never married, the two shared a cabin hideaway in New Jersey for many years before buying the house in Catskill where Camille did the cooking and cleaning, and supervised and mothered the boys.

During the 1940s Cus was learning the boxing business, sometimes the hard way. He had a young tough at his gym whom he thought would be his fighter when he turned pro, a kid named Rocky Graziano. But Graziano went with different management, including a 'silent' partner named Eddie Coco, a 'connected' hoodlum whose résumé listed more than a dozen arrests for rape, robbery, and felonious assault, and who eventually went to prison for life on a murder rap. Graziano went on to win the Middleweight Championship of the World in 1947, and Cus, having tasted sour grapes, spent the rest of his life knocking Graziano as a gutless guy who couldn't fight.

Another mistake that D'Amato made, besides losing Graziano, was to get involved with the International Boxing Guild, the so-called 'managers' guild', a large group of boxing managers who had organized themselves ostensibly to present a united front and gain better purses for those of their fighters who fought on the fledgling medium of television. At the time – the early 1950s – boxing could be seen on television three or four nights a week. The Guild filled its coffers by demanding payment from the manager of any fighter who appeared on TV, whether a Guild member or not. In those days, main event fighters on TV earned anything between $2,100 to $4,000. The customary tribute demanded by the Guild was $100. D'Amato, at a salary of $35 a week, became a 'collector' for the Guild, dunning managers at the various arenas around the City for their payments.

The Guild was controlled by mob-connected managers like 'Honest' Bill Daly, and it was less than a shining light. In 1953, the highly regarded trainer, Ray Arcel, and two partners went into boxing promotion with a contract for a weekly card of televised bouts. But for the first month of the new venture, each week they were forced to cancel their shows when one or another of the main event fighters pulled out for various reasons. Subsequently, Arcel would testify before the New York State Athletic Commission that when he and his group agreed to pay a tribute of $500 a week to the Guild, by some strange coincidence the health of the fighters suddenly improved and they were able to proceed with their matches without any further hitch.

When Joe Louis retired in 1949, an organization known as the International Boxing Club, through a complicated web of collusion, chicanery and quasi-legal manoeuvring, had gained a virtual monopoly on professional boxing in the United States. The head of the IBC was Jim Norris, a multi-millionaire in his 40s who, along with his father, James, and their partner, Arthur Wirtz, owned the Chicago Stadium, the Detroit Olympia Stadium, the St Louis Arena, and held the leases on the Omaha Coliseum and Indianapolis Coliseum. In addition, Norris owned the Detroit Redwings of the National Hickey League, and a substantial amount of stock in Madison Square Garden (eventually that amount would come to nearly 40 per cent). His other holdings, outside the world of sport, were equally formidable.

Norris was, to all intents and purposes, a legitimate businessman, but in his burning desire to monopolize boxing, he fell in with a good many people not so legitimate, chief among them a mobster named Frankie Carbo, who would become the real, underworld power behind the IBC, as Norris would become essentially a figurehead without the power to control Carbo. Paul John Carbo, alias Frankie, was born two years before Jim Norris, in 1904. By the time he was 45 years old, when the IBC was formed, he had quite an impressive rap sheet, beginning as a juvenile hoodlum, and progressing to felonious assault, grand larceny, robbery, and five arrests for murder. He served time in Sing Sing for manslaughter, but never actually did time for murder. Perhaps the following scenario explains why.

In 1939, a gentleman named Harry Shachter, alias Harry Greenberg, was shot down outside his house in Hollywood, California. Greenberg himself was no sweetheart, being a henchman of underworld figure Waxey Gordon, and a member of the gang with the colourful and notorious name of Murder, Inc. Frankie Carbo was indicted for the killing. Indicted with him was a who's who of crime that included 'Lepke' Louie Buchalter, 'Bugsy' Seigel, 'Mendy' Weiss and 'Champ' Segal. At the trial, a member of Murder, Inc. testified that Carbo did, indeed, along with 'Bugsy' Seigel, kill Greenberg. The witness, Al Tannenbaum, said that Seigel drove the getaway car, but it was Carbo who actually fired the five bullets that ended the less-than-exemplary life of Greenberg.

Nevertheless, the trial resulted in a hung jury. A retrial was set, for which the police had another witness against Carbo, a witness so valuable that he was being held under police guard in an upstairs room at the Half Moon Hotel in Coney Island. The witness was Abe 'Kid Twist' Reles. But shortly before the second trial of Carbo was to begin, Abe Reles went flying from the window of the Half Moon Hotel. His crushed and lifeless body was found on the street near the Coney Island boardwalk. It was never established whether Reles committed suicide or whether he was pushed from the safe haven of his hotel room while the police who were supposed to be guarding him conveniently looked the other way, although that theory still persists to this day. Whatever happened to Reles, without him there was no chance of prosecuting Carbo successfully. The trial was not held, Carbo was freed, to go on his merry way. As Barney Nagler wrote in his marvellous exposé of this era, *James Norris and the Decline of Boxing*, 'By 1947. . .[Frankie Carbo] had achieved widespread notoriety as the underworld's commissioner of boxing.'

An associate of Carbo's was a Philadelphia mobster named Frank 'Blinky' Palermo, with a dossier that included assault, car theft, violation of Pennsylvania's liquor laws, and operating a lottery, which meant, in reality, that Palermo ran the numbers rackets in Philadelphia. Palermo managed fighters like Ike Williams, legitimately one of the great champions of that era, and fighters like Billy Fox, whose careers were built on fixed fights, the most publicized of those being a bout in which Fox scored an upset TKO over the seemingly invincible 'Raging Bull', Jake LaMotta. It later came to light that LaMotta was forced to throw the fight in exchange for a chance at the Middleweight Championship, a chance he got and a title he won. Through the IBC, the mobsters dictated who should get title opportunities, and, in many cases, either by collusion with the fighters themselves or by paying off those who judged the bouts, who should win the titles. Of the 44 world championship fights held in the four years after the IBC was established, 80 per cent were essentially controlled by that organization, earning millions of dollars.

In 1952, the United States Department of Justice filed suit against the IBC and its front, Madison Square Garden, accusing the organization of 'conspiring to restrain and monopolize the promotion and broadcasting of professional championship boxing in the United States.' As Nagler states in his book, 'Undaunted by the shadow of federal law, Norris went right on with his business. He held all the weapons and appeared impregnable to assault by writ or competition. He controlled the activities of every champion. Those fighters that he did not control by contract he held in financial bondage, because the

IBC alone was in a position to promote important matches. And, through the International Boxing Guild he controlled the managers.' The government's lawsuit was dismissed, and the IBC and Madison Square Garden, which Norris by now controlled, continued to roll merrily along.

This was the unsavoury background to boxing in the post-World War II era when Cus D'Amato, a relative newcomer to the game, fell in with the Guild, a tie he would eventually sever long before the Guild was ordered to disband by Julius Helfand, Chairman of the New York State Athletic Commission, in 1955. Perhaps D'Amato knew no better at the time; possibly, as is most likely, he knew, as a small-time manager, that there was no alternative but to join the Guild; and maybe he learned from what he saw going on around him. Whatever his reasons for joining, D'Amato eventually became one of the most vocal critics of those who controlled the Guild, especially of Jim Norris and the IBC. In carving his own course, independent of the IBC, he would himself become a central figure in boxing surrounded by controversy. The ace-in-the-hole that permitted him to defy the powerful Norris emerged in 1952. His name was Floyd Patterson.

Like so many of the kids who eventually gravitated to D'Amato, Floyd Patterson came to him as a troubled youth who had spent time at the Wiltwyck School for Boys in upstate New York, since he was unable to get on either at school or in his family environment. Like Tyson three decades later, Patterson grew up in Brooklyn, where he was 'discovered' by a boxing coach named Frank LaVelle, who trained amateur kids at a YMCA. All three Patterson brothers started under LaVelle, who then brought them to D'Amato's Gramercy Gym. All LaVelle's better fighters – those with potential – moved on to the Gramercy, where they could receive better schooling.

D'Amato, meanwhile, having apparently learned his lesson from the experience of having Graziano poached from under his very nose, by this time had an understanding. Any boy could come to his gym and train for free. He would teach them, with no obligation on their part if they never fought, or if they only went to the level of amateur competition. But if they turned pro, they signed with Cus. 'I'm like a prospector,' he would say, 'and here is where I look for gold.' Patterson had an outstanding amateur career, which he capped in 1952 by winning a gold medal as a middleweight in the Olympics. When he turned pro, he went with Cus. LaVelle helped train Floyd, and worked his corner in many of his early fights. Later, the relationship between LaVelle and D'Amato soured, LaVelle claiming that Patterson had been his fighter.

D'Amato professed strong objections to the iron-fisted control of boxing by the IBC. As he began to develop Patterson into a contender, he endeavoured to chart his own independent course. Many of Floyd's early fights were at the Eastern Parkway Arena in Brooklyn, where promotor Emil Lence and matchmaker Teddy Brenner had no ties with the IBC. By fighting there, and later in places like Canada, California and even Kansas City, Cus was able to have the final say over Floyd's opponents. With the IBC he would have been forced to take fighters too tough for Patterson in his developing years, fighters who might have derailed him long before he could become a contender for the title. D'Amato ignored the frequent criticism that he matched Floyd too carefully, was too selective in handpicking his opponents; he knew a lot better than his critics how to develop his fighter into championship material. During this period of Patterson's development, the Heavyweight Champion of the World was Rocky Marciano, who was controlled by Al Weill. At that time, Weill had become the matchmaker for the IBC at Madison Square Garden. By law, he therefore could not function as a manager. He got around that simply enough by listing his son, Marty, as Rocky's manager. It was, however, an open secret in boxing that Al Weill controlled Marciano.

Because of this, D'Amato was forced several times along the way to do business with the IBC, because Weill's duality as the IBC/Madison Square Garden matchmaker and as Marciano's shadow manager meant he controlled the heavyweight championship and the road to it just about one hundred per cent. In the fall of 1954, D'Amato was forced to put Patterson in with Joe Gannon and Jimmy Slade. After Patterson beat Gannon, D'Amato accepted Slade as an opponent only after consulting with his fighter. Slade was then ranked number 4 in the world. It has long been a myth that D'Amato always decided himself whom his fighters would box, that their job was to do the fighting. In reality, D'Amato consulted more than once with Patterson, if he felt Floyd's delicate psyche would come into play, before making a fight with a particular opponent. In a terrible fight, with Slade running to survive, Patterson won a decision. In a rematch the next year in Los Angeles, Slade ran even more until Floyd stopped him in the seventh round.

Around this time, in early 1956, Rocky Marciano indicated he was going to retire as undefeated champion. Meanwhile, the government had appealed against the 1954 decision in favour of the IBC, and early in 1955 the Supreme Court decided in favour of the Justice Department in its suit against Norris and the IBC. In 1956, Norris, Wirtz and the IBC were facing charges in the Federal Court that they had conspired to monopolize championship boxing in the United States for four years beginning in mid 1949. While the trial was in progress, Marciano announced his retirement. This left Norris and the IBC vulnerable. Under the public and legal scrutiny of the trial, they could not move as aggressively to control the now vacant heavyweight championship.

The leading contenders for the title were Archie Moore, Patterson, and 'Hurricane' Jackson, an IBC-connected fighter. D'Amato agreed to have Patterson meet Jackson in an elimination bout promoted by the IBC – if he got his price. He wanted $50,000 for Patterson, an unheard-of amount at the time. The winner was to move on to a bout for the vacant World Championship. By all accounts, D'Amato got his $50,000 or, at the least, $40,000. 'I do not especially want to fight for the IBC,' he said, 'but such is the power of the IBC that independent promoters can't compete with it.' At his retirement press conference, Marciano had named Patterson as one of the top three contenders for the title, and D'Amato stated that the public knew that Patterson was the best and would demand that he get a crack at the title. D'Amato knew he had the weakened IBC on the ropes.

On June 8, 1956, at Madison Square Garden, Patterson administered a one-sided, 12-round beating to Jackson. Some six months later, a broken bone in his hand suffered in the Jackson fight having healed, Patterson met Archie Moore for the Heavyweight Championship on November 30, 1956, at Chicago Stadium. Moore was 39 years old, ancient by boxing standards. Patterson was 21. Moore went into the fight, nevertheless, as an 8-to-5 favourite. A professional only four years, Patterson was asked in one pre-fight interview how he expected to overcome the experience of a man who had been fighting for twenty years. Patterson, by no means a braggart but, despite being softspoken, confident of his abilities, answered, 'Well, maybe I learned as much in four years as it took him twenty years to learn.' Norris was quite certain that Moore would win, but he also felt sure, having dealt with D'Amato in the Jackson fight, that Cus would fall in line and support the IBC should Patterson take the title. Patterson knocked out Archie Moore in the sixth round to become the youngest heavyweight champion in history, an honour he would hold until D'Amato's next great heavyweight protégé, Mike Tyson, supplanted him thirty years later almost to the day. When Patterson knocked out Moore he also knocked Jim Norris and the IBC out of the heavyweight championship picture. The IBC would never promote another heavyweight title match, because despite whatever implied or hoped-for understanding Norris had with D'Amato, Cus was going his own independent way with Floyd Patterson. As the manager of the World Heavyweight Champion, he was now, suddenly, one of the most powerful men in the sport.

In 1956, before Patterson won the title, D'Amato had approached the IBC for two loans. He had already made up his mind never to do business with the IBC once Patterson won the title, but he was not above borrowing money from them, knowing they would not refuse, since Norris was very interested in Patterson as a future attraction. On June 7, saying he needed the money to pay tax debts, D'Amato took a $15,000 loan from the International Boxing Club. Two months later he requested an additional $5,000. The total of $20,000, for which he signed two IOUs, represented a considerable amount of cash by the standards of the 1950s.

Once Patterson had won the title and D'Amato had severed his ties with the IBC, he refused to repay the loans. When the money was demanded, Cus said he was keeping it for 'services rendered'. He was reminded that he and Patterson had been paid for their services rendered, and that the money was a personal loan to him, asked for and granted in good faith. Cus, in later years painted as a bastion of incorruptibility and honesty, refused to budge. He never returned the money to the IBC.

Harry Markson, who was eventually President of the Madison Square Garden Boxing Department in the post-IBC era, was an executive with the Garden during the reign of Jim Norris. Despite many Athletic Commission and Grand Jury investigations, Markson emerged completely clean. He had always refused to do business with Carbo and his mobster friends, yet somehow had managed to survive in the IBC hierarchy. Norris said he liked to keep Markson around as his conscience. Markson had many dealings over the years with

D'Amato. 'The picture of Mr Clean is false,' he says. 'Cus just wasn't that kind of a guy and did involve himself or allow himself to get involved, for what suited his purposes, with the bad guys of the business.'

Early in 1957, the courts ruled against Norris, the IBC, et al, saying they had acted as a monopoly in restraint of trade, and several months later Norris and Wirtz were ordered to divest themselves of all stock they owned in Madison Square Garden, to resign as officers and directors of the Garden, and not to promote more than two world championship fights a year for the next five years. In addition, Madison Square Garden was enjoined for five years from promoting more than two title fights a year. The judge further ordered that the IBC corporations be dissolved. Norris subsequently suffered a heart attack, and in the spring of 1958 he resigned as President of the IBC, but was still President of the Garden, which controlled the IBC. During all this time, the Federal Court decision ordering divestiture was under appeal, so it was business as usual.

Patterson, meanwhile, following a KO over 'Hurricane' Jackson in a rematch for the first defence of his title, was fighting an odd assortment of contenders. D'Amato maintained the IBC had a blacklist, and wouldn't let top contenders fight Patterson. He tried to make a fight between Patterson and Willie Pastrano. The challenger's managers accepted the fight, then, a short while later, when word got around, called back and said Pastrano couldn't fight Patterson. The IBC was calling in its chits. So instead, D'Amato signed with Pete Rademacher, the 1956 Olympic Champion, who, in a promotion unique in boxing history, fought Patterson for the heavyweight title in his first professional bout. Patterson stopped him in six rounds, then didn't fight for another year. When he did, it was against Roy Harris, a fringe contender from Cut 'N Shoot, Texas. Floyd stopped him in 12 in his only fight of 1958. The promoter of that fight was to have been, ironically, Al Weill, despite his former association with the IBC, and despite the fact that D'Amato was well aware of his close association with Frankie Carbo. The California Athlete Commission turned down Weill as a promoter, however. With the bout uncertain, a young executive with TelePrompTer Corporation named Bill Rosensohn approached D'Amato and asked him if he could promote the fight. Assured that Rosensohn had the money, D'Amato agreed, despite the fact that the young man had never promoted a bout before. But TelePrompTer was the company handling the new medium of closed-circuit theatre telecasts of fights. Rosensohn did better than expected with the venture, held at Wrigley Field in Los Angeles. It was very successful as a theatre-TV attraction. He asked D'Amato if he could promote another fight, and it was agreed, provided he came up with a viable contender who was free of any IBC entanglements. Rosensohn went to Sweden, saw Ingemar Johansson become the number one contender by knocking out the highly-regarded Eddie Machen in one round, and, having determined that the Swedish heavyweight had no association with Norris or the IBC, signed a forty-day option with Johansson and his management for ten thousand dollars, giving Rosensohn exclusive rights during that time to make a match for the title between Patterson and Ingemar.

Back in the United States, Rosensohn explained the situation to D'Amato, but as the days passed, D'Amato hedged on signing with Rosensohn. The young promoter was becoming increasingly worried. In a few more days, his option would expire and he would lose his ten grand. D'Amato only shrugged and told him he had signed the option on his own, and it was his problem if he lost his money, not D'Amato's.

Rosensohn did not know what to do, and so he consulted Charlie Antonucci, a.k.a. Charlie Black, a convicted small-time bookmaker and business associate of D'Amato's. Rosensohn, who had previously dealt with Black on the Roy Harris fight, explained his predicament, and Black suggested that the promoter might find it beneficial to meet with Tony Salerno. At this point, D'Amato was still refusing to sign the promotional agreement with Rosensohn. Salerno, who was a Mafia mobster known in the underworld as 'Fat Tony', told Rosensohn at their meeting that he was interested in investing in the promotion. For a one-third partnership, Salerno would put up all the money to back the promotion. There was one more thing. Salerno wanted his and Cus's buddy, Charlie Black, also cut in for a third. Rosensohn had no choice. It was either sign over two-thirds of the promotion to Salerno and Black, or lose the fight completely, and the ten thousand dollars he had paid to Johansson. He explained to Salerno that he didn't have an agreement with D'Amato for the fight, and his option was expiring in a few days. 'Fat Tony' told him not to worry. Rosensohn agreed to the deal, and within a day, as if by magic, Rosensohn had D'Amato's signature.

Before fighting Johansson, Patterson took a warm-up fight, a title defence against the British contender Brian London.

That fight was held amid a welter of suspicious circumstances. The fight, set for Las Vegas, was suddenly switched
to Indianapolis. The original promoter, Cecil Rhodes, Jr., a
Harvard-educated attorney and businessman, was apparently
dumped by D'Amato, who had Rosensohn step in to help
run the promotion. D'Amato later explained to Patterson that
agreements he had signed with Rhodes for the London fight and
subsequent bouts were not what he had thought they were, and
that Floyd wasn't going to get as much money for the bout with
Brian London as originally envisaged. When the British fighter
arrived in New York, he was met at the airport by a D'Amato
associate, and was immediately put under wraps so he could
not talk to the press about the business aspects of the bout.
He trained at D'Amato's Gramercy Gym, and used the same
sparring partners as Patterson. D'Amato also installed one of
his associates, veteran boxing man Nick Baffi, as London's
trainer, which created further suspicion. Patterson took eleven
rounds to knock out the mediocre but durable London, who
added more fuel to the fire by subsequently charging that he
had been promised a second shot at Floyd if he agreed to let
D'Amato take over his management. D'Amato denied this.
Patterson would later write, 'I was terribly embarrassed by that
fight and all the circumstances surrounding it.'

On June 26, 1959, under the promotional banner of Rosensohn Enterprises, Inc. (of which Bill Rosensohn was, by now a
minority owner, holding just 33 per cent), Floyd defended his
title against Johansson. In a major upset, Johansson knocked
Patterson down seven times in the third round to win the
World Heavyweight Championship. Patterson lost his title, the
promotion lost $70,000, because D'Amato, in the driver's seat,
contractually gave the promoters half of the net gate profits
only, of which there were none. He kept all the closed-circuit
TV revenue, of which there was plenty, for Patterson, himself,
and TelePrompTer.

Rosensohn still looked forward to promoting the Patterson–
Johansson rematch, to which he held the rights. He was in
for a rude awakening when he was informed by one Vincent
Velella, the attorney for Tony Salerno that he, Velella, was
in control of the 67 per cent of Rosensohn Enterprises given
over to Salerno and Charlie Black. Rosensohn sold out his
share to a newly-formed promotional group headed by the
New York power broker and attorney, Roy Cohn, Cohn's law
partner, Tom Bolan, and travel agency owner, Bill Fugazy. Also

forced to sell to the new promoters was Velella. Rosensohn had gone to the District Attorney's office in New York and told all about Salerno, Black and Velella taking over Rosensohn Enterprises. As a result, Velella was indicted for perjury, and though eventually cleared, he was in an untenable position regarding the running of Rosensohn Enterprises. Roy Cohn and his associates, under the banner of Feature Sports, Inc. now owned the contract to promote the return match in 1960.

D'Amato had made many enemies in the press during his long campaign against the IBC and his feud with Jim Norris. Some of the press's criticism of him was justified, but, in fairness to D'Amato, many of the journalists were on the IBC payroll, being paid off under the table by Norris, in return for giving the IBC a good press. Some of the newspapermen who were not 'on the take' just didn't like the oddball and unorthodox D'Amato.

Typical was the noted sports columnist, Jimmy Cannon, who constantly attacked D'Amato in his widely-read column. One example read: 'The manager of Floyd Patterson is as phony as snow on a Hollywood Christmas tree and his methods are as dirty as a coal miner's fingernails. . . .Cus D'Amato belongs in the fight racket because it has long been the sanctuary of the persuasive rogue. Seldom has deceit been practised with the suave hypocrisy of Cus the Mus, who is still Patterson's boss in all matters. In a foul business which has produced more fakers than all the quiz shows put together, the Mus is a spectacular blackguard. But the beneficiary of his surreptitious propositions has been Patterson, who is regarded as a decent kid mesmerized into a stupor of innocent acquiescence by the Mus' con.'

The esteemed Pulitzer-prizewinning columnist, Red Smith, also criticized D'Amato, writing, 'Who knows anything about Floyd Patterson?. . . .Hardly anybody, as a matter of fact, except Cus D'Amato, and whatever became of Cus? Every now and then, something. . . .serves as a reminder that there is a man named Floyd Patterson and that he really is the heavyweight champion – the most widely unknown, the least active, the most superbly concealed heavyweight champion since the birth of Jim Figg.'

A 1961 *Sports Illustrated* story by Robert Boyle referred to D'Amato as a 'tragic figure'. 'The press often reviles [him] as a crook. A crook he is not; a kook he may be. He fought the gangster-dominated IBC alone for such a long

spell that he wound up with a deep and permanent persecution complex. . . .He spends most of his time in his cluttered
two-room apartment at Broadway and 53rd Street, his main
companion a boxer dog. . . .he has a bed in the apartment, he
never sleeps there. He stays with friends, and he rarely spends
two nights in the same place. "I don't like my comings and going
to be predictable," he says. He is wary of what he says over the
phone because, he says, it may be being tapped. . . .He stays out
of bars for fear an enemy agent might stuff marijuana cigarettes
into his pockets, then whistle for the police.'

Jimmy Cannon, continuing his attack on D'Amato, wrote:
'Loyalty is a glorious trait and an uncommon one in the fight
racket where integrity is considered a defect. But Patterson
has been disgraced by his association with the Mus because
he hasn't repudiated any of the alliances which protected him
from people such as Pete Rademacher and Brian London. The
impression Patterson originally made on me must be altered
unless he expresses his independence and renovates his views
of the man who has provoked a national disgust with the fight
racket which may cause it to be voted a criminal act instead
of a sport.' One might well ask why Cannon chose to accuse
D'Amato of provoking 'a national disgust' with boxing when
he might better have directed his accusations at Frankie Carbo,
Jim Norris and others of their ilk.

Certainly, D'Amato was no innocent. He himself was
involved with numerous shady characters and underworld
figures with an interest in boxing, such as Weill, Salerno,
Black and so on. He was a sharp, veteran operator who had
his eyes wide open, and it suited his purpose very well to project
the image of a crusader against corrupt influences in the boxing world. His crusade against the IBC provided a convenient
means to accomplish one of his main goals: to keep Patterson
from fighting the legitimate top contenders for the title who
deserved but never got their chances against Patterson. Despite
his rhetoric to the press about Patterson's greatness, D'Amato
knew that his man was very limited as a heavyweight. He was
a good middleweight, a good light-heavyweight, but when the
top heavyweight contenders were men like Zora Folley, Eddie
Machen and Sonny Liston, D'Amato knew there was a good
chance of Patterson losing to any one of them. What better
way to shield his fighter than under the pretext of keeping
him away from IBC-controlled challengers? It was a brilliant
strategy; while adding to the legend of the honest, crusading

Cus D'Amato, it kept Patterson in the ring for years against safe opponents like Roy Harris, Tom McNeeley, Pete Rademacher and Brian London.

However, with his behind-the-scenes manoeuvring in the making of the first Patterson–Jahansson fight, his involvement in the promotion while at the same time being a manager, which was against the law, and the involvement of people like 'Fat Tony' Salerno in the promotion, D'Amato had made himself vulnerable. The press was eager to attack, and he had given them good cause.

Johansson fanned the flames by charging that in order to get his fight with Patterson he had had to agree to sign with Harry Davidow as his manager. Davidow was an old crony of D'Amato's, and had been one of Cus's original partners in the gym. He had dropped out to open a candy store in Brooklyn from which he ran a bookmaking operation. He had been out of boxing for fifteen years, yet here was his buddy Cus D'Amato securing him a deal that would give him ten per cent of Johansson's purses for the next five years. However, the deal went sour when the New York State Athletic Commission denied Davidow a manager's licence a month before the first scheduled fight, in response to Johansson's allegations.

On September 14, 1959, the State Athletic Commission began an inquiry into the matter of the Patterson–Johansson fight. D'Amato was accused of being the decision-maker behind Rosensohn Enterprises who had 'cut in' his colleague and friend, Charlie Black, 'a convicted gambler and associate of bookmakers', for a piece of the promotion, as well as attempting to force Davidow on Johansson and his Swedish manager. He was also accused of violating the rule that prevents a manager from being involved in the promotion of a fight. The Commission reached the following conclusions:

'D'Amato put Rosensohn in as a promoter of the [Patterson–Roy Harris] fight after Rosensohn had agreed to give Charlie Black, D'Amato's friend, fifty per cent of the profits. Charlie Black was also designated by D'Amato as the manager of Roy Harris, in the event of a return bout, and was to receive 10 per cent of Harris's purse of said match. This was a clear attempt by D'Amato to control the future heavyweight champion in the event that Harris succeeded in winning the title.

'Charlie Black, also known as Charles Antonucci, is D'Amato's trusted advisor and go-between. He has known

D'Amato for twenty-five years. Whenever there is a Patterson
fight, Black appears on the scene either with a part in the
promotion or in the boxer management. Black apparently has
no occupation. He is friendly with Tony Salerno and. . ."Trig-
ger" Mike Coppola for twenty-five years. . . .He, Black, does
not appear to be the type of personality whose presence would
inure to the best interest of boxing.

'In connection with the Patterson–Johansson fight, the
Commission denied an application for a licence to one Harry
Davidow as manager of Ingemar Johansson. The record in
that proceeding. . .supports the conclusion that D'Amato dictated the naming of Davidow as Johansson's manager. This
was another instance of D'Amato's attempt to control the
heavyweight title.

'This Commission cannot accept the fact that Salerno was
an innocent bystander at these meetings [involving the promotion of the Patterson–Johansson fight] and it believes that the
$10,000 loan was made by Salerno to Rosensohn in Velella's
office and that Salerno was a part of the promotion.'

Furthermore, D'Amato did not help his own cause by
boycotting the hearings. The Commission decision stated: 'Mr
D'Amato was directed. . .to appear at a hearing on September
14, 1959. . . .He failed to appear and was therefore suspended
by the Commission. Hearings were conducted until September
21 with no appearance by him. . . .The record amply sustains
the fact the D'Amato's failure to appear, pursuant to the direction of the Commission, was deliberate.'

D'Amato's licence to manage was revoked late in 1959. He
eventually took his case to the US Supreme Court, where
he won a minor victory on a technicality. It seems that his
manager's licence had expired before the Commission issued
the order to revoke it, so, technically, his licence had not been
taken away. But it was a Pyrrhic victory. Afraid that if he did
apply for and obtain another licence, it would then be taken
away, he never again held a licence as a manager.

Why D'Amato had acted in this manner will probably never
be known for sure. In view of his battle against the IBC, and
his loathing for the gangsters who exercised influence over the
sport, it doesn't seem credible that he would knowingly have
joined up with another band of mobsters. Yet he certainly knew
the backgrounds and reputations of Davidow and Black, long-
time friends, and of Salerno. Perhaps he acted out of loyalty to
old friends; perhaps it was because his pathological dislike of

the IBC closed many doors to him that might otherwise have
opened to offer lucrative bouts for Patterson. One thing is
almost certain: money was not D'Amato's incentive, as anyone
who knew him over the years will testify: he had no interest in it.
He enjoyed being a power in boxing, enjoyed being the manager
of the heavyweight champion, but money was generally the last
thing on his mind.

All the revelations that followed the London and Johansson
bouts served to create a strain between Patterson and Cus.
Floyd had certainly benefited financially from the fights. His
gross purse was over $600,000. But he was made to feel a fool
when, with each new revelation, he realized how much had gone
on without his knowledge. He would later write, 'I didn't mistrust Cus. . .but I did begin to develop a mistrust of the people
around him, for whom Cus always did favours.' He described
himself as 'horrified' when Salerno's name surfaced. In *Victory
Over Myself*, written while he was still at the peak of his career
as a fighter, Floyd said, 'I made up my mind to one. . .thing.
Nobody went down with me those seven times that I went down
to the canvas [against Johansson]. A fighter walks alone and
fights alone. If I could be successful the next time, I promised
myself I'd be my own man. The mistakes would be mine, the
decisions mine. . . .Nominally, at least, Cus continued to be
what he always was, but actually I tried to show him that too
many things had happened for me to allow myself ever to be
completely in anyone's control again. I was Cus's boy, but in
defeat and confusion I became my own man. I was hurt, very
badly, and maybe inadvertently by him, but whatever he did, I
know he thought he was doing it solely for my benefit.'

Roy Cohn et al went ahead and promoted the Patterson–
Johansson rematch on June 20, 1960, at the Polo Grounds in
New York. It was an historic fight, because in the fifth round,
Floyd knocked out Ingemar with one of the most devastating
left hooks ever thrown. By virtue of that punch, he was now not
only the youngest man ever to win the title, but the first fighter
in history to regain the Heavyweight Championship.

There's an old saying that just because someone is paranoid
doesn't necessarily mean someone isn't out to get them. This
was possibly the case when it came to D'Amato and Roy Cohn.
Cus's attorney, Julius November, also handled Patterson's
affairs. D'Amato now felt that Roy Cohn was using November as a wedge to get Patterson away from him and into his
own clutches. Knowing Cohn's propensity for deviousness, it is

likely that D'Amato had grounds for his accusations. Without a written contract with Patterson (it had expired and was never formally renewed), and without a licence to manage in New York, Cus was vulnerable. November moved in at this point to gain Floyd's trust. Fugazy, Cohn's partner in Feature Sports, called D'Amato 'mentally ill'. D'Amato countered by telling *Sports Illustrated* of Fugazy: 'This man has definite psychopathic leanings. The man has no principles. This man lies to your face, and he believes his own lies. A respectable racketeer. . . Compared to Fugazy, Norris is like a diamond in a coal pile.' There is little doubt that Cohn and Fugazy manoeuvred to win over Patterson. In this atmosphere, Patterson fought Johansson a third time, knocking him out to retain his title in 1961. Floyd had stated in his autobiography, '. . .my manager has been a suspicious man. Undoubtedly he had some reason to be, but over the years Cus allowed his suspicions about the IBC and his fight against its president, Jim Norris, to warp his thinking. Without question, it also warped my career. . . Let me say here, too, so that nobody gets any other ideas, that as long as I keep fighting, Cus will continue to be my manager.' But shortly after the third Johansson fight, Floyd broke with Cus, and was not to be reconciled with him for the duration of his fighting career.

In 1962 Floyd defended his title, without the guidance of D'Amato, against Charles 'Sonny' Liston, a sullen, one-time union thug and enforcer who had served 'hard time' in prison, and who was controlled in his climb up the boxing ladder by shadow managers (surprise, surprise!) Frankie Carbo and his associate, a Philadelphia mobster named Frank 'Blinky' Palermo. Patterson was knocked out in one round, losing his title to Liston, who stopped Floyd again in the first round a year later. Patterson would continue his career, losing a bid for the heavyweight title by TKO to Muhammad Ali, and failing in an attempt to win the WBA Heavyweight Championship against Jimmy Ellis in Sweden in a fight most observers thought Patterson had won, but, in one of the awful decisions you sometimes see in boxing, the only official under Swedish rules, American referee Harold Valan, raised Ellis's hand in victory. Patterson retired in 1972 after losing a second time to Ali in a bout at Madison Square Garden. He had never fought there in his days as champion, but, after leaving D'Amato, he fought there several times, long after its association with the IBC had ended. He went on to become a member of the New York State Athletic Commission and now, much as his mentor, Cus D'Amato did, he trains a stable of amateurs and professionals in a gym on his farm in upstate New York, not far from Catskill. Eventually, he became reconciled with Cus, and in the book, *In This Corner. . .*, he admitted that, if he had his career to do all over again, 'The only thing I would change in my whole entire life, I would never have gotten rid of Cus. . . .I don't think that there'll be another, in my opinion, man as Cus, with his witty ways, his cleverness, his shrewdness, how he was able to outmanoeuvre a whole organization, the IBC. You've got to have tremendous respect for a man like this.'

As for Norris, Carbo, Palermo and the IBC, on January 12, 1959, the United States Supreme Court upheld the decision ordering Norris and Wirtz to resign from their controlling positions at Madison Square Garden and divest themselves of all Garden stock. Within a month they had made a deal to sell the controlling interest in the Garden to the Graham–Paige Corporation, headed by Rear Admiral (Ret.) John Bergen, for just under four million dollars.

Determined to stay in big-time boxing, Norris then organized the National Boxing Enterprise. The Garden, free of its entanglements with him, formed Madison Square Garden Boxing, Inc. By the spring of 1959, the California Athletic Commission was investigating the attempt of Carbo and Palermo to strong-arm themselves into the management of World Welterweight Champion, Don Jordan. Then, in September, Carbo, Palermo and three of their associates were indicted by a federal grand jury in California on ten counts of extortion and conspiracy to violate federal anti-racketeering laws. The FBI arrested them the same day. Simultaneously, Carbo was under indictment in New York for conspiracy involving charges that he functioned as an unlicensed manager and matchmaker, and he was facing separate federal charges in connection with $750,000 in income taxes he had failed to pay.

Carbo switched his plea from not guilty to guilty in the New York case. Before he was sentenced, on November 30, 1959, Assistant D.A. Scotti said, in his statement to the court, 'The evil influence of this man has for many years permeated virtually the entire professional sport of boxing. I believe it is fair to say that the name of Frank Carbo today symbolizes the degeneration of professional boxing into a racket. This man is beyond redemption. He is completely impervious to public opinion.' Carbo was sentenced to two years in prison. When he was released, he went on trial in Los Angeles in 1961, along

with Palermo and their three associates, on the conspiracy
and racketeering charges. All five were found guilty. Carbo
received a twenty-five year sentence and a ten-thousand dollar
fine. He was sent to the notorious Alcatraz Federal Penitentiary
in San Francisco Bay.

In 1960, between Carbo's two trials, the so-called Kefauver
Committee (actually the US Senate's Subcommittee on Anti-
trust and Monopoly) conducted its own investigation into
underworld influence in boxing in the United States. Jake
LaMotta testified that he had been forced to take a dive in
his fight with Billy Fox (whose manager was Blinky Palermo)
in 1947. Jim Norris testified that he was hurt and embarrassed tremendously by his association with Frank Carbo,
which he said he discovered was a necessary evil if he were
to be able to function as a major promoter of boxing. The
Kefauver Committee heard a great deal more interesting testimony about mob influence in boxing. But by now, that underworld control had been broken, and was virtually a thing of
the past.

In the 1980s, justice finally caught up with 'Fat Tony' Salerno.
'Fat Tony', one of those indicted by the Federal government in
the highly-publicized Pizza Connection case, was sent away to
prison for life.

Cus D'Amato, sans licence, continued to manage and train
fighters. Most notable was Jose Torres, a Puerto Rican fighter
who won a silver medal as a middleweight in the 1956 Olympics.
After his split with Patterson, D'Amato developed Torres to
a point where he won the World Light-Heavyweight Championship in 1963 by knocking out Willie Pastrano. But while
Patterson was essentially a Spartan, Torres, a boxer of great
talent, did not like the rigours of training, his tastes running more to the sweet life and chasing women. Finally,
Cus sent his brother, Tony to training camp to drum some
discipline and obedience into Torres. 'I made him knuckle
down,' recalls Tony. 'I put the screws on him. I had to
stay practically night and day in order to watch the bum.'
It paid off when Torres went on to capture the title, but
within two years he lost it to Dick Tiger. An intelligent
man who gained additional insight from his association with
D'Amato, Torres matured following his boxing career and
became a successful newspaper columnist. Eventually, he was
named Chairman of the New York State Athletic Commission,

his deep understanding of the psychological elements that go into making a successful fighter – a critical aspect of boxing overlooked or ignored by many so-called trainers who never develop the perceptive qualities that made D'Amato unique – led many to seek his help and advice. Muhammad Ali invited Cus to his camp in Deer Lake, Pennsylvania, hoping that he would agree to stay on as a trainer. Ali told D'Amato he would pay him while continuing to retain his long-time trainer Angelo Dundee as well. But D'Amato refused, telling Ali that such an arrangement would be unfair to Dundee. However, he did work with Ali at his camp as an advisor. Some years later, Gerry Cooney was brought to Catskill and spent time there being advised and assessed by D'Amato. Cooney's managers, Mike Jones and Dennis Rappaport, were anxious to have D'Amato join them as Cooney's trainer. But D'Amato explained that he was a manager, not a trainer, and that in order to guide a fighter's career the way he thought it should go, he could not simply function as a trainer while leaving the crucial managerial decisions to others. Instead, he recommended Victor Valle, who became Cooney's trainer for his entire career, earning a small fortune along the way.

In general, life was comparatively quiet for Cus D'Amato. He had sold his Gramercy Gym. Norris, Carbo and the IBC were long gone; forgotten, too, in the public's mind, were D'Amato's crusades against them. Patterson and Torres were retired. Cus was slipping, perhaps not so gently, into old age. He had his little gym, his club of amateur boys where, legend has it, he helped troubled and underprivileged kids straighten out their lives and build character in the hope that they would leave there better people than when they arrived. However, there is another side to the story. D'Amato was not a trained psychologist, and sometimes his methods could be brutal. Often, if boys didn't have an interest in or an aptitude for boxing, they came and went quickly. One particularly sad case was that of Russ D'Amico, a stubborn 15-year-old who came to live with D'Amato, the alternative for him being reform school. D'Amico didn't like the way Cus was treating him; Cus felt the boy was bad, had no character. When the boy took it into his head to leave, D'Amato refused to take him back. Only the intercession of Teddy Atlas finally made him relent.

Unfortunately, as soon as D'Amico returned, Cus began to harass and badger him, calling him a liar, a weasel. After two weeks, the youngster couldn't take it any more. He told Teddy

he would rather be in prison than taking the constant harass-
ment from Cus. He left, and the courts sent him to reform
school. Soon after, Russ D'Amico committed suicide.

Another myth was that none of the boys who stayed at the
house paid, whereas in fact nearly all of them paid to stay there.
D'Amato was very good at finding out whether their parents
could afford to pay something. The other boys were sent out
to get part-time jobs locally. They all contributed financially
toward their keep.

Along with his amateur boys, D'Amato was developing his
young trainer, Teddy Atlas, and his young welterweight prospect, Kevin Rooney. Rooney and Atlas were best friends who
had grown up together on State Island in New York City. Like
so many of the young men who gravitated to D'Amato, they
came from troubled backgrounds. In 1975, Rooney had won
the 147-pound New York Golden Gloves novice championship.
A boxer with promise, he was nevertheless at a loose end. He
had had several run-ins with the law for brawling, and knew he
was heading for trouble and, eventually, prison.

The product of a broken, alcoholic home, Rooney would
even brawl on occasion with his father, and spent many nights
drinking and partying in bars till the wee hours. He was not yet
20 years old when a friend led him to D'Amato, who explained
the arrangement: Rooney could come and live in the house
and train at the gym for free, doing the yard work and other
chores around the house in exchange for his room and board.
Rooney recognized the opportunity, and grabbed it. 'Cus took
a personal interest in me,' he says. 'I was, like, his boy. He was
like a father. Cus was my friend. He made me go back to college,
get a two-year degree. He showed what I knew inside me, that
I was smart, but he brought it out. He'd tell me you're lucky if
you have one true friend who'll stand by you no matter what,
and I knew I had that in Cus.'

Like many of those who came before and after him, Rooney
was somewhat baffled by this strange old man who took such
a deep interest in developing him not only as a fighter but
as a person as well. 'Here was this guy so smart, a genius,
he knew about anything and everything, but, I said, this
guy doesn't care about money. At the time [I was] 19
years old, everything was about a buck. Here's this guy
who'd had the heavyweight champ, the light-heavyweight
champ of the world, but he didn't care about money. . .he
just cared about principle, which is very important. What's

right and wrong is what mattered to him. . . .He was a great man.'

About four months after Rooney arrived at Catskill, Teddy Atlas got into serious trouble with the police in Staten Island. Although his father was a physician, Atlas was a rough and wild kid who had been an amateur fighter in the same Police Athletic League gym as Kevin Rooney. When Rooney heard about it, he asked D'Amato to go out on a limb and appear before the judge on Atlas's behalf. Cus did so, offering to take Atlas in to his home in Catskill and help him develop his boxing skills if the court would consider it. The judge agreed to place the boy on five years' probation provided D'Amato took responsibility for him. As he had done before, and as he would do in the future with Mike Tyson, Cus D'Amato became a substitute father to both Rooney and Atlas, and played a major part in helping them to turn their lives around.

Under D'Amato's tutelage, the young men blossomed as amateur fighters, and showed great promise of a future professional career. But Cus soon noticed that when Teddy fought and trained, he would wince with pain. He discovered that the young fighter had a serious congenital problem with his spine that caused him great pain, although he had tried to conceal it because he was so keen to succeed as a fighter. Cus knew then that Teddy could never pursue a professional career in the ring, but he had another idea. He saw something in Atlas that made him believe he could teach him to become a good trainer, to work with other youngsters and in that way develop a career in boxing even though he himself couldn't fight. The idea did not appeal to Teddy at first. 'I was selfish and not ready or directed enough and not sure what I wanted to do. I had gone there to become a fighter and I wasn't prepared to dedicate myself to helping other people.' D'Amato later told film-maker Michael Marton: 'I tried to make him see, and I think I succeeded, that even if you're not a fighter yourself, you can become the same type of success through your fighter, because if you take a boy and teach him how to fight from beginning to end, part of you is in him, too, so that when he fights, part of you is in that ring. And suddenly I discovered [Teddy] had a real talent for teaching, a born teacher. He's the type of person that wants to help people, especially kids, and they come to depend on him and rely on him a great deal, so they become very close that way.'

In between the time his boxing career ended and he decided to take up D'Amato's offer to become a trainer, there was a year of aimlessness and confusion for Atlas. He left Catskill and returned to Staten Island. He was 20 years old and floundering. He got involved in a street altercation that nearly cost him his life. He was slashed by a knife down the side of his face nearly to his jugular vein. He spent eight days in the hospital, and thought about his future, finally realizing he had to make a decision on what direction the rest of his life would take. 'I made a phone call to Cus and said I'm ready now to take you up on your offer. I was prepared now, I was settled in my mind to do it. Cus was happy about it.'

D'Amato realized that Teddy had a very low sense of self-esteem, and decided to boost his morale by giving him more and more responsibility for the day-to-day running of the gym, as well as allowing him to take on much of the actual training of the boys. Teddy developed a rapport with the youngsters and they, in turn, responded very positively to him. D'Amato taught Atlas his own methods of training fighters. D'Amato had innovated what came to be known as the peek-a-boo style: both fists held high, tucked in alongside each cheek, elbows and arms tight to the ribs. From this defensive stance, peering over the tops of the gloves, a fighter was well protected. He also developed a punch-by-numbers system. Each punch, each part of the opponent's body, had a number assigned to it. The bags in the gym had the numbers written on them, and fighters had to land the right punches in the right place as the numbers were called out.

But the most important lessons were not learned in the gym. They were learned at the dinner table, or in the evening after the day's work was done. Sitting and talking with Cus, his young disciples learned the old man's philosophy of life as he applied it to life in the in ring. 'I never teach until I've spoken to the fighter,' he would say. 'I have to first determine his emotional state, get his background, to find out what I have to do, how many layers I have to keep peeling off so that I get to the core of the person so that he can recognize, as well as I, what is there.' The crucial lesson he taught, one he felt was generally ignored by other trainers, was the recognition of and acknowledgement of fear.

'Fear is the greatest obstacle to learning in any area, but particularly in boxing,' he said. 'For example, boxing is something you learn through repetition. You do it over and over and suddenly you've got it. . . . However, in the course of trying to learn, if you get hit and get hurt, this makes you cautious, and when you're cautious you can't repeat it, and when you can't repeat it, it's going to delay the learning process. . .When they. . .come up to the gym and say I want to be a fighter, the first thing I'd do was talk to them about fear. . . I would always use. . .the same example of the deer crossing an open field and upon approaching the clearing suddenly instinct tells him danger is there, and nature begins the survival process, which involves the body releasing adrenalin into the bloodstream, causing the heart to beat faster and enabling the deer to perform extraordinary feats of agility and strength. . . It enables the deer to get out of range of the danger, helps him escape to the safety of the forest across the clearing. . . .an example in which fear is your friend.

'The thing a kid in the street fears the most is to be called yellow or chicken, and sometimes a kid will do the most stupid, wild, crazy things just to hide how scared he is. I often tell them that while fear is such an obnoxious thing, an embarrassing thing. . .nevertheless it is your best friend, because anytime anyone saves your life perhaps a dozen times a day, no matter how obnoxious he is, you've got to look upon him as a friend, and this is what fear is. . . . Since nature gave us fear in order to help us survive, we cannot look upon it as an enemy. Just think how many times a day a person would die if he had no fear. He'd walk in front of cars, he'd die a dozen times a day. Fear is a protective mechanism. . . . By talking to the fighters about fear I cut the learning time maybe as much as half, sometimes more, depending on the individual.

'The next thing I do, I get them in excellent condition. . . . Knowing how the mind is and the tricks it plays on a person and how an individual will always look to avoid a confrontation with something that's intimidating, I remove all the possible excuses they're going to have before they get in there. By getting them in excellent condition, they can't say when they get tired that they're not in shape. When they're in excellent shape I put them into the ring to box for the first time, usually with an experienced fighter who won't take advantage of them. When the novice throws punches and nothing happens, and his opponent keeps coming at him. . .the new fighter becomes panicky. When he gets panicky he wants to quit, but he can't quit because his whole psychology from the time he's first been in the streets is to condemn a person who's yellow. So what does he do? He gets tired. This is what happens to fighters in the ring. They get tired, because they're getting afraid. . . .Now that he gets tired, people can't call him yellow. He's just too "tired" to go on. But let that same fighter strike back wildly with a visible effect on the opponent and suddenly that tired, exhausted guy becomes a tiger. . . . It's a psychological fatigue, that's all it is, but people in boxing don't understand that.'

By 1979, Kevin Rooney had developed to the point where D'Amato decided to turn him professional. D'Amato was unlicensed, so he could not work Rooney's corner. He would be managed by Jim Jacobs, an astute businessman and D'Amato's long-time friend, with Cus making all the boxing decisions. He entrusted Rooney's training to Teddy Atlas. It was not unusual for D'Amato to have another trainer handling the day-to-day routine with his fighters, even though he himself masterminded the overall strategy. Floyd Patterson had had Frank LaVelle, Buster Watson and Dan Florio training him. Jose Torres had had Joe Fariello, Tony D'Amato and Johnny Manzanet working with him. As for Atlas, D'Amato felt that working not just with kids but with a professional fighter would help centre him even more, since the young man was now determined to make a career for himself as a trainer.

When Mike Tyson burst upon the scene in 1980, Kevin Rooney had progressed through half a dozen fights. He and Tyson, along with the other boys, trained side by side, ate at the same table, and slept in the same house. Rooney, too, saw Tyson's potential from the very beginning: 'He had that power. Not too many guys have that one-punch knockout power. . . .I know this guy can't miss if he really wants it. . .'

5

The Catskill Years

A boy comes to me with a spark of interest. I feed the spark and it becomes a flame. I feed the flame and it becomes a fire. I feed the fire and it becomes a roaring blaze.

– CUS D'AMATO

THE RELATIVELY CALM and quiet life in the country surroundings of Catskill were totally alien to Mike Tyson, as well as the fact that for the first time in his life, most of those around this black kid from the city streets were white. It would require a big adjustment, one that at times proved very difficult for him. By his own admission, he was suspicious of this 'crazy old white dude' who kept telling him he could be the Heavyweight Champion of the World, and of his motives.

When Mike made his permanent move to Catskill, he had just passed his fourteenth birthday. 'I didn't want to be there,' he would later recall. 'I was a city boy. I wasn't used to that environment, [but] I had nowhere else to go.' There were house rules that all the boys had the follow, and Mike often chafed at having to live in a voluntary, cooperative arrangement with others, especially when those others were mostly white. But he knew his only alternative was to return to reform school.

Another thing that caused Mike to champ at the bit was the matter of his education. As a minor and a ward of the State, he was required to attend school. While running the streets of Brooklyn, he had been a truant, and so, despite Bobby Stewart's brief and successful effort to get him to knuckle down and learn, he had had relatively little formal education for a boy of fourteen. In September of 1980, when he arrived in Catskill, Cus enrolled Mike in the Catskill Junior High School, in the eighth grade. In the following two years, he created many problems at the school, although at least some of the trouble was provoked by other students.

Before his arrival in Catskill, the local schools had experienced several racial incidents and flare-ups. The black school population in this rural environment was less than ten per cent, and so perceived itself, with justification, as the underdog in any problems that occurred. As a result of the racial conflict prior

to Mike's enrolment, specific guidelines had been drafted by
school administrators to deal with any matters of discipline 'by
the book', so that all students, black or white, would receive
identical treatment. These regulations meant that Cus D'Amato
could expect no special treatment for Mike, despite his concern
that the teachers and administrators be made aware of the boy's
unique situation. He was coming there, with no family, from a
city childhood and reform school background; he was physically
much more mature than the other kids of his age; and he was
sorely lacking school experience.

The heightened racial awareness among students and teachers, together with Mike's imposing physical presence, and the
knowledge that he came from a tough institutionalized background, marked him out for more than his share of attention
from the day he enrolled. In 1980 there were no special or
alternative educational options available to administrators in
the Catskill community, as there are now, so Mike was main-
streamed into the normal school environment. Owing to his age
and his physical size (he was 5'8" and a hulking 200 pounds),
he was placed in the eighth grade, although his academic
skills hardly warranted such a placement. However, it was
felt that to place him with smaller and younger children in a
lower grade would have been more psychologically debilitating.
Also, although he did not have, say, the required knowledge
of social studies or science or history, he was assessed by Lee
Bordick, the Junior High School principal at the time, as being
'shrewd, very verbal, a con artist to some degree' and someone
who 'had a special quality about him that he was driven to be
successful. . . and those involved in education for many years
recognized that this was a special person, there was something
unique about him.' Bordick and other teachers who took an
interest in Mike during that first school year in Catskill felt he
had the native intelligence to catch on and catch up. Still, he had
to get used to some very basic things for the first time in his life,
such as sitting at a desk for an entire forty-minute period until
the bell rang and it was time to move on to your next class.

Mike had several quarrels during the eighth grade, but not
with other boys. Oddly enough, it was the black girls who tended
to taunt him. They were 'country', he was 'city', essentially a
new and mysterious and unknown quantity to them, a sudden,
unexpected intrusion on their little town. And, because he went
to the gym every day after school as well as at weekends, they
knew he was a boxer. He no doubt presented a paradox in being,

in some vague way, a threat, someone to be kept at arm's length, and yet, in another way, an irresistible attraction. Their way of dealing with their own confused feelings was to taunt him with jeering insults for no apparent reason about his mother, about whom they knew absolutely nothing. This would send Mike into rages, since he was particularly sensitive about his mother; he cared for her, and realized he had caused her much worry and grief. And while he never retaliated physically against the girls, his rage would cause him to become disobedient, resulting in a suspension for a day or two until he cooled off.

In addition, though more because of his imposing physical presence than any actual threat he made to them, several of the teachers were intimidated by Mike, worried about the consequences to themselves if he ever directed his rage at them. But Mike was on what was for him good behaviour. He didn't want to cross the line that would bring about the end of this new relationship with Cus and send him back to Tryon or the hopelessness of the streets, so he kept his temper in check for the most part.

One day, three black girls were harassing him once again about his mother, and Mike responded by chasing after them. They took refuge in the girls' lavatories, but Mike went right in after them. Lee Bordick, the principal, was summoned. As he was taking the boy outside to have a talk with him, one of the girls kicked Mike hard as he was walking past her. Mike spun round, his nostrils flaring, and glared at her, but then kept walking. Such was his strength at that age that if he had chosen to go after her, one or even two teachers would have been powerless to stop him without placing themselves at risk of physical injury. This occurrence came on the heels of other disciplinary incidents involving Mike over a period of several weeks, and Mike stormed off, ignoring the principal. Bordick went after him, determined to assert his authority. He could see Mike snorting with rage when he caught up with him. 'Mike,' he told him, 'I want you to run around the school campus until you calm down, and then we'll talk.' Mike obeyed, and a few minutes later he and Bordick talked things out. Under such provocation any kid might be forgiven for responding as Mike Tyson did.

Early in 1981, the school administered its annual New York State competency exam to students. It was a fairly tough test with perhaps an overall ten per cent failure rate, but Mike passed it, albeit narrowly, which was a good indication of his natural intelligence and how quickly he had managed to improve his reading and other academic skills in his few months at Catskill. Thanks to the interest taken in him by several teachers, Bordick's assessment was that 'Mike overall had a very successful eighth grade year. There were some problems, but they were certainly not the worst on the list. It was a matter of adjustment. Overall, one would have to be impressed with his incredible self-discipline and focus.' Bordick felt because Mike had a rigid routine of school, followed by the rigours of his training in the gym every afternoon, plus weekends, he was more disciplined than most of the kids his age in the school. He also appreciated Cus's influence on Mike: 'Cus became the consummate teacher, and I was very impressed with someone who was relatively uneducated but was fairly well read and was able to inculcate in a young fellow the things that we were trying to do with students in general, [which Cus] did very naturally.'

Cus remembered Mike's early days in Catskill this way: 'Things were rather difficult, because there was a lack of communication and I think he was a little apprehensive that we wouldn't get along. . . .He was accustomed to being in the company of different types of people, and as a result he didn't know how I would accept or be receptive to him because of that. He was coming there to be helped in every way. As a fighter, particularly, but in order to be helped as a fighter he had to be helped in every other way. His character had to be developed and strengthened, he had to learn discipline, and he had to learn to face his problems and not avoid them, which is an essential part of the character of any competitive athlete. The strengthening of character has been a slow process because the rules he had learned to live by were not those generally accepted by society. His life was a dog eat dog affair. But I can relate to someone of any age because I lived through all those periods. I grew up in a very tough neighbourhood. . . .People are people and boys are boys, and I know exactly how he feels. I know when to put a little pressure down to make him aware, perhaps to influence him in a particular direction. I also know when to lay off, because pressure at the wrong time may cause a certain amount of resentment in him to arise, which will delay the development.' Differences over when to 'lay off', and whether Tyson's character was being sufficiently 'developed and strengthened', would eventually lead to a growing rift between the young trainer, Teddy Atlas, and the old master.

D'Amato's methods for tutoring Tyson were those he had evolved and used over the years: 'I tell them the first time they're going to fight, the night before they probably won't sleep. I can't offer them any consolation other than the fact that the other guy went through the same thing, and when they get down to the fight and enter the dressing-room, especially if they're in an amateur fight, the room is full of possible opponents, because they don't know who they're going to fight, and everybody looks calm, confident and smiling and all the new boy is aware of is that terrible thump in his chest, and he's intimidated by their attitude and their confidence. What he doesn't realize is that they look at him and they see the same thing in him as he sees in them, because by an exercise of discipline he also puts on a superficial appearance of confidence. . . . We go on now to go into the ring. Half the time they're walking when they go down to the ring as though they're going to the gallows. So when they climb those stairs, I never call a fighter yellow. Knowing what he goes through, the very act of climbing into that ring stamps him a person of courage and discipline.

'So now they get into the ring. . . .The other guy probably looks bigger and stronger and better conditioned and real muscular and when he starts to loosen up he looks more experienced. This is the novice fighter's mind and imagination exaggerating everything, which is what the mind does. Nothing is ever as bad as the imagination makes it, not even death. A person doesn't realize what's making him nervous unless he understands why he's getting scared, which is the natural, normal thing. When he understands it he accepts it as such. Then it doesn't become as intimidating, which is the reason why I take the boy step by step until actually the bell rings to fight. I take them that way so that hopefully by the time they get to fight they've experienced these different feelings which are often intimidating by themselves. "Cus said it was going to be like this," so that they don't feel they are inferior or less prepared than their opponent.

'Now, when they go in and face the opponent and the bell rings, for the first time. . .they're facing reality, and suddenly a relative calmness comes over them. Relative. They're still scared but it isn't that terrible intimidating unknown thing. . . .But the moment the blows start to be thrown, the effort to throw punches has begun, he gets calm, because now this is something he's been prepared to cope with. . . .However, I should add that at no time does fear disappear. It's just as bad in the hundredth fight as it was in the first, except by the time he reaches a hundred fights or long before that he's developed enough discipline where he can learn to live with it, which is the object, to learn to live with it. . .

'Every fighter that ever lived had fear. A boy comes to me and tells me that he's not afraid, if I believed him I'd say he's a liar or there's something wrong with him. I'd send him to a doctor to find out what the hell's the matter with him, because this is not a normal reaction. The fighter that's gone into the ring and hasn't experienced fear is either a liar or a psychopath. . .'

Before Mike would be allowed to step into the ring for an actual fight, he would be prepared fully under D'Amato's guidance. D'Amato prepared those of his fighters who had the potential to become successful professionals, one way from the start: as professionals. In the short run, this would cause the fighter to suffer somewhat in his amateur career. He would win several national titles as an amateur, but never gain the wide public recognition of a Sugar Ray Leonard, a Mark Breland, a Henry Tillman, or a Tyrell Biggs. They all captured Olympic gold; Breland won a record five consecutive New York Golden Gloves Championships.

D'Amato was probably not especially interested in Tyson achieving greatness as an amateur. He knew that Mike's style was more suited to professional boxing, and schooling him too well as an amateur could adversely affect his adjustment to professional fighting later on. It's an accepted truth in boxing circles that fighters who spend too long in the amateur ranks don't achieve the same success in the professional arena. The theories vary: they burn themselves out with too many amateur bouts, they become too conditioned to being 'three-round fighters', the length of all amateur fights. But the main reason long conditioning as an amateur can stunt professional growth is the marked contrast between the rules amateur boxing is governed by as compared with professional boxing.

In any other major sport, the rules of the game and the way it is played remain virtually the same from high school and college to the minor leagues and on into the big-time professional competition. Boxing is the only major sport where the rules in the 'minor leagues', the amateur ranks, differ vastly from the professional side of the sport. In amateur boxing, with its convoluted scoring systems, the primary objective is to score points. In theory, a good job counts as much in a round as a knock blow. So if you're knocked down by a tremendous punch, you can get up at the count of nine, land three soft jabs on your opponent, and you've scored more points towards victory than he has! The front, or fist, portion of amateur gloves are painted white, and only punches that land on the white part of the glove count. Any others will not only not count in the scoring, but will usually result in the referee stopping the action to issue a warning to the fighter. Bending at the waist, bobbing and weaving, all effective defensive techniques for professionals, are frowned upon in amateur boxing. There are so many rules and regulations that it is rare to see amateur or Olympic fights where the action is not stopped numerous times in the course of just three rounds by the referee to issue warnings to the fighters that completely break up the flow of the action and, consequently, the excitement of the fight. The use of headgear in amateur boxing was also an aspect which did not meet with D'Amato's approval. He felt headgear gave fighters a false sense of security, and with good reason.

Headgear is perhaps the worst innovation introduced into amateur boxing by well-meaning but misguided amateur federation administrators. The casual boxing fan may think that headgear protects young fighters from damaging blows to the head, blows that critics of the sport are always quick to point to as the cause of injury. But nothing could be further from the truth. Headgear does not provide that kind of protection, nor was it ever intended to do so. The concussive force of a blow to the head is not lessened one bit by a piece of padded leather around the skull, because it is the impact of the blow and the resulting motion of the head that causes a knockout. Nor do gloves, which the uninformed may feel are also intended to soften the force of punches, serve any such purpose. Gloves are designed to protect the hand of the man throwing the punches, not the head of the man receiving them. The acceleration of the punch and the acceleration of the brain inside the skull are what cause damage in a fight, and padded hands or heads do not reduce that acceleration one iota. All headgear does, and all it was designed to do, is to protect the fighter from being cut, and this advantage is probably more than offset by the reduction in his peripheral vision which, ironically, makes him more vulnerable, since it can take him longer to see and therefore to avoid any punches heading his way. D'Amato believed that the fighter's restricted vision forced him to keep his head higher in order to see better, thus exposing his chin and making him even more vulnerable. From the beginning, Tyson was taught to train in the gym without headgear, and to this day, in his sparring sessions, no headgear is worn.

D'Amato insisted that the primary weapon, even for such a powerfully destructive machine as Tyson, was defence, and Tyson spent many hours in the ring during his early training not throwing a punch at sparring partners. D'Amato and Atlas just had him move, duck, bob, weave and practise lateral motion to avoid being hit. He paid for his lessons by catching punches every time he failed to make the proper defensive move, and he was not allowed to retaliate by throwing punches back at his opponents, who often were fast, smaller welterweights or middleweights.

Mickey Duff recalls seeing Tyson for the first time in a junior tournament in New York City: 'He paced up and down like a caged tiger and I thought at that time that he looked menacing. He looked a strong kid with not a lot of sophisticated talent yet. Natural talent, yes, but he didn't look to have any fine skills. He looked strong and awesome for his age. As I remember, he fought a kid about two years older than him. Knocked him out.'

D'Amato certainly knew how to turn a situation to his own advantage and help build his young fighter's confidence. Duff remembers one such occasion, when he had come to the United States with a young British heavyweight of his own, 22 years old, just in the early stages of a professional career. His name was Frank Bruno. Seven years later, when Tyson was Heavyweight Champion, he and Bruno would meet in the ring amidst the glamour and glitter of Las Vegas with millions of dollars and the world title at stake. But no one could foresee that when Duff brought Bruno to box with the 16-year-old Tyson, and perhaps was outsmarted by D'Amato. 'Cus called me to ask if Tyson could box with Bruno. I said yes. . . . Cus was very smart. Bruno was told twenty times before they started sparring, this is only a kid, don't go and hurt him. So Bruno went out mentally to just spar and suddenly finds this guy swarming all over him. The result was that Tyson had a good round, and when it was over, Cus said, "That was all I wanted him to box." He only let Mike box one round [*note*: it was actually two rounds], and he pounced out and jumped all over Bruno.' It must have given Tyson a boost of confidence then, and it certainly did when he was signed to fight Bruno in 1988, because he talked about how easily he had handled Bruno as an amateur those many years before.

At one point the quiet house in Catskill suffered an invasion that no one who was there at the time will ever forget. Wilfred Benitez came to train in Catskill. Benitez was managed by D'Amato's closest friend, Jim Jacobs, the first World Champion Jacobs would handle. The Puerto Rican native was a boxing prodigy. He won his first world title at the age of 17, making him the youngest professional champion in history. (Even Mike Tyson, who would become the youngest heavyweight champion ever, was still an amateur when he was 17 years old.) Benitez would go on to win two more titles in his career, making him one of a handful of men to hold championships in three different weight divisions. He did it all on natural talent, because his training habits and overall discipline were severely lacking. Benitez had the reputation in boxing circles of being a 'head case', a wacky, strutting, macho kid not playing with a full deck.

He began his career at age 14, managed by his father, Gregorio, who was heavily into horses and gambling. Within a few years, predictably, Gregorio was in debt and was forced to sell his son's contract to raise cash. Teddy Brenner, the matchmaker at the old Eastern Parkway Arena in Brooklyn who had started out Floyd Patterson, put Gregorio together with Jim Jacobs, who he knew had the money. Financially, it was a steal. Jacobs grabbed Benitez's contract for $75-thousand. Guided by Jacobs, the fighter would earn several million dollars over the next few years, and Jacobs's cut earned back his investment many times over. But handling Wilfred Benitez took its toll in aggravation, since the fighter's father insisted that he remain involved in his son's career as the boy's trainer. Father and son would prove to be their own worst enemies. Neither knew how to handle their new-found wealth, perhaps thinking those million-dollar purses would pour in forever. Eventually, a victim of his own profligate ways and milked by his father's continued gambling, Benitez would burn out while still in his twenties, his career over, and with virtually all his money gone.

When he and his entourage arrived in Catskill he was at the peak of his fighting powers preparing to challenge Carlos Palomino for the welterweight title. It was Jacobs's hope that the two men might gain some insight by training under the watchful eye of Cus. Apparently unfamiliar – or unconcerned – with the conventions of civilized society, the Puerto Ricans turned things upside down at the house. One member of the group would wake up between four and five every morning and begin to practise his martial arts, complete with loud screams and whoops, waking everyone up. He also had the charming habit of blowing snot from his nose right on to the floor, and leaving it there.

Wilfred himself would spit on the floor around his bed. He would also gorge himself on his favourite diet of chicken, beans and rice to the point where he would sometimes throw up, or get stomach cramps and shit all over the toilet, leaving his mess unflushed until someone would discover it the next morning.

Benitez also began a hot pursuit of a 13-year-old girl in town, until Cus put a halt to it by explaining that although this might be acceptable behaviour in the islands, in a small country town it could land you in jail for statutory rape, or perhaps provoke the girl's family to come after you with shotguns.

At dinnertime the Benitez entourage did not bother with utensils: they used their hands for everything. When the other boys in the house complained about this behaviour that was turning the place into a shambles, Cus tried to explain to them that these people came from a different culture. As Cus put it, all these people knew was how to cut sugar cane all day and screw their women at night.

However, the final straw came one day when Camille was trying to clean up. She had noticed that her expensive, monogrammed towels had been disappearing. While cleaning in Wilfred's room, she found a pile of them, along with a stench. When she examined more closely, she was repulsed. It seems that Wilfred had been using them to wipe his rear end after bowel movements, and then just dumped the excrement-covered towels in his room. Camille was enraged, and it was not long before Benitez and his merry men were sent packing.

When D'Amato came to the gym every few days, his professional eye watched and he tutored Tyson as he boxed. However, day to day, it was Teddy Atlas who was in the gym, delivering the same object lessons to Tyson and Rooney that he'd learned from Cus, week in and week out. As D'Amato told the documentary producer, Michael Marton: 'Teddy always

comes to me when he has some doubts or something important. Otherwise I let him do it because I know he can do it. I
wouldn't let him do it if I didn't know he could do it. I'm the
one that makes the final decision. Teddy and I are together.
We're synonymous. I'm Teddy, Teddy's me.'

'I'm not a creator,' Cus would often tell people. 'What I do
is discover and uncover. My job is, take the spark and fan it.
When it starts to become a little flame, I feed it. I feed the fire
until it becomes a roaring blaze, and then when it becomes a
roaring blaze, I pour huge logs on it, and then you really get
a fire going. That's what I do with these boys, that's what I
try to do.'

During these early months in Catskill, Tyson fought in a few
small tournaments, and also in 'smokers', amateur fight cards
often held in small gyms that were not sanctioned by any official
amateur organization, but a place for kids to get experience in
the ring, even though the fights would not go down on their
official amateur records. Mike won impressively every time.

Every fighter comes to a crossroads in the ring, a test which
he must pass if he is to progress up the ladder. Sometimes that
test is met in the gym, and many fighters have given up without
progressing beyond that point. Some fighters may meet their
first real challenge when it's too late, when they are ill-prepared
to cope with it, as happened with Gerry Cooney when he met
Larry Holmes for the Heavyweight Championship and found
he had not been properly prepared by facing tough opponents
on the way up, even though his managers had done a brilliant
job on the business side by manoeuvring him into a little fight
and a $10-million purse.

For Mike Tyson, the first test of his character, the first test
not of his natural ability but of his resolve and determination,
came on a forgotten night on a forgotten boxing show against
a forgotten opponent in Scranton, Pennsylvania. But it was a test
that proved crucial to his development, although only the inner
circle of Teddy, Cus and Mike himself would know it. They had
gone to Scranton because Kevin Rooney was booked to fight a
professional bout on a small card. Because of the realities of
promoting small-town boxing, the undercard would be made
up of amateur bouts, which served to give the local boys some
experience, while relieving the promoter of the burden of having to pay purses to pros in the prelims. Cus and Teddy brought
a couple of their amateurs along. Mike was one of them. He was
14 years old, and had not arrived at the point where he could

overcome his fear. Up till then he'd never had to, since things
had always gone his way in the few fights he'd had.

His opponent was a local white kid, not very skilled, but
tough. In the first round, Mike overwhelmed him, knocking
him down twice. But something unusual happened, something
that Mike was not used to. The kid got back on his feet both
times and instead of giving up, fought back hard. Mike came
back to his corner at the end of the first round, flopped on
the stool, and told Teddy he was very tired. Cus was watching
from ringside, and saw the fatigue Tyson was showing. But
Cus and Teddy knew that Mike was in great shape, and that
physically it was impossible for him to be tired after just three
minutes of boxing. 'Mike,' Teddy said as he sponged him off,
'you're not tired. You're letting your feelings get the better of
you. . . . You're better than this guy. You've got to concentrate,
just be steady, do the things we've worked on. . . . If you knock
him down and the guy gets up, knock him down again. And
don't let your imagination get the better of you.'

The bell rang for the second round, and Tyson went out
confidently. He put his opponent down for a third time, but
again he got up. Mike was dominating the round, and if the kid
hadn't been a local boy, the referee might even have stepped
in and stopped the fight. When the bell sounded, Mike came
back to the corner and dropped to his stool again, completely
exhausted. 'Teddy, my hand is broken,' he told his trainer.
Atlas knew better. His experience and judgment told him it was
Mike's will that was faltering. He had less than a minute to pull
his fighter together. It was critical. If Tyson came apart here, the
future they had anticipated for him would be in question. At the
very least, he would suffer a psychological setback that would
delay his development. In the corner, Mike was glazed, drifting
off, unfocused. His mind was out of control. Seconds were tick-
ing away. Teddy had to be sure his assessment was right. He
grabbed Tyson's gloved hand and squeezed it hard as he could.
Mike didn't even notice. The hand was obviously not broken.
Teddy twisted Mike's face toward his. He was nose to nose with
the panting fighter. He had to make his words count, make Mike
listen. 'Mike, there's nothing wrong with your hand,' Teddy told
him. 'What's broken is your spirit. All this crap about how you
want to become heavyweight champ of the world, here's your
heavyweight title. Go out and win the damn thing. Be a man,
damn it. This guy's falling down. If I was in the other corner I
would have stopped the damn fight already. Here's your first

test and you want to fail it. You want to quit. Now get out there, damn it, and keep doing what you been doing, which is knocking this guy down. If he gets up, you knock him down again. Otherwise all this work and all these dreams, it ends right here. You gotta want it. With all your skill, you just gotta want it. Now go out there and win the fight.' It was all the time Teddy had. He stuffed the mouthpiece between Mike's teeth and literally shoved him off the stool and into the centre of the ring.

Both fighters were spent, so neither was doing very much, groping and clinching, throwing harmless punches. Mike's mind was still not straight, despite Teddy's lecture. The white boy threw a few punches. Mike countered and hurt him again. They grabbed each other and staggered toward Tyson's corner. Cus had once told Teddy that when you get experienced enough as a trainer, you get to a point where you can almost see what's going on in the fighter's mind. Teddy suddenly knew what Mike was about to do. Although he wasn't being hit, Teddy knew that Mike was going to go down. He was going to quit, take the count on the canvas. His psychological exhaustion had got the better of him, his last ounce of resolve was gone. The crowd was going wild, rooting for their local boy. Teddy didn't have time to think. He had to react like a fighter, instinctively. He knew that in a more formal structure what he was about to do would result in the disqualification of his fighter, but something in that split second told him that here, in a small arena, with the crowd screaming, he might possible get away with it. By now, Mike was backed into the corner just above Teddy. His knees were beginning to buckle, and Teddy knew if he went down he wasn't going to get up. In an instant, Teddy jumped up on the ring apron, outside the ropes. He leaned in and shouted, 'Don't do it! Don't do it, goddam it!' Hearing him, Tyson grabbed his opponent and fell into a clinch. The two fighters staggered out of the corner, mauling and wrestling until the bell rang some 30 seconds later to end the fight. Teddy jumped into the ring, and Mike stumbled into his arms, hugging his trainer and mumbling, 'Thank you, thank you,' to him, again and again. Teddy knew what Mike meant. Without saying it, Mike understood that Teddy had saved him from himself, something much more important than the decision the judges awarded him after the final bell.

D'Amato, too, watching from ringside, knew that he had just witnessed a mental fight inside his young protégé much tougher than the outward, physical battle. One of D'Amato's

main axioms concerned the paramount importance of the will:
'When two men are fighting, what you're watching is more a
contest of wills than of skills, with the stronger will usually
overcoming the skill. The skill will prevail only when it is so
superior to the other man's skill that the will is not tested. . . .
As many times as you see a fellow get tired in the course of a
fight, note that he gets tired when pressure builds up, after he
gets hurt or he's been in some kind of doubtful situation, not
being able to control the situation. That's when he starts getting
tired. That's why when two good fighters get to fight, they're
head to head, so to speak, they won't give an inch and they're
using all their skill and ability, until maybe about the seventh
or eighth or ninth round, one fighter starts to visibly weaken. It
only means he's reached a point where he no longer can stand
the pressure. He's now become dominated, because when two
people fight it's very much like two armies. They seek to impose
their will on one another.'

Back in the dressing-room in Scranton, Teddy didn't have
much time. He had to get Kevin taped and gloved for his fight,
but he pulled Mike aside to talk with him briefly, while the
experience was fresh in their minds. Mike was still experiencing
his post-fight euphoria, still hugging and kissing and thanking
Ted, who calmed him down before telling him: 'Mike, look, I'm
only gonna say this once because it's not a thing I'm gonna keep
banging you over the head with, bringing up all the time. . . .
You were gonna give up out there. . . But you didn't. For the
first time you felt the feeling of a person when he felt he couldn't
control something and the only thing you could go on wasn't
your skill any more, it was your will. This is the first time you
were tested. . . . The weakness would have been if you had
given in and actually given up. You didn't. You felt it, so you
know you're human, you know like anyone else it's possible to
be vulnerable, and it's also possible to fight that vulnerability
off and overcome it. . . . In the future you can avoid getting
that close because you won't allow your imagination and the
unknown to get the better of you. You didn't quit. That's the
most important thing. . . .' Mike acknowledged that he understood what Teddy was telling him. Kevin went out and won his
fight, after which they all drove back to Catskill. Teddy never
spoke to Mike again about that night. He didn't have to. The
lesson had been learned.

A few months later, Tyson took his first big step up. He was
entered in the National Junior Olympics Tournament, held at

the USAF Academy in Colorado Springs, Colorado. This was a showcase for the best young fighters in the nation under the age of 16, and so not yet eligible to compete in senior amateur events. D'Amato sent Teddy Atlas alone with Mike to Colorado. Mike was not yet 15, but it was at this tournament that the 'Tyson mystique' truly began. It started even before Mike had his first fight. He stood out from all the other boys waiting in line to take their physical exams. Most of the other 14- and 15-year-olds still had baby fat. Their bodies were not fully formed yet, their muscles did not have the definition they would get as they matured. Mike, by contrast, looked as if he were sculpted out of rock, and attracted the attention of all the other fighters. His demeanour added to his mystique. Schooled by Cus in the tradition that the fighter did the fighting and the manager did the talking, Mike remained aloof, refusing to join in casual conversation with the other boys. If any of them asked him anything, he would just point to Teddy. He was scoring psychological points over them before they even saw him with a glove on. D'Amato had always maintained that you can build up a forbidding image, but you've got to be able to back it up when you step in the ring, or else it serves little purpose.

That night, Mike's first opponent was a hulking boy from Hawaii. He weighed 265 pounds, big but soft. Mike was small by comparison, barely 5'9" and under 200 pounds, but solid as a rock. In the first round, he hit the Hawaiian with a tremendous left hook to the liver. All 265 pounds of the youngster quivered, and he went down in a massive heap on the canvas. The arena, filled not only with spectators but coaches, officials and other fighters, was electrified. Everything they had feared and imagined about this unknown kid from back east was true.

The next night, Mike won his second fight, also by knockout. Suddenly, he was larger than life. He was still refusing to talk to anyone, trying to project an attitude of sullen invincibility. Out of earshot of Mike, the fighters were talking; 'See that Tyson who's knocking everyone out, he's Sonny Liston's nephew.' The rumour spread like wildfire, further intimidating the other heavyweights in the tournament: Mike Tyson was Sonny Liston's nephew, at least in their minds. The day before the finals, a black kid who had lost in the semis the night before was talking to the boy who'd beaten him. 'Man, you didn't beat me,' he said. 'I was just smarter than you. My momma didn't raise no fool. I knew if I won I'd have to fight that animal Tyson in the finals, so I quit. I let you beat me. Now what are you gonna do tomorrow night, man? You gotta fight Tyson.' The next night, Mike scored another knockout. He became the National Junior Olympics Heavyweight Champion, his first national amateur title, and as the word spread in amateur boxing circles about this 14-year-old destroyer, the Tyson legend was born.

Mike continued to develop as a fighter, knocking out virtually all of his opponents. In the fall of 1981, he entered Catskill High School, and during the course of the next year, a widening con-flict would develop between Cus and Teddy, fuelled largely by their differences concerning Mike's education and his overall discipline.

As he entered the high school to begin the ninth grade, racial tensions caused the school to be closed down for several days, according to a former school administrator. Some of the black students were concerned about where Mike stood *vis-à-vis* the situation, because of his close affiliation with whites at home and in the gym. Now that he was a national boxing champion, and had featured in the local newspapers, he was more and more the centre of attention at school, where he was still at a disadvantage academically, although the principal, Richard Stickles, feels that he did pretty well considering the circum-stances of his background.

However, the disciplinary incidents kept mounting, some-times because Mike was provoked into fighting. The black kids would taunt him, calling him 'whitey' because he lived with Cus, Camille, Teddy and Kevin. Mike's rage would sometimes reach flash-point. One black boy in particular, a school tough nicknamed 'God' because of his dominance over the other black kids, kept baiting Mike. One day he pushed him too far, and Mike pounced. Incredulously, one of the young blacks ran into the principal's office shouting, 'There's a fight outside – Mike's beatin' up God!'

There were also more serious incidents involving confronta-tions with teachers, as well as displays of temper such as the occasion when Mike entered the school cafeteria before lunchtime, saying he was hungry. When he was told the cafeteria wasn't open yet, he angrily grabbed several milk containers and splattered them against the walls. Some of the stories of his misbehaviour may have been overblown, but there is no doubt that he was a problem to the school as regards discipline. On numerous occasions he was suspended for brief periods, and several times he was the subject of Superintendent's hearings.

After one such hearing, Teddy Atlas said, 'Cus was heard leaving the school saying to Mike, "If they expel you, I'll get Jimmy [Jacobs] to get you a tutor". Then I went and confronted Cus with this and we had an argument because I said, "Cus, this is like giving him carte blanche to act any way he wants to with anybody, and I don't think it's healthy." To me, it was tantamount to saying, every time Mike threw his left jab and he was dropping his right hand, not to correct him. We would never let that happen. God forbid! He would have been jumped on by me and Cus. . . . I didn't think that we were giving him the same kind of time and direction and help in developing him personally as we were in the ring. We had a young man who had a background that wasn't the greatest, I know that. But still, there are certain standards and rules of discipline that we all have to adhere by.' Teddy believed that Mike needed a tighter rein than Cus was willing to give. 'Mike was learning,' says Teddy, 'there were certain things he didn't have to control in his temper, in his emotions outside the ring, and I thought he better learn that if he's going to be successful in a true sense. I even said to Cus, in a real self-serving way, "It's going to hurt us, because if we don't discipline him and guide him properly now, we're going to have problems with this guy after we've put in all our work. . .when we're supposed to be enjoying the fruits of this success financially and personally and professionally, we won't be able to. So if you just want to do it for selfish reasons, we have to give him the discipline, but I also think we have an obligation to do it. . . . He's learning to deal with his emotions outside the ring."' In the years that were to follow, Teddy's words would have a prophetic ring.

Eventually, Teddy felt he had to take matters into his own hands. If other youngsters had bad report cards, he would suspend them from the gym. He felt that to be consistent he had to deal with Mike in the same manner. He suspended him from the gym for two weeks, and told him he couldn't attend any boxing shows the other kids were fighting on during that time. But a couple of nights later, at an amateur show across the river in Hudson, Cus appeared with Mike in tow. And although for the most part Cus only came to the gym every week or so, relying on Teddy to run the daily training activities and getting reports from him over the dinner table, things suddenly changed. During Mike's suspension from the gym, Cus began bringing him there in the mornings, on his own, to train him. Again, it served as a definite signal to Mike that he need not abide by the rules so long as he kept up his progress in the boxing ring.

During Mike's freshman year in high school, he and Teddy returned to Colorado Springs for the 1982 National Junior Olympics Tournament, where Mike was to defend his title. Teddy told him, 'Just keep your mind where it's supposed to be and you'll be champ of the world some day.' In the days before departing for Colorado, Teddy intensified his physical and psychological work with Mike, understanding the fear that was inside his fighter. As Mike sparred, Teddy kept up a constant banter: 'That's it. . .bad intentions. . .who's the last guy to stop punching?. . .don't drop it, even half an inch. . .let it come in the same height as your shoulder. . .straight across. . .throw it with bad intentions, like you're hitting someone you want to hurt. . .throw it like you don't like somebody. . .that's it. . .throw it hard. . .that's better, see the difference?. . .It's in you all the time, it's just gotta come out. . .you better throw it with bad intentions. . .when you're in the ring you're not playing ping pong with the guy. . .that's it. . .good. . .now you gotta slip.'

Teddy told Michael Marton, who was travelling to Colorado with them in the course of producing a documentary: 'He's not as tough or hard as people think he is. Everyone that sees me, they say, "Oh, boy, you got that Tyson, you're lucky, he's an animal, he just loves to fight, he just loves to hurt people, he's not afraid of nothin'." Well, when we're done with him he won't look like he is, anyway. He's got the potential to go down as one of the greatest fighters ever, but he'll only reach that potential if he keeps his head screwed on straight.'

Marton observed, 'Whenever they travelled Teddy would always do this amazingly unending psychological job on Mike. He would always be with him, he always slept in the same room. He would give Mike some space to be with the kids and play pinball and stuff like that, but he would always be around him. And at that point Mike really needed that. Teddy carried that guy because that fear thing was so terrific. He was a very fragile guy.'

All eyes were on Tyson in this tournament because of his spectacular first appearance in it a year earlier. Mike did not disappoint. He won his first four bouts by knockout. Before his semi-final bout, Teddy could tell Mike was nervous. They went outside the arena to get some fresh air, away from all the tumult and noise in the dressing-room. 'Loosen up,' Teddy told Mike.

'Especially when you feel the tension mount. Motion relieves tension. You're the champ, they're the ones who gotta worry. If you weren't nervous, there'd be something wrong with ya. That nervous feeling is a sign you're gonna win, a sign you're ready, ready to win.' They returned to the arena. Teddy's pep talk was longer than the fight. With the first punch Mike landed, a tremendous shot to the head, he flattened his opponent. The referee didn't even bother to count. The boy was unconscious. Mike had won by knockout in an amazing eight seconds of the first round. It was the fastest knockout ever recorded in the history of the Junior Olympics tournament.

The next night, inside the arena waiting for the finals, Mike should have been the picture of confidence. He'd won all five of his bouts by KO, and he was the defending champion. But he wasn't. 'They want to take my title, but they're not gettin' it,' he kept muttering. He was tight and tense. Teddy coached him to 'box smart, like a hungry tiger, smart and calm. Once you get inside, set up those body punches, then switch up. Left jab, move your head, and cover. Win this title, then we'll go home to our friends.' Again, Teddy took him outside so he could walk and relieve the tension. 'Just relax, Mike, just relax,' Teddy told him. Then, suddenly, it all came out. Out of sight of all the fans and coaches and boxers who thought he was an indestructible fighting machine, Mike's body began heaving and he broke down in uncontrollable sobs. Teddy comforted him, knowing he had to remain calm, yet also realizing he only had a few minutes to bring Mike back under control. 'All it is is another boxing match. You done it already twenty times, you done it in the gym with better fighters than you're ever gonna fight here. It's always hard. . . .' Mike kept crying. In between sobs, he was muttering, 'I'm Mike Tyson. . .everyone likes me. . . .' What Mike was saying was that he was afraid, afraid that if he lost, everything he had would be taken away, the respect of Cus and the others back in Catskill, everything he had, which was wrapped up in his success in the ring. 'That's right,' Teddy assured him. 'You have a reason to be proud, and you'll continue to do it, as long as you don't let anything mess you up, as long as you don't let yourself mess you up, you'll continue to have people like you. Always remember, don't let your feelings get the better of you. Don't let things mix you up.' That was all he could say. He knew it was time. 'Now let's go get ready for a fight,' he said, and they went back into the crowded arena.

Mike's opponent, a 6'7", well-built youngster named Kelton
Brown, was already in the ring. The TV commentators were
telling their audience about Mike: 'There's a lot of noise being
made about this young man as a possible Olympic prospect and a
possible professional champion in years to come.' In the corner,
Teddy was giving his last words of instruction to Mike, 'Fight
smart, and like a tiger, and calm.' Mike kissed Ted on the cheek,
and the bell rang. Mike swarmed over Kelton Brown, throwing
punches from all angles, and just seconds into the bout, Brown
was taking a standing eight-count. A moment later, Tyson had
Brown pinned in the corner, and Brown's trainer threw in the
towel to spare his fighter any more serious punishment. In less
than one minute, it was over, and Mike was National Junior
Champion for the second straight year.

Back in Catskill, Mike displayed a lot more bravado than he
had outside the arena in Colorado Springs. He told Michael
Marton, 'I don't need nobody, I don't give a shit, anybody can
train me.' Marton was incredulous. 'Mike,' he said, 'I was there,
remember. I saw Teddy Atlas carrying you through that fight in
Colorado. You were hanging over the railing crying like a baby.
How could you talk like that?'

The question of Mike's education was coming to a head.
'Mike didn't want to go to school,' Camille Ewald acknowledges. Cus told Bobby Stewart, 'Look, the only time he gets
in trouble down here is in school.' Stewart agreed with Teddy
that disciplining himself to finish school was as important to
Mike as learning to fight, that he would need a high school
diploma if he didn't make it in boxing and wanted to take an
exam some day for a civil service job. Cus told him, 'This kid is
going to be the heavyweight champion of the world. Forget the
high school diploma. He's going to make so much money some
day he won't have to worry about getting a job.' According to
Richard Stickles, the principal, Mike was 'becoming restive. He
wanted out. . . . At this point, it was clear that the objective of
a high school graduation was not going to be attained within the
time frame Cus wanted.' And perhaps there were some ominous
indications, which Stickles only alluded to: 'If Michael was to
have any small problems. . .these continual things eventually
could lead to a hearing. . .a major thing, which would not be
in his best interests.' Stickles and Cus met, and it was decided
that it would be in the best interests of all concerned if Mike
continued his education outside the school environment. A
programme of home study, with a tutor coming to the house,

was arranged for him. Thus his formal schooling ended after his freshman year in high school.

As a school official, Stickles has to temper his words carefully. But a Catskill town official, able to speak more candidly, says 'I'm telling you, Mike Tyson was a major problem in that high school. . .and the fact that he was not thrown out of school was simply because Cus pulled him out under an ultimatum – "Get him out of here or we're going to take things in our own hands". . . .Cus's big concern was having that kid pulled back by the State. And once that happened, goodbye heavyweight champion. That was his major concern. . . .They had tremendous problems with Tyson in the local school system, with the local police, he was constantly in a jam.'

Before very long, Cus allowed the tutoring to lapse, and Mike's education became a thing of the past. Now Cus could concentrate full-time on his primary goal, which was to turn Mike Tyson into the Heavyweight Champion of the World. But even outside the school environment, Mike's troubles continued. Sometimes he would stay out all night, and he would be disrespectful to both Cus and Camille. One night when he arrived home very late, Cus confronted him and browbeat him to to the point where he had Mike crying. But often Cus would let things slide. One day when Mike was leaving the house, Cus asked him when he'd be home. 'I'll be home when I feel like it,' was the reply. Teddy grabbed Mike. 'What the hell are you talking to the man like that for? Talk to him respectfully,' Atlas ordered. Mike put his head down, embarrassed and contrite, but Teddy noticed that Cus did not appear to be angry. Later, he asked Cus how he could allow Mike to talk to him that way. But Teddy knew that Cus was wrestling with his own conscience, realizing perhaps that if he disciplined Mike too harshly, he might open a Pandora's box and risk losing Mike back to the State reform school system or to the streets of Brooklyn.

Mike had a habit of not bathing. Often he would come home from the gym, and not change his sweaty work-out clothes. One day Camille told him to take a bath. Mike tore into the 78-year-old woman: 'Fuck you, you piece of shit,' he told her. 'You take a bath.' Teddy chased after him, but Cus intervened and said he'd handle things his way. Nothing was done of any significance, and once again Mike Tyson's behaviour was conveniently overlooked.

'For the years I was there before Tyson came,' says Teddy, 'I developed a lot of these kids. There was an atmosphere of discipline, we had harmony, and there was a set of rules that was consistent for everybody. Now there was two sets of rules, one for everybody and one for Mike Tyson, and I didn't think that was healthy for Tyson or the rest of the fighters or for us. There was a lack of discipline. . . .I'm sure Cus's judgment was a lot more experienced than mine. He helped a lot of kids and he obviously knew that Mike still needed development as a person. He was afraid that maybe he wouldn't keep him as a fighter.'

Around this time, the summer and fall of 1982, several events occurred. Teddy married a local girl, Elaine, over the objections of D'Amato. At the same time, Mike's mother, still living in Brooklyn, died of cancer. The caring people in Catskill dumped Mike on a train alone and sent him back to Brooklyn by himself to attend his mother's funeral.

With Mike's mother dead, Cus began proceedings to become his legal guardian. The story, effectively fed to the press over the years to the point where it became part of the myth, was that the kindly old man adopted the poor young black boy because he had been left an orphan. While it is true that Cus did care very much for Michael, he may have had less altruistic motives in quickly moving in to gain custody of the boy.

During the two years he had lived in Catskill, Tyson was still a ward of the State, and therefore subject to the authority and possible whims of the State. Since Mike's arrival, D'Amato had done an effective job of keeping the State's interference to a minimum. As one person close to the situation put it, 'There were a couple of caseworkers that were supposed to be keeping tabs on [Mike's] progress. They used to come around once in a while, but Cus was a pretty persuasive man. . . .He went to work on these caseworkers in his charming way, sincerely, he won their confidence, so they didn't feel they had to come around. So visits became phone calls. The only one to inform them of any misbehaviour. . .was Cus. Obviously they got sent clippings on his success in winning tournaments, when he knocked somebody out, but they didn't get sent the reports from the dean's office. And of course, once he was out of school there was no contact with anyone official anymore. The State never knew that he was out of school. If they knew, it's very possible they would have taken action because it was their responsibility. The State was paying Cus for Mike's boarding and his rooming and his clothing. They didn't know he was out of school or about any of the problems and his aggressive behaviour, rude remarks to girls, to physically putting his hands [on them], being forceable with girls, taking kids' lunch money, threatening kids, things like that. The State was paying his freight. And there were certain responsibilities that had to go along with that. His behaviour had to be in line, and his education had to come first.'

Cus knew that if he became Mike's legal guardian, he could then control the boy and his future in the manner he thought best, a way which did not necessarily coincide with what the State youth authorities might think were in Mike's own best interests.

D'Amato had brought Mike a long way. From the outset he had recognized the boy's potential, and he did not want to risk losing everything now. He had developed two world champions, had seen the boxing game pass him by, and now, suddenly, in the December of his life, he had found a youngster who could be one of the best of all time, a fighter who would allow D'Amato to go out in a final burst of glory, his self-perpetuated reputation as a genius assured. Teddy Atlas observed that 'Cus had a hunger to get another champion at an increasing age. Because he knew he was against the clock, Cus felt that exceptions had to be made with Mike, where otherwise he would have taken the time and made sure that the guy was also proceeding along the right way socially and personally. But Cus needed a champion.'

There was another reason why D'Amato wanted legal custody of Mike. Cus's friends and business associates, Jim Jacobs and Bill Cayton, had been paying the taxes and fuel bills for the house, and financing D'Amato in other ways. They were experienced in boxing and in negotiating business deals, and they were, above all, honest. They had already managed several world-class fighters, as well as three-times world champion Wilfred Benitez (with D'Amato calling the shots as a behind-the-scenes advisor). The understanding was that Mike's future would be in their hands once he turned pro, and Cus had to protect him from the scum of boxing that was already beginning to sniff around the young phenomenon. With his lifelong paranoia that everyone was constantly out to steal his fighters, D'Amato believed he would be under siege for eventual control of Tyson. As events following his death would prove, his fears may have been well founded. Bobby Stewart, who remained in close touch with Cus, said, 'Mike was drawing a lot of attention in national tournaments, and guys like Don King were already taking notice. Cus told me that "Jimmy has a lot of money invested in this kid, I'm going to adopt the kid legally." He loved the kid, but he was doing it for financial reasons also. Why see Jimmy or any of them get screwed because a scumbag like Don King comes in and robs them of the fighter?'

If one were still looking for a purely altruistic motive in D'Amato's behaviour, one need simply ask the question: in the previous seventy-five years of his life, how many other needy kids did he adopt? The answer, of course, is none. The bottom line is, Cus D'Amato wanted to adopt Mike Tyson because Mike Tyson could hit like a mule and he was going to be heavyweight champion some day.

Mike gave him a reason to live. D'Amato explained it this way: 'I often say to Mike, "You know, I owe you a lot," and he doesn't know what I mean. . . . If he weren't here, I probably wouldn't be alive today. . . . Nature is smarter than people think. Little by little we lose our friends that we care about and little by little we lose our interest until finally we say what the devil am I doing around here if I have no reason to go on? You get used to everything. Even the idea of dying is something a person gets used too, and he accepts it. I believe that people die because they no longer want to live, they have no motivation to stay alive. But I have a reason with Mike here, and he gives me the motivation. I will stay alive and I will watch him become a success, because I will not leave until that happens, because when I leave he not only will know how to fight, he'll be able to take care of himself. I don't succeed when I help make a guy become Champion of the World. I succeed when I make that fellow become Champion of the World and independent of me. . .'

One evening, when Bill Hagan, the Greene County (Catskill) Supervisor and a friend of D'Amato's, was dining with friends in a restaurant, the waitress came to tell him that an old man was asking to see him right away. Hagan was surprised to find it was D'Amato, in a state of some agitation. 'Bill,' he said, 'I have a problem. The wise guys just gave their telephone numbers to Tyson. They're trying to get to him. I've got to get guardianship of him.' Hagan told Cus to go home, that he would call him in twenty minutes. One of those dining with Hagan happened to be his attorney. Hagan explained the problem, and the lawyer told him to have Cus in his office the next morning at 10 o'clock. In a small town, local powers can pull together and close ranks quickly if need be. At 10 a.m. the following day, D'Amato was in the offices of Pulver and Stiefel, Attorneys.

By 10:30, they were in the local court offices, the papers were presented, the judge banged down his gavel and Cus had been granted guardianship of Mike Tyson.

It was not the first favour Bill Hagan had done for Cus. Earlier he had cut through Washington red tape and approached a friend of his, a former congressman, who was the Deputy Director of the Community Services Administration. As Hagan himself puts it, 'In the waning days of the Carter Administration, we played a little shenanigans with the CSA and got a grant. . .which essentially put 25,000 bucks in Cus's pocket to run his boxing club.' Unfortunately, there is no evidence to show that the money was ever used for its intended purpose. A few new pieces of equipment were purchased for the gym, a used van to transport the boys to and from amateur tournaments was obtained, for about $2,000. The bulk of the money has never been accounted for, and evidence points to the fact that a large part of it may well have been misappropriated by D'Amato.

The proposal for the grant said that part of the funds were needed to pay the gym's one full-time trainer, Teddy Atlas, a salary, but Teddy never saw a dime of the money. County Supervisor Hagan confirms this is true. Atlas was told by one of D'Amato's associates that since the grant had been obtained under the pretence of paying him a salary, it would have to appear as such. He was asked to sign tax papers showing he was receiving a salary, and told that at the end of the year he would have to file an income tax return, but as he was not actually receiving payments, he would be indemnified against any actual tax liability. Since his concern was taking care of the boys in the gym, not financial gain, Atlas did as he was asked. It didn't matter to him at the time whether he was paid for the work he was doing or not. He trusted Cus, and believed Cus would do the right thing.

D'Amato used at least $2,000 of the government grant funds to make an illegal loan to a friend of his in New York City. And there is also evidence to support the contention that two or three of his most trusted cronies in Catskill were handed cash payments by D'Amato for their loyalty to him and for services rendered, payments he may well have believed were legitimate because they helped further his goals concerning the Catskill Boxing Club and Mike Tyson, but which nevertheless are decidedly suspect.

When D'Amato received the periodic $3,000 cheques from the Community Services Administration, he would immediately go to the bank and cash them, rather than deposit them. Perhaps his paranoia extended to banks, too, or perhaps cash rather than cheques, which are traceable, made it a lot easier for him to use the money without being accountable to anyone.

One of Cus's rules was that no one should ever enter his room when he wasn't there, or without knocking and waiting to be asked in when he was. But one evening Camille opened the door unannounced. D'Amato was sitting on the bed, together with one of his local cronies, with about $10,000 spread out over the mattress. It was the government grant money, which, unbeknown to anyone, he kept stashed under his mattress. Frantically, he tried to gather up the bills, scooping them in his arms, while launching a tirade at the woman who had shared his life for forty years for having the nerve to come into the room without knocking. Camille made a hasty exit, and so was unable to determine whether the money was simply being counted, or whether Cus's buddy was there to receive a payment for 'services rendered'.

Some of the funds may well have been used to support Tyson, which in Cus's mind was justifiable since, after all, wasn't Tyson part of the Catskill Boxing Club, even the major part of it? It is quite clear that if Tyson was not involved in a project, any expenditure of money from the grant was deemed not worthy in D'Amato's judgment. When the Federal grant money came through, Cus allotted $2,000 of it for a trip to the Ohio State Fair where, each summer, one of the most important national amateur boxing tournaments takes place, with top fighters from throughout the US taking part. D'Amato arranged for Teddy Atlas to take five fighters from Catskill. To eke out the $2,000 for six people for a week to ten days, it was determined they would drive to Ohio, and stay in the dorms at Ohio State University, rather than pay air fares and motel costs. One of the five fighters was Mike Tyson, but shortly before they were due to leave a chronic wrist problem flared up, rendering him unable to compete. D'Amato immediately cancelled the trip, despite the disappointment of the four other boys.

Around this time, Kevin Rooney was preparing to fight three-times world champion, Alexis Arguello. Although no title was at stake, a victory for Rooney would be a tremendous boost and propel him to the top of the division and into big-money welterweight bouts. But Teddy, both his friend and trainer, detected that Rooney was not ready for the fight. Rooney had to make weight according to the contract, and was forced to lose the excess by daily sessions in a steam bath which weakened him. Teddy brought him to a doctor who knew both young men very well. The physician told Atlas, after examining Rooney, that there was no way he should be allowed to step into the ring in his condition. Teddy went and confronted Cus, but the old man would not budge. The fight was in a couple of days, it would be on national TV, Rooney would earn his best purse, and there was no way Cus was going to pull him out. The result was not surprising. Arguello knocked Rooney out cold with one of the most powerful punches ever landed by a welterweight. To all intents and purposes, it ended Kevin Rooney's career as a viable contender, and it served to trouble Atlas further and alienate him from the man whose opinions and principles he had previously admired for years.

The final split between Cus and Teddy Atlas came in November 1982. Teddy had banned Mike from the gym until he learned to accept the same rules of behaviour the others were required to live by, but Cus again overrode Teddy's ban and started bringing Mike to the gym and training him on his own, and a major rift developed between them. Teddy, married, was no longer living at the house. Then he and Cus began avoiding each other at the gym. In the morning, D'Amato would bring Tyson there and work there with him. Later in the day, when they were gone, Teddy became the bad guy, the enforcer to Mike, the only one demanding that he abide by the rules of society. Cus wanted the title. He sided with Mike.

As Atlas maintains, 'it came to the point where Mike became more and more bold with his actions, and got bold to where it was becoming dangerous. Up to that point, I was giving Mike a fair mixture of support, emotional support and backing, and discipline at the right time. Cus started bringing Mike to the gym. He went against me. It was obvious to me that I was going to have to make a decision. I obviously couldn't stay involved in a situation like that. I wasn't going to compromise myself and be in an uncomfortable position. Tyson started getting out of hand, and it would come to my attention that he was being abusive to people, and it was getting to a point where he was getting completely disrespectful, unrefined in his choices of what he was doing. . .I just felt betrayed, felt that the situation was brought on by Cus not being loyal to our partnership. We were partners in the gym with the dream of developing fighters, and we had been doing this for six years together, and I felt that Cus walked out on me.'

'Mike was a ghetto kid, and so his behaviour was not unusual,' observes Fred Chetti, an influential citizen in Catskill who was friends with both D'Amato and Atlas, and whose sons were part of the boxing club. 'That's what you expect from a kid from Bedford–Stuyvesant and Tryon. The behaviour was not unusual for him, but it was unacceptable for the society he was living in. The things he's doing today (as champion) and paying his way out of is what he did then.'

Kevin Rooney followed D'Amato blindly. He saw it differently. He felt Cus knew what he was doing to accomplish his goals, and felt Teddy was being disloyal to Cus and had no right to question D'Amato's methods or motives. Rooney sided with Cus, and a rift developed between himself and his old Staten Island Street pal, a rift that eventually grew and became bitter and irrevocable, despite their lifelong friendship and Teddy's having been in Rooney's corner throughout his professional career.

Parents in town, who had seen the caring and concern which Teddy employed when working with their youngsters, and trusted him, came to him with their complaints about Mike; Cus, in turn, always said he'd handle it his own way, but the anti-social behaviour continued. Finally, all the pressure and tension was brought to a head when Mike made lewd and suggestive remarks to a 12-year-old girl. Teddy found out about it one evening, and was enraged. No doubt part of his reaction came from his being on emotional overload from his perceived rejection by D'Amato, his feeling of betrayal that Tyson was wooing Cus away from him, and the incident became the straw that broke the camel's back. The previous year, Teddy had turned a blind eye when the mother of a 13-year-old girl who lived in the same road as the D'Amato ménage complained to Camille that Mike was screwing her daughter. Since the girl was a willing partner, and the situation did not involve coercion, Teddy decided the affair was a part of growing up and was best left to take its own course. But this time it was different, and Teddy ran from his house, looking for Mike.

He found Tyson and took him to the gym. All Teddy will say of the incident is that 'Cus allowed a situation to get to where a guy was really getting very dangerous and very abusive to more than himself, to other people's well-being. . . . It came to a head through letting Mike get away with these things, and it came to a showdown, so to speak, where finally he abused someone, some of it verbal abuse, along with physical, and I had to go and confront him.' Tyson himself has never spoken about the incident, turning away all questions about it. But what happened was that Teddy pulled a gun on Mike Tyson, put it to his head, and threatened to blow his brains out if he didn't change his behaviour towards people. Tyson panicked. He bolted from the back of the gym and ran full speed down the hill and home to Cus.

That incident ended things once and for all between Cus D'Amato, Mike Tyson and Teddy Atlas. According to Jay Bright, who was living at the house then, and indeed still does, Mike planned to get his revenge on the trainer he was once devoted to. Tyson confided to Bright that he was going to kill Teddy: 'Teddy should thank God he's alive. . . . Michael wanted to go and in no uncertain terms get rid of the guy, really, and Cus talked him out of doing what he wanted to do. . . . I know exactly what Michael was going to do, and no one would be able to trace it back to Michael. No one would have known.'

What D'Amato did do was get Tyson out of Catskill for a couple of weeks until the volatile situation was defused and Teddy had gone. He called Bobby Stewart, and asked him to take Mike back up to Johnstown to Tryon School, a procedure Cus had followed several times in the past when Mike had problems in Catskill.

Under Teddy's guidance, Mike had more than twenty sanctioned fights, plus numerous 'bootleg' bouts. He lost just one and that was a disputed decision to an amateur named Ernie Bennett in Rhode Island. At the time, Bennett had close to two hundred fights and was 20 years old. Mike was fifteen and had engaged in fewer than fifteen bouts. If you go through the old newspaper clippings from the two years that Mike spent with Teddy in Catskill, you'll find stories that speak of the bond between the two:

'Tyson works out two hours a day in D'Amato's downtown Catskill gym. His trainer is Ted Atlas, a former fighter. "Teddy has taught me everything I know," Tyson said. . ."Back when I was in New York, nobody encouraged me. . .If I stayed in New York I might have become a fighter but it wouldn't have been the Mike Tyson you see now. I learn more here in one month than some guys do in two years."'

'The people I train with are good people and Teddy, he's great. I love him to death.'

There are the other images: Teddy saving Mike from giving up and quitting in the ring in Scranton; Teddy pulling Mike together when he broke down minutes before his championship bout in the Junior Olympics; Teddy and Mike hugging and kissing after victories; Teddy giving Mike his last $50 so he could buy a clean warm-up suit to wear to his mother's funeral. Yet today, Teddy Atlas is a forbidden subject in the presence of Mike Tyson, who will go so far as to deny that Atlas was ever even his trainer, despite the proof that exists on film and video tape.

It may be that Mike Tyson is afraid of Teddy Atlas, afraid to look his ex-trainer and teacher in the eye when their paths have occasionally and accidentally crossed in the years since 1982, afraid of the 145-pound ex-amateur fighter with a bad back – not in a physical way, but for a much deeper, more significant reason. Teddy Atlas, the one person who would not bow to expediency, represents a portion of whatever conscience Mike Tyson may have. The easiest way to deal with his uncomfortable feelings was to make Teddy, once and for all, a non-person, since he knows his first trainer was the one person who would not compromise what he expected of Mike as a person for the sake of expediency. Today, Atlas's friends joke with him about how he has become the invisible man in the Tyson saga. 'Hey, Teddy,' they tease him, 'when they make the Mike Tyson movie, who's going to play you? Claude Rains?'

The D'Amato loyalists, who have formed an almost cultish devotion to the late trainer, dismiss Atlas's contribution to the development of Mike Tyson. Jay Bright says, 'Everything was orchestrated by Cus one hundred per cent. Cus was the genius behind the whole thing.' But there are others with perhaps a more objective view who feel differently.

The British promoter, Mickey Duff, maintains that D'Amato was forced to choose where his loyalties would go, to Mike or Teddy. 'Cus wrongly chased [away] Teddy. Cus had a decision to make whether he was going to have this world heavyweight champion or stay loyal to Teddy, and he had no choice really.'

At the time of the break-up, D'Amato did not have legal custody of Mike quite yet. That would come a few weeks later. In the meantime, concerned that problems might arise if any of the news of Mike's behaviour or the resulting showdown with Teddy got out, he sent an intermediary to Teddy with an offer: if Teddy left quietly and made no waves, he had Cus's word that he would receive five per cent of Tyson's earnings for the rest of Mike's career once he turned pro. Atlas, mixed up, confused, hurt by his parting with Cus, wasn't interested. The fact that his relationship with D'Amato had ended meant more to him than the offer of money. He left quietly out of loyalty and respect for what he and Cus had built together, and never said anything which might have brought the State youth authorities back to Catskill. Subsequently, when Tyson turned pro, the promise made to Atlas was conveniently forgotten, and he never received a penny from the fighter he had helped develop.

The end of the story, however, had not quite yet been written. Many of the boys involved at the Boxing Club and their parents came to Teddy and said they wanted to go with him, he could open another gym in town, and they'd leave the Catskill Club and join him there. It was Teddy who had won their respect and affection, not Cus. If they had problems outside the gym, at home, in school, Teddy was always ready to help them. If the poorer ones couldn't afford groceries, he would buy a bag of staples for their family. But Teddy told them that it was Cus's gym, his club, and it would be disloyal of them, and him, to leave and start another gym. Stay with Cus, that's the right thing, Teddy told them.

The parents then called a meeting with Cus. And here D'Amato made a mistake. He told them the reason Teddy had left was to take a job in New York for pay as a pro trainer, and there was nothing he could do to persuade him to stay on. But the boys knew what Cus didn't – that Teddy was still in town, that he had never left – and they confronted him with the truth. They also knew he was willing to stay in Catskill if given the chance.

D'Amato was shaken by being caught in a lie. Perceiving that Teddy presented a threat, fearing that his authority was being eroded and that 'his fighters' (except for Mike, of course) wanted to leave him, he took vindictive action against Teddy. Insidious and untrue rumours began to circulate: that Teddy was a psychopath, Teddy was involved with drugs, Teddy was involved with the Mafia. Atlas, completely unaware these rumours were going around, was befuddled when he kept running into dead ends at gyms and with boxing managers in New York City. One night, speaking with Fred Chetti on a return visit to Catskill, Teddy expressed his confusion as to why he couldn't land any fighters to train. Chetti, an IBM executive and a member of the Town Recreation Board, had been instrumental in D'Amato getting the gym twelve years earlier. He had become a friend of Cus's, spending evenings at the house talking boxing and watching fight films with him. He had also become friendly with Teddy, and so was undecided as to whose side he was on in the split between them. He remained friendly with both.

Chetti went to Cus's house one evening to ask him about the break. Cus spent the entire evening telling him all the negative things in Teddy's past. D'Amato filibustered, Chetti hardly getting a word in for two hours. True, Teddy in his earlier years had personal problems, problems with the law. But so had every boy who had come there. Teddy, after all, had turned his life around. He was now 26 years old. What did his youthful past have to do with the present? 'I had difficulty deciding who was right,' Chetti acknowledges, 'but the one thing I didn't like was the fact that Cus was trying to convince me he was right by telling me all the bad things Teddy did when he was a teenager. That wasn't the way to convince me.' Chetti did not like the rumours that were circulating about Teddy, and he was convinced it was D'Amato who was floating them. He decided to run a litmus test.

He told a fighter in the club that he was going to use his political influence in town to have the gym closed down. Chetti knew this youngster was a talker, and that word would spread. 'I wasn't serious. I was just trying to scare Cus,' Chetti admits.

Sure enough, word got back to D'Amato, because the very next day, one of his emissaries phoned Chetti and said he wanted to come over and talk to him. He was Joe Colangelo, President of the Catskill Boxing Club, a title D'Amato had bestowed on him. Colangelo's son was a member of the club and he had been nurtured by Teddy Atlas. Yet when Colangelo got to Chetti's house, it was obvious he was speaking for D'Amato. He told Chetti how important the gym was to the kids, how much his son had been helped there, how Teddy had been a bad influence and how it was would be for the best if he went. Chetti became enraged over the convenient lapse of memory Colangelo was displaying. 'Joe,' he said, anger boiling over in his voice, 'I've heard enough. It's time for you to leave. You go back and tell Cus that sending you here to convince me to keep my hands off the gym is not going to work.' Colangelo protested that Cus hadn't sent him. 'Bullshit,' Chetti told him. 'I told the kid yesterday

I'd have the gym closed down, and today you're here. Who are you kidding! You tell Cus one thing. If he doesn't leave Teddy Atlas alone, stop spreading lies about him and just let him get on with his life, that goddamn gym is gone.' Atlas, who was unaware of all that was taking place, phoned Chetti several days later, completely confused. He told Chetti he had no idea what was going on, but suddenly, as if out of the blue, people were calling him to talk about his working with their fighters. Fred Chetti knew why.

Today, Teddy Atlas is one of the most respected trainers in boxing. Jim Jacobs himself recommended him to friends, saying, 'Forget about everyone else, Ted Atlas is the best trainer in boxing.' Working out of the famed Gleason's Gym in Brooklyn, New York, his stable of top-notch pros have included contenders Chris Reid, Felix Santiago, Tyrone Jackson, and Art Tucker, plus world champions Donny Lalonde and Simon Brown. He played an instrumental role in Ireland's Barry McGuigan winning the World Featherweight Championship, and he will no doubt develop many more contenders and champions in the years ahead.

All the same, the break with D'Amato was painful for Teddy, and it still hurts. 'When I first went up there I was fighting, having problems, getting in trouble,' he says. 'Cus did help me. Nobody ever denied that. That had nothing to do with our falling out. I'm the first one to say I'm grateful to Cus for being a friend and for being a helpful person at that time in my life. . . . When it came to a head with me and Tyson, Cus, of course, was in the middle of it. Cus had to make a decision, either me or Tyson. Because of what Tyson could be, because of Cus's need at that point, it was natural it would be Mike. I left out of some degree of what I owed Cus, loyalty to the things we had together. . . .It was never a part of why I left that I got what I needed and no longer had a need for Cus or I was ungrateful and I walked out on him. It had nothing to do with it. It was falling out. I didn't even want to leave at that time. It was an unhappy break.'

6

Turning Pro

There is no such thing as a natural puncher. There is a natural aptitude for punching and that is different. Nobody is born the best. You have to practice and train to become the best.

– CUS D'AMATO

WITH THE DEPARTURE of Ted Atlas, Cus needed someone to step in and undertake the day-to-day chores of training Mike. He turned to Kevin Rooney, who had remained intensely loyal to him during the turmoil of the previous weeks. Rooney's career had reached a crossroads. He had climbed the welterweight rankings until his crushing knockout loss to Alexis Arguello caused a major setback to his career, and although he continued to fight for a while longer ('We'd fight on the same card,' Tyson would recall. 'He'd train me, then fight himself'), he agreed to help Cus train Mike, since it was apparent to everyone at this point that Mike's career potential was much brighter than his own. 'Mike was 15 when I started working with him,' notes Rooney. 'I had him for all his senior fights as an amateur.' And Rooney, with the advantage of having been a fighter, began to learn the nuances of training from D'Amato. 'You cannot be around a man like Cus D'Amato,' he points out today, 'with his genius, and not learn something. I was Cus's eyes and hands and Cus was the mind.' When Tyson had first come to Catskill, Rooney was a bit suspicious. 'I figured he just wanted to come out of the can and go home. Then he started winning fights and I said, this kid is gonna make it. He was so fast, and he had that punch. I saw the potential. He was 14, but he was so big and strong, he picked things up so quickly.' This quickness was what had impressed Bobby Stewart when he or Cus would show Mike techniques while he was still at Tryon. Kevin and Mike were close, having lived together for more than two years, and Kevin had been doing some training all along, helping Cus in the gym and working with the boys when Teddy took Mike or the others to tournaments out of town.

Perhaps, however, the adjustment to a new trainer was too abrupt for Mike, who was now sixteen. He was stepping into the seniors bracket now, and Cus entered him in the 1982 United States Championships. The fighters he would meet there were much more seasoned than those he had faced in the juniors. Before going to the US Championships, Mike did not get a lot of good, tough sparring in the gym, and he had just emerged from the emotional upheaval of the break with Atlas, which may well have had an unsettling effect on him. He paid the price at the tournament. He faced an experienced heavyweight named Al Evans, a mature man ten years older than himself. In the third round, Evans pulled a shocker. He dropped Tyson three times, scoring a knockout victory.

The loss was a temporary setback. Cus, with Kevin, continued the teaching process, determined to instil in Mike a professional attitude. To D'Amato, being a professional had nothing to do with whether or not you were paid. He believed that what set the true professional apart from the amateur was the way the professional thinks. 'I believe a man is a professional,' he would often say, 'when he can do what needs to be done no matter how he feels within. An amateur is an amateur in his attitude emotionally. A professional is a professional in the way he thinks and feels and in his ability to execute under the most trying conditions. The ability to do what needs to be done regardless of the pressure and do it with poise, with no reflection of his inner feeling or conflict if it exists, is what makes a professional. It has nothing to do with their knowledge. I'll show you many amateurs with far superior knowledge and ability than top professionals.'

'When you get hit,' Cus would drill into Mike, 'that's when you've got to be calm. A professional fighter has got to learn how to hit and not get hit, and at the same time be exciting. That's what professional boxing is about. You've got to be clever, you've got to be smart, and not get hit, and when you're able to do this, you're a fighter.' Another rule was, 'if you can hit your opponent with two punches, you don't hit him with one. Get off with some bad intentions in there. Believe in yourself. A guy can feel it if you don't believe in yourself. Set your mind to make yourself do it.'

Over the years, Cus would use the example of the hero and the coward in teaching all his fighters how to perform even under adverse circumstances. It was a lesson so indelibly drilled into Mike's conscious and subconscious mind that he can repeat it by rote to this day. Here's how Cus would explain it: 'I tell my kids, what is the difference between a hero and a coward? What is the difference between being yellow and being brave? No difference. Only what you do. They both feel the same. They both fear dying and getting hurt. The man who is yellow refuses to face up to what he's got to face. The hero is more disciplined and he fights those feelings off and he does what he has to do. But they both feel the same, the hero and the coward. People who watch you judge you on what you do, not how you feel.'

In 1983, Mike continued his sweep through the amateur ranks, losing only in the finals of the National Golden Gloves tournament, where, according to Kevin Rooney, he was 'robbed' by the amateur rules officiating, to which Mike's style, by Cus's design, had never adapted. In one nine-day period, he swept through two tournaments a thousand miles apart, mowing down every opponent he faced and capturing two national titles.

Beginning on August 12, with a first-round KO that took him just 44 seconds, he began his march through the Ohio State Fair national tournament. In his next bout, on August 13, he met Jerry Goff, a veteran of some 150 fights. He knocked Goff out in the second round with a combination so devastating that Goff lost two front teeth and was unconscious for close to ten minutes. In the finals, on August 14, Mike was set to face National Golden Gloves Champion Olian Alexander, but Alexander did not turn up for the bout, claiming he had a bad hand. Many fighters along the way suddenly found they had bad hands or sore shoulders when they discovered they had to tangle with Tyson. By default, Mike won the Ohio State Fair crown.

The next day, he and Kevin flew to Colorado for the 1983 US National Championships, which began on August 16. When Mike arrived four of the six other fighters entered in the heavyweight division withdrew, perhaps with good reason. Mike automatically advanced to the semi-finals, where he met 250-pound Dave Yonko. He knocked out Yonko at 1:38 of the first round. In the finals he didn't waste as much time. He stopped Mark Scott at 54 seconds of round one, returning to Catskill with the Ohio State Fair and US National Championship titles.

Cus was extremely pleased with Mike's progress in such a short time. Though Tyson was still an amateur, Cus offered this appraisal of him: 'The boy can do everything a champion is required to do, and if he does everything that he's capable of doing, I tell you he may go down as one of the greatest fighters of all time. . .as a professional my judgments of a fighter are detached. I never allow my personal feelings to get involved, no matter how much affection I may have for him, and I can honestly say I have a very deep affection for him, and an admiration, having watched him come from where he was to what he is, because I know what it takes to do what he's done and what he's doing. I feel I was a part of it. It's almost like watching yourself. You never know how much you contributed to it, but the result is there and you like to think you had something to do with it.'

Mike, too, had a deep feeling for Cus. He knew just how much this man had helped him. 'People think I was born this way,' he said. 'They don't know what it took to get this way. The training, when you have to do things over and over again until you're sore. Deep in your mind you say, God, I don't want to do this no more, and then you push. I always used to think I was a coward because of the way I felt. Cus was there when I needed him. . .he was the one. Cus would always explain you should always do things to build your character and make you a better individual. He was different than anyone I'd ever met, because principle meant more than anything to him, more than money, more than health, more than his life. He would sacrifice anything for principle, for what he believed was right.'

But there was still much of the streets, much of the uncontrolled wildness in Mike, and often he would lapse from the lofty principles that Cus strove to inculcate in him. He continued to have difficulty in showing respect for those in authority, including Cus. One member of the household said Tyson even spat on Cus. Another acknowledged that there were many times Cus got so angry he wanted to toss Mike out and be done with him.

There were other problems. One person, who requested anonymity, said: 'I overheard Cus talking to Jimmy on the phone. I know that Cus and Jimmy paid off a woman five or ten thousand dollars, a poor woman in the Catskill area, because Mike knocked up her daughter when he was living up there, and they decided it wouldn't look good because he was going to be heavyweight champ some day. I'm not sure if the girl had the baby or had an abortion. But Tyson may have a kid out there somewhere. And then they deny pay-offs were made to cover things up that Mike did!'

Mickey Duff, who was very aware of the situation with Tyson from the beginning because of his close friendship with Jim

Jacobs, says, 'Mike Tyson has been nothing but a pain in the ass since day one, in my opinion. And Mike Tyson has been a far more sophisticated user of people than anybody ever gave him credit for until recently. He has that habit of putting his head on your shoulder like a little boy. I think that Jim Jacobs and Bill Cayton genuinely hoped that success would lead to making him a nicer person, a better person, a more responsible person. They also hoped and believed that success would introduce him to a nicer group of people and disassociate him from some of the people they felt he shouldn't associate with.'

In the summer of 1984, after winning the National Golden Gloves Championship, Mike was entered in the United States Olympic Trials. It was, for some reason, a time of tension between D'Amato and Tyson. Sitting with two friends at the Trials in Las Vegas, Cus turned to them and said, 'If Jimmy and Bill didn't have so much money invested in this kid, I'd get rid of the son of a bitch right now.' But now, no matter what his personal feelings, there was no turning back. The commitment had been made – to Mike, to Jacobs and Cayton, and mostly to himself. After four years of blood and sweat, drilling and teaching anguish and frustration, it was almost time. Mike would go to the Olympics in Los Angeles; without the Cubans and East Germans and Soviets there (they were boycotting the Games), he would sweep through the heavyweight division and win a gold medal, watched by millions of his countrymen and millions of others around the world on television. It would make Mike Tyson a household name and provide the ideal launch pad for the professional career that was to come. But it was not to be. In the trials, he was beaten by Henry Tillman, who repeated his victory over Tyson a week later in the Olympic box-off. There was griping by D'Amato after Tillman won the decision that kept Mike out the Olympics. It was a close fight, but Mike was not effectual against the 6'3", 195-pound Tillman, who, he said, 'kept pushing me and trying to stick his thumbs in my eye.' Tillman said Tyson was just jumping at him and jabbing with his feet in the air instead of being solidly planted on the canvas. Tillman's trainer acknowledged that Tyson was strong, but called him excitable and mechanical, 'a doer, not a thinker. . . . There's more to boxing than being able to bang.' Tyson certainly did not fight with his mind and physical skills together, and Tillman took advantage of his own height and reach to outbox him.

Tillman went on to win the Olympic gold medal in the 201-pound heavyweight division. Mike went as a spectator to Los Angeles, where, frustrated at not making the Olympic team, he managed to stir up a little unpublicized trouble by pouring a can of beer over security guards at the Athletes' Village while visiting a friend, fellow Brooklynite Mark Breland, then taunted them, telling them: 'Go fuck yourselves, white boys.'

In the long run, his failure to make the Olympic team would not matter. Tillman, after winning the gold medal, was knocked out in his only important fights, including a cruiserweight title bout against friend and fellow Olympic gold medallist, Evander Holyfield, and faded from the scene, talk of an eventual professional title showdown against Tyson forgotten. While there is no doubt that the publicity attendant upon an Olympic appearance is tremendously valuable, if a fighter can fight, it is not of paramount importance. Some of the greatest fighters of the past two decades, including Roberto Duran, Alexis Arguello, Thomas Hearns, Marvin Hagler, Larry Hueries, Michael Nunn, Matthew Saad Muhammad, and Julio Caesar Chavez, have not been Olympic champions.

In the short run, it changed the strategy of how to market Mike Tyson. Without the Olympic fanfare behind him, Tyson would turn pro quietly, almost unnoticed. D'Amato was the architect of these plans; now, however, Jim Jacobs and Bill Cayton would move to the forefront. They would become Mike Tyson's co-managers, and their brilliant manoeuvring on behalf of their fighter on all fronts would make him, in less than two years, the Heavyweight Champion of the World, and in just over three years the best-known and most financially successful athlete in the world.

Jim Jacobs was born in 1930 in St Louis. When he was five years old, his family moved to Los Angeles. As a boy, he had an avid interest in comic books. During the War, he worked as a volunteer on paper-collection drives. In sorting through the old newspapers and magazines donated by people to aid the war effort, he would take home the discarded comic books that caught his interest. These finds, along with purchases and trades he made as a youngster, helped form the nucleus of a comic book collection that contained duplicates of many rare first and early editions, including *Superman* and *Batman*. Jacobs maintained and built the collection for more than 40 years. At the time of his death it was probably the largest and most valuable collection of its kind anywhere, containing some 800,000 comic books warehoused in Los Angeles with a value of perhaps two million dollars.

During his adolescent years, Jim lived somewhat in a fantasy world with his comic books. 'I always pretended that I was Robin, the Boy Wonder,' he said. 'Superman I admired, but Batman and Robin were human, and everything athletic that Robin did, I tried to do. He threw a boomerang, I learned how to throw a boomerang. Robin was an excellent tumbler, and so I would run off diving boards to practise double flips. Robin swam underwater for two minutes. . .I learned how to hold my breath underwater. Before long I could swim underwater for two minutes. I didn't want to admit that Robin could do something I couldn't do. Being Robin, the Boy Wonder, was a tremendous help to me in sports. All of us are susceptible to our emotions when under stress, and when I was younger I would think: What would Robin do? Instead of succumbing to nervous apprehension, I would transform myself into this other character who was emotionally unaffected.' It's interesting how, through the device of using Robin, Jacobs arrived at a means of controlling his emotions and 'performing in a professional manner' – something so close to the theory of Cus D'Amato, whom he was not to meet for many years.

Jacobs was a natural athlete. Tales of his exploits in high school still survive. He was an outstanding basketball player, reportedly good enough to be invited to try out for the Olympic team. He excelled in track, running the 100-yard dash in 9.8 seconds, second in the city among high schoolers at the time. He was also a top-notch baseball, football, tennis and table tennis player. A friend of his related a story once about Jim that gives a clue to his natural athletic talents and his incredible hand–eye coordination. According to his friend, Jim, strictly as a challenge, decided to see if he could take up and master the sport of skeet shooting. Within a relatively short time, he became so proficient that he was able to win a major skeet shooting championship, after which he put his shotguns aside, satisfied that he had mastered his own challenge, and never pursued the sport again. He also shot in the low 70s in golf.

Jacobs, along with his sister, Dorothy, was brought up by his mother after his parents' marriage ended in divorce. He remained extremely close and devoted to his mother, often visiting her in Los Angeles following his move to New York, until her death in December, 1986. Although an excellent athlete, he was less than devoted to the academic rigours of school, and was close to flunking out of Los Angeles High School when he apparently dropped out. He never completed his high school education.

By this time, in the late 1940's when he left school, Jacobs had developed two consuming passions that would lead, respectively, to his putting his own name in the sports record books and to building his own fortune. They were handball and collecting boxing films. He began playing four-wall handball at the Hollywood YMCA. His climb to the top of that sport was interrupted by the Korean War. He was drafted, served two years in the infantry with the First Cavalry Division and earned a Purple Heart, although he maintained that he wasn't a very good soldier. In 1953, representing the Los Angeles Athletic Club, he competed in his first national championship, finishing fifth. The following year he finished third. In 1955, he was matched in the finals of the United States Championships with his idol, Vic Hershkowitz, one of the legendary names in the sport, but who was now 37 years old and past his prime. Jacobs defeated Hershkowitz to win his first national singles title. It was the beginning of a run which would match Joe Louis's reign as Heavyweight Champion in both dominance and duration. The *Guinness Book of World Sports Records*, under a photograph of Jim Jacobs in action on the handball court with the caption 'Handball Master', lists Jacobs as the record-holder for titles won. He captured six United States Handball Association National Four-Wall Championships from 1955 to 1965. In addition, from 1960 to 1968, he won six doubles titles, most of those with playing partner and friend Marty Decatur. He also won the three-wall championship three times, the AAU four-wall title twice, and was one-wall singles champion six times. He was inducted into the Jewish Sports Hall of Fame in Israel and the Helms Hall of Fame in Los Angeles.

In a story published in 1966 in *Sports Illustrated* magazine, Robert Boyle wrote: 'There is no athlete in the world who dominates his sport with the supremacy that Jimmy Jacobs of Los Angeles and New York enjoys in four-wall handball. . .Jacobs is generally hailed as the finest player of all time. Indeed, there are those who say Jacobs is the best athlete, regardless of sport, in the country.'

It was while still a teenager that Jacobs became equally obsessed with boxing films. He had heard about the controversial decision in the December 5, 1947 bout between Joe Louis and Jersey Joe Walcott, and he set out to obtain a copy of the film so he could judge for himself. After that, he was hooked. He began seeking out and buying whatever old and rare boxing films he could find, often spending his free time while playing handball exhibitions overseas in this pursuit.

During the reign of the controversial first black World Heavyweight Champion, Jack Johnson, from 1908 to 1915, several of his victories over white opponents had touched off race riots in American cities. So as not to inflame the passions of fans both black and white who viewed the films of these fights in movie theatres, the Federal Government passed a law banning the interstate transport of boxing motion pictures. This law remained on the books for decades, and so hundreds and hundreds of old fight films lay for years unused and uncared for, decaying in vaults and archives and storage rooms. Jacobs rescued most of these films from decaying to the point where they would have been lost forever. In the years that followed, he and his partner, Bill Cayton, would invest much money in restoring these brittle old nitrate negatives so that the rich legacy of the sport could be preserved forever. For this, boxing historians, journalists and fans owe these two men an eternal debt of gratitude, for without their efforts no one now would be able to see many of the films of Jack Johnson, Jack Dempsey, even nineteenth-century champions like Bob Fitzsimmons and Gentleman Jim Corbett, plus scores of other great champions, in action.

Jim's consuming passion was to build the world's greatest archive of boxing films. In 1970, a young writer set out to do a book on boxing history. It involved travelling around the United States to interview champions of the past. Jacobs advanced the writer, who was a friend of his, the money for a major trip around the country. He requested just one thing in return: that the writer ask all the champions he interviewed if they had any old films of themselves boxing, and if he could borrow them to reproduce prints. The writer turned up two gems. One was a brief film of the World Flyweight Champion, Corporal Izzy Schwartz, in Paris in 1928, training and boxing a humorous sparring session with a giant heavyweight for the benefit of the newsreel cameras. The heavyweight was a young and still unknown Primo Carnera, who was just beginning his professional career. It provided a first look at Carnera, long before he became Heavyweight Champion, as well as being the only film that exists of Schwartz. The film had been gathering

dust for more than 40 years in a closet in Schwartz's Bronx
apartment, just twelve miles from the offices of Cayton and
Jacobs in Manhattan. The other find was a complete print
of the 1913 World Lightweight Championship fight between
Willie Ritchie and challenger 'Mexican' Joe Rivers. Until then,
Jacobs had no film of Ritchie in his library. Now he not only had
one, but it was Ritchie in top form, defending his crown against
a great challenger by a knockout. Jacobs was ecstatic.

'I always wanted to have the greatest collection of fight films
in the world,' Jacobs said. 'I wanted to own the most comic
books. I wanted to be the greatest handball player in the
world. I wanted to be a millionaire. . . . I've always been very
complusive about everything. . .I can't explain why.'

Jacobs, in many ways, presented an enigma. He was very
loyal to friends, accessible, helpful, friendly. Yet he kept a good
part of himself closed off from the outside world. Mickey Duff,
a longtime friend and associate, says, 'Jim was a very private
person, and it was very difficult to get through to him.' Jacobs's
sister, Dorothy, with whom he did not have a particularly tight
relationship, termed him 'close to the vest'. Perhaps the biggest
conundrum was the story that Jim came from a wealthy family.
Over the years he himself carefully and deliberately spread the
word that he had inherited a considerable fortune from his
father. At the time of his death, one New York sportswriter
wrote that Jacobs 'inherited hundreds of millions from his
family, St Louis department store moguls and Los Angeles real
estate giants.' Nat Loubet, longtime editor of *Ring* magazine
who knew Jim since the 1940s, said that when he talked to Jim
about the expense of buying boxing films, 'Jim would say, "Don't
worry about it. Mom's loaded".' Top Rank matchmaker Teddy
Brenner, who also knew Jim for years, remembers the time
he asked him, 'Jimmy, is it true, they tell me that when your
father died he left you $9-million? He said to me, "Not only is it
true, but what you didn't know is when my grandfather died, he
left me $20-million".' Another source said Jacobs's family had
owned a chain of St Louis-based stores named Stix, Baer and
Fuller, but that the estate left by his father was at most two or
three million dollars.

In tracing Jacobs's life, however, the evidence does not support the lifestyle of someone who had money, at least until he
made his own fortune as an adult. For one thing, he attended
public schools in Los Angeles, and even when he was in
academic trouble, he was not moved to a private school or

academy. When he began playing handball at the Hollywood YMCA as a teenager, one of those he often played against was the television personality Art Linkletter, who beat him quite often in those early days. Jacobs, determined to improve, practised for hours in front of a mirror until his weaker left arm was virtually as good as his right. In a short time he was able to beat Linkletter and just about everyone else. Seeing Jim as a prodigy, Linkletter got together with several other backers and put up the money that financed Jim's first trip to a major tournament, the Junior Nationals in Bremerton, Washington. There, he won the Junior singles championship. If his family had had money, Jim would hardly have needed the financial backing of Linkletter to travel from Los Angeles to Bremerton.

In 1950, Jacobs, then 20, went to Chicago. While there, he was able to arrange a game against former national champion Gus Lewis. To say the least, Lewis was impressed. He telephoned Robert Kendler and told him, 'I just played a kid who doesn't know what he's doing, and for a kid who doesn't know what he's doing, he's a hell of a handball player.' Kendler, a multi-millionaire businessman who had a passion for handball, asked to meet Jacobs. He had gathered up twelve or thirteen of the country's best players and given them jobs in his home remodelling business. He then built the Town Club of Chicago so his 'team' would have a place to practise and play. He offered Jacobs the chance to do the same. Jacobs went to work for Kendler as a home remodelling salesman, practising his handball in his off-hours. He stayed in Chicago for a year and a half with Kendler, until he was drafted. Again, one might question the need to work as a salesman to support himself during his stay in Chicago if there was great wealth in the family.

After his service in Korea, he returned to Los Angeles and became a salesman with a business machine company. He said it was his father he worked for, that his father owned a business machine and supplies company. But his business partner of 28 years, Bill Cayton, who knew Jim perhaps better than anyone, told Phil Berger of *The New York Times*: 'I know Jim said that, but it wasn't so.'

One of Jacobs's oldest and most trusted friends and business associates, a true member of his small inner circle who admired him and was truly devoted to him over the course of their nearly thirty-year friendship, nevertheless had this observation: '[There is one thing] I've tried to find the answer to with Jim, and I can't, that completely astounds me. He lived in this world of make believe. And it turned out to be bullshit. He'd have you believe that he came from very wealthy parents. The funny thing is, he did it to everybody. I [believed it] and it's totally untrue. . . .

'He told me that when his mother died, from the time she died until the time they settled her estate, that the interest on the money was six million dollars. We were talking one day and I said, "Everything is for sale. There's not a thing in this world that's not for sale for the right price. Do you want to sell your fight film business?" He said that's not for sale. I said, "If somebody came along and gave you $100-million it would be for sale." He said, "No it wouldn't, because I already have $100-million." He told me that when his father died he was left a chain of stores, for him and his sister, but he had total control, and he couldn't stand the sight of the stores, so he sold them to the manager and the manager paid him back the money over a period of years. And he said that when his parents divorced they were both independently so rich that they didn't even have a settlement. He said his mother came from rich people. It's all bullshit.'

In an interview with United Press some years ago concerning his success, Jim said, 'I always wanted to be a millionaire.' That is not the aspiration of someone who has already inherited millions. Possibly the most revealing comment came from his sister, Dorothy, to Phil Berger in *The New York Times* on June 28, 1988. 'My father was a salesman for Alfred Hart distilleries, a liquor salesman,' she told Berger. 'Before we came to LA, he had been in ladies' ready-to-wear in St Louis. When my father was old and retired and had nothing, Jim sent him a check every month.' Berger went on to write: 'Whatever his reason, Jacobs was uneasy about what his father did for a living.'

It was lack of finances that resulted in Jacobs meeting and eventually forming a business partnership with Bill Cayton. In 1959, Jacobs found out that a collector in Australia had the only known copy of Jess Willard's knockout over Jack Johnson in Havana in 1915, a copy that included the actual sequence of the knockout. For years controversy had swirled around this fight, Johnson claiming that he was pressured by financial problems and legal persecution to 'throw' his heavyweight title to Willard. Jacobs felt the film could help solve this mystery, and he had to have it. The price was five thousand dollars. Jim needed the money, so he called Bill Cayton, knowing that Cayton had a sizeable library of boxing films and had been the producer of the fight film series 'Greatest Fights of the Century'. Cayton agreed to advance Jacobs the money. He went to Australia and obtained the Johnson-Willard film. Many years later, Jacobs would acknowledge that 'my partner, Bill Cayton, and Cus D'Amato. . .took those energies that I had given to handball and re-directed them to business.' In 1960, Jim Jacobs would combine his library and go into partnership with Bill Cayton, a partnership that would last for 28 years until Jacobs's death. During that time they would build a successful boxing film syndication business throughout the world, their boxing documentaries would win numerous awards, including two Academy Award nominations, they would manage a stable of top contenders and world champions, and they would develop Mike Tyson into the most financially-successful athlete of all time, growing rich themselves along the way.

Bill Cayton was a dozen years older than Jim Jacobs. He was 42 years old when they began their partnership in 1960. Cayton was in many ways different from Jacobs, which made for an effective symbiotic relationship between the two over the years of their association. Never having any athletic prowess to speak of, Cayton was, on the other hand, a good student. He grew up in Brooklyn, the son of a stockbroker, and graduated from the University of Maryland with a degree in chemical engineering. He then went to work as a technical report writer for the DuPont Chemical company for $35 a week in the Depression years of the late 1930s. From DuPont, he went to work for an advertising agency, and by the end of the Second World War he had his own advertising agency in Manhattan – Cayton, Inc. Television was then in its infancy, and one of his clients wanted to sponsor some sort of sports show on TV. Cayton thought boxing would be ideal, and in 1948 he began obtaining the rights to vintage boxing films and launched the TV series 'Greatest Fights of the Century,' which followed the Gillette Friday Night Fights. The programme, often giving viewers their first glimpses of legendary champions on film, proved to be immensely popular. When he and Jacobs joined forces and combined their respective fight film libraries and then purchased the vast collection of boxing and other sports films that belonged to Madison Square Garden, they eventually built a library of nearly 20,000 boxing films. Over the years, Jacobs carved out a reputation as a boxing historian, and was the 'up front' man, the spokesman for the company, the manager-of-record for their eventual stable of fighters. Jim enjoyed this role, guesting on boxing broadcasts, being sought out for his opinions on upcoming bouts or the great fighters of the past. Cayton, meanwhile, enjoyed functioning in relative anonymity, handling the nuts-and-bolts detail work of their companies. Bill handled the matters concerning contracts and negotiations, although Jim, of course, was always involved as well. 'Jim knew nothing about contracts. I'm an expert,' Cayton told an interviewer. And Jim agreed. 'Bill is an excellent contract man,' he would say.

Around the same time as he met Bill Cayton, Jacobs met the other man who would have a profound influence on his life. That was Cus D'Amato. They met at a screening of old boxing films Jim was presenting one night. Afterwards, they began talking about the merits of various past champions, and the two hit it off. Jacobs was about to begin his business association with Bill Cayton, and was therefore moving to New York. Jim and Cus quickly developed an extremely close bond. D'Amato admired not only Jim's serious interest in and knowledge of boxing, but he admired Jim because he excelled at everything he did, especially pursuits involving athletic prowess. Jim was fascinated with the complex man that was Cus D'Amato. He saw that this was a unique individual, a man he regarded as brilliant and someone he admired for his principles. At this time, around 1960, D'Amato was in the midst of his battle against the IBC, and Jacobs became convinced that Cus, despite some detours he might have taken, was on the side of right. D'Amato may have served another purpose at well. He was in his early 50s when they met. Jacobs was barely 30 years old. Because Jacobs came from a broken home and was raised by his mother, he lacked a strong father figure in his life. D'Amato filled that psychological and emotional void. He became Jacobs's mentor, and not only in matters pertaining to boxing. Jacobs moved in with D'Amato, and the two, despite differences in age, upbringing, ethnic background and just about every other surface consideration, shared something much deeper, a sympatico. They were kindred spirits, and Jacobs in large part formed his life-view through the eyes of Cus D'Amato. Over the years, many people who knew both of them would remark that when you listened to Jimmy what you were hearing was Cus. It was an observation that no doubt pleased Jim Jacobs. Eventually, D'Amato moved to Catskill, and Jim, after dating a variety of women over the years, settled

down and married Lorraine Atter, a businesswoman from New
York.

When it was time for Mike Tyson to turn pro, perhaps
the best team in the history of boxing was standing by and
ready – Cayton the negotiator, Jacobs the publicity and boxing strategist, and D'Amato, the trainer, teacher and boxing mastermind. Combined with Tyson's fierce and visceral
determination and ability, it was as near to a sure thing as is
possible to be.

Cus was still concerned about Mike's behaviour. He knew the
boy still had a 'street' mentality. Cus confided in one friend that
every time Mike was out of the house and the phone rang, he
worried that the call might mean trouble of one sort or another.
At the end of 1984, as preparations were being made to turn
Mike pro, Cus told Alex Wallau of ABC Sports, 'Many people who have been around boxing all those years never had a
champion, certainly a heavyweight champion. . . . For that to
happen in one's lifetime is so improbable. I got Floyd Patterson,
then, here, at the age of 76, I was fortunate to come in contact
with this young man who has, in my opinion, all the require-
ments to be the great champion that I believe he's going to be,
maybe the best that ever lived.' D'Amato realized that if he
were to fulfil his dream of masterminding another heavyweight
champion to the top, he had to move with cautious haste to
achieve the agenda. He and Jacobs mapped out a strategy
unique in modern-day boxing. Tyson, while being carefully
matched, would fight every two to three weeks. In other eras,
this would not have been unusual. In the 1980s, however, no
contender climbing to the top kept up that active a schedule.
However, apart from enabling D'Amato to move Tyson up the
ladder quickly, keeping him in the ring would serve another
important purpose. It would use up Mike's time and energies,
leaving him less of either to get into trouble. Certainly if a
fighter engaged in gruelling, bruising fights every two or three
weeks over a long period he would burn himself out quickly.
But Team Tyson did not plan to put Mike in with anyone who
was likely to give him a hard time or last very long, so the fights
themselves would be much easier and quicker than the long,
tiring sessions in the gym. The fights would present Mike with
opponents who had differing styles; they would get him used to
performing under pressure in the professional arena, and build
him up in the public's eyes as an invincible destroyer.

For Jim Jacobs, like D'Amato, the success of Mike Tyson would fulfil a dream. In the late 1960s when he had reached the heights in the handball world, and his career on the court was winding down, and when he had achieved his goal of being independently wealthy, for by then his film partnership with Bill Cayton was thriving, he told a friend, Judd Maze, that he now had one driving ambition: he wanted someday to manage the Heavyweight Champion of the World. This ambition perhaps predated his conversation with Maze, since his friendship with D'Amato may have ignited that spark a decade earlier. There was even a story that at one point Jacobs, with his bull-like strength, tenacity and natural athletic ability, under D'Amato's guidance, would take a crack at becoming a fighter himself. The scenario was that Jim would be taught by D'Amato, would practise in closed-door gymnasium 'bouts', and then would put up $100,000 to challenge Archie Moore for the Light-Heavyweight Championship in his first professional fight, much as Rademacher had done in his pro debut against Floyd Patterson. Only in this case, D'Amato felt Jacobs could defeat the clever but ageing Moore. For some reason – if indeed the story was true – it never happened. In the late 1970s, when he was already a fight manager, Jacobs became the international booking agent for highly-rated South African heavyweight, Kallie Knoetze. He was optimistic that with D'Amato's behind-the-scenes help in tutoring Knoetze, he would achieve his goal. 'He reminds me of Rocky Marciano,' Jacobs said, perhaps a little over-enthusiastically, '. . .there is no question that Knoetze will be the Heavyweight Champion of the World before the end of 1978.' However, Knoetze was knocked out by John Tate and then, in rapid succession, by journeymen Mike Koranicki and Jimmy Abbott, and Jacobs's hope of finding a second Marciano was gone. Now, the better part of a decade later, he had the genuine article in Tyson: now, he told Maze, his revised goal was not only to manage the Heavyweight Champion, but to make him the most financially successful champion in the history of boxing in all weight divisions.

D'Amato knew of a local husband-and-wife team, Bob and Loraine Miller, who promoted small boxing shows in the area around Albany. Raising a house full of kids, working as a receptionist near their home in Troy, New York, Loraine Miller got involved in the sport through her husband, who had fought while in the service, then trained her brother, who was a fighter for a while. Developing local amateur kids, Bob bought

an old, decrepit building, gutted it, and turned it into a gym. He
also managed local pros. Loraine took out a promoter's licence
to keep the business in the family, and they began running
shows in their spare time, since Bob also had a full-time job
in the local high school. D'Amato asked them to meet him and
told them, 'I've watched you and Bob for a number of years
running shows. I like the way you do things. You're honest,
you try and keep things running smoothly, you watch out for
the fighters. I'd like to turn Mike Tyson pro. I've had a lot
of offers, but I want him to go with you. I feel that Mike
will be champ of the world one day, and I'd like you people
to promote him. I'm not saying that along the line I won't
have other promoters, but if Mike makes it to the top, we
all make it to the top. There'll be other people involved,
but we'll all make money.' They shook hands, Cus kissed
Loraine, and everything was set. Cus had what he wanted
– local promoters who could build Mike as a local attraction
while keeping him away out of the limelight until the time was
right.

Mike's first fight was fought on the undercard of a Miller
promotion on March 6, 1985. His opponent was a harmless
trialhorse named Hector Mercedes. Mike attacked him as he
would all his early opponents, with a vengeance. Digging right
uppercuts, he pinned Mercedes on the ropes, then pounded
left uppercuts to his ribs. Mercedes went down from this
relentless barrage, and took the ten-count on his knee, getting up immediately after he heard 'ten' and knew he was
safe from any further onslaught. At the age of 18 years and
9 months, Mike Tyson had successfully made his debut as a
professional.

The deal with Millers was that they would not lose any
money promoting Mike Tyson. If they made money on their
shows, fine. If not, their losses would be covered by Jacobs
and Cayton. After the Mercedes fight, there was no profit and
so the Millers could not pay Tyson a purse. Jacobs and Cayton
chipped in and covered a $500 purse for Mike. The money went
to D'Amato, so that Mike wouldn't blow it all at once. Kevin
Rooney got his traditional trainer's cut of ten per cent. Cus gave
Mike $100, and Tyson was thrilled. The rest of the money was
put aside for him.

A month later, again on a Miller-promoted show, Tyson did
away with Trent Singleton. A furious flurry dropped Singleton
barely more than ten seconds into the bout, and when he rose,

a winging left hand ended things a few seconds later, less than one minute into the first round. On May 23, Don Halpin gave Tyson a longer fight than any he had ever been in outside his gym sparring sessions. Halpin lasted into the fourth round, until a crushing right to the face put him down, followed by a smashing left-right combination when he arose that put him into the ropes and ended matters.

At this point, Team Tyson was ready to reveal their tiger a little more to the world. Despite a previous conflict with Bob Arum stemming from a contractual battle over control of Wilfred Benitez, they were willing to let bygones be bygones for the sake of advancing Tyson's career. Arum had a valuable outlet for exposing Mike Tyson. His organization presented a weekly series of live bouts called 'Top Rank Boxing' on the ESPN national cable-TV network. Arum was being given the chance to get in on the ground floor where Mike Tyson's promotion was concerned, an opportunity he would take but later fail to follow through and capitalize on, and while no one will ever have to throw any benefits for Arum, who grew rich promoting major fights with Tommy Hearns, Marvin Hagler and Sugar Ray Leonard, it nevertheless cost him financially as well as losing him the high profile he would have had in promoting Tyson once Mike reached the top.

Arum agreed to use Tyson on his cable-TV shows. Mike's first fight before a television audience was set for the undercard of Arum's show at Resorts International in Atlantic City on June 20, 1985, against Rick Spain who was 33 pounds lighter than Tyson. Mike overwhelmed Spain from the opening bell, dropping him with a right hand. Spain beat the count, only to be flattened by the first left hand that hit him after he arose. The fight was over at: 38 of the first round. Three weeks later on another Arum promotion in Atlantic City, Tyson met a big, awkward white opponent named John Alderson who, at 6'4" and 226 pounds, towered over him. Alderson managed to last two rounds before Tyson stopped him. Just eight days later, Tyson was back in the ring, this time on his familiar turf in upstate New York, where he knocked out Larry Sims in three rounds. Four weeks after that, it was back with Top Rank in Atlantic City, where Lorenzo Canaday was his next victim, going down just ten seconds into the first round from an overhand left, and finished by Tyson less than a minute later.

Despite the strategy of keeping him busy, Mike managed to

find time to seek out trouble. Although now a professional fighter in the early stages of his career, he reverted to the behaviour that had landed him in the Tryon School as a 12-year-old. He and a former street buddy of his, who later told this story, were back in their old neighbourhood in Brooklyn, where Mike frequently went after fights to alleviate the boredom and routine of Catskill. On this particular day, the boys had about $10 between them, but Mike got it into his head that he had to have a radio. The two were riding in the elevator of an apartment building when another person got in. According to Tyson's friend, Mike 'yoked' the guy around the neck, grabbing him in a stranglehold. The pair then went through the victim's pockets, coming up with about $80. Instead of letting the man go, Tyson's mean streak emerged, and he began banging his face into the elevator wall. Mike's buddy, incredulous, intervened. Mike stopped, the two made off, and later that day, Mike bought his radio.

There were two more fights in Atlantic City for Top Rank, and one for a new promoter, Jeff Levine. Tyson scored two knockdowns in rapid succession, the first with a devastating left to the ribs, and the second with a right hand that left Michael Jack Johnson prone on the canvas for several minutes. That fight lasted 39 seconds. A month later, Tyson was matched with a solid veteran of 18 fights, Donnie Long. Teddy Brenner, Arum's matchmaker, had been dubious about Tyson's abilities. In Long, he felt Mike would meet his match. Long had gone ten rounds with both James Broad and John Tate, ranked heavyweights. He was 6'2", and weighed 215 pounds, the same as Tyson. Tyson destroyed Long in less than a minute and a half, knocking him down three times in that short span of time.

It was around this time that Arum allowed Mike Tyson, the biggest fish in the shark-infested waters of boxing, to get off the hook. Bill Cayton maintains that he and Jim were prepared to continue to do business with Arum because of the help he was giving them in exposing Mike Tyson on the ESPN network. 'We would have stayed with Arum,' says Cayton, 'but it would have been fight by fight. We don't make any long range commitments.' However, a snag developed. For some reason, Arum's matchmakers were not cooperating in making available opportunities for Mike to fight as often as Team Tyson wanted him to. Cayton went to Arum and said, in effect, 'You're the Chairman of the Board [of Top Rank], it's your decision.' But Arum protested that his matchmakers ran that end of the business, and it was up to them. As a result, after six appearances on 'Top Rank Boxing', Jacobs and Cayton met with Jeff Levine, who was then affiliated to the Houston Boxing Association, and made a deal with him to become Tyson's promoter. Years later, after the Tyson-Spinks fight that grossed some $70 million, Arum, in an interview with sportscaster Bill Mazer on WFAN Radio in New York, lamented the loss of Tyson to Top Rank, blaming his match-makers for underestimating Tyson's potential. He told Mazer that Teddy Brenner and Bruce Trampler, Top Rank's match-makers, didn't think much of Tyson as a fighter. They said his style was 'too wide open', that he was a marginal talent who didn't warrant the amount of on-air exposure Cayton, Jacobs and D'Amato were asking for, and so Arum, on their advice, let Tyson slip through his fingers.

Less than three weeks after disposing of Donnie Long, Tyson was back in the ring at the Atlantis Hotel in Atlan-tic City to face Robert Colay, a 14-and-5 fighter, under Jeff Levine's promotional banner. Tyson made Levine's debut as his promoter a brief one. The first clean punch Tyson landed, a pulverizing left hand, sent Colay down. He barely beat the count, but was helpless, and the referee quickly jumped in and waved the fight over. It had lasted 39 seconds.

Mike Tyson was now a perfect 10-and-0 as a pro, with 10 knockouts, in just eight months. Seven of his ten KOs had come in the first round, although, as with any fight-er being properly advanced, none of the ten opponents presented any real threat to Tyson. Perhaps a little de-fensively, Cayton, while acknowledging that Mike's opponents were 'very carefully selected', nevertheless maintains, 'There was never a "tomato can" in the whole group. . .We always wanted a fighter who Mike would beat [but] that Mike could learn something from.' However, Jacobs privately admitted that some of Mike's early opponents were 'embarrassing' in their lack of boxing ability. Despite the fact that they had the best talent in the heavyweight division to come along in years, one whom they were moving along with great speed, they were extremely cautious in their matchmaking, following D'Amato's advice.

Each day, as he had done for the previous twenty-five years, Jacobs would start the morning over coffee in Bill Cayton's Manhattan office. In the past, it was their film business, or

boxing that they would talk about. Now the sole topic was Mike
Tyson. They would consult a variety of trainers and promoters
around the country about the merits of prospective opponents.
Whenever possible, they would obtain video cassettes of those
fighters, send a copy to D'Amato, and study their various
styles. While many of the opponents chosen for Mike did not
have a lot of ability, most were selected for a particular reason,
to expose Mike to fighters with different styles. Many of the
opponents were obtained through Johnny Bos, a booking agent
with the reputation for providing any type of opponent needed
in any weight division. Jacobs had tremendous respect for the
job Bos performed, saying, 'There are people who are geniuses
in different areas. Johnny Bos is a genius when it comes to shit.'
And Jacobs meant it as a strong compliment and endorsement
of Bos, recommending Bos to any manager who needed help in
building his fighter's ability and record. Bos could deliver just
the right type of mediocre opponent.

For every much-vaunted new boxer who appears on the scene
with a 22-and-0 record, or 18 straight knockouts, you can bet
there's a trail of nonentity opponents with unrecognizable
names in his wake. Any manager or promoter developing a
kid with potential will stress how important opponents are,
especially in the heavyweight division, where there seems to
be a scarcity of fighters upon whom aspiring champions can
fatten their records. In the case of Mike Tyson, it quickly
became difficult to find opponents willing to step into the ring
with him. When a willing fighter was located, he or his manager
wanted more than $500, sometimes $1,000, even for undercard
prelim fights, to risk life and limb with a monster like Tyson.
Jacobs and Cayton soon learned they would have to foot the
bill for these purses. Fortunately, they had the financial means
to do so, ensuring that the Mike Tyson bandwagon would keep
rolling along. Jacobs handled the actual procuring of opponents
on behalf of D'Amato and Cayton, and he could be a stern
taskmaster when it came to his fighter. Nothing was left to
chance. Loraine Miller recalls hours spent phoning around
the country, trying to locate someone to face Mike in one of
her upstate shows, restricted in terms of the type of opponent
Jacobs had specified for that particular fight. When she found
a fighter, she would call Jacobs and Cayton. 'I would say, I
have a kid, I think his record is seven and five.' Jim would
then demand more precise information. 'You don't "think",
with Jimmy. You "know". Everything had to be just perfect.'

The development of Mike Tyson was brilliantly orchestrated not only in the ring, but outside it as well by Jacobs and Cayton. They scheduled his fights early enough in the evening for sports-casters to have highlights in plenty of time for their 11 p.m. newscasts. They compiled a list of the top sports writers and sportscasters in the country, and, after Tyson's third fight, began sending them video tapes of each of his knockouts to view or use on their news programmes. Stills of Mike in action were also supplied to newspapers and magazines. And, always, the story of 'Mike and Cus' was played to the hilt, how the brilliant, ageing guru had found this troubled but talented black youth, how they had developed a father and son relationship that res-cued him from reform school, and how D'Amato had taken this rough diamond and not only developed him as a fighter on the verge of greatness, but had instilled in him a sense of values and loyalty as well. It was great public relations job, and it paid off.

For a quarter of a century, as purveyors of boxing films, as packagers of billiards tournaments on network television, as managers of world champions and contenders who often fought on network TV, Jacobs and Cayton had made many friends and developed many valuable business and press con-tacts. As a result, Mike was featured on the covers or in major stories in over a hundred sports and general-interest magazines, extraordinary for any fighter, especially one who had not won an Olympic medal. 'They've done the best marketing job ever done on a fighter,' says Mickey Duff. 'The fighter was good enough to stand up to it, but they saw it very early and they got him all this publicity well before he deserved it.' At a time when the heavyweight division was weak in terms of viable contenders, when Larry Holmes was reaching the end of his long and distinguished reign as champion, when the title was divided among three champions, each recognized by a different sanctioning group, and when most people didn't really care who was the champion anyway, Mike Tyson was sold and quickly adopted by the media and fans as the saviour of the heavyweight division, the fighter who would bring excitement and magic back to what had traditionally been considered boxing's most glamorous division. Everything was going right for Mike Tyson, and then tragedy struck.

* * *

Cus D'Amato was attending a boxing convention in upstate New York. He was ill, but had insisted upon going despite Camille's objections. While there, he collapsed, and was taken to a hospital in Albany, where he spent a week. He was diagnosed as having a form of pneumonia, and his condition did not improve. He was transferred at the insistence of Jacobs to Mount Sinai Hospital in New York, but he continued to deteriorate. Tyson went to visit him in the hospital, where they has an emotional scene. Mike told him that without him he couldn't go on, that there would be no purpose in his continuing to fight. 'It would be tough fighting without you,' Mike said. 'tough remembering the things you taught me, tough not having you to stay on my back. I can't fight if you're not around.' D'Amato told him that was nonsense. 'If you don't continue fighting when I'm gone,' he said, 'we're going to find out if people can come back from the dead, because if I can, I'm going to come back and get you if you give up, or if you do anything wrong.' A few days later, on November 1, in Latham, New York, Mike won his eleventh fight, destroying Sterling Benjamin in the first round in under a minute, knocking him down with a left to the face and then finishing him with a dazzling flurry of a dozen punches, crunching body shots sending him down for the second, and final, knockdown. It was the first time D'Amato was not at one of Mike's fights, sitting at ringside, supporting the three-man corner of Kevin Rooney, Steve Lott and cut-man Matt Baranski.

D'Amato continued to weaken, yet his instincts caused him to resist efforts to put an oxygen mask on him. He fought off three hospital attendants with a final burst of strength, and they had to sedate him. Cus lapsed into a coma from which he never emerged. On November 4, 1985 two months short of his 78th birthday, Cus D'Amato died of interstitial pulmonary fibrosis, just a few miles from where he had drawn his first breath nearly eight decades earlier. Both Tyson and Jacobs were distraught. Each had lost a man who had had a profound influence on his life. At Cus's funeral, on a crisp autumn day in Catskill, Tyson stood alongside Jacobs and Rooney, Jay Bright and Tom Patti, another of Cus's boys, Floyd Patterson and Jose Torres. Each was lost in his own private thoughts. It's certain that each in his own way felt diminished by the loss of this man. Miles away, in New York City, Teddy Atlas's thoughts also dwelled that day on Cus D'Amato, and what might have been.

* * *

Mike's next fight was scheduled for just a week after Cus's funeral. Of course, he had the opportunity to cancel it, but he didn't. Continuing his training and going through with the fight was his way, and Rooney's, of working through their grief. Mike knew that it was Cus's wish that he continue. The old man had said he would live to see Mike become a success, and he had. Mike was 11-and-0. He was on the threshold. Cus hadn't quite made it all the way with him, but Mike could repay him by fulfilling his dream, so he would fight on. He and his team went to Houston to meet Eddie Richardson. Now it was up to Mike to apply the lessons he had been taught. What's the difference between an amateur and a professional? A professional can perform no matter what he's feeling inside. Eight seconds after the opening bell, Eddie Richardson was on the canvas. For the better part of the next minute, Mike was all over him, a left hand finally sending Richardson's 6'6" body toppling like a felled tree. It was over at 1:17.

Nine days later, back home in upstate New York, Conroy Nelson became ring victim number 13, going down in the second round from a right-left combination after absorbing a brutal body beating throughout most of the first round. By now, Tyson was playing to full houses in such upstate arenas as the Latham Coliseum and the Rensselaer Polytechnic Institute stadium. Although the rest of the country and the world had not quite caught on yet, Tyson mania was rampant in the Albany-Troy area. The fans wore T-shirts that proclaimed 'Mike Tyson – Future Heavyweight Champion'. It was a far cry from the previous spring, when Mike was just turning pro, and Loraine and Bob Miller would hustle tickets for the shows featuring Tyson on the undercard and Kevin Rooney in the main event, the days when a local sportscaster told her Mike Tyson was a nobody, but be sure to call him if he ever got anywhere. Tyson had now been featured on CBS 'Sunday Morning', with a profile of himself and D'Amato. The networks and magazines were clamouring to set up stories about him. Suddenly, the sportscaster from the Albany TV station was calling the Millers. Tyson was hot, and he wanted to be in on the story. The Millers were only too pleased to oblige, because they had been given a promise. If Mike Tyson made it to the title, he would come back home to defend the crown at least once in the Albany area, and the Millers would be given the chance to promote a World Heavyweight Championship bout. After scraping by all these years with club shows, they would at last get a piece of the big-time pie.

Now it was time for another step for Tyson. He would make his New York City debut, at Madison Square Garden, with all the New York sports media on hand. His New York 'coming out' party was a spectacular one. On December 6, against huge and ponderous Sammy Scaff, a journeyman opponent, Tyson drew blood in the first 20 seconds of the bout, rocking Scaff with a left hook to the nose. The fury of his attack overwhelmed the lumbering Scaff, who was pounded relentlessly until his face was a bloody mess. Mercifully, it ended quickly, with a final left hook at just 1:15 of the first round.

Next, it was back to Latham, New York, to close out 1985. Two days after Christmas, Tyson was presented with a foe who showed no fear of him. Short, compact Mark Young, at 207 pounds, was built in much the same way as Tyson, but there the similarity ended. To his credit, Young came right at Tyson and at last tried to challenge him. However, he just did not have the tools required, and a right uppercut sent him flying across the ring. He was counted out 50 seconds into round one, raising Tyson's record to 15-and-0, all by KO. The demand for stories about Tyson increased every day. NBC's 'Today' programme and ABC's 'Good Morning America' interviewed him at breakfast time, and the 'CBS Evening News' profiled him at dinner time. The *Sports Illustrated* hit the stands in the new year with a cover that featured Tyson under the banner, 'Kid Dynamite', and Mike Tyson, who had still not defeated a ranked fighter and who had been fighting professionally for less than a year, was being touted as the hottest attraction to come down the boxing pipe since Sugar Ray Leonard.

On January 11, in Albany, David Jaco was the opponent. A lanky, frail-looking white kid, he proved to be amazingly resilient during his brief time in the ring with Mike. Less than a minute into the bout, he dropped like a strand of wet spaghetti when Tyson nailed him with a left, but he rose, took an 8-count, and came back at Mike. Just seconds later, another left toppled him face forward, and it seemed certain that the evening was over. Surprisingly, Jaco got to his feet a second time, and still attempted to fight back. Only when a right hand sent him down a third time did the fight finally end, with the three-knockdown rule forcing a mandatory finish at 2:14 into the opening round. Two weeks later, Mike got a few rounds of work in down at Trump Plaza in Atlantic City. Mike Jameson survived a fourth round knockdown, then was blasted out by Tyson in round five. It was the furthest Tyson had ever been extended by any opponent.

Mike's next fight would give the entire country its first chance to see him. Until now, his bouts had been seen on cable-TV, but a good portion of the US was not yet cabled, and even in those regions that were, many people did not subscribe to the service. However, late in 1985, ABC-TV Sports approached Cayton and Jacobs about a deal for Tyson to fight on the network. They made a solid offer, but Cayton felt his fighter was worth more, even though he was not yet ranked in the top ten. Cayton knew that TV was starved for an exciting new boxing face. Until that time, ABC had made long-term deals almost exclusively with fighters who had the glamour of Olympic gold attached to them, such as Sugar Ray Leonard, or the 1984 US Olympic crop that included Meldrick Taylor, Evander Holyfield, Tyrell Biggs and the most celebrated amateur of all time, Mark Breland. Yet Cayton's clever bargaining enabled him to make a deal for Tyson's services that doubled what ABC had paid to get Breland. For five fights, with Jeff Levine as the promoter, Mike Tyson would be paid one million dollars by ABC, on a graduated scale, as the level of his opposition increased. It was a sensational deal on behalf of a fighter who, though attracting a lot of publicity, was essentially unproven against any opposition of note.

Tyson's first fight for ABC was set for February 16, a Saturday, and would be broadcast on ABC's 'Wide World of Sports'. The opponent, while not top-ten ranked, was placed among the twenty or so best heavyweights in the world, and would certainly be a step up for Tyson. His name was Jesse Ferguson. Both ABC and Team Tyson wanted the fight away from the bland casino setting in Atlantic City that had become so familiar for the staging of fights. To show off Tyson to full advantage, and exploit the excitement he was generating among his growing army of fans, as well as for a 'small town' atmosphere, the location selected was the Rensselaer Polytechnic Institute fieldhouse in Troy. Tyson's fans would pour in from Albany, Catskill, Rotterdam, Schenectady, Watervliet, Cohoes and all the other nearby cities and towns. The Millers would run the local promotion, in cooperation with Jeff Levine.

On the day of the fight, the RPI fieldhouse was packed to the rafters with a 7,600-strong crowd. Several million more people around the country were tuned in at home. Outside, the weather was freezing, but in the fieldhouse things were hot. When Tyson entered the arena, the crowd erupted with deafening cheers that were repeated when the ring announcer introduced him a few minutes later. Ferguson must have felt as though he were in the lion's den, but he proved to be a game opponent, fighting back through the first four rounds as Tyson piled up the points and pursued him around the ring. In the fifth round, one of the patented Tyson combinations finally connected solidly, a right to the ribs and then immediately a right uppercut with the worst of bad intentions that sent Ferguson sprawling on the canvas. He barely beat the count, rising as the referee, Luis Rivera, reached nine. For the rest of the round, it was bombs away, as Ferguson absorbed a terrific pounding that took away any desire to fight that may have been left in him. When he answered the bell for the sixth round, his only thought was to survive. He grabbed Tyson and would not let go. When Rivera tried to break the clinches, he had to struggle time and again as Ferguson refused to release his grip. Finally, after Rivera had battled to pull Ferguson off Tyson one final time, he waved his arms in the air, pointing at Ferguson, and indicated the fight was over. ABC's commentator, Alex Wallau, quickly shouted, 'He's disqualified him!' and pointed out that this would end Tyson's run of consecutive knockouts at seventeen. However, Rivera, perhaps suddenly aware that a highly visible heavyweight did have a knockout streak at stake, explained that he was awarding the fight to Tyson on a technical knockout, not a disqualification. In his judgment, Ferguson was hurt and therefore refusing to fight. It was a close judgment call, but that is how it went down in the record books, and Tyson had stopped his 18th opponent in as many bouts.

The victory was almost overshadowed by Mike's post-fight interview with the press, where he made a statement that shocked most of those who heard it. Speaking of Ferguson, he said, 'I tried to punch him and drive the bone of his nose back into his brain.' The admission of such murderous intent provoked reactions ranging from raised eyebrows to out-and-out incredulity, and over the next few days, Jacobs had his work cut out trying to limit the damage, explaining to reporters who called his office that it was an unfortunate statement, that Mike had not meant it literally, and so on. Nevertheless, it was widely reported and it certainly stuck in people's minds. Long after the Ferguson fight, the 'nose bone into the brain' statement would continually resurface in stories written about Tyson.

The morning after the fight, Tyson headed to New York City to appear on a couple of local TV shows. An Albany station wanted him for their show. No, Jacobs said, after a couple of days off in New York City, Mike would be returning to Catskill to resume training; his strict rules would not permit Mike to break his routine. The producer was persistent, assuring him that Mike could be finished and on his way back to Catskill by eight in the morning. Jacobs was polite but adamant. Mike's routine could not be interrupted. The media blitz was on in full force, and Jacobs was determined to control it as best he could so that Mike's concentration remained on track.

Four days after defeating Jesse Ferguson, the concern D'Amato had always felt about Mike's activities and whereabouts when he was away from the house once again proved well founded. Tyson and a friend were asked to leave the Crossgates Mall in Albany after creating a disturbance. Word got out, and a reporter for Albany's *Knickerbocker News* investigated, and reported in the paper's February 23 edition that a mall security officer said Tyson 'made lewd and obscene comments to female customers and was throwing clothes around.' The details (not reported in the paper) according to another reporter covering the story were that Tyson allegedly propositioned a young white salesgirl in Filene's department store in blunt language rife with four letter words. She, in turn, told him just what she thought of him, sending the fighter into a rage. He reportedly grabbed a rack of clothing and threw it towards her, scattering garments around the store, and exploding in a torrent of filthy gutter language directed at the girl and whatever customers happened to be in his vicinity. Mall security responded to a call for help and when they arrived Tyson and his friend were ordered off the premises. Everyone was well aware of who he was, having been a local celebrity for several years and having fought on national TV the previous weekend.

Crossgates Mall personnel did not press charges, anxious to just let the incident die and avoid adverse publicity. Team Tyson quickly closed ranks, trying to protect their fighter's well guarded image. Jim Jacobs said Mike had done nothing wrong. Albany *Times-Union* reporter, Paul Grondahl, went to the mall several days later to dig a little further into the story. Kevin Rooney had denied to Grondahl that Tyson had caused a problem, instead placing blame for the disturbance on Tyson's friend according to what Rooney said the fighter had told him. At the Mall, Grondahl ran up against a stone wall. All he got were either denials or people suddenly unwilling to talk. He located a Filene's security manager who refused to give her name, but who termed the incident 'a very minor thing'. Grondahl pressed her for details, but she told him that if she spoke to him about what had taken place with Tyson, she risked losing her job. Obviously, someone had contacted her superiors and succeeded in suppressing the story. Grondahl says that he then asked her if the original account in the *Knickerbocker News* was accurate. Nervously, she looked around and then nodded at him. Another Mike Tyson cover-up had succeeded. It would not be the last – not by a long shot.

On March 10, at the Nassau Coliseum, Mike completed his first year as a professional. Steve Zouski has a solid 25-and-9 record and claimed he had never been knocked down in his entire career; however he had lost 8 of his previous 10 fights and was definitely on the downslide. After absorbing a non-stop pounding, Zouski went down and out in round three. It was Mike's 19th straight knockout. He had averaged a fight just about every three weeks, right on target with the schedule D'Amato, Jacobs and Cayton had hoped to maintain for him. He was now poised for an assault on the top-ten rankings.

7

Contender

First, to the Fight, advanc'd the Charioteer,
High Hopes of Glory on his Brow appear;
Terror vindictive flashes from his Eye;
(To one the Fates the visual Ray deny)
Fierce glow'd his Looks, which spoke his
inward rage,
He leaps the Bar, and bounds upon the Stage.

– GYMNASIAD
PAUL WHITEHEAD

THE TYSON EXPRESS slowed down slightly, as the fighter suffered an ear infection that landed him in hospital early in the spring of 1986, and kept him out of the ring for two months, his longest stretch of inactivity since turning pro. While Tyson convalesced, the people looking out for his best interests were busy at work. When Cayton had negotiated their million-dollar deal with ABC, the network had wanted Mike's services on an exclusive basis for the seven figures they were paying. Cayton and Jacobs demurred. They wanted to be free to expose Mike elsewhere, as long as it did not adversely affect ABC, with whom they had had a long relationship leasing boxing films. Many meetings took place over a period of weeks, and shortly before the Ferguson fight they arrived at an agreement. Tyson would fight three times for the Home Box Office cable network, while ABC would have exclusive use of his services on non-cable, over-the-air TV.

Once that problem was resolved, Cayton went to work. Tyson had not made it yet into the top-ten world rankings, yet the deal Cayton negotiated with HBO called for him to receive half a million dollars a fight. The purse for the opponent – $50,000 in each case – would come out of that, leaving Tyson a gross of $450,000 for each of the bouts in the three-fight HBO package. He had earned $150,000 for the Ferguson fight from ABC, along with a percentage of the live gate of $170,000. Few champions earned these kinds of paydays, let alone fighters in the top ten. For a fighter still not even No. 10 in the world, the deals Cayton and Jacobs were making were unprecedented. Teddy Brenner, known as a tough negotiator himself, said the trouble with Bill was, 'When Cayton made a deal it was always 99-to-one in his favour.' Brenner may not have meant it as a compliment, but when it came to serving Tyson's interests, Cayton could not have been paid a better one. And ABC and HBO certainly never complained that they did not get their money's worth.

Mike was far from polished, but his lethal punching power and his tremendous will to win overcame any possible lack of technical skills. Although he'd won 19 fights, because so many had ended early, the cumulative time he had spent in the ring added up to less than an hour and a half of actual combat. He was still learning, although to the public he was already an indestructible fighting machine. His victims added to his reputation by the comments they made to the press. Sammy Scaff said he'd boxed with world champions Tim Witherspoon and Greg Page, but Tyson had hit him harder than anyone in his entire life. Eddie Richardson, whose fight with Tyson lasted :02 longer than Scaff's, was asked if he'd ever been hit as hard as Mike hit him. 'Yeah,' he said, 'about a year ago. I was hit by a truck.' Someone asked one of Mike's sparring partners if he'd ever really tried to open up on Mike and get the best of him in the ring. 'I'm no fool,' he said. 'I'm paid to survive, not to commit suicide.'

Jacobs and Cayton – especially Jacobs – were sensitive to criticism in the press. When it was written on more than one occasion that Tyson's opponents were a bunch of hand-picked nobodies, Jacobs reacted defensively by referring writers to the record books to look up the calibre of Joe Louis's or Sugar Ray Robinson's first 19 opponents. When they were criticized for putting Tyson in the ring so often he might burn out, Jacobs was stung into responding that, regardless of whether you were a boxer, a brain surgeon or a plumber, the more often you practised your trade, the better you were at it. To rest is to rust. Tyson was criticized as being too small to make it to the top as a heavyweight. Jacobs maintained that his size was actually an advantage, not a disadvantage. By punching upwards at most of his opponents, with the force generated by his tree-trunk thighs, he was able to hit with much more power. Jacobs took much of the criticism personally, and felt obliged to reply to it whenever it caught his eye. Journalists and reporters began to refer to him and to Cayton as 'arrogant', 'condescending', 'stuffed shirts'.

There may have been some strategy behind Jacobs's behaviour. D'Amato had always felt it was his job to shield his fighter, to deflect criticism from his boxer to himself, to make himself out to be the 'bad guy' to the press. Jacobs may well have decided to adopt the same attitude. The bottom line was, *he* managed Tyson, not the press, and *he* would make the decisions that affected his fighter's future, not the newspapermen. Significantly, no one criticized the way Jacobs and Cayton were managing their charge. Everyone, either admiringly or begrudgingly, admitted they were doing the most efficient and effective job of building a heavyweight champion, both in the ring and in the bank account, that anyone had ever done. Tyson was becoming a serious contender for the Heavyweight Championship, and he was still just 19 years old. Now it was time for the next step, and it would be a big one.

Tyson's ear infection, the result of an injury he suffered to the cartilage on his right ear when he banged it accidentally in his pigeon coop, had cleared up. He was set to fight the shrewd veteran James 'Quick' Tillis, once a legitimate contender for the heavyweight title and though now 28 years old and somewhat past his prime, still top-ten calibre. His wars with Carl Williams, Earnie Shavers, and Former Champions, Mike Weaver, Pinklon Thomas and Gerrie Coetzee had gained him invaluable experience, and he and manager Beau Williford knew that an upset over Tyson on national TV would catapult Tillis right back into the title picture and some big paydays.

The Tillis fight had been set for March, three weeks after Mike had demolished Zouski, but the ear injury and infection had forced a five-week delay. The bout was rescheduled for May 3 in the Glens Falls (NY) Civic Center, fifty miles north of Albany. Tyson Territory. During his convalescence, when the monotony of his enforced idleness got too much, Tyson had done some unscheduled travelling, disappearing down to Brooklyn without Rooney's knowledge in pursuit of girls and the smell of the streets. When he returned to Catskill, it was time to knuckle down and do some serious work. Tillis was tricky, and Rooney knew he would be no walkover like Dave Jaco or Steve Zouski. Rooney had also seen things during the Ferguson fight that he did not like. After digging Ferguson to the body in the first round to the point where he was wincing, Mike had let up in the second round, and he and Ferguson had ended up clinching, mauling and holding. Mike had had no spark, he had forgotten about his lateral movement and his sharp combinations. Later, he had become careless and had been on the receiving end of a few good shots to the head by Ferguson. They hadn't done any harm, but Rooney was not happy, and he applied pressure to Mike during their training for

Tillis. Tyson responded by getting mean. He knocked several teeth loose on one sparring partner, knocked another down twice, and knocked a third unconscious.

One day, Tyson did another disappearing act, chasing girls somewhere in Albany while Rooney waited, impatient and embarrassed, at the gym – embarrassed because his non-appearance was being documented by an NBC-TV crew and a reporter for the *New York Daily News*. Rooney's discomfort was compounded by the fact that when the reporters asked him where Mike was, and when he would be there, he had absolutely no idea.

In a jam-packed Civic Center in Glens Falls and in front of millions of ABC viewers, 'Quick' Tillis managed to do, over the first four rounds, what none of Tyson's previous opponents had been able to. He made Mike back up. He confused him. He threw off Tyson's timing with his own well-timed jabs, which Mike ate as he fell behind on the scorecards. Then, with 15 seconds left in the fourth round, Tillis decided the time was right to take a shot and test Tyson's chin. He fired a big left hook, but it missed, carrying him off balance and leaving his face momentarily unprotected. Instinctively, Tyson seized the moment. He shot a short left hook to Tillis's jaw, and Tillis went down hard. He was hurt, but not enough to stay down, and luckily the bell rang before Tyson could follow up. For the rest of the fight, Tillis adopted a more cautions demeanour, making sure he was safe before firing combinations at Tyson. He continued to have his moments, but they were fewer and further between. Tyson kept the pressure on, and piled up points to draw even on the scorecards. Tillis still had the tools of the trade, and he knew how to use them to survive, how to tie Tyson up on the inside. When the bell rang ending the tenth round, Tillis was still standing, still fighting back. He had never been in serious danger after the fourth round knockdown, and Tyson's KO streak was over at nineteen. The decision was unanimous, but very narrow, for Tyson. He had just pulled away from Tillis with a strong finish. If one round had been different on the scorecards, Tillis would have held him to a draw. Instead, Mike had his twentieth victory, the first time he had been forced to go the distance. He had failed to impress the national audience except for his brief flash of power early in the bout. His shortcomings were still apparent to observers, his trainer, and his managers. Jacobs had admittedly underestimated Tillis. He would later confide to a friend, '"Quick" Tillis was a mistake, a big mistake. And it was my mistake as the manager.'

Mike's next fight was set for May 20, just seventeen days after the Tillis bout. His bout against Sammy Scaff had taken place in the Felt Forum, Madison Square Garden's small auxiliary arena. Now he would appear for the first time in the main 22,000-seat arena of the Garden, for decades the fabled 'Mecca of Boxing', and he would be fighting the main event, which Home Box Office would televise live. His opponent was Mitch 'Blood' Green, a talented fighter but a 'head case' who had had some trouble with the law. Green was ranked No. 7 in the world by the World Boxing Council. He had a solid record of 16–1–1, with 10 of his victories by knockout. Before the fight, Green talked long and loud about what he would do to Tyson, but in the ring the name of his game boiled down to one word – survival. Green took no chances with Tyson. He was big enough and experienced enough to avoid Mike's power, and Tyson allowed himself once again to be frustrated by a big, durable opponent. However, unlike Tillis, Green was unable or unwilling to mount any kind of an effective attack. The fight was less than a pleasing aesthetic experience, but at the final bell there was no doubt this time about the winner. Tyson had achieved a near walk-over. The three judges, scoring by rounds, had the bout 8–2, 9–1, and 9–1. Tyson had won a total of 26 out of a possible 30 rounds on the three scorecards, easily handling the man the WBC considered the seventh-best contender in the world. Two years later, Tyson and Green would meet in an unscheduled fight on a Harlem street that would earn them both headlines far outstripping the ones that followed their meeting in the ring at the Garden.

Three weeks later Mike returned to the Garden's main arena, this time on the undercard, facing Reggie Gross. Tyson's wins over Tillis and Green had catapulted him to the No. 4 position in the WBC ratings. He was determined to get back on the KO track. Gross was a solid pro, a spoiler, with an 18-and-4 record. The fight was exciting while it lasted. Gross came out winging, unleashing a rapid-fire flurry at Tyson, an offensive that had the crowd screaming encouragement to the lopsided underdog. What many failed to notice as they cheered a rare display of courage by an opponent against Tyson was that Gross failed to land solidly a single punch from his entire barrage. Tyson's great upper-body movement, his vastly underrated defensive abilities, took over, and he bobbed and weaved away from

Gross's fists. Biding his time, not getting rattled, he waited for an opportunity. Suddenly, as Gross persevered with his volley of punches, Mike unleashed a solitary, lightning left hand seemingly from nowhere, and Gross was sent sprawling on to the canvas, in serious trouble. When the referee completed the count, Tyson closed in for the kill. It came at the end of another left hand, and the evening had ended for Tyson – and Gross – at 2:36 of the first round. The crowd was awed at this first-hand look at Tyson's power. Mike showered and dressed, and then returned to the ringside to cheer on his stablemate, Edwin Rosario, who was challenging Hector 'Macho' Camacho in the main event for the World Lightweight Championship. Rosario lost a hotly contested and controversial decision to the 'Macho Man', after which he and Mike and Team Tyson left the arena. It was Tyson's last fight at Madison Square Garden. A few more appearances in the upstate arenas, and then it would be on to the big fights in the gambling capitals of Atlantic City and Las Vegas.

The next venue was a return to Troy two weeks after the Reggie Gross fight, for a quick dispatching of William Hosea, who decided discretion was the better part of valour after tasting Tyson's fists. He listened intently on one knee while the referee counted him out, then got up the instant he heard that comforting word, 'ten', which came exactly 2:03 after the opening bell. Thirteen days later, at the Stevensville Hotel in the resort region of the Catskill Mountains, with the summer vacation crowd eager for an evening's entertainment, Tyson was booked to fight Lorenzo Boyd. Strolling on the road outside the hotel grounds on the warm summer evening several hours before the fight, Tyson and Rooney encountered one of the judges assigned to the bouts that night. They knew each other, and after exchanging a greeting the judge ribbed Tyson, 'You know, I'm judging your fight tonight, so I shouldn't be talking to you. People might get the wrong idea.' Tyson smiled, and turned to Rooney. 'Hey, Kevin, look who's here. Maybe if we give him something. . . .' he joked. 'Mike,' said the judge, 'if you need to rely on my scorecard tonight to win this fight, I've got the biggest sports story of the year.' The judge was right. Mike celebrated his elevation to the No. 2 slot in the WBC rankings by taking Boyd out in the second round with a lightning-fast 6–4 combination – right to the ribs, and then the right immediately whipped to the chin.

   Joe Frazier was a brave warrior who feared no man during his days in the ring. He still feared no man in 1986, long after his career was over. Unfortunately for his son, Marvis, whose boxing career he was now managing, this fearless attitude led him to accept the offer of a chance for Marvis to fight Tyson on July 26 at the Glens Falls Civic Center. It was a bad move. Nearly three years earlier, Marvis had been knocked out in one round by Larry Holmes in a bid for Holmes's title. True, it was Frazier's only loss in 17 fights, but Holmes did not have the same reputation as a puncher of 'bad intentions' as Tyson did, and if Holmes could polish Marvis off in one round, it did not bode well for his chances against Tyson. Joe was training his son, and tried to mould Marvis after himself, which was a mistake, because Marvis had neither the grit nor the firepower that his father had possessed. The strategy they devised was to bob and weave and slip, the way Joe had fought, but Tyson and Rooney had worked out an effective plan to counter any bobbing and weaving Marvis Frazier might do. In the locker room shortly before the fight, Tyson told Jacobs exactly what was going to happen. 'When you jab him,' Tyson said, 'he bends forward at the waist, like he's bowin', just bends straight over. He doesn't bend his knees. When I jab and he bends over, I'm gonna catch him with the right uppercut.'

   ABC's cameras were on hand to televise the bout live to the nation. This fight, under the terms negotiated by Cayton, would earn Tyson $250,000 from the TV network. True to form, Mike entered the ring without robe, without socks, just black trunks and black leather shoes. He paced the ring like a caged animal once he had climbed through the ropes. His mouth curved in a snarling sneer. When the bell rang, he moved quickly at Frazier and immediately backed him against the ropes. In a lightning burst of controlled fury and power, Tyson pinned him in a neutral corner with a series of jabs. Sure enough, as Tyson had predicted, Frazier bent forward, and, planting his massive legs for optimum leverage, Tyson fired a right uppercut that caught his opponent flush on the jaw and effectively ended the fight then and there. Frazier was stunned and in the corner with no place to retreat, a bad situation to be in with Tyson. Instinctively, he tried to bob and weave away from Tyson's fists, but was caught by a second right uppercut. Frazier was now semi-conscious although still standing. He was in that in-between world where, as Muhammad Ali told author Thomas Hauser,'you see black light, the black light of unconsciousness'.

Tyson shoved Frazier's gloves away to get another clear shot at
the helpless fighter, and for the third time in a matter of seconds,
Tyson's right fist crashed into Frazier's head. As he started to
topple, a left hook provided the unnecessary finishing punch.
Frazier went down in a sitting position, his legs folded under-
neath him, his upper body propped up by the two lower ring
ropes. Referee Joe Cortez jumped in and began his count. Seeing it was pointless to continue, he waved the fight over. Just
30 seconds had elapsed from the bell to the end of the fight,
Tyson's quickest and most impressive outing in 25 fights. Mike
moved across the ring to Joe Frazier and, concerned about
Marvis, asked him to check his son. 'I'm sorry it had to happen
like this,' he said to the former great heavyweight champion.

The Marvis Frazier fight marked the end of two promotional
relationships. Gone was Jeff Levine. Jacobs had felt that Levine
had crossed him, and vowed never to do business with him
again. The parting had nothing to do with Tyson. Levine had
obtained promotional rights to Hector Camacho, and intervened when a match was about to be made between Camacho
and Jacobs's and Cayton's other fighter, Edwin Rosario, for
Camacho's lightweight title, killing the match. 'Jim never for-
gave him,' says Cayton. 'Jim laid it out, he said Jeff had done
the wrong thing, that he was interested in a few bucks instead
of a relationship with us. . . . I never felt that way about Jeff.
I didn't think he should have done it, but I rationalized, I
understood, while I did not like it.' Jacobs's extreme displeasure was enough to shut Levine out of any future dealings
concerning Mike Tyson. Levine has, naturally, his own view
of what transpired between himself and Jacobs: 'I promoted
Mike's early fights. Jim assured me, "As long as we have no
problems working together, you'll be with Mike Tyson for his
entire career." With all the things written about Jim's integrity,
"his handshake was his bond, he never broke his word", Jim's
memory could conveniently lapse when it suited his purposes.
When he needed Don King to join the HBO tournament
[which Tyson entered and in which he won the heavyweight
title] he dropped me. I understood his reasons, because this
business is like this. But they were in the driver's seat with
Tyson. All they would have had to say was, "Jeff Levine is our
promoter, so he has to be in for a $25,000 fee for each fight."
Jim didn't.' Subsequently, Levine says, Jacobs asked him not
to get involved with Camacho in jeopardizing the fight he was
trying to make for his lightweight, Rosario. 'If I'd been in still

with Tyson, OK,' says Levine. 'But I had nothing else to fall back on. I'm a promoter. Camacho came to me to do business. I have a mortgage to pay, kids to feed. I'm not a millionaire like Jim. Later, Jim didn't want Tyson to fight Tony Tucker because I stood to profit from the promotion. But he finally relented because he wanted Tyson desperately to have all three title belts.' Jacobs also told Judd Maze that Carl 'The Truth' Williams would never get a title fight with Tyson as long as Jeff Levine was involved with him.

Just as surprising was their parting with Loraine Miller. She had done her job in the belief that she would share in the big time when Tyson made it. Instead, she found herself shut out. She says that she received payments to cover her losses on Tyson shows she promoted upstate, as per her agreement. But when she informed them in the summer of 1986 that the combined losses on the Hosea-RPI and Boyd-Stevensville shows were $22,000, she received a cheque for only $4,000. She called Jacobs for an explanation. 'He said, "You can just consider that a gift,"' Miller recalls of their conversations. 'I said, "But that wasn't our agreement." And he said, "Well, Loraine, you're a promoter. That's the chance a promoter takes." I trust people in general, I try to stay honest with people, and I just figured that's the way everything is in return. I didn't realize they had gotten TV money from [those shows]. They're cheap. . .I felt they did wrong to me. . .When Mike got a chance to fight for the title, Bob and I never as so much got a phone call to say, look, you have to buy your own seats, pay your own fare, but we'll save you two seats if you'd like to come down. Not even as much as a thought. . . .'

Jacobs may have grown disenchanted with the Millers after Loraine made a mistake with the seating arrangements for his wife and some friends at one of Mike's fights, inconsequential as that may seem. 'We got back back to the Holiday Inn in Latham,' Loraine Miller recalls, 'and Jimmy said, "Loraine, I'd like to speak to you." We went over to one of the corners and Jimmy said, "I want you to remember something. Who is the most important person in the world?". . . . I just looked at him, and he said, "I am, and I never want you to forget that. I am the most important person in the world, and my loved ones, and that means my wife. . . . Don't you ever mess up those [tickets]." Don't forget, Bob and I aren't a Don King. . .my twins were two years old, my little girl was three, plus my other three kids, so it was like a zoo. My phone is ringing, I had people coming in my front door to buy tickets. . . It's only Bob and I doing this, it's not a Don King promotion. . . . With them, it wasn't feelings. It was strictly business.'

Bill Cayton acknowledges that 'Jim was a little hard on her', but is nevertheless surprised to hear of Loraine Miller's dissatisfaction. 'I thought we treated them extremely well. . . . When they were short, Jim and I put the money out of our own pockets. . . . They were on a fee basis on most of the fights [*note*: when Jeff Levine joined Team Tyson as a promoter, he paid the Millers for several of the ABC-TV fights on a flat fee basis, rather than working on a profit basis from the live gates], where she got a very substantial fee and she was very happy.'

One of the things the Millers had been promised for their promotional work when Tyson was climbing the ladder was the chance to promote a Heavyweight Championship fight in the Albany area when he became champion. That promise was never fulfilled.

Three weeks after his dramatic disposal of Marvis Frazier, it was time for Tyson to fulfil the second part of his three-fight commitment to HBO, against Jose Ribalta, a Cuban-born, Miami-based, 6'6" fighter with a top-ten ranking and a solid 23–3 record. The fight was held at Trump Plaza in Atlantic City. Tyson floored Ribalta for the first of three knockdowns with his now familiar rapid-fire combination of a right to the ribs and a right uppercut to the jaw. Ribalta was up quickly at the count of two. Later, Tyson dropped him for the second time, but his opponent was game, and was still there to answer the bell for the tenth and final round. A left hook to the head dropped him for the third time in the fight. Again, he arose quickly, and said, 'Hell, yes,' when the referee asked him if he wanted to continue. Tyson quickly backed him up against the ropes and landed a right-left-right combination to the head, all the punches landing on target, unanswered by Ribalta. At that point the referee jumped in and stopped the fight over Ribalta's strong protests that he was all right and wanted to continue. Tyson now had his 24th KO in 26 fights. He was the No. 1 contender in the world, ready to challenge for the heavyweight title.

8

The Youngest Heavyweight Champion

A little man against a big one, and the chances are in favour of the little one. The cat has the best of it with a dog. Goliaths are always vanquished by Davids.

– THE MAN WHO LAUGHS
VICTOR HUGO

WHEN MIKE TYSON came on the scene, the heavyweight division had fallen on hard times due to the activities of promoter Don King, who controlled most of the top heavyweights, and the three sanctioning bodies that effectively ran the sport on the championship level, where the money was. Nearly a decade earlier, when, after upsetting Muhammad Ali, Leon Spinks refused to fight the WBC's top contender, signing instead for a more lucrative rematch with Ali, the title had been fragmented, leading to confusion and apathy among much of the public. That same year, 1978, Larry Holmes won recognition as the WBC Champion by defeating Ken Norton. Ali regained the title by a decision over Spinks on September 15, 1978, although by then it was only the WBA version of the crown that he regained. However, the following year, without fighting again, Ali announced he was retiring, leaving the WBA title vacant. Boxing's third sanctioning organization, the International Boxing Federation was not in existence at this time. Over the next half-dozen years, a motley assortment of relative unknowns played musical chairs with the WBA belt, winning it and then, inevitably, losing it, often in their first defence, months later. To say that any of them failed to capture the imagination of the public would be an understatement. Among the WBA Heavyweight Champions were such names as John Tate, Mike Weaver, Michael Dokes, Tony Tubbs, Greg Page, and Gerrie Coetzee.

Holmes, meanwhile, gained wide public acceptance as the real Heavyweight Champion. He defeated Ali when, a mere shell of his former magnificent self, Ali attempted a comeback, and then polished off a succession of top contenders including Leon Spinks, Earnie Shavers, Renaldo Snipes, Carl Williams, Mike Weaver, Trevor Berbick and Gerry Cooney. During this period, the IBF, with its base in America, was formed to counterbalance the strong influence of the WBA and WBC, which were controlled by Mexican and Latin-American interests and often acted in ways prejudicial to US interests in boxing.

When Holmes defied a WBC dictum on which opponent he should fight, instead deciding to follow his own course, the WBC withdrew recognition from him, leaving their title vacant. The IBF, which needed a recognized champion to give its organization instant credibility, jumped into the void, according him recognition as champion. The WBC then filled its vacant title with a succession of champions that, like the WBA, the public could not have cared less about, champions such as Pinklon Thomas, Tim Witherspoon and Trevor Berbick. By overwhelming public consensus, Larry Holmes, by virtue of his performances in the ring and the continuity of his reign, was the true champion. After ruling the division for more than seven years, Holmes was upset by Michael Spinks late in 1985, losing his title by decision to the former Olympic champion. Spinks became the first Light-Heavyweight Champion to successfully challenge for the heavyweight title.

Thus, as 1985 was drawing to a close, the heavyweight division was in some confusion. Michael Spinks was the IBF champion, the man who had defeated the true champion, Larry Holmes, in the ring, and so many felt he had a legitimate claim to the title. However, he held only one-third of it. The WBA Champion was Tim Witherspoon (who had previously held the WBC title briefly). The WBC Championship belonged to Pinklon Thomas at this time.

Seth Abraham, a 39-year-old one-time Brooklyn street kid who had risen to become head of sports programming at the HBO cable-TV network, conceived the idea of a tournament to crown one undisputed Heavyweight Champion. Abraham had become a friendly adversary of Don King's, buying scores of fights for HBO from the promoter. In 1985, when King was visiting Abraham's apartment to see his new baby daughter, Abraham made his pitch. They stayed up until 2:30 a.m. discussing it. As Abraham recalls, 'With King, I appealed to his sense of history, believe it or not. Don really wants to be, when he's all done, recognized as the greatest promoter of all time. Just saying to Don, "This can't be done, this can't be done – can it?" appealed to Don's sense of the impossible, and for him it was, in a sense, his Mount Everest. That's not to say he was philanthropic about it, but it was not money that drove King. He loved the challenge. . . .To Butch Lewis [promoter of Michael Spinks, the IBF Champion] it had nothing to do with history. Butch was new . . . to wealth after Michael beat Larry Holmes in September of '85. For him, [it was] strictly money. As we put the deal together, I was able to show them . . . fight by fight what they could amass, and it became dollars and cents.'

After a succession of marathon meetings, the deal was made. Then it was up to King to deal with the WBA and WBC, and Lewis to bring the IBF into the fold. HBO did not get involved directly in negotiations with the sanctioning organizations, but King and Lewis did their jobs. Now everything was in place. Home Box Office would put up $16-million dollars for the rights to televise the 18-month-long series of round-robin bouts that would lead to the unification of the heavyweight title. It was a major coup for HBO, since King and Lewis usually wouldn't even set foot in the same room together, let alone work cooperatively as co-promoters, and the WBA, WBC and IBF were constantly at each other's throats.

In 1920, in the United States, the National Boxing Association was formed. Like most attempts at organization within the sport of boxing, it was a less than cohesive, well-oiled cooperative effort, involving various state and local boxing commissions and officials. In 1962, the NBA, which sanctioned title fights and recognized dozens of its own NBA 'world' champions over the years, changed its name to the World Boxing Association. At that time, despite its new, global name, the WBA was firmly centred and rooted in the US, which was, in fact, the world centre of boxing. In 1962, the Heavyweight Champions were Floyd Patterson and Sonny Liston, the Light-Heavyweight Champions were Archie Moore and Harold Johnson, portions of the Middleweight Championship belonged to Gene Fullmer and Paul Pender, the Junior Middleweight Champion was Denny Moyer, the Welterweight Champion was Emile Griffith, the Lightweight Champions were Joe Brown and Carlos Ortiz, the Featherweight Champion was Davey Moore. All were Americans. Only a portion of the Middleweight Championship (won by Dick Tiger, a Nigerian who was under American management and was based in the United States for much of his career), the Bantamweight Championship, the Flyweight Championship, and a couple of junior championships in the lighter weight divisions were held by foreign fighters. The United States was the dominant power in boxing.

In 1963, the rival World Boxing Council was organized, in large part by George Parnassus, a leading boxing promoter in California. Parnassus, a Greek immigrant, promoted shows in the lighter weight divisions dominated by Mexican, Latin-American and other non-USA fighters. He became fed up with the pro-American bias he perceived in the actions of the NBA/WBA. The WBC, which was Mexican-run, virtually excluded the United States from any position of power. It was divided up into seven geographic regions. Each region had two votes. The United States was part of the North American region. But because that region, or 'federation', as the WBC termed it, also included Mexico and Canada, the United States – which generated an estimated 80 per cent of world wide boxing revenue – wound up with two-thirds of one vote!

In 1974, control of the WBA was also removed from the hands of American interests, as a cabal of Panamanians was voted in. This bloodless coup was accomplished through a clever manipulation of the organization's very own rules – one rule in particular, which said, basically, that the athletic commission or any other duly authorized body that existed for the purpose of regulating boxing in any country, *territorial or political subdivision, province or city* is eligible for membership in the WBA and is *entitled to one vote*. Another key portion of the rules stated that only delegates who were actually in attendance at the annual convention were eligible to vote. Utilizing this rule, dozens of newly-discovered delegates from Latin-American and the Caribbean turned up, with small countries like Panama, Venezuela and even the Virgin Islands having three, four, five or even six delegates each, every one of them entitled to a vote. A well-documented 1981 exposé by Pat Putnam in *Sports Illustrated*, stated bluntly: 'many of the WBA's delegates since 1974 have been shipped in [to annual conventions] prepaid, or have been outright phonies. . . At the 1979 convention in Miami Beach, as an example, there were three delegates from the Virgin Islands. . . .If the credentials committee had bothered to check, it would have discovered that there has never been an official boxing commission in the Virgin Islands.' With technicalities conveniently cast aside, the WBA has been controlled lock, stock and barrel ever since by a succession of Latin-American interests.

In the years since, these organizations have been run with banana-republic mentality in keeping with the geographic makeup of their top leaderships. World rankings and lucrative title fights go to those managers and fighters with the right friends or connections, whether deserved or not, plum 'junket' assignments have frequently gone to officials, it's been alleged numerous times, who score bouts the 'right' way for the 'house' fighter. The WBA and WBC have watered down the sport by adding, collectively, a dozen new and unnecessary in-between weight divisions such as strawweight, super-bantamweight, junior-lightweight, and super-middleweight. This demeans the sport but is all important to the sanctioning groups since more weight divisions mean more champions, more title fights, and thus more sanctioning fees to fill the WBA and WBC pockets – those fees being two and a half per cent of the gross purse of each fighter in a championship bout! Allegations of wrongdoing or strange coincidences are legion. Some examples:

According to promoter Bob Arum, he had to agree to pay Pepe Cordero, a boxing manager and henchman for the WBA leadership, $85,000 to obtain a crack at the WBA Lightweight Championship for Ray Mancini, plus, when Mancini won the title, Arum had to give Ernesto Espana, an over-the-hill, shot fighter, a title bout with Mancini and a quarter of a million dollar purse. Espana was managed by Cordero, and the manager collects one-third of his fighter's earnings. 'There's one bagman in the WBA,' Arum has stated, 'and that's Pepe Cordero. Anytime you want a fix in the WBA, you bribe Cordero and he takes care of it. When I want something done, I have to pay off Cordero. We shouldn't really call it a bribe, because you can't bribe a person who's not in a position of authority. Cordero has no office at all in the WBA. . . But anyone who wants anything done in the WBA has to pay Cordero.'

An American boxing judge who used to officiate at WBA bouts told *Sports Illustrated*'s Pat Putnam: 'I was officiating a fight in Puerto Rico and Dr Elias Cordova [then the most powerful figure in the WBA] came over to me just before round one, touched my arm and said, "Remember who you are working for. We want to keep the championship here." The fight was between a Latin American and a US fighter. Later, at another fight that year, Dr Cordova told me that the reason I wasn't used much was because I wasn't a house referee. I had just voted against one of their fighters. The WBA has never called me to work again.'

In 1979, a mediocre club fighter, 'Irish' Mike Baker, was suddenly ranked No. 7 in the world by the WBC in the junior middleweight division and given a title fight with World Champion Maurice Hope of Great Britain. Baker didn't belong in the same ring as Hope. He was beaten badly and stopped in the seventh round. Baker's manager was the powerful Washington, DC attorney Edwards Bennett Williams. Coincidentally, Williams represented in his law practice both Don King and the WBC's President, Jose Sulaiman.

Bob Busse, who has served as President of the North American Boxing Federation and chairman of the WBC Ratings Committee, has said, 'One of the WBC's problems is that it refuses to recognize that the United States represents the heart of professional boxing. Jose [Sulaiman] will say time and time again that the United States is only one of 104 countries, but that's ridiculous. You can't compare boxing in the United States with boxing in Barbados, and, too often, American fighters are treated unfairly by the WBC as the price of appeasing other countries.' Busse said that while he was chairman of the WBC Ratings Committee, 90 per cent of the ratings were established by Sulaiman, without any consultation with Busse or the Committee. 'How some of the people get into our ratings I couldn't tell you,' Busse told *Sports Illustrated*. 'Promoters call me and ask about fighters they say we have ranked, and I didn't even know they were ranked.'

The WBA rules states that a champion must defend his title once every six months against the leading available contender. Yet, from 1977 to 1979, Ayub Kalule was the top contender for the Junior Middleweight Championship, and the WBA did everything in its power to keep Kalule from getting a title opportunity, in direct violation of its own rules. Their apparent purpose was to protect a mediocre Latin-American fighter, Eddie Gazo, from having to risk his title against Kalule, an African fighter living in and fighting out of Denmark. Finally, only after pressure on the WBA mounted to the point where Kalule could no longer be avoided, and long after Gazo had lost his title to a Japanese fighter, Masashi Kudo, did Kalule get his long-overdue title shot. He easily defeated Kudo to win the World Championship.

As recounted by Pat Putnam in his *Sports Illustrated* exposé, in 1977, Dr Elias Cordova, the WBA President, told a Japanese promoter of a world title fight that the WBA would not sanction the fight unless the organization was provided with seven round-trip airline tickets to Tokyo, along with first-class hotel and dining accommodation. Included in the WBA party that arrived in Tokyo, all expenses paid, were two wives, including Cordova's, and Pepe Cordero, who held no official position with the WBA. The day after the party arrived, the Japanese promoter took them all to a shop in Tokyo where they picked out pearls, silks, and other gifts, all of which were paid for in cash by the Japanese 'host'.

In Columbia, a fight manager wanted very much to have his boxer rated, but did not have the cash necessary. A WBA official told him, not very subtly, that his daughter liked emerald earrings. In Colombia, emeralds are relatively inexpensive. The official's daughter got a set of beautiful earrings. The fighter got rated.

When Mandry Galindez replaced Cordova as President of the WBA, he travelled to Korea, where he was surprised to find managers and promoters trying to give him money. He didn't know what they were doing, until one of them asked him, 'Are you the man we now pay for the ratings?'

In the WBC Welterweight Championship fight in Montreal in 1980 between Roberto Duran and Sugar Ray Leonard, one official assigned scored the fight 3 rounds Duran, 2 rounds Leonard, 10 rounds even: Despite this unprecedented monument to indecision in a major title match, the official continued to be given world title matches to judge, along with the travel, hotel and meal allowances, and the $1,200 fee that goes along with such assignments.

In 1988, when Sugar Ray Leonard decided once again to come out of retirement and challenge Donny Lalonde for the WBC Light-Heavyweight Championship, the WBC created a new 168-pound Super-Middleweight division and declared that this new title, as well as Lalonde's 175-pound Light-Heavyweight title, would be on the line in the fight. This virtually handed to Leonard the opportunity to become the first boxer to win titles in five different weight divisions, even though it violated WBC rules which stated that a fighter could only hold one title at a time.

These examples, plus numerous others documented by Pat Putnam, Thomas Hauser, and other journalists over the years, point to an obvious pattern of rules violations, incompetence and, in some cases, outright corruption. Putnam concluded in

1981 that 'the WBC and WBA are failures', yet they continue to flourish right up to the present day, with the WBC the dominant organization.

Don King aligned himself closely with the WBC and its President, Jose Sulaiman, while also maintaining ties with the WBA. British promoter Mickey Duff said, 'My complaint is that Jose Sulaiman is not happy his friend Don King is the biggest promoter in boxing. Sulaiman will only be happy when Don King is the only promoter in boxing.' *Ring* magazine termed Sulaiman King's 'personal lap dog'. But because King has controlled many of the fighters over the years who were WBC champions or challengers, and therefore has emerged as the promoter of many lucrative WBC title bouts, the organization relies heavily on him for its economic survival. It is a perfect symbiotic relationship.

As there seemed no chance of things changing, Bob Lee, at that time the Boxing Commissioner in the state of New Jersey, and President of the United States Boxing Association, began in 1983 to set up a third global sanctioning organization: the International Boxing Federation. Seeing this as a potential threat to Latin-American and third-world dominance in controlling boxing, the WBC and WBA, traditional rivals, have, in recent years, begun a rapprochement in the hope that some degree of unity will limit the power and influence of the IBF, with its strong American bias.

All three independent organizations continue to exist because of the demand for 'world championship' matches by the American television networks. For years, boxing reformers have proposed the simplest of solutions for doing away with the undue influence of these organizations, a solution that would relegate the WBC and WBA to the backwaters of boxing beyond the US borders, and eventually to virtual extinction. The proposal calls for the establishment of a Federal Boxing Commissioner with the power to appoint qualified officials; to control boxing in all fifty states and US territories, such as Puerto Rico, under one uniform set of rules; to institute strict licensing and medical procedures in order to ensure the calibre and safety of fighters, as well as the competence of trainers, managers and promoters; and to sanction US-recognized world championship bouts. With 80 per cent of boxing revenues originating in the United States, such a move would quickly bring government-regulated control of the sport back into American hands. Whatever its reasons, congress has failed to act on such a proposal, however, and so boxing continues on its merry, laissez-faire way, with the IBF, the WBC, the WBA, Don King and Bob Arum at the controls. It was against this backdrop that Home Box Office brought all parties together (except for Arum, who did not figure in the heavyweight picture) to create the Heavyweight Championship Unification Tournament.

The Heavyweight Unification Tournament began in the early spring of 1986. Mike Tyson was not included at that time, for several reasons. Firstly, Don King was not interested in having him in it: King controlled the WBC champion, Pinklon Thomas; he controlled the WBA Champion, Tim Witherspoon; he did not exercise any control over Tyson. Jacobs and Cayton were running an independent course with Tyson, and this made King uncomfortable. If he can help it, King only promotes fighters he can control. Secondly, Tyson had been fighting for only a year, and he wasn't quite ready to face the mental pressure of fighting for the title, his toughest opponent to date having been Jesse Ferguson. Thirdly, Jacobs and Cayton knew they had the hottest property in the heavyweight division, and if they continued to bring him along slowly and successfully, they could step in and challenge for the title when their fighter was ready and it suited their schedule.

On March 22, 1986, in the first bout of the HBO tournament, Trevor Berbick upset Pinklon Thomas to win the WBC Heavyweight Championship. Both fighters were controlled by Don King. Berbick had been the Canadian Heavyweight Champion. In 1980 he'd knocked out a washed-up John Tate. In 1981, he won a decision over a washed-up Muhammad Ali in what was to be Ali's last fight. Subsequently, he'd gone 15 rounds with Larry Holmes in a title bid, losing the decision. Now he was the new WBC World Champion.

A month later, on April 19, Michael Spinks defended the IBF version of the title on a narrow, controversial decision over Larry Holmes, the man he had taken it from the previous September. Next on the list was the WBA title. On July 19, in London, a less than well-conditioned Tim Witherspoon, trailing on points, came back to knock out British challenger, Frank Bruno, late in the fight to retain his crown. On September 6, Michael Spinks defended his IBF title in a walk-over, knocking out Scandinavian challenger, Steffen Tangstad, in four rounds. The fight drew little interest. Most people had never heard

of Tangstad, and those who had knew he didn't belong in
the same ring with Spinks. What did attract interest was the
presence of Mike Tyson on the same card. HBO, knowing that
Spinks-Tangstad alone could not sustain their national telecast,
added Tyson to the card. Before his name was added, a little
over $200,000 in tickets had been sold at the Las Vegas Hilton.
Once Tyson was on the show, the live gate came to a near sell-
out of $1.1-million.

Tyson's opponent was Alfonzo Ratliff, the former WBC
Cruiserweight Champion. Ratliff tried to run, but, as they
say, he couldn't hide. In the second round, a Tyson left hook
dropped him. He was up at the count of nine, but Mike pinned
him on the ropes, and a right hand sent him careening, only the
ropes holding him up. A combination with a right-hand *coup de
grâce* ended the fight. A few weeks earlier, Jim Jacobs had said
there was no pressing need to put Tyson into the Heavyweight
Tournament. 'Mike can make a lot of money while a unified
champion is determined,' he reasoned. 'If Mike continues as he
has, he will be the number one contender in all three organizations by then. There are a lot of big fights for Mike without
going after the title – Holmes, Tyrell Biggs, Gerry Cooney' –
although Jacobs was also quick to point out that Mike would
have no trouble fighting the reigning champions if he were to
enter the tournament – 'After all, we are not talking about
Jack Dempsey and Joe Louis.' Jacobs invited critics to look at
films from his vast library to see for themselves if Tyson didn't
surpass them all at the same stage of development. However,
they realized that keeping Mike out of the Tournament was
not the right way to go. As Seth Abraham said, 'Jimmy and
Bill. . .were very, very practical. . .and practically speaking, it
would have taken Mike Tyson years to get all three belts.'

HBO wanted Tyson in the Tournament because, as Abraham
frankly acknowledges, 'Tyson out of the series really jeopardized the credibility of the series because Jimmy and Bill had
done such a remarkable job in marketing him, he had already
been on HBO twice, and every boxing writer was writing that
this man indeed may be the real champion, and if you want
credibility, so that people believe this is legitimate, that it's
not a "Don King series", let's go out and get this man in. It
was something we turned our attention to in earnest in June
[1986].'

Of course, nothing is simple, and protracted negotiations
were to take place throughout the summer. Abraham spent

much of his time at Wimbledon in July in transatlantic telephone conversations with Jacobs, Cayton, King and Lewis, including one with Cayton and Jacobs that lasted for five hours. On his return from Wimbledon (which HBO televises in the US) Abraham went on vacation to Fire Island, from where the long-distance negotiations continued. HBO offered to sweeten the pot, adding additional millions to the $16-million they had already invested in order to lure Tyson into the Tournament.

There was yet another marathon meeting at the Home Box Office headquarters in Manhattan. This one lasted fourteen hours, with Don King, Butch Lewis, Jacobs and Cayton and their respective attorneys present. According to Abraham, King was anxious to have Tyson in the HBO series, seeing it as a way to legitimize his involvement as Tyson's promoter in the future. Lewis was opposed to Tyson's inclusion, which he saw as a block to his man, Spinks, eventually unifying the title. Finally, an agreement was reached. A meeting was set for August 20, 1986, at Cayton and Jacobs's office at which all parties involved were to sign a memorandum of agreement. At the very last moment, Butch Lewis balked, and only a stern talking to by Abraham, who pulled him aside, caused him to relent. But Abraham is convinced that the seeds that eventually led to Lewis pulling Spinks out of the Tournament were sown that day, when Mike Tyson came into it.

D'Amato had predicted that Mike would be ready to fight for the Heavyweight Championship by the end of 1986. Jacobs had often said, when asked when Tyson would be ready to fight for the title, 'The aim is not for Mike to fight for the title. The aim is for Mike to win the title.' Now they believed he was ready. His fighting skills were not fully polished yet, but he was mentally tough, physically the most powerful of the heavyweights, and what he lacked in experience he made up with what might be termed his intimidation factor. Tyson's image, backed by his impressive performances in the ring, had been carefully cultivated to the point where there was an aura of invincibility around him that had his opponents psyched-out before they even set foot in the ring against him. Jacobs used to describe it as the 'Joe Louis syndrome', since Louis had the same effect on many of his opponents; however, by the time Tyson had moved to the top of the heavyweight division, Jacobs had renamed it 'Tysonitis'. And Tysonitis was racing like an epidemic through the heavyweight ranks.

Mike Tyson was now in the Heavyweight Elimination Tournament. On November 22, 1986 he would step into the ring at the Las Vegas Hilton to challenge Trevor Berbick for the WBC Heavyweight Championship. Tyson would be 20 years and 5 months of age. It would be only the 21st month of his professional career. He had boxed only 75 rounds in his 27 fights, and 25 of those rounds were only partial rounds because knockouts brought them to an end before their three-minute duration. He had two and a half months to prepare, following his KO of Ratliff. Some of that time would be spent in isolation, working in the quiet confines of Catskill with Kevin Rooney. Then, about a month before the fight, they would move more into the spotlight, shifting their base of operations to Las Vegas where he could become acclimatized to the desert conditions and where – although it did not please Tyson – the media would have easier access to both him and Berbick.

Away from that spotlight, yet with Tyson every day in the weeks leading up to the fight, was a member of his entourage somewhat unique to the training camp of a fighter. His name is John Halpin. He remained quietly in the background, out of reach of the curious and inquiring press, which was always looking for a story or an 'angle'. John Halpin had been with Mike Tyson since his very first fight as a professional, brought in by Cus D'Amato, who had been using Halpin's expertise for his fighters for nearly 20 years. John Halpin was a hypnotherapist. From his office on West 72nd Street in Manhattan, just off Central Park West, Halpin spent most of his time working with patients to help them lose weight or quit smoking through hypnotic suggestion. D'Amato believed in the value of hypnosis to help his fighters overcome doubts, fears and lack of confidence. He would often bring boys down from Catskill, three or four at a time, to have Halpin work with them in his office. Along with D'Amato's fighters, D'Amato disciples such as Joey Fariello and Teddy Atlas have brought their boxers to Halpin as well, and he has worked with Canada's Hilton brothers, heavyweight Art Tucker, Canadian champion Donny Poole, Light-Heavyweight Champion Donny Lalonde and Welterweight Champion Mark Breland.

Hypnosis is as old as recorded time, dating back to the 'sleep temples' of ancient Egypt, where women went to give birth after being placed in hypnotic trances. But hypnosis has suffered from a lack of understanding by those unfamiliar with its sound therapeutic foundation, in large part due to the false image presented in the Boris Karloff-genre of Hollywood horror and melodrama films in the 1930s and 40s. There is really nothing mysterious, supernatural or occult about hypnotism. It is simply a means of placing a subject in an altered state, resembling sleep but not really sleep. Under hypnosis, an individual's awareness can be dealt with on a subconscious level, usually more effectively than when the subject is conscious, because in a hypnotic state the subject is focused and free from distraction.

John Halpin has been a successful practitioner of hypnotherapy for years. A distinguished looking man of middle age with a penchant for conservative grey suits, white shirts and tailored topcoats, with a clear and resonant speaking voice, he is quick to point out that 'The person under hypnosis is not the pawn of the hypnotist. The person under hypnosis has his mind moved to a different, altered state, other than the active, conscious state. In that state, where he is so suggestible, he is not without his protections of self. He has his morals, his ethics, his principles, his understandings of legality.' Meaning, basically, a person under hypnosis cannot be made to do anything he or she would not ordinarily do while fully conscious.

Halpin first worked with Tyson when D'Amato brought him down from Catskill to the hypnotist's Manhattan office, along with the Hilton brothers, when Mike was sixteen years old, but his regular work with Mike began when Tyson turned pro in 1985. Except for a few of the easy fights Mike had to keep him busy on the way up, Halpin has worked with him for every important fight along the way. 'Cus believed in the hypnotist's ability to reinforce the lessons of the trainer. . .Usually a man is brought to me who does have great basic mechanics but has fears that are overwhelming and are handicapping him. Unless a man has the mechanics, I can't help him. I can help him overcome his psychological obstacles so that he can develop the mechanics much more quickly,' says Halpin.

D'Amato would often be present at the sessions, and when Halpin had Tyson under hypnosis, he would get D'Amato to talk directly to the fighter, to reassure him that whatever doubts he had were unfounded. 'You have a wonderful right hand,' he would say. 'You haven't believed in it, but now you're going to.'

Now, as the fight approached, Halpin was constantly working with Tyson, as often as twice a day. His procedure was always the same. He would get Mike in a relaxed, comfortable position, lying on a bed or perhaps on the floor. He would then

place him under hypnosis and proceed to talk to him about
his fears, about how his doubts and concerns were unfounded,
emphasizing how good, how talented he was, perhaps talking
him through how he was going to perform in the fight. After his
session, he would generally leave Mike in a deep sleep, telling
him how refreshed he was going to feel when he awoke.

'Every fighter has fear. That's part of the reason why I see
a fighter a lot in the weeks before a fight. I want to work with
him two times a day for four or five days while he's in training.
Then I want to work with him four or five days right before the
fight. The reason for all of my activity on that level is because
of the incredible emotional level a fighter experiences even two
weeks before the fight, then a week before the fight, then the
days leading up to the fight, whether he knows it or not. He
can be walking around in a daze. It may not hit him as a big,
fearful emotion, but rather as an underlying uneasiness, and
that's why he needs me. It is ever-building toward the climax.
It isn't on an even keel.' That is why, Halpin says, it requires
more intense work as the fight draws closer. He has worked
with inducing a hypnotic trance in Tyson as close as two hours
before a fight, but he is quick to point out that Mike never fights
while under hypnosis. At fight time, Halpin will be in his seat
at ringside, near Cayton and Jacobs. Like the managers, once
it is fight time, he can do nothing. Their jobs are done,and all
they can do is watch. The only difference is that Jacobs and
Cayton are known, are recognized, are greeted, interviewed,
photographed. John Halpin remains anonymous. The public
watches the invincible Mike Tyson, unaware that a hypnotist
has been constantly at his side helping him to prepare for his
fights. It's one of the things Jacobs and Cayton did not make
public, feeling, perhaps, that it had no part in the Tyson myth.

As November 22 drew near, opinion was divided. Many were
giving Berbick a good chance to beat Tyson, reasoning that he
was durable; he had gone 15 tough rounds with Larry Holmes;
he had the edge in experience and was used to the pressure;
he'd been in big fights besides Holmes – his KO of Tate, his win
over Ali, his title victory against Pinklon Thomas, all proved he
could stand up to the pressure of a big fight, he had the stamina
and mental toughness to go the distance. Tyson had fought
nobodies or over-the-hill fighters. The two best fighters he'd
fought, Green and Tillis, had extended him the full distance,
had negated the power with which he had dominated lesser

fighters. Berbick had an awkward style that could keep Tyson off balance, frustrate him, and perhaps take away his punching power. This was going to be Tyson's toughest test, with the new and added pressure of a championship fight weighing heavily on his mind.

The flighty Berbick made one strategic move not to his advantage. When he had defeated Pinklon Thomas and won the title eight months earlier, he had had the great trainer Eddie Futch, considered a master, working with him and making him toe the line. Berbick needed this, since he had proved to be an in-and-out fighter, depending on where his mind was. He had shown well in losing to Holmes, he had beaten Tate, Ali, Greg Page and Thomas in an upset for the title, but he had lost decisions to Renaldo Snipes, a good and unorthodox heavyweight, and to S.T. Gordon, a cruiserweight, and been knocked out by hard-punching but mediocre Bernardo Mercado. Now, in the most important fight of his life, his biggest payday (he was getting $2.1-million to fight Tyson, and would be a star with more million-dollar purses on the horizon if he could beat him), he stubbornly refused to come to a financial agreement with Futch, and so did not have the venerable trainer with him as he prepared for Tyson. Although he brought in another top trainer, Angelo Dundee, he did so only two and a half weeks before the fight, and so Dundee's contribution was severely limited by time.

Futch, now an impartial outside observer, told *Sports Illustrated*: 'Tyson has wonderful attacking abilities. His hands are tremendously fast for a man with that kind of upper body and he can really punch with either hand. God, he can punch. His right uppercut especially will take your head off. But so far he has had a big psychological edge. He has intimidated his opponents, made them freeze and wait to be slaughtered. I think you have to go to him, back him up, never let him take you into the corners or on to the ropes, keep him in the middle of the ring where you can use mobility against him. I believe Berbick has the nerve and the equipment to make a good attempt at all that, to have a real chance of pulling it off. But Trevor is never sure to be the same fighter twice in a row. You never know how he will be.'

Dundee talked up his man, saying Tyson was only a kid about to fight the most important fight of his life against the best heavyweight he'd met in his career. 'Berbick has the style to do a number on him. . .Tyson won't find Berbick running, like all those guys he's been knocking over.' Dundee predicted Berbick would stop Tyson late in the fight. Jacobs simply said he had no worries: 'Mike Tyson is the best heavyweight in the world, and he is about to prove it.' Tyson volunteered that while he did not think D'Amato would be there in the ring with him, he would go into the fight taking with him everything he had been taught by his late mentor.

Tyson's routine in Las Vegas was laid back. He lived in a private house with his small entourage, which included trainer Kevin Rooney and assistant manager Steve Lott. The house belonged to a friend of Jim Jacobs. In it, Mike could keep himself isolated from the press and the public, both of which he found irksome. His days began with roadwork early in the morning. In the afternoon, he trained in closed sessions at Johnny Tocco's Gym. The rest of the time, apart from sessions with his hypnotherapist, he spent relaxing, killing time by watching television and video cassettes, preferably cartoons and kung fu movies. Steve Lott had the most difficult job in camp. It was up to him to see that everything functioned smoothly, that Mike had all his creature comforts taken care of, that he had all the training equipment he needed, that he got to his training sessions and anywhere else he needed to be, that press interviews were duly scheduled, that good sparring partners were hired, that plane reservations, accommodation and meals were properly arranged, and that whatever Mike needed or wanted in order to keep him happy and focus his mind on preparing for the fight, free of worries, was done. His was the least noticed, yet the most taxing job in camp. Jacobs and Cayton arrived a week before fight time, but Lott was there right through from beginning to end, coping in a professional manner with the vagaries of Tyson's childish and often nasty mood swings.

Berbick, a native of Jamaica, spent part of his time off in Las Vegas at the Moments of Miracles Church. An ordained minister who described himself as a 'soldier of the cross', Berbick would preach the gospel there in his lilting island accent. Another part of his time off from Johnny Tocco's Gym, where he, too, was training, was spent in responding to legal depositions just when he did not need such a distraction. Five days before the fight he was in court, being sued by a Texas promoter named Tom Prendergast who claimed that Berbick (and heavyweight Randy 'Tex' Cobb) had pulled out of a fight show he was promoting four years earlier. Possibly due to the emotional overload of the forthcoming fight and his legal entanglements, Berbick experienced some respiratory problems the day after his court appearance, and ran around town all day going to doctors trying to get medicine that would alleviate his condition. His quest was made more difficult because of the necessity of obtaining a medicine that the Nevada boxing commission would allow him to have in his system when he fought. Berbick's mental state must have been further adversely affected two days before the fight when he learned that the district court judge had attached his purse to the tune of nearly half a million dollars until the lawsuit with Prendergast was resolved at some future date.

On fight night, Tyson was the 3-to-1 favourite on the betting boards. While still pretty strong odds, they were down considerably from their original high of 6-to-1 for the challenger. Tyson would be earning his largest purse to date, a million and a half dollars. The celebrities were out in force at ringside. From Hollywood there was Kirk Douglas, Eddie Murphy, Tony Danza, Rob Lowe, Sylvester Stallone. The world of boxing was represented by Hector Camacho, Tommy Hearns, Archie Moore, and heavyweight champions Michael Spinks, Larry Holmes and Muhammad Ali. All were there, fenced off in the $1,000-a-seat VIP section, to witness, as one of the TV commentators put it, 'a coronation'. Berbick wore the crown, but at 10:20 p.m. Eastern time, it was the crown prince, Mike Tyson, who made his way to the ring first, with Kevin Rooney leading the way. Tyson wore a terrycloth towel over his chest and shoulders. A hole had been cut in the middle of it so he could slip it over his head like a poncho, a concession to the chilly November night air of the desert, since he customarily entered robeless, but this was the first time he was fighting outdoors so late in the year. Steve Lott and cut-man Matt Baranski followed Mike up the ring steps. Already in the ring were a host of officials, and the adversarial Dynamic Duo of Don King and Butch Lewis. The only reason Lewis was involved in the Heavyweight Elimination Tournament was because he controlled Michael Spinks, and Spinks's participation was necessary to make it a true attempt at unifying the title. To King, Lewis was simply a thorn in his side. Tyson moved around, getting the feel of the ring.

Moments later, Dundee brought the champion into the ring. The crowd was amazingly silent and indifferent. There was no cheering for Berbick, who was dressed all in black, including a

black satin robe with a hood that covered his head. Also with
Berbick was his nominal manager, Carl King, the promoter's
son. Both fighters wore black trunks, different only in that
Berbick's carried the symbol of his religion, a small red cross.
Traditionally, the champion has the choice of trunks. Knowing
Tyson always wears black, Dundee had Berbick wear black.
Under the rules Tyson was obliged to select a different colour.
Instead, he opted for his customary black. It cost him a $5,000
fine from the Nevada Athletic Commission, but that mattered
little to Jacobs and Cayton. Mike had worn black prior to this
fight, and he would wear black this night as well, fine or no
fine. Berbick, variously stated to be 32, 33 or 34 years old,
had weighed in at 218 pounds. At 6'2½" he was half a head
taller than Tyson, who claimed to be 5'11½" but looked closer
to 5'10". After giving both men their instructions in the centre of
the ring, Mills Lane, a veteran Nevada referee who had handled
many world title fights, uttered his traditional 'Let's get it on' to
both men. They returned to their corners. Dundee reminded
Berbick not to get in a slugging match with Tyson. 'Box him,
move side to side,' were his final words, while across the ring,
in what had become an odd tradition in the Tyson corner, Mike
and Rooney kissed on the lips. Kevin then hugged him, and the
bell rang.

Tyson moved out fast, bobbing. Both men were tight, and a
right by Berbick drove a slightly off-balance Tyson back. Tyson
answered with a left hook that landed. Berbick was trying to
keep the young bull off him, but Tyson kept coming forward.
Berbick threw a quick flurry of half a dozen punches, digging
an uppercut to Tyson's body. A right and left by Tyson landed
solidly to Berbick's head and then, 1:15 into the round, Tyson
was on target with a clubbing right to Berbick's skull. The
fighters clinched, Berbick holding on to clear his head. When
they broke, Tyson shot a left hook to Berbick's jaw. They then
fought on the inside, but with just under 30 seconds left in the
first round, a quick right-left-right-left combination by Tyson
sent Berbick stumbling backwards. He was groggy and hurt.
A final left hand shortly before the bell sent Berbick back to
his corner stunned, although, in a show of bravado, he stuck
his chin out in the direction of Tyson's corner as he made his
way back to his stool.

Dundee was more agitated than he usually had reason to
be after just one round, screaming at his cornermen for the
sponge, then spending what remained of the one minute rest

trying to revive and advise his champion, who was in serious trouble. In Tyson's corner, Rooney was calm. 'You're head hunting,' he told Mike. 'Use the jab, stay calm. Body shots first, then the head.' The bell sounded for round two, Berbick's last as a world champion.

Just seconds after the bell, a big right to Berbick's head rocked him back on his heels, and he stumbled off balance. Two more rights followed, and Berbick was down, just 8 seconds into the round. He jumped to his feet immediately, but his legs were unsteady. A left-right combination by Tyson forced him to hold, and he spent most of the next minute clinching and holding, trying to regroup his senses and figure out a battle plan to counteract this relentless young warrior, the likes of which he had never encountered before. Halfway through the round, Tyson buried a right hand to the champion's ribs, then shot a right to his jaw and a clubbing, hurting right hand to his head, forcing Berbick once again to grab the smaller man he had boldly said would not beat him. Lying on Berbick's chest, Tyson blasted his opponent's body with a right, then bounced a short left hook to the top of his head. The force of that punch rearranged Berbick's equilibrium in a way that most viewers had never before seen. The champion toppled on to his back like a tree. At the count of three, he tried to get up, but stumbled on ankles that bent like rubber tubes, and tumbled back down, for a second time, into the lower strand of ropes. Again he tried to rise, and did make it to his feet momentarily, but the liquids in his inner ear must have been swirling like a whirlpool, and his legs would not – could not – follow the commands his brain was issuing. He buckled at the knees and stumbled forward, across the ring, falling and rolling over on his back. It was the third time he had hit the canvas in less than ten seconds, all from the pulverizing force of just one punch. Those who witnessed it will never forget the sight of Berbick stumbling helplessly out of control around the ring. By sheer force of will, he managed to rise at the count of nine, but Mills Lane was there to referee a fight, not be party to a murder, and so he wisely draped his arms around Berbick's neck to help support and steady the big man from Jamaica, and waved the evening's proceedings over. At 2:35 seconds into the second round, Mike Tyson had become the new – and youngest – Heavyweight Champion of the World. Mike raised a glove fist and pointed out into the crowd, then shrugged his shoulders as if to say, 'No fuss, no bother. I did what I came here to do.

End of story.' Tyson, as he had seen Jack Dempsey and others do in the hours of films he had watched over the years, went to help Berbick back to his corner, a courtesy to the fallen ex-champion. Jimmy Jacobs entered the ring, and Mike kissed him. Also there, inexplicably, was Jose Torres, who blatantly disregarded the impartiality he was duty-bound to exercise as Chairman of the New York State Athletic Commission, and openly rooted for Tyson at all his fights. Now, he was here in Las Vegas to see 'his fighter' crowned champion, and he was in the ring as a member of Tyson's entourage. Tyson posed for the ringside photographers while Berbick sat on his stool, being checked by the ringside physician. The new champion was flanked by Rooney and Lott and Jacobs, and, of course, a beaming Don King. The goal had been achieved, but at what price. For now Don King was in the picture. The octopus of the boxing world had been, of necessity, permitted to wind his tentacles gently around Mike Tyson, and when events less than a year and a half later afforded him the opportunity he was waiting for, King would tighten those tentacles around the most valuable athlete in the world until his grip could not be loosened.

His victory achieved, Tyson opened the floodgates of emotion as he talked with reporters. 'This is the moment I waited for all my life since I started boxing. . .Berbick was very strong . . . I never expected him to be as strong as me. . .every punch I threw with bad intentions to a vital area. . .I aimed for his ear. . .I wanted to bust his eardrum. . .Every punch had bad intentions. . .My record will last for immortality, it'll never be broken. . .I want to live forever. . .I refused to lose. . .I would have had to be carried out dead to lose. . .I was coming to destroy and win the Heavyweight Championship of the World, which I done. . .I'd like to dedicate my fight to my great guardian, Cus D'Amato. I'm sure he's up there and he's looking down and he's talking to all the great fighters and he's saying his boy did it. . .I thought he was a crazy white dude. . .he was a genius. . .everything he said would happen happened.'

The comments and observations from the opposing side were more restrained. Berbick acknowledged he'd made a 'silly mistake' by trying to punch with Tyson. 'I tried to prove my manhood,' he said. However, Angelo Dundee expressed awe: 'He throws combinations I never saw before. I was stunned. Nothing is supposed to bother me. I've worked with Ali and Sugar Ray Leonard, but I'm seeing [from Tyson] a three-punch combination second to none. When have you seen a guy throw a right hand to the kidney, come up the middle with an uppercut, then throw a left hook?'

What amazed many who were seeing Tyson for the first time was his remarkable defensive ability. The impression given by reports of his exploits in the ring was that he was a slugger and nothing else. In reality, he had tremendous defensive skills every bit as good as his power of attack. It was extremely difficult to hit Mike Tyson with a clean shot. 'From 13 to 18,' Jim Jacobs said, 'Mike was taught by Cus D'Amato that the object was not to get hit. He learned nothing but how to avoid getting hit.' Jacobs explained that because of his height and reach disadvantages, Mike had to expose himself to potential danger by getting closer to his opponents in order to land his shots. Therefore, 'when he fights, he gets down in a crouch. People have to punch down, which makes their punches ineffective.'

Mike Tyson was the Heavyweight Champion of the World (at least according to the WBC), and a fully-fledged millionaire. No matinee idol when it came to looks, uneducated and unread, for the most part unpolished and uncomfortable in the presence of others, Tyson nevertheless, owing to his new-found fame and fortune, suddenly had access to the attractive and desirable women with whom he had always been obsessed, but who, until now, had not been available to him. The world was at his feet. The task ahead of him in the ring was to unify the heavyweight championship in the coming year of 1987 and become the first undisputed Heavyweight Champion in nearly a decade.

9

Unification . . . and Robin Givens

Boxing is much more a battle of wills than of skills. Given fighters with equal skills, the one with the stronger will inevitably will win.

– CUS D'AMATO

THREE WEEKS AFTER Tyson took the WBC crown, the stage was set for the next fight in the Unification Tournament. The scene shifted to Madison Square Garden, where, on December 5, 1986, Tim Witherspoon was scheduled to defend his WBA title against Tony Tubbs. But Tubbs withdrew from the bout, claiming an injured shoulder, and King, against the will of Witherspoon, whom he controlled, forced the WBA Champion to accept James 'Bonecrusher' Smith as a substitute opponent. (More on the questionable circumstances surrounding this fight later.) Witherspoon had previously defeated Smith and did not want to fight him again at such short notice because he had prepared physically and psychologically to do battle with Tubbs. But Witherspoon had nowhere to turn. Usually a fighter when disputing with a promoter has the backing of his manager. In this case, Witherspoon's promoter was Don King, and his manager was Carl King, Don King's son. With no one, including the New York State Athletic Commission, willing to take his side, Witherspoon had no choice but to capitulate. The fight was postponed one week, and re-set for the night of December 12 at the Garden.

'Bonecrusher' Smith got his chance of a lifetime for two reasons. Firstly, he was actually in training to fight Mitch Green for a $35,000 purse, so he had the advantage of being ready and in shape, and did possess the requisite top-ten ranking, which qualified him for a title fight. But most importantly, Smith got the fight because he and his manager, Alan Kornberg, were willing to do 'business' with Don King. In other words, to no one's surprise, it was announced shortly before Smith was signed to meet Witherspoon that Smith had signed over 50 per cent of his contract to the promoter's son. Presto! Smith had the title shot and a $230,000 purse. On the night of the fight, there was an audience of barely 5,000, leaving 17,000 empty

seats. After all, it was winter; you could stay at home and
see the fight for free if you subscribed to the HBO cable-TV
service; and, in any case, who cared about Tim Witherspoon
vs. Bonecrusher Smith? Whether there were 5,000 or 500 or
50,000 people present didn't matter one jot to Smith. He was
earning a lot more money than he would have received fighting
Mitch Green in Fayetteville, North Carolina, and he had the
chance to win the world title. He made the most of it. He
went out at the opening bell and took his best shots, and
they landed. Witherspoon, his mind distracted by his disputes
with the Kings, was a listless and uninterested participant.
Unfortunately for him, his title was on the line. Smith blasted
Witherspoon with right-hand bombs to the head. Witherspoon
was knocked down four times in less than three minutes, and,
having struck like lightning, Bonecrusher Smith was the new
WBA Heavyweight Champion of the World at the advanced
age of 33, with his next fight a WBC-WBA unification bout
against Mike Tyson with a million-dollar purse.

The Kings were in a no-lose situation in this fight, since they
controlled not only Witherspoon, but now Smith as well.
They were winners no matter who won. The only loser was
Witherspoon. He was fed up with the games he said the
Kings had played with his purse monies over the years. 'I
been Heavyweight Champion of the World twice, and I live
in an apartment in Philadelphia I'd be embarrassed for you
to see. I got nothing to show for it,' he told a friend from
the media. He then handed the same person a souvenir of
the fight that had ended less than an hour ago. It was one
of his front teeth, complete with root, that had been knocked
out by one of Smith's punches. Witherspoon, his trainer, 'Slim'
Jim Robinson, and his small group of friends and family then
stepped on to the Garden's service elevator, rode downstairs
to the street level, and stepped out into the cold night.

What nearly everyone hoped for was that Tyson and Spinks
would eventually meet in the final bout of the Tournament.
Spinks had name value, as well as a legitimate claim to the
title since he had won it from Holmes. While Tyson was next to
meet Smith, Spinks was due to meet the IBF's No. 1 contender,
Tony Tucker. It was here, in the early weeks of 1987, that
the Unification Tournament went topsy-turvy. Butch Lewis,
Spinks's promoter and de facto manager, decided that instead
of making the mandatory defence against Tucker, which would

have been televised by HBO as part of the Tournament, he would take Spinks out of the Tournament for a more lucrative and possibly safer match against the unranked Gerry Cooney who was making a comeback. Lewis maintained his contract allowed him to take his fighter out of the Tournament for one bout and then rejoin it. He might have negotiated a financial settlement with Tucker and his people to step aside temporarily from their mandatory fight with Spinks, but Tucker demanded a ridiculously huge amount of money, and they were unable to work out an agreement. Lewis still felt that Bob Lee, President of the IBF, could grant Spinks an extension on his obligation to fight Tucker; however, Lee refused, and when Lewis went ahead with his arrangements for Spinks to meet Cooney in June, Lee directed the IBF to strip Spinks of his IBF heavyweight title. Spinks would now earn $4-million in fighting Cooney, but he was out of the Elimination Tournament, and no longer held any official recognition as champion. This would eventually bring Spinks and Lewis a financial windfall far beyond what they might have earned had they remained in the Tournament. It would also bring down on Lewis's head several lawsuits that would be contested through 1989, as well as the wrath of HBO, King, and Jacobs and Cayton. For by lifting his fighter out of the Tournament, it seemed that he was taking a tremendous amount of glamour and prestige away from it, and losing the hoped-for Tyson–Spinks showdown for the undisputed title in 1987.

The fight to unify two-thirds of the title was set for March 7, 1987, at the Las Vegas Hilton. While the IBF manoeuvred to arrange a fight to fill its vacant title, Mike Tyson and Bonecrusher Smith would face off with two title belts at stake. Smith was a 7-to-1 underdog in the posted odds, but it mattered little to him, for overcoming odds had become a way of life to this most unlikely of Heavyweight Champions. He was born, and still lived, in the small town of Magnolia, North Carolina. His parents were poor sharecroppers who believed that education would provide the road out of the fields for their children. Smith's younger sister became a doctor, while he himself graduated in business administration. When he upset Witherspoon to win the WBA crown, he became the first and only college graduate in boxing history to win the Heavyweight Championship.

Smith never laced on a boxing glove until he was doing his national service, and did not have a pro fight until the age of 28, when, in 1981, ill-prepared, facing an experienced fighter, he was knocked out by James Broad in four rounds. Ready to quit, Smith reconsidered, put together a string of victories, and, after joining up with manager Kornberg, took on the respected trainer and former world champion, Emile Griffith, who taught him how to refine his style. Ready to face Tyson, Smith had compiled an unimpressive record of 19–5 in his five-year pro career. On May 13, 1984, trailing on the scorecards in London, he came back with his great equalizer, his knockout punch, to stop Frank Bruno. That same year he fought Larry Holmes for the heavyweight title. He was stopped by Holmes in the 12th round of a 15-round fight. He lost a decision to Witherspoon, then, in 1986, he knocked out ex-WBA Heavyweight Champion, Mike Weaver, in one round.

His fight with Tyson was a major disappointment. Instead of taking his best shot and going for broke, Smith played it cautiously. He was in there to survive, to avoid being knocked out. It was 12 rounds of driving a standard-shift car – clutch, clutch, clutch all night. Smith spent the evening grabbing and holding. Tyson did nothing to overcome Smith's survival tactics. He allowed himself to be grabbed and held, did not fight his way out of the clinches, and did not punch inside to Smith's body when he was being held. While Smith was intent on survival, Tyson was lacklustre. There was no sign of the hand speed, the devastating body punches, the combinations to the head. Tyson plodded through the 12 rounds, building up points on his attempts at aggression and for the punches he was able to land, which was more than Smith was doing. The best punch of the fight was thrown by Smith. It momentarily stunned Tyson, but unfortunately for those spectators struggling to stay awake during the 48 boring minutes the fight lasted, the punch came in the final 10 seconds of the last round, when it was too late to make a difference. Tyson was declared the winner on a unanimous decision, the scores being 120–106, 119–107, 119–107 (the maximum each judge could award Tyson was 120), but his reputation had suffered. He did not look invincible. Jacobs put the blame on Smith for fighting the way he did and making Tyson look bad. To punish the Bonecrusher, Jacobs had him banned from a subsequent Tyson undercard, telling Don King that he had damaged Tyson's ring reputation, and so he did not want him appearing in the future on any Tyson cards.

* * *

Mike Tyson was now the Heavyweight Champion of the World, recognized by the WBA and the WBC. As a matter of fact, with the IBF title vacant, he was the only heavyweight champion. He had the trappings of success: an apartment in an exclusive building on Manhattan's chic East Side, the same building in which Jim Jacobs, assistant manager Steve Lott, and British promoter Mickey Duff lived; a bachelor pad in Albany, near Catskill; gold and diamond jewellery galore; more automobiles than he needed, including a Rolls-Royce, Jaguar, Corvette and Mercedes-Benz. He was also bored. Winning the title wasn't the thrill he had thought it would be. 'I was happy to win the title,' he said early in 1987, 'but it wasn't a big anything because I knew I was going to win the championship when I went in the ring, as soon as I stepped in the ring.' He described himself as 'moody' and 'grumpy'. He didn't like too many people around him, and was ill at ease in public. Whereas Larry Holmes stood joking with fans and admirers, signing autographs while attending a fight one night at Madison Square Garden, Tyson, in a ringside seat, began to take on the look of a caged animal when people approached him to say hello or shake his hand. Finally, he broke off a conversation with a friend and retreated to the shelter of the ringside press area, which was fenced in and beyond the reach of the public. Holmes continued to accommodate every autograph request he was presented with. Muhammad Ali has always, at least until his health began to fail, been equally accessible. Mike Tyson had not learned, and still has not, that fame and publicity entail certain responsibilities and duties.

Though saying he was reasonably content, Tyson was at a loose end. He suddenly had fame and wealth, but had never had the time, education or grooming to develop a sense of values or indeed any interests beyond watching mindless action films and satisfying himself with as many women as he could. He had always had problems relating to women; once, he had lamented to Cus that girls wouldn't pay any attention to him, wouldn't talk to him, much less go out with him. He was depressed, and felt no girl would ever be interested in him. D'Amato went into town and bought a baseball bat. Returning home, he gave the bat to Mike, saying it was a present. 'Save the bat,' he said. 'Someday, when you're the heavyweight champion and you're rich, you're going to need it to beat away all the women who'll want to be with you then.' Now he was the champion, and the women, indeed, were there. Mike's obsession was to have beautiful women, women recognized by the public, high profile women whom the world would see at his side, and who would make him the envy of the world. His goal was to marry a beautiful woman. He fantasized about the singer, Whitney Houston. He then became obsessed with the TV actress, Lisa Bonet, then co-starring in *The Cosby Show*, once remarking, half-jokingly, that he would give up all he had if only he could meet her. Finally, he zeroed-in on a then little-known TV actress, and made conquering her his goal. Her name was Robin Givens.

Givens was part of an ensemble cast of the ABC TV sitcom, *Head of the Class*. Tyson spotted her and was irresistibly attracted by this light-complexioned black woman a year older than himself with her high cheekbones, pouting lips, long, flowing hair, and petite figure. He managed to arrange a meeting with her early in 1987. It took place at a Los Angeles restaurant. Mike was somewhat surprised when Robin arrived with an entourage that included her mother, her publicist, and several other people. It was a portent of things to come.

Tyson and Givens began a roller-coaster relationship. Robin played hard-to-get until she could twist Tyson around her little finger. After a while, Mike didn't know if he was coming or going. The couple presented an incongruous picture. Tyson was huge, massive, a hulk. Givens was small, delicate. Tyson was rough, unpolished, crude, from the streets. Givens was refined, well-spoken, educated. Tyson shunned the limelight, Givens relished it, lived for it. But each had what the other wanted. For Tyson, Givens represented everything that had been missing from his life – beauty, refinement, education. For Givens, Tyson was the means to get what she desired – fame, wealth, a ticket out of the ensemble casts and on, perhaps, to stardom. Robin Givens was an ambitious girl, with an even more ambitious mother behind her, pushing. Mike Tyson could be their passport to the big time.

When Mike arrived for the press conference to announce his title defence against former Heavyweight Champion Pinklon Thomas, Robin was in tow. No one in the media really knew who she was then, but it was obvious Mike was anxious to show her off. Press conferences were the bane of Mike's existence. He hated attending them, answering questions, sitting on the dais listening to Don King and Las Vegas hotel executives and closed-circuit TV entrepreneurs drone on and on. Often, Jim Jacobs had to implore Mike to attend, apprehensively urging on him the necessity of participating in these media circuses. Mike wanted to get in the ring. That he enjoyed. That he looked forward to with relish. That gave him pleasure. Attending news conferences did not. His usual demeanour was that of a bored child. He would either be fingering some trinket, or reading a boxing magazine someone had handed him, totally ignoring the proceedings, or else he would fix his gaze on the ceiling. Often he would lean over and rest his head on Jim Jacobs's shoulder, and close his eyes, or put his head down on his arms on the table in front of him, as if by shutting his eyes he could shut out all that was going on around him and make it disappear. All this in full view of several hundred boxing and media people, not to mention those on the dais whose combined efforts were going to pay him three, or eight, or ten, or 22-million dollars. Certainly they had the right to expect at least some interest on Mike's part, but that was never forthcoming. He felt they would get their money's worth from him when he stepped into the ring, and as far as he was concerned, that was all he owed them. Mike was also conspicuous by his lack of sartorial elegance. He would inevitably arrive in a sweatsuit, or rumpled slacks and a T-shirt of some sort, or jeans and a wool training-sweater. Invariably, he would look as though he had just came from a gym workout or had just fallen out of bed, while everyone else was dressed as befitted the formality of the occasion, the setting for which was usually a posh Manhattan hotel. Basically, Mike didn't give a damn. But now, with Robin, he had a new interest that sparked his enthusiasm. He wanted everyone to see her, to see him with her. The media, looking for new stories, jumped on it. The day after the news conference, the stories were full of Mike's new girlfriend, along with photos of Robin Givens, the Hollywood starlet.

Mike's defence of his WBA-WBC titles was set for May 30, back at the Las Vegas Hilton. It would be a double-header. On that same night, the IBF would fill its vacant Heavyweight Championship so that the tournament could proceed later in the summer with its concluding unification bout. Pinklon Thomas was regarded by many as a tough, solid test for Tyson, although some boxing insiders believed that Thomas had had a relapse of a problem involving drug use, and that he was essentially a 'shot' fighter and no real challenge for Tyson. Regardless, Mike had to show well against Thomas if he was to restore the damage done to his reputation by his lacklustre performance against Bonecrusher Smith. 'Bottom line, people pay to see

Mike knock someone out,' said Jacobs, and that was the truth. Angelo Dundee was training Thomas. The 29-year-old former champion was a big heavyweight, at 6'3". Despite the skills he possessed, or had once possessed, depending on who you believed, he was a 5-to-1 underdog, which was especially remarkable considering that he had an outstanding record of 29–1–1 with 24 KO's, and was ranked No. 1 by the WBC.

In the first of the evening's two main events, Tony Tucker, whom Michael Spinks had ducked in order to fight Gerry Cooney, won the vacant IBF Championship by knocking out James 'Buster' Douglas in the 10th round. Tucker improved his record to 35–0 with 29 KOs, and moved into line for the finals of the Unification Tournament.

Next into the ring came Pinklon Thomas, followed moments later by Tyson. When the bell rang, Mike went right at him. In the final minute of the round, Tyson connected solidly with a left to Thomas's jaw, followed it with a right to the same spot, and Thomas sagged backwards into the ropes. He was hurt, and Tyson followed up with another right and left to the jaw. At ringside, once again abandoning any appearance of impartiality, Jose Torres jumped to his feet, cupped his hands around his mouth, and shouted instructions to Tyson, calling out 'five-six, five-six', D'Amato's number combinations, to the young champion. Thomas was in serious trouble, but managed to land a right hand to Tyson's head in the closing seconds and survived the round.

Back in the corner, Dundee worked furiously to revive his man. The ringside physician came up to the corner to check Thomas and see if he was badly damaged. Dundee, who had seen Berbick destroyed by Tyson six months earlier and was now experiencing *déjà vu* with Thomas, let slip a torrent of misplaced aggression at the doctor, screaming at him to leave Thomas alone, utterly frustrated at the inability of his warriors to stop the relentless onslaught of the 20-year-old boxing monster.

Surprisingly, Thomas was able to pull himself together, and began to land an effective jab, keeping Tyson a bit off balance and enabling the challenger to survive a bit longer. Basically, though, he was postponing the inevitable. At the end of round five, the customary one-minute rest was extended to two and a half minutes while a torn glove was replaced on Thomas. Veteran ringsiders chuckled. They remembered a similar incident involving Dundee in London twenty-four years earlier.

A young Muhammad Ali, a.k.a. Cassius Clay, was fighting Henry Cooper. Ali, who had not yet won the Heavyweight Championship, was rolling along when suddenly Cooper landed a tremendous left hook flush on the brash young American's jaw. Ali went down hard on the seat of his pants. He was hurt badly, and fortunately for him, the bell rang as he got up, saving him from a possible knockout. Dundee worked furiously over Ali, when he suddenly noticed a small split along the seam of one of his gloves and – as Dundee admits in his autobiography – stuck his finger in the split, 'helping it along'. It took several minutes to find another glove, remove the torn one, lace it up and tape it around Ali's hand. By that time, Ali had rested and recovered all his scrambled senses. The deliciously devious strategy worked. Ali came back to TKO Cooper on cuts. Now, in Thomas's corner, history was perhaps repeating itself. Meanwhile, in Tyson's corner, the extra rest was also giving the champion time to regain his strength. Rooney told him it was time to 'start throwing punches with mean intentions'. When the sixth round started, that's what Tyson did. A left drove Thomas back. As soon as Tyson saw he had staggered the ex-champion, he closed in for the kill. He fired hurting punches like a machine gun, 16 unanswered shots to the head, finishing with a pulverizing left to Thomas's forehead, and a left hook flush on the side of the face that shook Pinklon like a cannon ball, and knocked him flat on his back. As Thomas struggled to his feet, attempting to beat the count, Angelo Dundee had seen enough. He jumped into the ring to rescue his fighter and spare him any more punishment. Pinklon Thomas had become victim number 30 for Mike Tyson.

The fight over with, Tyson turned his attention once again to his pursuit of Robin Givens. It blew hot and cold, as Robin turned the emotional taps on and off at will to control the flow of the affair with the emotionally immature and insecure young champion. Her mother was against the relationship. A wilful woman, Ruth Roper had seen to it, by hook or by crook, that Robin and her sister went to the best schools, lived in the best neighbourhoods, had the best clothes. And now she wanted the best husband for her daughter, a doctor or a lawyer, not a hardly-reformed juvenile delinquent, ex-reform school inmate, high school drop-out, ghetto-raised prizefighter.

Mike's next fight was to be on August 1, 1987. His opponent would be the IBF Champion, 6'8" Tony Tucker, and the fight would be the culmination of the HBO Unification Tournament, all three titles on the line, the winner to be the undisputed Heavyweight Champion. The news conference to announce the fight was held in June in New York. A sullen and depressed Tyson turned up alone. The night before, Robin had broken up with him, and given him back the diamond friendship ring he had given her. Now, waiting for the news conference with Tucker to start, he stood alone, fingering the ring. When a friend asked him what was wrong, he said, 'I don't have a girlfriend anymore. Robin broke up with me. I was doggin' her a little bit because she wouldn't give me any pussy all this time. I kept askin' her, Robin, what's goin' on? So I dogged her a little bit, and she broke up with me.' She was clever enough to realize that if she gave in too easily, she would just be another Tyson conquest, to be discarded, and that was not what she had in mind.

Several days later, on June 21, Tyson's rage and frustration boiled over. He was in Los Angeles, no doubt in pursuit of Robin. He attended a rap music show at the Greek Theatre in Hollywood. Afterwards, in the parking lot, Tyson spotted an attractive female attendant. Without bothering to check whether his advances were welcome or not, he grabbed her around the waist, pulled her close to him, and laughingly demanded a kiss. She began screaming at him to let go and leave her alone. A co-worker, 20-year-old Jonathan Casares, seeing her struggling, gallantly but foolishly intervened. Tyson turned his rage on Casares, slapping him across the face several times, a slap from Mike Tyson being sufficient to rattle the average person's teeth. Tyson's friends stepped in and calmed him down, and the situation was defused. Jim Jacobs attempted to play the incident down, saying it was just a misunderstanding blown out of proportion. But this time the attempt to cover up another Tyson indiscretion and preserve the champion's 'image' did not work. After conducting an inquiry, the Los Angeles City Attorney's office found sufficient grounds to file charges against Tyson. Early in July, the Heavyweight Champion of the World, who apparently couldn't control his libido, was charged with one count of assault with a deadly weapon (his fists) and one count of battery. Tyson was ordered to appear in court in late August to face the charges. He never did. The two parking lot attendants were bought off. For payments totalling $105,000, they withdrew their charges and Tyson's lucrative commercial marketability was not compromised by a court appearance.

Tyson and Robin were reconciled, and during a hiatus in the taping of her series, she joined him in Catskill, where he had returned to begin training for the Tucker fight. But all was still not well. A friend, visiting one day, asked Mike how things were with Robin. Out of earshot of her, he indicated that things weren't smooth because 'Her mother doesn't like me much.' But even in the gym, he couldn't keep his hands off her. He took her off to a quiet corner, leaned against a wall, pulled her to him, and kissed her passionately for several minutes.

Robin returned to Los Angeles to resume taping her series, and a lonely and lovesick champion continued his training in Catskill. About a month before the fight, he shifted his camp to Las Vegas, staying with Rooney and Steve Lott in the private house they customarily used to avoid the tumult and chaos and distractions at the Hilton. Tensions always built up inside Tyson in the weeks leading up to a fight until they literally got to breaking point. However, in Las Vegas, before the Tucker fight, he was especially tense, perhaps because of the turbulent state of his emotions owing to Robin's manipulation. This time, his temper kept exploding in confrontations with Rooney during his gym workouts in Vegas, behind closed doors. In public, they kept up the facade of brotherly love, with Jacobs denying to the press there was any rift between the fighter and trainer.

Two weeks before the fight, when Mike's emotional and psychological state usually reached the lowest point, it happened. He disappeared, amid rumours that he was upset with Rooney. He turned up 2,500 miles away, in Albany, where he had an apartment. He was seen at a night club he sometimes frequented, a hangout for local drug dealers and users. He told friends there that he'd had it with boxing, and that he was retiring. But bolting from camp was something Mike frequently did when the pressure got too much for him. After four days around Albany and Catskill, he was ready to return to Las Vegas and resume training.

On the night of August 1, both fighters weighed 221 pounds. That was the only similarity. Tucker, tall and handsome, entered the ring in a dazzling robe of sparkling gold sequins, trimmed in red, over red Spartan trunks. Though he had fought in relative obscurity, his professional record was as sparkling as his robe – 35-and-0. Tyson, by contrast, ever the gladiator, entered robeless in his customary black leather shoes with no socks and plain black trunks.

What no one knew was that Tucker was coming into the fight with a badly injured right hand, an injury sustained in training. His father, who managed him, foolishly kept the injury a secret instead of bringing it to the attention of the Nevada Athletic Commission physicians and requesting a postponement. In the first round, Tucker showed that he had come to fight. As Tyson charged in, a ripping left uppercut by Tucker caught him flush and sent him reeling backwards, the hardest punch Tyson had received in his pro career. Tucker then bombarded him with rights to the head until the bell ended the round.

Watching the action from on high were two interested spectators, Butch Lewis and Michael Spinks. Since their withdrawal from the Tournament and the stripping of the IBF crown from Spinks, he was no longer a champion. But Lewis knew that down the line, although it was Tucker in the ring on this night defending the IBF title, the economics of the situation would dictate a meeting between his man and Tyson, and he was astute enough to keep Spinks's name and face in the public eye. Michael, he declared, was the 'People's Champion', never defeated in the ring but stripped of his title by decree of a sanctioning organization. He therefore sat with his fighter where the common man was sitting, high in the gods in the cheapest $50 seats. In the months ahead, Lewis would proclaim loudly and often that Michael Spinks was the true champion who had followed the line of succession by defeating Larry Holmes, and that Tyson had to prove himself by beating Spinks. By doing so, Lewis helped feed the flames and create the demand for a Tyson-Spinks showdown.

On this night, Lewis and Spinks were shown that Tyson was not invincible. Dancing, moving, boxing, holding. Tucker was able to bother Tyson enough to throw off his timing and render his power largely ineffective. Lateral movement, the observers said, would always be the key to beating Tyson eventually. Unfortunately for Tucker, one of the right hands he bounced off Tyson's skull early in the bout re-injured the hand, and after the fifth round he was reduced to fighting a battle of survival. Still, he was able to prevent Tyson from landing any effective combinations throughout most of the 12 rounds. Tyson fired hard jabs, then came in and banged to Tucker's body in the early rounds. Finding his range, he then slammed shots to Tucker's head, effectively building points on the scorecards of the three judges. In the twelfth round, Tyson banged a left hand off Tucker's head, sending a spray of sweat and water flying into the air, but Tucker shook his head to say it didn't hurt (usually a good sign that it did).

When the bell ended the bout, both men were on their feet. There had been no knockdowns, neither fighter had been in serious trouble. Tyson's relentless pressure and aggression had made the difference. The scores were 119–111, 118–113, and 116–112, all in Tyson's favour, and so, via a unanimous decision, Mike Tyson was now the undisputed Heavyweight Champion of the World. He had already fought four title bouts to defend and unify the Championship, and, at 21 years and 1 month, he was still not the age Floyd Patterson had been when he had gone down in history as the youngest fighter to win the crown. He had earned $2½-million for this bout (Tucker's purse had been just under $2-million) bringing his ring earnings to $14-million in just 2½ years as a professional, a remarkable tribute not only to his fighting skills, but to the way Jacobs and Gayton had marketed their fighter. And now, the road to even greater riches lay before them, for now he held universal recognition as Champion. The day following his victory, an embarrassed-looking Tyson was the focal point of a 'coronation' ceremony only a Don King could stage. At the hotel, with boxing officials, press, hangers-on, and even Muhammad Ali on hand, Tyson, wrapped in a fur robe and with jewelled sceptre in hand, was crowned the new 'King of the Heavyweights'.

For Tyson's next fight, his first defence of the undisputed title, the venue would change, thanks to the entrance on the scene of a new power in boxing, 41-year-old Donald Trump, hardly the type one would expect to find mixed up in a sport that Mike Tyson himself said attracts 'scum'. ('All my life,' he had once said, 'I've been dealing with scum.') Now Tyson would be dealing with a different 'player', one of America's youngest and wealthiest entrepreneurs, who would eventually make his own power play for control of the champion.

Donald John Trump is not the wealthiest billionaire in the United States. He's not even the youngest. He is, however, without a doubt, the best known and the most flamboyant. Born in 1946 in the exclusive Jamaica Estates of New York City, he was one of five children of Fred and Mary Trump. His father was a real estate developer who built 24,000 apartments in Brooklyn, Queens and Staten Island, amassing a fortune of $20-million. Having learned the hard realities of the real estate wars from his father, Donald then went out to see what he could do on his own.

In 1976, he persuaded the bankrupt Penn Central Railroad to sell him the ageing and run down Commodore Hotel on 42nd Street, adjoining Grand Central Terminal, for $10-million, as well as an option on their Hudson River Railroad yards, a now prime piece of mid-Manhattan real estate which is currently the site of the showcase Javits Convention Center. With the option on the Commodore, and using his father's powerful political and financial connections to smooth the way, he secured $80-million in loans and a $120-million tax abatement, and set about renovating the Commodore. Not knowing much about hotels, he entered into partnership with the Hyatt Corporation, and in 1980 the old Commodore was reopened as the showplace Grand Hyatt Hotel with 1,347 rooms. Today it provides Trump with $30-million in profits annually. It was just his starting point.

In 1982, on Fifth Avenue, he built the skyscraper Trump Tower. Its lower floors house some of Manhattan's most exclusive and expensive shops, plus an atrium complete with an 80-foot waterfall, and walls of pink marble. The apartments sold for upwards of $4-million apiece to people like TV superstar Johnny Carson and film-maker Steven Spielberg. He sold out the condominiums for a total of $275-million.

Trump also owns numerous other hotels and properties in New York and Florida, including the landmark Plaza Hotel on Central Park South, together with one of the primest pieces of undeveloped real estate in the world, a 76-acre parcel stretching from 59th Street to 72nd Street along the Hudson River waterfront on Manhattan's West Side, where he plans to develop a $5-billion Trump City, a complex of luxury apartments, shops, restaurants and parks, and the world's tallest building.

His personal lifestyle is one of unimagined luxury. He dresses in $2,000 Brioni suits, $350 shirts and $100 ties. His wife, Ivana, a Czechoslovakian-born former Olympic skiier and fashion model, reportedly purchases $1.5 million worth of clothing each year! He boasts that his private French Puma helicopter, capable of 180 m.p.h. speeds and with passenger space for ten, is used by the Queen of England when she visits the US because of its speed and safety. For longer trips, Trump owns his own Boeing 727 jet. Several years ago, he picked up the crowning glory of his private holdings, the 282-foot long Trump Princess yacht, at a 'bargain' $29-million from financially strapped international wheeler-dealer Adnan

Khashoggi. Said to be the world's largest, it contains 100 rooms, including eleven guest suites. The walls are covered in chamois leather, the baths are gold and onyx.

On dry land, the Trumps and their three children divide their time between three homes: a 45-room estate on ten acres in Greenwich, Connecticut; the 118-room Mar-a-Lago landmark estate in Palm Beach, Florida, set on 17 acres with its own golf course and 400 feet of private ocean beachfront (built in the 1920s for cereal heiress Marjorie Merriweather Post); and their main residence in Trump Towers, a 50-room triplex worth between $15- and $20-million, which has among its features an 80-foot-long living room which includes a 12-foot-high onyx waterfall, hand-carved marble columns, pure gold leaf-covered ceiling mouldings; a bathroom with a bathtub carved from lilac onyx; and ceilings adorned with hand-painted murals.

Trump has little free time, however, to enjoy the luxuries he has amassed. He is essentially a workaholic who doesn't particularly enjoy vacations and gets his true pleasure from his business dealings. To get the jump on his competitors, he sleeps just four hours a night and is already up, planning his deals, at 4 am. Ten law firms handle his business affairs. In the 1980s he challenged the supremacy of the National Football League by helping to organize the United States Football League and luring top college prospects to sign with his team, the New Jersey Generals, with the offer of multi-million dollar contracts. The NFL proved too big to take on, and the USFL eventually folded, but it provided an insight into Trump's fiercely competitive nature. In his spare time, Trump has dabbled in corporate raiding, moving to take over major companies, acquiring large blocks of their stock, then selling out at inflated prices. From 1986 to 1988 he earned 'pocket change' profits of $137-million in this manner.

His wealth has been estimated at a low $1.3-billion by journalists on *Forbes* magazine, whom he calls 'idiots'. *Business Week* puts his worth at just over $3-billion. *Fortune* magazine says it's just under $1.6-billion. Trump himself says it's all rubbish. 'I know what I'm worth,' he says, and puts his total net worth at $3.7-billion, including liquid cash assets of nearly $700-million, then candidly acknowledges, 'Who the fuck really knows?'

So why would this fabulously wealthy and successful real estate entrepreneur become the world's unlikeliest boxing promoter? The answer lies in Trump's other holdings, those in the East Coast gambling capital of Atlantic City, New Jersey.

Trump is a major player – probably *the* major player – in the Atlantic City casino sweepstakes. He owns two hotel casino complexes, Trump's Castle and the Trump Plaza, which provide him with a major source of his income, an estimated yearly profit of $100-million. In addition, in 1990, he will open the Taj Mahal, the world's largest hotel-casino complex, bigger than anything in Las Vegas, which will cost $750-million to complete.

Although Atlantic City had hosted many championship fights, all the major bouts for years had been co-opted by the casinos in Las Vegas. With his enormous holdings in Atlantic City, always looked upon as a shabby, poor cousin to the glitzy Las Vegas, Trump decided to turn the city's image around. One of the ways to do this, he decided, was to bring in the big fights. They would focus worldwide attention on Atlantic City, take the play away from Las Vegas, and also, not incidentally, ring up tremendously increased casino profits, as the high rollers, traditionally attracted by the glamour of the big fights, brought their money to Atlantic City instead of Vegas. Trump, who has said 'I just keep pushing and pushing to get what I'm after . . . I like beating my enemies to the ground', decided to take on Las Vegas and beat them at their own game. He did it the old-fashioned way. He opened his chequebook and outbid the Vegas interests, and so he snagged the hottest property in sport, Mike Tyson, in a glamour bout. Tyson would defend his title on October 16, 1987, for the first time in Atlantic City, against the undefeated 1984 Olympic gold medallist, Tyrell Biggs. The fight would actually take place in the venerable Convention Hall, but that was adjacent to, and was actually connected by a walkway with, Trump Plaza, and to all intents and purposes, it was Trump's hotel that was the site of the fight. Don King, with an option on Tyson's services, would be the promoter.

Fighting Tyrell Biggs was something Mike Tyson looked forward to with relish. He had wanted the chance to win a gold medal at the Olympics; he had never got it, and he was always jealous of the attention given to those who did win gold, especially Biggs in the glamorous super-heavyweight division. Tyson was disdainful of the stand-up style of jabbing and moving that won points in the amateurs, a style he did not use and for which he felt he was unfairly penalized by the judges in the Olympic trials and box-off against Henry Tillman. The style Tyson most admired was epitomized by the contemporary fighter he most respected, Roberto Duran, a no-holds-barred, two-fisted slugger. In the past, Tyson had tried to goad Biggs into fistfights by taunting him when they had had chance encounters. Now Tyson would get his chance to show up this Olympic pretty-boy in the ring, in front of millions of spectators. 'I want to give him a good lesson. I want to hurt him real bad,' he said, with undisguised evil in his eye.

With fewer than 20 professional fights to his credit, Biggs was rushed into the bout with Tyson by his managers before he was ready. Theirs was a calculated business decision, nothing more. The talented Biggs was regarded by many in boxing as a 'head case'. He had had problems with drug abuse, and privately, Shelly Finkel, Lou and Dan Duva, who oversaw his career, didn't know how much longer they could keep his fragile psyche in one piece. Finkel, a friend of Jim Jacobs, confided to him that it was best to grab the payday against Tyson now, while they could, while he was still undefeated, while he was off drugs, before who-knows-what might happen. With Jacobs's cooperation, the favour was done and the match was made. It was like feeding a lamb to a lion.

There was the dream, always the same dream. He was about to fight Mike Tyson, the Heavyweight Champion of the World, and he was afraid. Who wouldn't be? The bell rang. He was terrified. He didn't know what to do. He just went out and started throwing punches. Did he win? He never knew. He woke up. He was Mike Tyson! But in the dream, he was someone else, his mind, its deep recesses freed by the narcotic of sleep, showing him what it might be like to face himself in the ring. A fantasy about fighting himself, this was always Mike Tyson's dream.

In training, Tyson was his usual abusive self. Steve Lott, who, along with Rooney, was the target of most of Tyson's boorishness until he was summarily dismissed without so much as a goodbye after the Spinks fight, Tyson's usual pattern of behaviour: 'The middle three weeks, especially two weeks before the fight, he got very surly, and that would happen every fight, and then the last week he knew the fight was getting so close, the last couple of days he was fine. When training was over, that's when he was most relaxed. Two weeks, three weeks before the fight, that's when . . . he would treat Kevin and me like shit. That was his style. "Mike, would you like to have some dinner with us?" He wouldn't say a word, walk back into his room. "Time to go to the gym" – he wouldn't say a word. He'd leave the house without telling us where he was going, take the day off all by himself. Kevin would give him instructions during the round [while sparring], Mike would ignore him completely. The round would be over, Mike would walk back to the corner, Kevin would start talking, Mike would walk away, indifferent, wouldn't listen to Kevin. The sparring would be over, Mike would start to take the gloves off himself, throw them on the floor and walk away, take the wraps off with his teeth, not let Kevin do it, walk away, not even change his clothes, just leave the place. Completely indifferent to everyone around him. . . . He's just a surly motherfucker during that time. Mike knows. He says, "Steve, you know I'm an asshole, but that's my style." I said, hey, it's no big deal, forget about it. He knows he's an asshole, I know it, Kevin knows it. So what? Let's just get the job done. Everyone else does their job, when they go home to go to sleep, then they're personal. But when it comes to boxing it's a job, and he does his job. He's not expected to behave himself like Sir Laurence Olivier. He's supposed to fight. I don't think [there's] anything Cus could have done or Jimmy or Kevin or anyone to help him rid himself of that mood he had three weeks before a fight. . . . He was too young. He hadn't experienced enough life, he hadn't been a professional long enough, he wasn't a human being with the objectivity of a 30-year-old person knowing how he should be perceived and how he is perceived and how he should treat people. That wasn't his job. His job was to fight, and then, as he gets older, then he starts to think, "You know, I don't want to go down in his history as an asshole. I better cool it a little bit. Maybe it'll hurt my boxing, but I can't treat people like this." The only thing that mattered is, what did he do in the ring. That's the bottom line, and he did OK. Now, could he have done better outside the ring? I'd take that two week period anytime, of him being surly, if he puts on those type of performances [when he fights].'

Tyson also played psychological tricks on himself. He would deliberately slack off on his training until the fight drew close, then, realizing the danger that his opponent was likely to be better prepared and would therefore have the edge, he would feel challenged, threatened, and come on strong, whipping himself into fighting shape. Not being ready, in his own mind, would serve for him as a self-imposed prod, forcing him to knuckle under and concentrate.

With Donald Trump, his wife and family ensconced at ringside, along with a host of celebrities, Mike Tyson gave them what they had all come to see, a show of controlled violence, legalized brutality, blood and, finally, the kill. Biggs began the fight moving, dancing, jabbing nicely. Tyson just applied the pressure and kept coming forward. He didn't want to finish Biggs too soon. He wanted to savour this one, torture his opponent a little before finishing him off. Biggs's number-one rating was a joke. He had had just 15 fights, none of them against any top-notch contenders. His number-one ranking owed more to the ability of the Duvas and Finkel to pull strings and exert their influence with the sanctioning bodies than to his true abilities after just 15 bouts. Tyson kept cutting the 6'5" Biggs down to size, methodically chopping away at him. Finally, late in the seventh round, Tyson had had enough fun. He whacked a vicious elbow into Biggs's mouth, illegal, but a customary Tyson tactic nevertheless. He then banged a left off Biggs's head, then, as Biggs attempted to dig a left uppercut to Tyson's body, the champion fired a left hook to Biggs's jaw, and the Olympic champion crumpled backwards and through the lower ropes, his head out on the ring apron. As Biggs was going down, Tyson tried another left, which missed, and the momentum of the punch carried him, off balance, stumbling into the ropes directly over the fallen Biggs. The challenger just beat the count, rising at the count of nine, a cut above his left eye pouring blood down the side of his face. He was a tired, beaten fighter. Tyson swarmed in for the *coup de grâce*, throwing a flurry of punches from every angle, finally landing a left hand flush on the jaw of the battle-weary Biggs. He went down hard, on the seat of his pants, in a corner. His upper body was supported by the turnbuckles that held the ropes. There was no count. Referee Tony Orlando had seen enough. He dropped to his knees alongside Biggs and waved it over.

Mike Tyson, now 32-and-0, had had his revenge over the Olympic gold medal winner who had stolen all the attention three years earlier. He had also picked up some extra spending money. Cayton and Jacobs had negotiated a seven-fight deal for Tyson with HBO for $26.5-million.

10

Hello to Robin, Goodbye to Jimmy

A fairy-tale proposition: The heavyweight champion is the most dangerous man on earth: the most feared, the most manly. His proper mate is very likely the fairytale princess whom the mirrors declare the fairest woman on earth.

– ON BOXING
JOYCE CAROL OATES

STEVE LOTT SAT up in bed with a start. He thought he must be dreaming. He had heard screams. Awake now, he knew it wasn't a dream, because the screams persisted. They were coming from the next room in his Manhattan apartment, the apartment Tyson shared when he was in New York City, as he was on this night. Staying with him and sharing his bedroom was Robin Givens. Something was obviously wrong. Lott got up to investigate. He opened the door to Tyson's room, and got a sinking feeling in his stomach. Robin had been screaming for help. Mike had apparently gone into a fit of rage and had been hitting her. Lott didn't know what to do. If Tyson resumed, Lott thought, he would be facing the unpleasant task of having to help her by taking on Mike Tyson in a fight. He knew the odds were not in his favour. Instead, much to his relief, Mike picked up the telephone and called for a car to come and fetch Robin. He wanted her out of his sight, out of the apartment, away from him. He saw Lott's questioning expression. 'Everything's cool, Steve. No problem,' he said, so Lott left the room and closed the door. Lott never knew the extent of the physical attack by Mike on Robin. The next day, Mike said to him, 'Steve, just remember one thing. Robin's an actress, a good actress.' But the incident was definitely a portent of things to come.

Robin's mother, Ruth Roper, was a woman driven by the desire to succeed, to get on at any cost, to achieve success for both herself and her daughters. 'I raised my daughters,' she would say, 'to be smart, beautiful and gutsy – everything that can be intimidating to a man.' Ruth Roper wanted her girls to have it all. She was born Ruth Newby in October, 1946. Her family

was from Lexington, Kentucky, then a part of the South of
segregation, the South before the 1964 Civil Rights Act. Her
grandfather owned a successful garbage-carting business, and
so she was spared the abject poverty that afflicted many black
families in that era. After her parents divorced, Ruth was raised
in New York City by her mother. As a teenager, she went to
visit her father in Lexington, where she met Reuben Givens, a
local high school basketball star two years her senior. The two
fell in love, and Ruth stayed in Lexington, transferring into the
high school there in order to be near Reuben. Not only was
Givens a top athlete, he came from an athletically prominent
family: his brother, Jack, was a star player for the University
of Kentucky Wildcats in the 1960s, and helped lead them to the
NCAA basketball championship. A cousin, Lou Johnson, was
a major league baseball player.

Reuben gave up any chance he might have had to play college basketball when he and Ruth got married on the day they
graduated from high school, June 6, 1964. They had to. Robin
was born five and a half months later, on November 27, 1964.
Two years later, her sister, Stephanie, was born. A year after
that, the marriage broke up, although it took an additional
two years for them to obtain a divorce. Ruth was 17 when
she married Reuben. At 20 she was a single parent with two
little girls.

'I told her,' says Reuben Givens, 'that I didn't want to have
to live up to her standards. When our marriage broke up, I
told Ruth to go home to her mother, because her mother
kept interfering with our lives.' Obviously, Ruth had goals
and ambitions that Reuben could not, or would not, try to
keep up with. She also had a domineering mother to set the
pattern for her own behaviour.

They had moved north to New York, and now Ruth was raising the two girls in the Bronx, but not for long. She went to work
for Trans World Airlines, learned about travel, then opened her
own travel agency. She married businessman Phil Roper, but,
according to Reuben Givens, the marriage lasted only a few
weeks, and was annulled. She began to move up in the world
as fast as her brightening economic situation allowed her to.
She left the decaying Bronx, then moved to the Westchester
suburb of Mount Vernon. Although an improvement over the
Bronx, that, too, was largely blue-collar working class, so as
soon as she could, Ruth moved on to the much more affluent
(and largely white) suburban town of New Rochelle. Her girls

were not sent to public school. They were enrolled in the more exclusive, private New Rochelle Academy, and Ruth worked hard to pay for the Westchester County lifestyle, the private school tuition, and the preppy clothes the girls needed in order to blend in. Although she had never attended college, she was a shrewd businesswoman. Armed with some knowledge of data processing, she formed her own highly successful computer consulting company.

She continued to drill into her daughters the urgent necessity to succeed. Robin's sister, Stephanie, a professional tennis player on the US Tennis Association's satellite tour, told *Vanity Fair* magazine, 'It was like a plan. Robin was going to be a doctor. My mother worked very hard to put her through the best schools. It was like a dream for her because she didn't have the opportunity herself. . . .Both of us have a tremendous amount of faith in our mother. We think there's nothing she can't do. But it's true she doesn't want us to grow up.'

All was not complete sweetness and light as Ruth Roper climbed the ladder of success toward the American dream, however. Roper was sued in New York State Supreme Court by a former business partner; an ex-husband also sued her, saying she had failed to pay him 50 per cent of the proceeds of the sale of their former home; but she drew most public attention when she went to court herself to sue Dave Winfield, a superstar with the New York Yankees and one of the most famous athletes in America, with whom she had had a three-year affair during the mid-1980s, and whom when the relationship ended she charged with giving her a sexually-transmitted disease, believed to be herpes. The case ended when Roper and Winfield reached an out-of-court settlement, with no admission of guilt by Winfield, who, according to his attorney, categorically denied all of Roper's allegations. No more details are known, the court papers in the case having been sealed. A former employee said of Roper, 'She doesn't flinch. You cross her and she'll hurt you. . . .Ruth is vindictive.'

And what of Reuben Givens? Left behind by the ambitious Ruth, he remained behind. He remarried and fathered several more children, but never got out of the Bronx. Contact with his successful daughter, Robin, has been minimal. He is a self-confessed 'street person', while Robin was raised in a different world with different values and standards far away from the run-down tenements of the Bronx. When Tyson and Givens and Ruth Roper began making the headlines almost daily in

1988, amid all the accusations, charges, innuendo, rumours, counter-charges and allegations, Reuben Givens said he felt it was important to separate Robin from his ex-wife in the public's mind, to 'let them know what really the real deal is, who the real person who's doing the dirty work out here [is].'

For Robin, a bright student in private school, the next step was to attend a top college. The best schools were actively seeking qualified minority applicants, and Robin had no problems, with her grades and colour both working in her favour. She was accepted at the unusually early age of 15 by Sarah Lawrence, in Bronxville, NY, just a short drive from her home in nearby New Rochelle. Sarah Lawrence is considered one of the most prestigious colleges in America, and competition for admission is stiff. Black, aggressive and strikingly pretty, Robin made her mark quickly, and became unpopular on campus before very much time had passed. She recalls her four years there as being miserable, and returned home at weekends to sit with her mother and sister watching television.

Coincidentally, two classmates of hers, Lauren Holly and Holly Robinson, also went into the world of television. Neither has fond memories of her. Lauren Holly roomed with Robin before going on to prominence in the ABC-TV daytime soap opera *All My Children*. She says that she and Givens were once close friends, although today they no longer speak. She told newspaper columnist Cindy Adams, 'You just knew she'd make it. Nothing would stop Robin. Robin was determined to get ahead. She has a vibrant personality. She's smart, literate and went about life with a vengeance. . . .She was focused positively. She wanted to be educated. . . .I can't say she was really popular – either with boys or girls. . . .Robin is very controlled, even emotionally. It's important to her to remain cool.' When Givens and Tyson split up in the fall of 1988, Lauren Holly was not surprised. Lauren commented, 'All I'll say is that, relative to the Tyson story, I'm seeing a familiar pattern in her.'

Holly Robinson, who went on to become the star of the TV detective drama, *21 Jump Street*, and who is the daughter of Delores Robinson, a Hollywood talent agent, got to know Robin Givens quickly when she entered Sarah Lawrence two years after Givens had started there. Robinson, a smart and beautiful young black woman, says it was only natural that she and Givens should become friendly, since Sarah Lawrence is a small campus, with only a handful of black students. Delores

Robinson recalls being surprised at Ruth Roper's frankness when the two met for the first time. Roper told her that now she had got Robin into a good school where she was getting a good education, her next job was to find her a rich husband.

The friendship between Holly and Robin ended spectacularly after Robin was invited to spend the Christmas recess with Holly in California at her mother's home in the exclusive show business colony of Malibu. According to Holly, when they got back to college, Givens went around telling people on campus that Holly and her mother had stolen money from her wallet in California. Delores Robinson and Ruth Roper spoke on the phone about Robin's accusations, and Ruth laughed it off. 'You know how Robin can be,' she said. 'She didn't mean it.' She suggested they all meet for lunch to sort the matter out. But Holly had different ideas. Finding Givens in the dormitory, she punched her in the face, and the two wrestled to the ground, screaming and rolling around until the fight was broken up.

Despite her mother's wish that she pursue a career in medicine, where she could find a nice Ivy League-educated doctor or lawyer to marry, Robin had been bitten by the show business bug. She decided to try her luck in Hollywood. Once she saw Robin was determined to make it in acting, Ruth Roper headed for Hollywood with her daughter, rather than loosen her controlling grip. She auditioned for a small role on *The Cosby Show*, and Bill Cosby was impressed with her. He made Robin's still doubtful mother an offer: if Robin didn't make it in show business, he would pay for the rest of her education when she returned to graduate school. However, the offer would not be necessary. Givens's agent at William Morris was quick to spot the 19-year-old's 'fierce' desire to make it as an actress. Before long, she landed the part of a brilliant high school student in the ABC-TV series, *Head of the Class*, and her career was launched.

Supplied with information from Robin, her official studio biography read: 'Robin's academic excellence was almost surpassed by her love for the theatre.' Listing her work in films and television, it pointed out that she had been 'one of the top young models at New York's Ford Agency'. It also mentioned that she had attended the prestigious American Academy of Dramatic Arts as a youngster, and after graduating from Sarah Lawrence College, had gone on to further her education at the Harvard University Medical School, dropping out to pursue her acting career. Eileen Ford, founder and owner of the famous modelling agency which bears her name, says Givens was never a model with her company. A director of the American Academy of Dramatic Arts says Givens attended for five Saturday sessions, then dropped out. Most significantly, Harvard University's Graduate School of Medicine says Robin Givens never dropped out of its medical school, because she never attended Harvard to begin with. Other than that, the biography was accurate!

Once she settled into the Hollywood scene, Givens moved on the fast track. Run-of-the-mill successful men weren't good enough for her, apparently. Her sights were set higher. The hottest star in basketball was Michael Jordan of the Chicago Bulls in the National Basketball Association. He is one of perhaps half a dozen superstars of American sports. A spokesman for the agency that represents Jordan acknowledges that Givens 'wanted to meet him because of who he was'. She sent them some photos of herself, and asked that they be passed along to Jordan, along with her wishes to get together with him. Jordan's people say they only met a couple of times, and that was it. In reality, the two shared a hot and heavy relationship over a period of time longer than just two of three meetings. But Jordan quickly bailed out of the relationship.

Another of Givens's paramours was one of Hollywood's hottest box office attractions, Eddie Murphy. Givens set her sights on landing this most eligible bachelor, and Reuben Givens told a TV interviewer he thought for a while that Eddie Murphy was indeed going to be his son-in-law, but his relationship with Givens also came to an end.

Tyson was certainly unaware of his girlfriend's checkered past, along with that of her domineering mother, when he became involved. Even had he known, it's doubtful the unsophisticated young man would have believed any of it or indeed cared, so obsessed was he with possessing this delicate, feminine creature. Their relationship continued on its bumpy course for eleven months, interrupted constantly by his training schedule and fights, her television commitments in Hollywood, both necessitating long separations, and by their regular heated arguments, usually provoked by Mike's keeping a stable of girlfriends on the side while he pursued Robin. But he pursued her relentlessly, and she said she liked that, that she had never had a man so bent on 'claiming her' as his own. Tyson set out to win her affection by lavishing gifts on her. Starting with a five-carat diamond ring, the jewellery and other baubles piled up, hundreds of thousands of dollars' worth. For the first time in his life, Mike was able to give expensive, material tokens of his love to someone, and he liked the feeling. So did Robin. Now, however, as 1988 loomed on the horizon, so did Tyson's biggest professional challenge to date, and he had to divert his attention from Robin to face it head on. Larry Holmes, the great former champion who had dominated the division for seven years until his narrow loss to Michael Spinks in 1985, was coming out of retirement to challenge Tyson's claim to the title.

On June 9, 1978, Larry Holmes had pounded out a 15-round decision over Ken Norton in one of the classic toe-to-toe heavyweight slugfests of all time to win the WBC Heavyweight Championship. Over the next seven years, he had ducked no challengers. Taking on all comers, he had carved out widespread recognition as the real heavyweight champion, while the WBA belt was passed back and forth among a host of heavyweight nonentities. Holmes won 48 consecutive fights without a loss, and grew rich defending his title. At the age of 35, he had one more goal in boxing, to surpass the record of Rocky Marciano, who retired as undefeated champion in 1956 with a perfect 49-and-0 record. Holmes aimed to have two more fights, then retire with an unblemished 50-and-0 record to oversee his varied business interests. For his 49th fight, the one that would put him even with Marciano, his opponent was Michael Spinks. Either way, it would be a history-making fight, for if Spinks won, he would become the first light-heavyweight champion in history to win the heavyweight title. They met on September 22, 1985, and on that night, the years caught up with Larry Holmes. Out-hustled by Spinks, Holmes lost a close but unanimous decision in Las Vegas, and with it went his Heavyweight Championship and his hopes of wiping the great Marciano's record off the books. Afterwards, a bitter and intemperate Holmes lashed out, saying that, if the truth be known, 'Rocky Marciano couldn't carry my jock strap'. His ill-conceived remarks, directed at a dead man and an icon of the sport, caused him some unpopularity. But for someone intent on continuing his career, he made an even bigger strategic mistake: he openly criticized the Nevada boxing judges who he felt had robbed him of his title, saying they were drunks and incompetents. The judges had long memories, and when Holmes signed to fight Spinks in a rematch at Las Vegas, his fate was essentially sealed. The second time around, on April 19, 1986, Holmes defeated Spinks fairly handily, and most independent observers acknowledged Larry's superiority that night. When the decision was announced, however, the Nevada judges, by a 2-to-1 vote, had seen to it that the title stayed with Spinks. Always conscious of his inability to capture the public imagination the way his predecessor, Muhammad Ali, had done, Holmes was now more bitter than ever. With the boxing establishment obviously out to get him – at least in his own mind – he had no choice but to announce his retirement. Back in his home town of Easton, Pennsylvania with his wife and children, he watched over his business investments. He had done well. He had achieved fame in the ring as 'The Easton Assassin', and the fruits of his blood-and-sweat labour were apparent. He lived in a $1.5 million home, and had an automobile and motorcycle collection worth a million dollars. He had invested his money in his home town while he was fighting, and owned several properties including a night club/disco, a restaurant, a $1.5-million office building, and a 130-room hotel in nearby Phillipsburg, New Jersey, and he was in the process of putting up a $10-million complex of offices and luxury apartments. But more and more, he was drawn to his modern gym and training facility. At first, it was just to lose weight, but increasingly he was feeling the urge to return to the ring. Tyson had now come on the scene, and throughout 1987, Holmes played a cat-and-mouse game with Jacobs and Cayton, engaging in an on-again, off-again series of negotiations with them concerning a fight with Tyson. But each time he was about to sign on the dotted line, something inside him made him back off. Still, in the end, he wanted to do it, wanted to lance the festering boil that his two losses had become in his psyche. He told people, 'I hated the way I lost against Spinks. I want to get back what was taken from me. I'm coming back to prove something.'

Gene Tunney and Rocky Marciano walked away from the sport at their peaks, retiring with the title, but they were exceptions. Most fighters stay around too long for their own good, finding ways to justify to themselves their reasons for doing so. Certainly Larry Holmes must have thought back to that day in 1980 when he stood in the ring to face the faded legend that was Muhammad Ali. On that October night in Las Vegas, Holmes mercilessly pummelled perhaps the greatest heavyweight of all time. Ali had nothing, no jab, no legs, no reflexes, and suffered the first and only knockout of his career, quitting on his stool. Afterwards, one wag remarked, 'Ali still has a million-dollar punch. He got paid 8-million dollars and he threw eight punches all night.' Ali was 38 years old on that night. Now Larry Holmes was 38 years old, now he was the former champion coming back to challenge the young kid. Despite all this, he had to do it or he would never be able to enjoy a peaceful retirement. For his own satisfaction, he had to try.

Holmes signed with his old nemesis, Don King, and the fight was made for January 22, 1988. Once again, Donald Trump had taken the action away from Las Vegas, and had put up the multi-million-dollar site fee to bring the bout to Atlantic City. Holmes had to bring himself down from 250 pounds, and shake off the ring rust which built up over his 21 months of inactivity. Yes, he was 38, just like Ali had been on the night he had humiliated the former champion, but, he rationalized, he hadn't been through the battles with Frazier and Norton and Foreman and Spinks and Bonavena and all the others that Ali had. Yes, he was 38, but he was a young 38. Conveniently, he chose to overlook the signs of age – the difficulty in getting up and running the miles every morning, how much harder it was to take off the pounds – the fact that his first grandchild had just been born. In his gym every day, he worked with Richie Giachetti, one of King's men, to try and get it all back, to somehow recapture the past.

For Tyson, the fight would be the first in his seven-bout, $26.5-million new contract with HBO. Specifically, his payday for this one would be $5-million, but he would also receive site fee money and foreign television rights fees that would double the HBO $5-million. The game plan laid out by Cayton and Jacobs for Tyson in 1988 would bring the 21-year-old fighter a mind-boggling $50-million in gross earnings, more in one year than Dempsey, Louis, Marciano and Ali combined had earned in their entire careers! But also, a victory over Holmes would be a rite of passage for the young champion. Many experts were saying this could be his toughest test, facing a clever and experienced veteran of ring wars who had been a proud and skilled champion. So many of the great fighters had moved to the forefront with victories over once-great heroes of the past. Jack Johnson had beated Jim Jeffries. Louis had risen with victories over Carnera, Sharkey and Baer. Marciano, in turn, had knocked out Louis. Ali had done it to Archie Moore, who was nearing his 50th birthday at the time, and then Holmes had done it to Ali.

Jacobs, Cayton, Rooney and Tyson knew that Holmes, despite his age, would be no push-over. They knew he was smart. They knew he was durable. They knew he had power in his sneaky right hand, behind his pulverizing jab, power enough to stop 34 of his 50 opponents. And echoing in the minds of Jacobs and Tyson were the words of Cus D'Amato, who had told both of them many times his theory about once-great but ageing fighters. D'Amato always said that on any given night, a fighter who had known greatness could recapture that, and so should never be underestimated.

During his preparation for Larry Holmes, Tyson's attention was diverted by something unexpected. Jim Jacobs, not only his manager but his closest friend and confidant since the death of D'Amato, was taken ill and hospitalized. Although nearing his 58th birthday, Jacobs had always been vigorous, the picture of health, the supreme athlete himself. Only a few trusted friends knew that for nine years, he had suffered from lymphocytic leukaemia, a secret he kept even from Tyson. Previously, when he had disappeared, he had told friends he was going to Texas on business, or to London to work on some Olympics film deal. In reality, he had gone into hospital for chemotherapy treatments. Now, as the Holmes fight approached, he had developed further complications, and although he chose to keep the nature of his problem a secret once again, he was going into hospital for surgery to have his spleen removed. It was nip and tuck whether he'd be discharged from hospital and in time to travel to Atlantic City for the fight.

Every year, during the Chanukah and Christmas holidays, Jacobs would travel to California to visit his mother. In December of 1985, a month after D'Amato's death, Jacobs was in Los Angeles. He had never told his mother or other family members of his illness, not wanting to cause them grief or worry. On that visit, however, perhaps made more aware of his own mortality by the recent death of his mentor, Jacobs took his lifelong friend, Nick Beck, aside, and told him: 'I have lymphocytic cancer. The prognosis once you're diagnosed is about seven and a half years. I was diagnosed seven years ago. I'm telling you because if anything happens to me I want you to keep in touch with my mother.' His mother and her welfare were one of his main concerns in life, but she was spared the knowledge of her son's illness, for the following December she passed away.

Just as Tyson's career was beginning, the illness worsened. In London on business, Jacobs had an attack in Mickey Duff's office. He grew weak and broke out in a cold sweat, telling Duff he had a blood problem and needed a doctor. Duff arranged for him to see a specialist. The next morning, Jacobs was fine. Duff never knew the true nature of his ailment, despite the nearly 30-year friendship between them.

Following Tyson's victory over Pinklon Thomas in May of 1987, Jacobs suffered another attack on the trip back to New York. He started shaking at the airport in Las Vegas, and grew so weak that he had to ask his wife to hold a small bag he was carrying. On the flight home, he sweated profusely, but rode out the attack, and by the end of the day, once he was home, his condition had improved.

Jacobs could not ignore the fact that his health was now deteriorating rapidly. Following the surgery for the removal of his spleen early in January, his recovery was slow. His release from the hospital came only days before the Holmes fight, and when he arrived in Atlantic City two days before the bout, those who knew him were shocked. He looked very ill; his skin had taken on a sallow complexion, he had lost a substantial amount of weight, and patches of hair had fallen out as a result of his chemotherapy.

On fight night, January 22, Robin Givens was among the celebrities at ringside. Inside his dressing-room, Mike Tyson was ready. His gloves were on, and he wanted to do damage. Minutes before it was time to enter the arena, while warming up, he threw a right hand at the ¾ inch-thick plasterboard wall, which exploded from the force of his punch. Tyson's fist went right through it, leaving huge, jagged hole. Mike Tyson was indeed ready to do damage.

Holmes had vowed to use 'all my old tricks' in the ring against the powerful young champion. He knew he couldn't match Tyson for strength, but he felt he had a marked advantage in experience that could turn the fight in his favour. He was 226 pounds, the heaviest of his career. Tyson was 10 pounds lighter, and won the first two rounds, pressing the former title-holder, landing some big punches, with Holmes holding off the charging Tyson by keeping his left hand in Mike's face, or grabbing and forcing clinches. But when they clinched, Tyson twisted his way out, compelling Holmes to use extra energy to hold on to him. In the third round, Holmes landed some uppercuts and this, combined with his controlling the tempo

of the round, won it for him on the scorecards of two of the
judges.

The final moment of glory for Holmes in a professional
ring career which had spanned nearly fifteen years came in
the first half-minute of the fourth round, which would prove
to be the final round for Larry. He came out dancing, moving, recapturing for a moment the old footwork and the fast
hands. He pumped sharp jabs into Tyson's face, one, two,
three. . .six jabs landed crisply. The crowd responded with
cheers for the old warrior. Sugar Ray Leonard, one of the
HBO TV commentators, was awed. 'Look at the jab, look at
the jab,' he kept repeating. The two fighters fell into a clinch,
during which Tyson popped an illegal but by now familiar elbow
into Holmes's face. Fifty-five seconds into the round, Tyson
landed a left hook to the head, forcing Holmes once again to
clinch. Then, suddenly, out of nowhere, Tyson saw an opening,
and sent a right hand crashing off Holmes's head, clipping the
ex-champion with another elbow to the face for good measure
on the follow-through. Holmes toppled backwards as if he had
been shot. Grabbing the ring ropes, he pulled himself to his feet
at the count of four, shaking his head to try and clear it. He
was obviously hurt, and Tyson knew it. Not wanting to give the
clever Holmes any chance to recover, he moved in quickly. Two
left hands rocked Holmes again, and when a Tyson right grazed
off the top of Larry's head, he went down for the second time.
His champion's heart brought him to his feet again, although
the end was now inevitable. Hurt and dazed, he stumbled into
the ropes and then, finding his feet, walked around the ring to
try to bring the feeling back to his legs while referee Joe Cortez
counted off the mandatory eight-count.

Now, it was time for the kill, and Tyson pounced like the
hungry predator he becomes in the ring, throwing a barrage
of punches. Holmes was very unsteady. He tried to hold
Tyson, to find some way to tie him up and somehow survive to the bell, but Tyson would not be denied. Holmes
did manage to parry a good many of Tyson's punches, but
caught a big right hand that wobbled him once again and
sent him reeling crazily for a moment. That was followed by
another crisp Tyson right to the head. Holmes tried to punch
back and move, but he ran out of room. Tyson pinned him
on the ropes, landing another tremendous right to his jaw.
Now there were less than 10 seconds remaining in the round,
and it looked as though Holmes might somehow survive. If

he could just land one more good shot, take the offensive for a moment, the saving bell and a much-needed minute's rest on his stool would be his reward. He reached back to launch a right uppercut to Tyson's jaw, but the unexpected happened. His right hand, on the backswing, got caught in the third strand of the ring ropes, and for an instant he was a fighter with one hand literally tied behind his back. Tyson fired a right hand at that same second at Holmes's jaw, but it missed and went sailing by. Tyson's speed and reflexes were so uncanny, however, that even as Holmes freed his arm and slid down the ropes, away from him, the young champion was back in position and ready to fire the right hand again. He had re-cocked his shotgun. With Holmes pulling away, Tyson's pulverizing right, with the full extension of his arm, landed flush on his jaw, and he went down hard on his back, the third knockdown of the fight. Joe Cortez had seen enough. He dropped to his knees, straddling the fallen ex-champion's body, and pulled out his mouthpiece so the semi-conscious fighter could breathe more easily. The fight was over.

Larry's two cornermen, Richie Giachetti and his brother, Jake Holmes, ran across the ring to their man, as did the ring physician. 'I want to get up. Please let me stand up,' Holmes insisted, but referee Cortez kept him pinned to the canvas until the doctor had a chance to look at him. 'Richie, get me off the goddam floor,' said Holmes, trying to regain a last moment of dignity in the ring. He was helped to his feet, and went to find Tyson and congratulate him. 'You're a great champion,' Holmes said to the younger man. 'Thank you, you're a great champion, too,' replied Tyson. After regaining his senses on his stool, Holmes wrapped himself in his fighter's robe for the last time, and took his final climb down the ring steps. The crowd gave him a warm ovation, to send him into retirement, and Larry responded by saluting them with one of his still-gloved hands. Holmes said he had no regrets: 'The guy beat me legitimately. I can't make no excuses for that. I just got caught. People will say Tyson beat my ass, and he did. He beat me good. As we all go along, someone eventually gets us, and he got me tonight.'

Mike's next fight was set for March 21, exactly two months away. The circumstances were extraordinary. Tyson would be fighting in Tokyo, Japan. Although he had never been to that country, the Japanese had become Tyson-crazy. Stories about him were flooding Japanese publications, his picture was on magazine covers throughout the country, and the people couldn't get enough information about him. Michael Jackson, the black American entertainer, had had a similar effect on the Japanese, although their homogeneous society, isolated for centuries, otherwise harboured a strong racist attitude toward blacks, Jews, and even other non-Japanese Asians. In 1987, Prime Minister Yasuhiro Nakasone had said that Japanese society was 'more intelligent' than the United States because 'blacks, Mexicans and Puerto Ricans lowered [the] level of intelligence' and literacy rates in the US. The following year, Michio Watanabe, a senior official of the ruling Liberal Democratic Party, who had apparently not learned a lesson from the furore caused by Nakasone's indiscretion, said that American blacks were irresponsible because they tended to accumulate bills on their credit cards that they could not repay and did not intend to repay. Nevertheless, their attitude, it seemed, was different when it came to black celebrities, and they had to have Mike Tyson in Tokyo no matter what the cost. Cayton and Jacobs were able to cut an almost unbelievable deal for their fighter.

Within a few months, egged on by those around him, Mike Tyson would begin making wild, irrational, unsubstantiated charges about the way Cayton and, by implication, Jacobs, had mishandled his money. In point of fact, however, they handled his fight deals, his endorsement deals, and the resulting income with impeccable scrupulousness and integrity, making him the richest athlete in history. Far from keeping him in the dark where money was concerned, shortly after the Holmes fight, Cayton sat down with Tyson in his 40th Street office and spelled out for him the deal they had cut in Japan. The fight would take place at a brand new, $465-million stadium in Tokyo. Cayton had tied in the stadium interests with Nippon TV, the country's largest network, along with the major advertising interests. Mike's money had been guaranteed, secured in letters of credit. When it was all counted, Mike would gross some $10-million, and the Japanese did not even care who the opponent was! It was a $10-million payday for Tyson against anybody they named! Tyson spent more than an hour listening to Cayton's patient explanation. When he returned to Catskill, he made a point of telling Camille Ewald how much he loved and respected Cayton, how patient Bill was in teaching him the business side of things.

Finished with the Larry Holmes fight, a month away from beginning serious training for his Tokyo bout, Mike was free to continue his pursuit of Robin Givens. The previous June, he had told Wally Matthew of *Newsday,* 'I'm never going to get married. These women are all just after my money. If I wasn't rich and famous, they wouldn't want no part of me, and I know it.' In Atlantic City that January he had essentially repeated the same words, yet he was besotted by Givens. He would phone her constantly when they were apart. Her phone might ring at three in the morning, with Mike asking her if she was ready to marry him. Minutes later he'd call back and say, 'Are you ready now?'

On February 7, Mike and Robin were in Chicago to attend the National Basketball Association All-Star Game. Shots of them sitting at courtside and enjoying the game were shown on national TV periodically during the telecast. Only six or seven people were aware of what happened after the game. Mike Tyson and Robin Givens eloped. With just a few friends in attendance, they were married early that Sunday evening in a Chicago church. Afterwards they went out to a local nightclub, where Mike had the band play 'My Girl' in tribute to his new bride. He had acted on impulse. When Robin had finally said yes, he had jumped. He did not even phone Steve Lott or Jim Jacobs to let them know. Had he done so, Jacobs would doubtless have counselled him not to rush out and get married that night, but to plan things more carefully. And most certainly, Jacobs would have strongly advised that the couple enter into a pre-nuptial agreement, so that Mike's assets would be protected. After all, Mike had said over and over that women were just after him for his money.

The next day, when word of the marriage leaked out, Jacobs said he was surprised. All he would say publicly was that he and Mike had a great deal to talk about when Mike returned to New York. Reading between the lines, it was obvious that Jacobs was very perturbed by Tyson's impulsive and secret nuptials. Bill Cayton reportedly said, 'Mike is in love, and the woman he is in love with has ideas.' Both men had Givens and her mother pretty well sized up, and were upset that Mike had now left himself financially vulnerable. But they were caught in a dilemma. Mike was smitten not only by Robin, but by her mother, and so to criticize, or even appear to question anything the two women did, might alienate Mike. And, in any event, he wouldn't want to listen to anything they, or anyone else, might have to say about them. He told *Life* magazine that Ruth and Robin 'display so much class I hope it rubs off on me'. Back in New York, Mike and Robin repeated their wedding vows in a civil ceremony, since, in their romantic fervour, they had failed to obtain a marriage licence in Illinois prior to their spur-of-the-moment Chicago wedding. A couple of weeks later, it was time to head for Toyko, but before they left, the self-willed Givens made sure she asserted herself. She phoned Bill Cayton and told him, 'I'm Mrs Mike Tyson and I'm taking over.'

Tyson went off to Tokyo with Givens at his side, while his two managers went off to hospital. Jacobs's leukaemia was advancing, and more chemotherapy was needed. Cayton had suffered a relapse of endocarditis, a serious heart infection which had plagued him. Don King, the nominal promoter because of his options on Tyson's services, was having his own problems. He was being paid on a flat fee basis by Jacobs and Cayton, and so was not skimming off the millions of dollars he had been able to with previous fighters. The Japanese were making it clear that this was their show, and no interference from King would be tolerated. For a while, they were reluctant even to allow King into the country because of his unsavoury background, and they made it clear that his role would be very limited.

Tyson's challenger would be Tony Tubbs, a notoriously overweight fighter who had held a piece of the revolving-door title for a few months before Tyson came on the scene. It was a fight that would have been hard to sell in the United States, but the Japanese, hungry for a Tyson appearance, were willing to accept Tubbs. So concerned were Cayton and Jacobs that Tubbs should not be a bloated embarrassment, the services of Jose Ribalta, a top-ten heavyweight whom Tyson had beaten on his way to the title, were secured on a stand-by basis. Ribalta would receive a substantial payday just for waiting in the wings. If Tubbs showed he was not making an effort to get in shape, Ribalta would be substituted as the opponent and he, instead of Tubbs, would receive a $1-million purse. To give Tubbs more incentive to take off the extra poundage, a clause in his contract guaranteed him a $50-thousand bonus if he weighed in at 230 pounds. At the weigh-in, he tipped the scales at 238 pounds, thus blowing his bonus money. With the weigh-in taking place a day before the fight, it's safe to assume that by the time he stepped into the ring, Tubbs was comfortably over 240 pounds.

At ringside was co-manager Bill Cayton, his wife, and Camille Ewald, who had travelled from Catskill to see her 'son' defend his title. Ominously absent, however, was Jimmy Jacobs. He and Cayton had kept in touch by phone from their hospital beds in the weeks preceding the fight. They felt that Jim would be out of hospital and in sufficient health in time to travel to Tokyo, although Cayton's situation was more uncertain. As it turned out, Cayton had improved enough to make the trip, but Jacobs had taken an unexpected and serious turn for the worse. Weakened by his chemotherapy treatments, he had developed pneumonia, and so, for the first time in 34 outings, he would not be at ringside for a Mike Tyson fight.

Mike wanted to get the fight over with and then head home. He didn't much like being away from friends and familiar surroundings. He was concerned about Jacobs. And he was bored in Japan. He wasn't there to sightsee, to observe a different culture, to enjoy the adulation of the Japanese masses. He was there to fight, collect his $10-million, and go. Except for a few carefully orchestrated excursions – to the Tokyo Zoo with Robin, to visit some sumo wrestlers for a press photo, to see the film, *The Last Emperor*, which put him to sleep, to attend a Tina Turner concert, which he left after twenty minutes, and to film a Suntory beer commercial, which took him two hours and for which he was paid more than $600-thousand – Tyson spent most of his five weeks in Japan training and holed-up in his hotel room, watching the usual genre of action films that he enjoys. He took most of his meals in his room.

There were two more reasons why he wanted to get home quickly. He had sent Robin and her mother off on a mission while in Tokyo: find a home for himself and his bride. Ruth had picked out a $4.5-million dollar estate, and Robin flew back to sign the papers on it. Mike also wanted to get home to await the birth of his first child. He boasted that Robin was pregnant, although she was evasive when asked directly about it in Tokyo, and her publicist issued the curious statement that the pregnancy 'was not official', whatever that meant.

For only the second time in history, Japan was hosting a heavyweight title fight, the first time in fifteen years, since George Foreman had knocked out the grossly overmatched Joe 'King' Roman in the first round. Tony 'TNT' Tubbs came

into the ring with a No.2 world ranking, and an impressive
24-and-1 record. For a big man – a fat man – his punches
were surprisingly crisp and fast. Using his jab, he fought
Tyson on even terms in the first round, but felt the champion's
power, as Tyson dug rights to his flabby body. He, in turn,
landed squarely with several short, punishing hooks to Tyson's
head.

At the start of round two, Tubbs continued to pump his
jabs into Tyson's face, successfully fending off the champion's
attack. Tyson then landed a solid uppercut, but Tubbs answered
with a right uppercut of his own. The two men then proceeded
to fight on the inside. Tubbs whipped a left hook and a right
to Tyson's head. Tyson came back with a left that grazed
Tubbs's head, but still landed with enough power to knock
the challenger off balance with one minute to go in round two.
Tyson then pinned Tubbs on the ropes, and landed several
clubbing shots to his head. Suddenly, a crisp left hook found
the mark on the top of Tubbs's skull and he slumped back into
the ropes as Tyson dug a right hand to his body. Tubbs was hurt,
and forced a clinch. He then shot a good left hook to Tyson's
head, and followed with a right to the face. Tyson blasted his
familiar combination of a right to the ribs and then a right
uppercut to the jaw. It landed hard and flush, hurting Tubbs
again, taking the fight out of him, and Tubbs fell into another
clinch, trying to earn time to recover, with less than 30 seconds
remaining in the round. When referee Arthur Mercante broke
the clinch, it was apparent how much that right hand combination of Tyson's had hurt Tubbs. The challenger stumbled on
unsteady legs into the ropes. Tyson stepped toward him and
banged a single left hook off the side of his head, opening
an ugly cut over his right eye. Tubbs did a drunken dance,
stumbling across the ring. He grabbed the ropes for an instant,
instinctively trying to stay on his feet, but his legs collapsed and
he tumbled on to his back. Tyson, in pursuit, took four quick
steps toward Tubbs and threw a final left hook, which missed
as Tubbs sank to the canvas. Even as Tubbs was beginning to
fall, his trainer, Odell Hadley, was jumping into the ring to end
the fight. Tubbs probably could have made it to his feet and
survived into the third round, but to what purpose? He and
Hadley had no doubt agreed before the fight that the trainer
would stop it as soon as there were any signs Tubbs was hurt.
He was earning the same million dollars whether he took more
punishment or less, so why not opt for less, grab the money, and

In 1982 at the US Junior Olympics in Colorado, a 16-year-old Mike Tyson breaks down and cries before his championship fight and is comforted by trainer Teddy Atlas. (*'Watch Me Now'/Michael Marton*)

16-year-old Mike Tyson gives an affectionate kiss to his trainer, Teddy Atlas, before his 1982 championship victory in the US Junior Olympics. (*'Watch Me Now'/Michael Marton*)

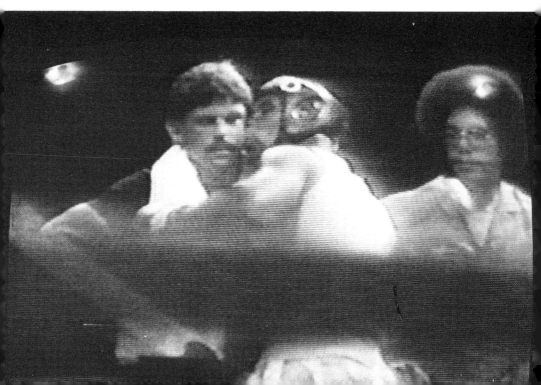

Mike Tyson shares a quiet moment in Catskill with his pigeons. When he needs to escape from the pressures and tensions of life, he retreats to Catskill and spends time with his birds. (*Peter Heller*)

From left to right: Cus D'Amato is joined by Floyd Patterson, Mike Tyson and Jose Torres after an early Tyson victory in 1985. (*The Big Fights, Inc.*)

Tyson practises his defensive moves by bobbing and weaving away from a small sandbag in the gym above the police station on Catskill's Main Street. (*Peter Heller*)

The morning after his title victory over Trevor Berbick, a smiling Mike Tyson is flanked by co-managers Bill Cayton (left) and Jim Jacobs on the flight back to New York. Tyson is wearing his newly-won WBC title belt. (*The Big Fights, Inc.*)

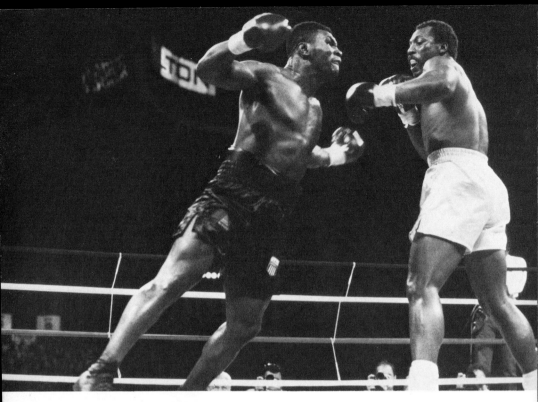

Tyson launches a furious attack to knock out former champion Pinklon
Thomas in a 1987 title defence at Las Vegas. (*The Big Fights, Inc.*)

Tyson's January 1988 title defence against once-great but faded former
champion Larry Holmes ended in a fourth round KO at Atlantic City.
(*Don King Productions*)

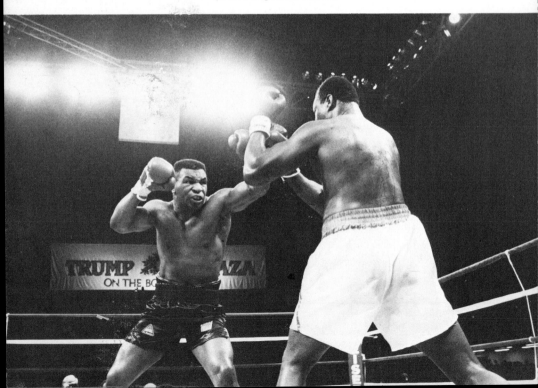

Tyson works out in his Catskill gym with trainer Kevin Rooney. Rooney took Tyson through the latter part of his amateur career and through his first 35 professional fights, including eight heavyweight championship bouts, until the two split before the Frank Bruno fight. (*Peter Heller*)

Tyson shares a happy moment with his then-wife Robin Givens at their Bernardsville, New Jersey estate during the summer of 1988. (*ABC Television*)

Mitch Green delivers a right hand to the face of Mike Tyson in their 1986 Madison Square Garden main event. Two years later, in a Harlem street fight, Tyson delivered a punch to Green's face resulting in a broken hand for the heavyweight champion. (*George Kalinsky/Major League Graphics*)

After five postponements and eight months of inactivity, Tyson's return to the ring on February 25, 1989, was successful. He stopped Frank Bruno in five rounds to make his record a perfect 36-0. (*The Big Fights, Inc.*)

Tyson, in full Muslim attire, on release from prison, March 25, 1995. Met by Don King and assorted bodyguards, the world waited to find out whether Tyson still had what it took. (*Todd Rosenberg/Allsport*)

Tyson in training. On August 19, 1995, Tyson walked in to the ring against Peter McNeeley. That controversial fight was over within one minute and 29-seconds of the first round, after McNeeley was disqualified. (*Lonsdale Sports*)

head home? Sometimes discretion is, indeed, the better part of valour.

As Tubbs lay on the canvas, his eye dripping blood, and Mercante waved the bout over, Tyson stood in the centre of the ring, legs spread apart, hands on hips. It wasn't the first time he had struck this pose. He had done it two months earlier, after stopping Larry Holmes. It was Tyson's tribute to a great champion of a bygone era. Much taken with the history of his sport, Tyson enjoyed reading about and viewing films of the old-time champions. He felt a direct connection to them. He often wore his hair cropped closely around the sides and back, because that was the way Dempsey wore his. He dressed in newsboy caps and thick wool sweaters with buttons up the front, because that was how the old-time greats appeared in the still photographs and flickering motion pictures he studied. Often he helped lift his fallen opponents to their feet once a fight had ended, because he had seen Dempsey and others do it. And shortly before the Holmes fight, he had seen an old photograph that intrigued him. It showed the great lightweight champion, Battling Nelson, in 1910, standing over a knockout victim, legs spread, gloved fists resting on his hips. Tyson loved it, the champion posing in triumph, and he made a conscious decision to strike the same pose.

On Tuesday, March 22, Tyson returned to the United States from Tokyo. The following day, at Mount Sinai Hospital in Manhattan, Jimmy Jacobs died at the age of 58. Having never realized how seriously ill Jimmy was, Mike was shaken and distraught. In little more than a year he had lost the two guiding, stabilizing figures in his life.

The tributes to Jacobs showed how highly he was regarded in the boxing world. Howard Cosell, writing in the *New York Daily News*, said, 'In the dirty world of boxing Jacobs was a clean man, a man of character. He was proof that boxing and character need not be mutually exclusive. . . .And boxing is that much less a sport without his presence.' Doug Krikorian, in the Los Angeles *Herald-Examiner*, wrote, 'The beleaguered sport [of boxing] suffered another damaging blow the other day when it lost its most eloquent spokesman, Jimmy Jacobs. . . .He was respected and trusted by bitterly divisive factions and his sound reputation was never tainted by rumours of dishonesty – rumours that inevitably curse everyone in the sport, who reaches Jacobs' lofty status. . . . "I never heard a

bad word about him," says Don Fraser, veteran fight promoter. . . ."If there is anyone in boxing who didn't like Jimmy
Jacobs, then he didn't like him because Jimmy wouldn't sell
out," says Gene Kilroy, charter member of the old Muhammad
Ali entourage and long-time Jacobs friend. "Jimmy was very
honest and very honorable".' Ali himself said, 'Jimmy Jacobs
has always been a good friend of mine. I will truly miss him. I
not only respect him, I had great admiration, compassion and
love for this man.' Ali recalled that Jacobs was one of the
few who stood by him in the late 1960s when he was stripped
of his title for refusing to serve in the Armed Forces. Even
Wally Matthews of *Newsday*, who was often critical of Jacobs's
personal style, wrote: 'Nobody had anything bad to say about
Jacobs the manager. . . .[he] was the consummate professional manager. . .as Jacobs liked to say, his only obligations
were to his fighters, and he fulfilled those very well indeed. For
the sake of the fighters, boxing could use more managers like
Jim Jacobs.'

Jim's funeral was set for Friday, March 25. He was to be
buried alongside his mother at the Hillside Memorial Park in
Los Angeles. A sobbing Mike Tyson sat in the chapel during
the service. He was alone. His wife and mother-in-law had
chosen not to accompany him to the funeral of the man who
had played a major role in turning this kid of the streets into
the most successful athlete in the world. Instead, Ruth Roper
and Robin Givens spent the day in New York. Even as Jacobs
was being laid to rest, Givens was storming into the offices
of Merrill Lynch, where Cayton and Jacobs had established a
trust account for Tyson worth several million dollars. Givens
wanted access to the account although it was in her husband's
name. She angrily demanded 'my money' in a confrontation
with Merrill Lynch officials.

Anticipating the worst, Jacobs and Cayton had taken pre-
cautions to protect themselves and their wives in the event
of the death of one of the partners. On February 12, five
days after his marriage to Givens, and six weeks before the
passing of Jacobs, the two managers and Tyson had signed
a new contractual agreement in the offices of the New York
State Athletic Commission. The contract stipulated that if
either manager should die, his 50 per cent interest in Tyson
would pass to his widow. The duration of the new contract was
a standard four years. Tyson signed it with no reservations. He
had complete faith and trust in Jacobs and Cayton, and they

had never done anything to cause him to question that faith and trust. Jose Torres, acting in his capacity as Chairman of the Athletic Commission, but also a friend of all the parties involved, witnessed the proceedings and affixed his signature to the new documents. The contract was watertight, and would presumably keep anyone from trying to muscle in on Mike Tyson if anything happened to Jacobs or Cayton. Looming on the horizon, as both men well knew, was Don King.

The bushy-haired promoter's options on Mike Tyson had come to an end. Jacobs and Cayton, in the weeks prior to Jim's death, had been putting together the deal for Tyson to meet Michael Spinks in a super-showdown in June. They had once anticipated making Spinks and his promoter, Butch Lewis, wait, sweat it out, until 1989, but it was THE match, the big one, one that Jacobs wanted to see happen, and his rapidly declining health made them put Spinks on their immediate agenda. Jacobs wanted to live to see the fight that would cement Tyson's place among the great heavyweights. Don King would be part of the deal, co-promoter along with Butch Lewis and Donald Trump, but King knew that it had long been the intention of the Tyson camp eventually to move from promoter to promoter, making the best deals on the open market. That could ultimately put him on the outside looking in. He knew control of Mike Tyson was essential to his survival in big-time boxing, and he set out to gain that control any way he could.

11

Don King: 'Only in America'

You can't believe anything anybody tells you in boxing. The business is predicated on lies. You are dealing with people who very rarely tell the truth.

– DON KING
promoter

DON KING IS like a vulture, circling his prey, always looking for signs of weakness; waiting, never far away, until he determines it's the right time to close in. In the case of Mike Tyson, King literally did not even wait for the body to get cold. On the day of Jim Jacobs's funeral in Los Angeles, Jacobs's friends, relatives and colleagues gathered at the Beverly Hilton Hotel, before proceeding to the memorial service. Among the mourners was Don King, but his mind was more on 'trickeration', as he terms it, than on mourning. In the hotel lobby, he and a henchman homed in on Tyson, and King told him he did not have to go through with the Spinks fight, even though plans were being finalized. He offered an alternative: he would put together a five-fight deal for the champion at $5-million a fight. A business associate of Jacobs, noticing that King had Tyson's ear, signalled Mike that he wanted to talk to him. Mike came over, and Jacobs's friend told him, 'Mike, just be aware of one thing. Now that Jim is gone, people are going to be making moves on you.' Gesturing toward King across the lobby, Tyson replied, 'I know it. That motherfucker is trying already.' Jay Bright, one of Cus's 'boys' from Catskill, also saw what was going on and warned Tyson. But Mike Tyson was fresh meat, and Don King was determined to hook his talons into him as quickly as possible. King had proved over the years that once he set his mind on something, his will was formidable.

Don King was born in 1932 in Cleveland, Ohio, one of six children. On December 7, 1941, the day the Japanese attacked Pearl Harbor, tragedy struck the King family in a more personal way. Don's father was killed in a horrible steel mill accident. He was incinerated by molten metal. The family received a $10,000 insurance settlement, which Mrs King used to move her family to a better, although modest, neighbourhood. She baked and sold pies as well as roasted peanuts to support her family.

Don graduated from John Adams High School in Cleveland and says he planned to attend Kent State University in Ohio. In order to earn tuition money, he began running numbers. The numbers racket, nothing more than an illegal lottery, flourishes to this day in the poor neighbourhoods of virtually every city in America. As a runner, it was King's job to pick up the $1 or $2 or $5 bets from people, then deliver the money to the numbers boss. According to King, one day he did not deliver a bet and that number turned out to be the winner. He had to pay the better out of his own pocket, thus wiping out his college savings. That story should be taken with a grain of salt.

Betting the numbers is a way of life in the inner city, and King in later years explained his involvement, with some justification, by saying that regardless of the law, black people bet the numbers the way whites are allowed to go to church or parlours legally and play bingo for money. Why shouldn't blacks, in their neighbourhoods, be allowed the chance to relieve a little of their poverty by hitting on a number and maybe winning a few hundred dollars?

King rose rapidly from his days as a teenage runner. By the time he was in his mid-thirties, he was the undisputed 'policy' or numbers racketeer in Cleveland. Along the way, in 1954, he had shot a man who was trying to rob a numbers house operated by King. The killing was ruled a justifiable homicide.

In 1966, King hired an ex-convict named Sam Garrett to help him with his thriving numbers business. King drove around his Cleveland neighbourhood in a big Cadillac, flashing huge wads of money as he paid off his winners. One day, King discovered that Garrett had not laid off some bets with other policy operators, and the number hit. It was a similar situation to the one King said he had been in as a young man. But he stopped his Cadillac and confronted Garrett in the street, accusing him of cheating him out of $350. King, weighing about 250 pounds and variously described as standing 6'1", 6'2", or 6'4" tall, became involved in a brawl with the much smaller Garrett which ended with Garrett's head banging on the concrete, causing a severe brain injury. A week later, Sam Garrett died, and King was tried and convicted of second-degree murder. Subsequently, the murder conviction was reduced to manslaughter. King was sentenced to serve ten years in the Marion, Ohio, Correctional Institute.

He used his time in prison to read and study, and he was paroled on September 30, 1971, after serving just 3 years and 11 months of his sentence (years later, an outgoing Governor of Ohio, in his final week in office, would grant the successful boxing promoter a pardon). Exactly four years to the day after his release from prison, Don King would be the promoter of the climactic 'Thrilla in Manila', the classic third meeting between Muhammad Ali and Joe Frazier, for the Heavyweight Championship of the World. His meteoric rise to the top of the boxing world is a remarkable story, and was achieved through a combination of his considerable intelligence, his seemingly limitless energy, his driving ambition, his predatory nature, the clever use of his colour to develop bonds with important blacks in boxing, and his instinctive ability to exploit to his advantage the laissez-faire atmosphere in the sport. 'All the way through boxing I have played by the rules,' he has said. The trouble is, in boxing there are few rules, and fewer still that can't be bent and manipulated.

Deciding to get involved in boxing after his release from prison, he bought in on the career of rising heavyweight Earnie Shavers, who was then managed by Blackie Gennaro of Youngstown, Ohio, and former Major League pitcher Dean Chance. King bought Chance out for $8-thousand, then acquired the contracts of two more fighters, heavyweight Jeff Merritt, who had the potential to become a top contender but eventually fell by the wayside after developing a drug habit, and light-heavyweight contender Ray Anderson, who rose eventually to a number-one world ranking and a title shot. Thus was launched the career of Don King.

In addition, King approached Muhammad Ali and asked him if he would take part in a charity boxing exhibition to benefit Forest City Hospital. Ali initially did not want to get involved with King, saying the fledgling boxing manager was a mobster. But having checked around and found out that the hospital benefit was a legitimate charity affair, Ali agreed to take part. In this way, King got to know Ali, and Ali's manager, Herbert Muhammad.

At the time, Joe Frazier was champion, and King succeeded in getting an introduction to Smokin' Joe through Ohio boxing promoter Don Elbaum, who promoted Shavers's fights. King flew to Jamaica when Frazier was to defend his title in Kingston against George Foreman. He walked to the ring with Frazier and his entourage. Less than fifteen minutes later, Frazier was an ex-champion, knocked out in the second round by Foreman. King quickly switched allegiance, turning up with a big smile on his face among the celebrants in the new champion's corner.

The following year, 1974, King became involved in a company called Video Techniques, which promoted and handled the closed-circuit TV of Foreman's title defence against Ken Norton in Caracas, Venezuela. King says he was the company's 'token nigger', but said he needed the association with Video Techniques and a major fight in order to establish his credibility and make himself in the eyes of the boxing world more than just 'a wild nigger from Cleveland'.

King next went to Ali's manager, Herbert Muhammad, and told this son of the Black Muslim leader, Elijah Muhammad, that he wanted the chance to promote a fight between Ali and Foreman. He told Herbert, 'God has put me here to do this. You must give me the chance because your father said in his holy words that if you find a black man comparable to a white man in doing his duties you must give the black man the chance, or else how will he ever get the chance?' Herbert Muhammad may have been a Black Muslim, but he was also a very practical businessman. He told King he could promote the fight if he could come up with the money.

King offered Foreman and Ali $5-million each, a vast amount of money far beyond what any fighter had ever been paid before. Not surprisingly, both fighters found the amount acceptable. Now all King had to do was to come up with the $10-million in guarantees. He went first to Britain's Hemdale Corporation and got them to back the promotion with $1-million in front money. King, always thinking, then came up with another idea. He would make this a black event, two black men fighting for the heavyweight crown, both managed by black men, in a fight promoted by a black man, so what better place to stage it than in the heart of a black consciousness and black history – Africa? King took off for Zaire, and arranged an audience with President Mobutu Sese Seko. He proposed that President Mobutu back the fight with $10-million of his poverty-stricken country's money, telling him that world attention would be focused on Zaire in the months and weeks leading to the fight, which would give the new nation worldwide prestige. The name of Zaire (and, by the way, that of Mobutu) would become known throughout the globe. Mobutu agreed to put up the $10-million to bring the Foreman-Ali fight to the capital city of Kinshasa. And so, the 'Rumble in the Jungle', as it was billed, had been made, and a new company, Don King Productions, was in the boxing business in a big way.

When Muhammad Ali was champion, Bob Arum promoted many of his title fights. King and Arum had had a few conflicts in the early 1970s, when Arum was the dominant promotional power in the heavyweight division and King was starting to climb the ladder. On October 30, 1974, Ali knocked out Foreman in a major upset to regain the heavyweight title, and now it was Don King, not Bob Arum, who had the inside track with Muhammad Ali and Herbert Muhammad.

King promoted Ali's title defences against Chuck Wepner, Ron Lyle and Joe Bugner. Then, on October 1, 1975 (September 30 in the US, across the International Date Line) in Manila, he staged Ali-Frazier III, considered to be one of the greatest heavyweight fights of all time. As he had done in Zaire, he persuaded Filipino President Ferdinand Marcos to foot the bill for the big show in exchange for worldwide exposure for his nation and himself.

Whereas Jim Jacobs and Bill Cayton prided themselves on having concern for their fighters as people and on looking out for their financial welfare, and were respected in boxing circles for doing so, Don King treats the fighters he has been involved with simply as commodities to be used for his advantage, and to be discarded when their commercial usefulness has been sucked dry. This pattern of operating can be traced back to King's earliest days in boxing.

Ernie Butler, an elderly black man, was the first to experience Don King's methods. A small-time trainer in the small town of Easton, Pennsylvania, Butler has spent his life in boxing. In the late 1960s, he found a young boy on the streets of Easton who showed some promise. His name was Larry Holmes. Butler took the youngster and nurtured him through the amateurs, then turned him pro in 1972. Holmes began winning consistently, and became a local attraction around Scranton, a hotbed of boxing in eastern Pennsylvania. One night in 1973 Don King was there and saw him in action. He liked what he saw, and talked to Butler about becoming involved with Holmes. As Butler was to discover when it was too late, 'all the talk he was giving me was trickery talk. He didn't do anything he agreed to do.'

Butler liked Holmes to box with top heavyweights in the gym, believing it was valuable experience. He would bring Larry to New York City to spar at Gleason's Gym, and he also took him to Muhammad Ali's training camp in nearby Deer Lake, Pennsylvania, to work as a sparring partner with The Greatest. King had a chance to see Holmes in with Ali, and became more determined than ever to latch on to the young heavyweight. He asked Butler to bring Holmes to Grossinger's resort in the Catskill Mountains to spar with Earnie Shavers. Butler agreed, since it would not only be a good opportunity for Larry to learn, but King also promised them a fight on the undercard when Shavers fought Jerry Quarry at Madison Square Garden.

Butler had to leave Holmes at Grossinger's while he returned to his regular job in Easton, and this gave King his chance without Butler around to interfere. He began to sweet-talk Holmes with promises about what he could do for the young boxer's career. When Butler returned to Grossinger's, he and Larry had their first argument. Butler had a contract with Holmes, but King found a loophole. The contract had never been executed with the Pennsylvania Athletic Commission, as required. It was simply a contract between Butler and Holmes. King had the contract declared invalid, and signed Larry Holmes.

While Holmes went on to earn millions, Butler was left in the cold. When he began to make noises about the way Holmes had been taken from him, he received an anonymous threat. 'I don't know who it was. . .but I got a threat over the telephone. The guy told me to lay off, or else. I got a wife, two kids, and a house. I don't want nobody to blow up my house, kill my kids, nothing like that. So, naturally, I begin to back off more then, and stop fightin'. . . .How are you going to take a sport like boxing,' asks Butler, 'that's supposed to be so corrupted, how you going to take a sport like that and let a man come out of prison and run it?'

Although Holmes became a multi-millionaire during his seven and a half years as heavyweight champion, Richie Giachetti, who worked with King for years as Holmes's trainer, then had a bitter parting with the promoter but has since gone back to work for him, has charged that King cost him $6-million and Holmes about $20-million by skimming from the fighter's purses. During his separation from King, Giachetti said, 'Don King is a crook. You've got to get burned by Don King to really know Don King. . . .Don King is a liar and a thief, the greediest bastard I've ever known. This guy wants all the money and all the fighters. He talks about fairness and equality, but he wants everything for himself and doesn't want to give anything to anybody.' But Giachetti also acknowledged, 'If I was a fighter and needed a promoter, who would I take? Don King. The man is the best. Don King delivers.'

Holmes's attorney, Charles Spaziani, says that King would take 25 per cent fees for consultation or advisory services. Spaziani told *Newsday*'s Wally Matthews, 'Early in Larry's career we had to make a decision. Either you let Don King take advantage of you and make half a million dollars or stay away from Don King and get no fights that are above the $20-thousand to $25-thousand range, because Don had all the heavyweights tied up.'

Holmes had a love/hate relationship with King throughout his career. Now that he is retired from boxing and financially secure, Holmes is more willing to talk freely: 'Don would say, "I'm going to give you $3-million for a fight," and I'd say, "Great." Then Don would say, "I got to get 25 per cent of that." That's the way Don did it. . . .The only mistake I made in my whole career was getting tied up with Don King. I was exploited, used and abused,' he told Matthews. 'I listened to all of King's black talk. . .he sells it to you. He tells you, "We're both brothers, let's get all the money we can together." I thought I would be protected.'

Over the years, King has been nothing if not resilient. He is the Teflon Man of boxing. Nothing sticks to him. He has demonstrated a remarkable ability to slide out of jams with minimal damage to himself. Twice he was investigated by grand juries, but was never indicted. In 1983, it was reported that King was the central figure in an investigation into boxing being conducted by the US Attorney's Organized Crime Strike Force unit. He was not indicted. The FBI also investigated him. Joe Spinelli, who spearheaded that operation for the FBI, spent a considerable amount of time in Catskill talking with Cus D'Amato about Don King and about the involvement of organized crime in boxing, going back to the days of the IBC. D'Amato must have been convinced that the FBI was going to nail King: he confided to intimates that when King went to jail, Jimmy Jacobs would move in to fill the vacuum and become the main power in boxing. Cus would then regain his manager's licence and once again move to the forefront, handling much of boxing's top talent. This was in the early 1980s, and it proved a pipe dream. The FBI investigation came to nothing, and King remained firmly in control of the heavyweight division and many fighters and champions in other weight divisions as well.

On December 13, 1984, King and his assistant, Connie Harper, were indicted by a federal grand jury on 23 counts of income tax evasion, filing false and fraudulent income tax returns, and conspiring to conceal more than $1-million in unreported income. The case went to trial. When it was over, King walked away a free man, while Miss Harper was convicted and went to prison for several years.

Publicly, King makes light of his situations. 'I'm a victim of trickeration. I think I'm destined to be investigated until I die,' he says, and blames his plight on the fact that he is a black man whom the establishment is out to get. But when it comes down to brass tacks, King plays hardball when cornered. In one lawsuit filed against him, he refused to answer any questions, pleading the Fifth Amendment against self-incrimination no fewer than 364 times.

Perhaps the best example of King's ability to rise like a phoenix from the ashes occurred in 1977. He had gone to ABC Sports in 1976 and sold the television network a new concept in boxing he had dreamed up, the United States Boxing Championships. The tournament would begin in January, 1977, and would eventually crown US Champions in eight major weight divisions. It would provide young fighters on the rise with an opportunity to move to the forefront of boxing, gain valuable national TV exposure, and earn modest but substantial purses as they progressed through the competition. ABC agreed to finance the tournament with an investment of between $1.5- and $2-million, and committed 23 hours of national broadcast time to televising it over the course of six months. To give the tournament credibility, King had enlisted the services of 'The Bible of Boxing', the prestigious *Ring* magazine, whose ratings of fighters had been widely respected for more than fifty years. At this time, 1976, few in boxing paid much attention to the banana-republic WBC and WBA. *Ring* was to be paid a fee of $70,000 in exchange for providing special ratings of just US fighters, from whom the tournament participants would be selected. The association of *Ring* with the tournament would ensure the integrity of the US Championships, which was critical to ABC.

The tournament had barely got off the ground when charges of all sorts of irregularities began flying about. It was later established that, as a pre-condition, any fighter invited to participate had to sign a contract giving Don King the option on three fights should he win the tournament. The editor at *Ring* magazine in charge of the ratings was John Ort. It was also established that King had paid Ort $5,000 in cash. It has been alleged that Ort played all sorts of games with the ratings, although he always vigorously denied any wrongdoings. Two King associates, boxing managers Paddy Flood and Al Braverman, were paid $20-thousand fees each to help administer the tournament and serve as consultants. Eight middleweights were invited to participate, but they did not include one of the best in the division, Marvin Hagler, despite Hagler's 38-and-2 record. However, three fighters Hagler had beaten were invited to take part. Hagler charged that he was blacklisted from the tournament because he had refused an ultimatum to take Flood and Braverman as his new managers.

In December, 1976, ABC's boxing consultant, Alex Wallau, sent two memos to one of the sports department's senior executives, outlining other flagrant examples of how the tournament was being rigged with fighters who did not deserve rankings but who received them because they were in some way connected with King and his cronies. Among the examples cited by Wallau were: Mike Colbert, 'a Portland prospect who has been unconscionably promoted by Ort on behalf of his rumoured partner Mike Morton of Seattle who manages Colbert. His number one ranking in *Ring* Magazine is laughable'; Paddy Dolan, managed by Paddy Flood, and John Sullivan, 'White club fighters who have never fought a main event or an opponent of any reputation. . . .two disgraceful examples of King handing $15,000 to Paddy Flood and his friends'; Hilbert Stevenson, 'an unknown unproven nonentity'; Juan Cantres, '[An] embarrassment. . .an unskilled club fighter'; Biff Cline, 'Perhaps the greatest example of King's pay-offs to Ort and Ort's lack of integrity lies in the inclusion of Donald "Biff" Cline in the light-heavyweight division. He has never even fought as a light-heavyweight. The only reason he will collect a paycheck of $10,000 is his father, Chris Cline.' Chris Cline was a Baltimore manager rumoured to be a business partner of John Ort.

In addition to Wallau's conclusion that 31 of the 56 fighters invited to participate were not qualified, it was shown that at least eleven of them had been credited with phoney victories to beef up their records. Ike Fluellen of Houston, Texas, had not fought in more than a year, yet was credited with two victories in 1976 and received an honourable mention by Ort in *Ring* for the 1976 *Ring* Progress Award! Fluellen subsequently told ABC executives that he had received a call from Chris Cline, who told him he could get the inactive fighter ranked in *Ring*'s US top-ten ratings, which would earn him a place in the tournament and some good money. Fluellen therefore told Cline he could represent him. Sure enough, the next month, Fluellen was rated number ten. Cline then told Fluellen he would be moved up in the ratings; without a fight, he was jumped to number three in the February 1977 issue of *Ring*, and was even more surprised to see that he had also been added to the world rankings, without having fought in more than a year! Fluellen was in the tournament, and, of course, the 'connected' Cline would be getting a big cut of his purse money. But when ABC made inquiries about Fluellen's charges, word got out that the fighter was causing trouble, and he was dropped from the tournament by Don King Productions. Fluellen subsequently charged that he had received threats over the phone.

Despite all these revelations, ABC went ahead and began televising the tournament. King picked some very interesting locations for some of the bouts, including a US aircraft carrier anchored in the waters off Florida, the US Naval Academy campus, and King's own former campus, inside the walls of the Marion Correctional Institution. Coincidentally these locations were on turf outside the jurisdiction of any potentially interfering state boxing commissions.

During the second telecast, on February 13 (during which, to no one's great surprise, Biff Cline was knocked out in his first bout), heavyweight Johnny Boudreaux was awarded a controversial decision over Scott LeDoux. Following the announcement of the decision, LeDoux became enraged and declared on national TV that the fight had been fixed. This served to focus more press and public attention on the charges swirling around the tournament.

Two fighters directly controlled by King, future World Champions Larry Holmes and lightweight Esteban DeJesus, were in the tournament. That fact, along with the options King had extracted from every other participant, prompted *Sports Illustrated* magazine to charge, 'For a promoter to control – or be in a position to gain control of – fighters in his own tournament is at best unethical. In some jurisdictions, it would be illegal.' The manager of one participant came forward and alleged that he was forced to kick back 40 per cent of his fighter's purse. Then ABC turned up hard evidence of records of participants being faked: Paddy Dolan, credited with four phoney wins in 1975; Hilbert Stevenson, five fake wins in 1976; Anthony House, seven non-existent wins in 1975 and '76, plus similar examples involving at least five other fighters.

ABC persisted with the tournament telecasts until April 10. On April 14, Nat Loubet, editor of *Ring* magazine, admitted that *Ring* had published records that were not accurate, but he put the blame on managers who had supplied false records for their fighters. He told *Sports Illustrated* that King tried to persuade him to fire John Ort. 'The idea was that he could pile everything on John, use him as the scapegoat. . . .His lawyer was on the other phone. I said, "I will not. You're just looking for a scapegoat." All the things he's worried about in his own background, he's trying to keep covered by throwing all the attention on us,' Loubet charged.

King had to do something. He announced he was suspending his 'consultants', Al Braverman and Paddy Flood. It was to late, however. ABC announced on April 16 that it was suspending telecasts of the US Boxing Championships. ABC issued a statement saying, in part, 'ABC believes that the very basis of the tournament has been severely compromised.'

Three days later, ABC retained former prosecutor Michael Armstrong to conduct its own investigation. Armstrong, then in private practice, had considerable credentials. As a prosecutor, he had broken the New York Police Department's Serpico case. Armstrong and seventeen of his law firm's partners and associates conducted the investigation. King, meanwhile, cried race persecution once again, saying it was all an attempt 'to fry this coon'. Because the ABC investigation was a private one, Armstong was at a disadvantage. He was not able to subpoena people to compel their testimony, nor could he obtain documents. Despite this handicap, he and his colleagues conducted the most thorough investigation possible. The 450 page report conceded that many people were reluctant voluntarily to discuss their involvement in the tournament in detail, but maintained that King and his associates, Flood and Braverman, had a financial interest in at least 14 fighters involved in the US Championships.

Here is a summary of some of the findings contained in the Armstrong Report: The US Boxing Championships included 'a good deal of unethical behaviour by individuals involved with the administration and organization of the tournament. . .in a number of instances, Don King Productions failed to take even the minimal steps to secure the participation of well-qualified fighters. . . .In six cases the evidence indicates that improper payments were paid or requested, purportedly in return for getting fighters into the tournament. . . .It is clear that Flood and Braverman, both of whom had financial interests in fighters, had serious conflicts of interest in carrying out their assigned roles in the tournament. King was aware of the facts giving rise to the conflicts of interest, but failed to take appropriate steps to deal with the problems. . . .we believe that in some cases the evidence established deliberate manipulation of the process [of choosing fighters for the tournament] in order to assure the inclusion of fighters whose managers or representatives were associated with or friendly to King, Ort, Flood or Braverman at the expense of other more highly qualified fighters. . . .The most disturbing action by King for which we were able to acquire direct evidence of personal involvement was his clearly improper payment of $5,000 to John Ort which seriously compromised the integrity of the selection process. . .and the credibility of the tournament was seriously impaired by allegations regarding King's interests in fighters.'

The Armstrong investigation lacked the power of the law to back it up, however, and no legally-empowered body chose to pursue the matter, even though seventeen years earlier the IBC was prosecuted by a variety of different legal entities. Although King continued to make charges of racism whenever he came under attack, it might well be that because he was so visible, and the first black to achieve such a high level of success in boxing, an attitude of positive discrimination was adopted when it came to dealing with him. Whatever the reasons, no one involved with the fraudulent tournament was prosecuted, and business at Don King Productions continued as usual. Braverman, for his part, termed the findings of the investigation 'Hogwash and bullshit', although he did acknowledge that he and Flood, who is now dead, were suspended briefly by King. As a result of *Ring* magazine's loss of credibility because of the part it played, the networks had no choice now but to rely on the ratings of the WBC and WBA, thus giving those groups the power base they expanded and still enjoy to this day.

King has carved out his empire by writing his own rules in a sport where he knew he could get away with it because boxing lacks a central governing body or a much-needed Federal Commissioner. Bob Arum is in favour of a federal boxing authority, King is opposed. Those who have done business with King over the years, including numerous disgruntled fighters, say he has established a virtual monopoly by employing the same techniques over and over again. He promises fighters a quick road to a title shot if they sign with him, then gains control over them by including option clauses in his contracts. 'There's nothing wrong with options,' he says. 'Options are everywhere. In movies, in sports. I need to pay overhead. I invest a lot of time and money in developing a fighter and then I deserve to reap the rewards.' But there is, indeed, a problem with options. It leaves a fighter under contract to King with no bargaining power. He has to accept the purse King is offering, or not fight. He cannot sell his services and talents on the open market, choosing the best deal from among the offers of a variety of different promoters.

King has also been accused by many of his fighters of having them sign blank contracts. Another of his consistent methods is to cut a fighter's purse at the last minute, saying the promotion didn't do as well as expected financially and so the fighter must accept less money. And, of course, he will do whatever he can to induce a fighter to sign a contract with him. 'Don King buys whoever he has to buy,' said Larry Holmes. 'He takes a young fighter that doesn't have any money and he puts a thousand dollars or maybe twenty thousand on the table. Boy, then you do anything. Only later do you realize he bought you, he owns you, and it wasn't the right thing to do.' As Jack Newfield wrote in his 1983 *Village Voice* exposé of King entitled 'Don King's Boxing Monopoly': 'King's most successful promotion has been himself. His investors have lost money on most of King's major fights. . .King makes his profit from closed-circuit franchising, subsidies from TV networks. . .and from Las Vegas casinos. . .King is essentially a brilliant con man, who uses what he calls "OPM – other people's money" to make deals as a broker. . . .three champions say King cut their purses after their fights. Larry Holmes, Thomas Hearns and Juan LaPorte all report they were paid less money by King than their pre-fight contracts promised them.'

And then there is King's use of his stepson, Carl, to help him control fighters. Don King moved in with Carl's mother, Henrietta, in 1961 when Carl was four years old. Carl graduated from college with a degree in marketing and management, and Don promptly put his stepson in business. The business was boxing management, and Carl King got very lucky very quickly. Although many veteran boxing managers go a lifetime without ever handling a top contender or a world champion, within a few short years, while still in his twenties, Carl King miraculously ended up as the manager of world champions Bonecrusher Smith, Julian Jackson, Tim Witherspoon, 'Irish' Leroy Haley, Carlos DeLeon, Leon Spinks, Azumah Nelson. Saoul Mamby, and Michael Dokes, among others. Of course, it is not miraculous at all. Carl King works hand-in-hand with his father, since boxing commissions do not allow a promoter to manage fighters.

Saoul Mamby told author Thomas Hauser how he came under the promotional and management wing of the Kings.

When Mamby's manager died, King asked to meet with him and proposed that the fighter sign a promotional agreement with him and a management agreement with his son. Mamby signed the promotional contract with Don, but did not want to sign with Carl as his manager. King used Mamby, a world-class fighter, exactly once in nearly a year, in an undercard fight. Finally, Mamby got the message. He signed with Carl King, even though he had never met him. Immediately, he was offered two easy fights for good paydays by the Kings, and then got a fight shortly thereafter for the junior welterweight title. The bout was in South Korea. Carl King did not even go to Korea with his fighter. Nevertheless, Mamby knocked out Sang-Hyun Kim in 1980 and became a world champion. After five successful title defences, he was matched against 'Irish' Leroy Haley, a black fighter with a distinctly Celtic name, on June 26, 1982. 'Just before the fight,' Mamby told Hauser, 'Carl King came into the dressing-room and told me he couldn't work my corner. I asked why, and he mumbled something about rules and regulations or some kind of obligation. The fight went on. I lost a decision. And after the decision was announced – here I am, I've just lost my title'– I look across the ring, and there's Carl King hugging Haley. I looked over there and said, "What the fuck is going on?" Then I realized that Carl King might have been my manager, but he was also managing Haley. Why is Carl King still my manager? His daddy is the man. Business is business.'

In another King exposé, by the Philadelphia *Inquirer*'s Glen Macnow, a second fighter managed by Carl King and promoted by Don King had much the same to say. Alfonso Ratliff, the

former World Cruiserweight Champion, said, 'Carl became
my manager because Don King said the only way he would
promote me was to have his son be my manager. I didn't want
anything to do with Carl King, but I had no choice.' When the
Kings put Ratliff in against Mike Tyson, he says he received
only $20-thousand of the $75-thousand he signed for. 'He's like
a spider who pulls you in with his money. Before you know it,
you're all caught up in the web and you're at his mercy, and this
man has no mercy.'

In 1986, Eddie Gregg, a fringe contender under promotional
contract to Don King, received a lucrative offer to fight Gerry
Cooney. He was to receive $50-thousand, and the most money
by far he'd ever been offered for a fight, but the Cooney bout
was not being promoted by King, and King refused to let Gregg
take the offer. Gregg signed for the fight regardless, and King
sued in an effort to stop the bout from taking place. Gregg and
his manager, Tommy Gallagher, testified in court that King had
got Gregg just two fights in 1985, although King's own contract
with the fighter guaranteed him four fights a year. Gregg and
Gallagher further testified that they had not been allowed to
read the King contracts thoroughly, and that the contracts they
had signed with the promoter were blank. Martin Stecher, Justice of the New York State Supreme Court, had heard enough.
He ruled against King, criticizing him for compelling the fighter
to sign 'harsh' and 'one-sided' blank contracts, with King left
to fill them in any way he chose. Stecher also noted that in
the previous year, the two fights King had provided for Gregg
paid him just $12,500, one-third of which had to be paid to
his manager, Tommy Gallagher. 'There is no demonstration,'
Justice Stecher stated, 'of devotion of a single dollar or a single
hour to Gregg's career.' Gregg fought Cooney and was stopped
in the first round, but at least the $50-thousand he earned gave
him a little nest egg to retire on.

British promoter and manager Mickey Duff has had numerous run-ins with King. He says King stole top featherweight
contender Azumah Nelson from him after Nelson looked
tremendous in a narrow loss to Salvador Sanchez for the
Featherweight Championship at Madison Square Garden in
1982. Nelson won the title after the untimely death of Sanchez
in a car accident in Mexico. Duff also tells a humorous story of
how Don King tried to steal Duff's top middleweight contender,
John 'The Beast' Mugabi. Duff had Mugabi fighting in Atlantic City on a King-promoted card early in the African boxer's

career, when Duff wanted him to get experience fighting tough American opponents. Duff had other business in England, so reluctantly left Mugabi and trainer George Francis alone. Mugabi looked sensational knocking out tough Curtis Ramsey in one round. Duff got a transatlantic phone call after the fight. King was on the line, saying, 'Mickey, we got a problem. Mugabi is begging me to take over his career, but I told him no. I said you and I are friends, Mickey, so I wouldn't take him on unless he agreed to keep you as a 50-per cent partner.' Duff responded, 'Don, I didn't know you spoke Swahili.' King said he didn't. 'That's very interesting,' said Duff, 'because Mugabi doesn't speak a word of English.'

Rival promoter Butch Lewis sued Don King in 1983 for stealing a fighter from him. When Lewis left Bob Arum's Top Rank and went out on his own, he handled the careers of the two Spinks brothers and heavyweight Greg Page, who rose through the rankings and became a top contender. Lewis testified that King offered him $200-thousand in cash to join Don King Productions and bring Page with him. Lewis turned down the offer. He charged that King then inter-fered with the exclusive promotional contract he held with Page and induced the fighter to leave him and sign with DKP. Lewis said King did it by promising to advance Page's career, and also by spreading about $50-thousand in cash among Page's friends, and especially Page's parents, until they all began telling him that King was the man to go with. Lewis also charged that King seduced Page with a $300-thousand payment.

King's defence in Manhattan Supreme Court was nothing if not bold and frank. He said he did not interfere with Lewis's contract, but that Page came to him because he knew King was the man who held the key in the heavyweight division. To illustrate this, King proceeded to show the court how he controlled, either exclusively or in partnership, not only the champion, Larry Holmes, but all of the top-ten heavyweights in the division. Gerry Cooney, Michael Dokes, Trevor Berbick, Tex Cobb, Leon Spinks, Renaldo Snipes, Jimmy Young, Lynn Ball, Bernardo Mercado and Quick Tillis all were under con-tract to Don King Productions. Therefore, King reasoned, 'Greg Page must, if his career is to develop properly, fight only top ranked opponents. I respectfully submit that, unless Greg Page can fight opponents who are under contract to DKP, his career will be at a standstill. And under DKP's promotional contracts with top contenders, they cannot fight for any other promoter without DKP's consent. In light of Butch Lewis's past and present conduct toward both me and Greg Page, such consent will not be forthcoming.' In other words, to justify his co-opting of Page, King used as his defence the very fact that he already held a virtual monopoly on the heavyweight division! The jury ruled for Lewis, but Page wanted to stay with King, so Lewis accepted a $200-thousand settlement. As far as King is concerned, compromise settlements are part of his business costs, just like rent or staff salaries. He went on to earn much more than $200-thousand with Greg Page.

In 1982, former World Featherweight Champion Bobby Chacon of California, then 30 years old, was offered the chance to fight Bazooka Limon for Limon's WBC Super-Featherweight title. To get the fight, Chacon, a gutsy little scrapper, had to sign a three-fight option contract with Don King in the event he beat Limon. In what was perhaps the most sensational fight of 1982, the plucky Chacon, badly battered, rallied in the late rounds to earn a close decision and take the title.

In the spring of 1983, NBC Sports was planning to televise Chacon's first defence, against Cornelius Boza-Edwards, another of Mickey Duff's fighters. Edwards was ranked No.1 by the WBC, so he was a mandatory challenger. But King decided he wanted Chacon's opponent to be Hector Camacho instead. Coincidentally, King had just signed Camacho to a six-fight promotional deal. NBC said no, Boza-Edwards was the top contender, and they wanted to televise Chacon–Boza. The network did not take into account the power King wielded with his close ally, WBC President Jose Sulaiman. Even though Boza, according the WBC's own rules, was due the title match, Sulaiman withdrew WBC sanction from the bout, and NBC no longer had a world championship match.

Independent promoters then offered Chacon $1-million to fight Camacho, but King, with his three-option contract on Chacon in hand (even though WBC rules allowed a promoter only one option), told Chacon he couldn't take either of the $1-million offers. King said he would promote the Chacon–Camacho title fight, and pay Chacon $450-thousand. Chacon refused to accept King's much smaller offer, so Jose Sulaiman, who brags about all the gifts he has received from his friend Don King, stripped Chacon of his title. Not surprisingly, King's fighter, Hector Camacho, was handed the crown in an easy fight for the vacant title which the dangerous Boza-Edwards was not invited to take part in. As Jack Newfield further pointed out in his *Village Voice* exposé of King, the WBC Constitution said the very multi-option contract that King had trapped Chacon with was against the organization's rules in order 'to promote and preserve competition and deter monopoly in the sport of boxing'. And in addition, multi-option contracts were illegal in California, where King had signed with Chacon but then conveniently failed to file the contract with the California Athletic Commission.

On November 26, 1982, a tough and durable fighter with limited talent named Randall 'Tex' Cobb fought Larry Holmes for the Heavyweight Championship in Houston, Texas. Holmes took an easy, lopsided decision in a fight promoted, naturally, by Don King. Cobb's contract called for him to receive $700-thousand or 30 per cent of all gross revenues, whichever figure was the larger. Cobb figured that the 30 per cent should have earned him as much as $1.3-million. Instead, Cobb says, a week before the fight his manager, Joe Gramby, came to him and said the bout would be cancelled unless he agreed to accept a flat purse of $500-thousand. Cobb wanted the shot at the title, so agreed and signed the new contract for the smaller amount. Cobb charges that, after the fight, Gramby received $200-thousand as a 'consultant's fee' from Don King Productions, coincidentally on the same day he persuaded his fighter to sign the reduced-purse contract with King. Cobb couldn't figure out what consulting services his manager could have performed for King that would have been worth $200-thousand. Subsequently, a letter turned up on Don King's corporate letterhead dated November 13, 1982, which was thirteen days before the Holmes–Cobb fight. The letter is addressed to Mr Joe Gramby, and reads: 'This letter serves as an agreement between Don King Productions (DKP) and Joe Gramby for the Randy "Tex" Cobb vs Larry Holmes WBC World Heavyweight Championship bout, scheduled to take place on November 26, 1982 at the Houston Astrodome in Houston, Texas. This letter will confirm our understanding that in addition to $500,000.00 (Five Hundred Thousand) dollars being paid to Randy Cobb as his purse under contract dated August 25, 1982, DKP agrees to pay $200,000.00 (Two Hundred Thousand) dollars to Joe Gramby for consult-ant services.' The letter is signed by Don King Produc-tions, Inc., and also signed 'Accepted and agreed' by Joseph Gramby and dated November 15th, 1982 in the same hand.

Joe Gramby says he never received any money from Don
King. He says he does not know about the letter purportedly
signed by him. He says Cobb's purse was reduced by $200-
thousand because Cobb did not arrive in Houston two weeks
before the fight, as agreed, in order to help publicize the
bout. Gramby said, 'It was a penalty and it was justified. . .he
deserved it.' This rings hollow in the light of the fact that a
manager is supposed to argue on behalf of his fighter, not on
behalf of the promoter, and also because the $200-thousand
cut would have cost Gramby about $65,000 as his one-third
share, so one would think it hardly in his interest to justify the
purse cut. King has changed his story several times concerning
how much money Cobb was due and why his purse was cut,
but he has always denied all Cobb's allegations. It will be
left for a court in Texas to decide exactly what happened,
because Cobb has brought suit against both King and Gramby,
charging that 'In return for a $200,000 payoff [Gramby] was
to instruct his fighter that a new agreement was needed and
that Plaintiff [Cobb] would need to accept a reduction in
his compensation or the fight would be called off. . . .The
agreement between Don King and Joe Gramby was not intended
to be a contract for legitimate services to be rendered, rather
it was designed as a pay-off to Joe Gramby for his assistance
in inducing Plaintiff to accept a reduction in compensation.'
The case was due to be heard at the time of writing (March
1989).

Playing games with fighter's purses has been a long-standing
business practice of King's. Mitch Green, under promotional
contract to Don King Productions, signed to fight Mike Tyson
at Madison Square Garden in 1986 for $50-thousand. But
Green says shortly before the fight, Don and Carl King came
to him and told him he had to take $30-thousand or there would
be no fight. No reason was given. Green protested and said he
wouldn't fight. King went to New York boxing commissioner
Jose Torres, and Torres came to Green's dressing-room and,
instead of looking into Green's charges, told the fighter if he
didn't go through with the bout he would be suspended and
Torres would see to it that he never fought again in the United
States. Torres, of course, was wearing two hats: he was a boxing
official, but he was also a member of Tyson's inner circle. The
fight went on, since Green felt he had no alternative. He lost
a 10-round decision to Tyson, and claims he was given only
$7,500 of the $30-thousand purse.

In 1986, Green was set to fight Bonecrusher Smith. King was not involved in that fight. But when the promoter needed a substitute to fight Tim Witherspoon at Madison Square Garden, he obtained the services of Smith, who withdrew from his scheduled fight with Green. Mitch Green then filed a lawsuit against Don King, claiming that he had suffered financially when his fight with Smith was called off. Green, himself a 'head case', also confronted and threatened King at a Madison Square Garden news conference. King attempted to have the lawsuit dismissed, but New York State Supreme Court Justice Beatrice Shainswit denied the motion, saying the Kings, father and son, 'juggled contractual relationships when it served their economic purposes'. Justice Shainswit also said the rights of Mitch Green were 'mocked' as the Kings 'charted their respective courses'. Green's case thus remained on the court docket, but the problem with suing King, it seems, is that you have to get in line and wait your turn.

One of the biggest jokes in boxing circles for years has been the use of Carl King as a boxing manager by his father. An effective manager must function in an adversarial position with a promoter. It is a manager's job to negotiate every financial and other advantage he can for his fighter, looking out for his man's best interests and making the best deals for him. As many of King's fighters have asked over the years, how could they possibly expect Carl King to go to his father and negotiate faithfully on their behalf, when controlling those fighters was a family business? Carl King insists he operates in his fighters' best interests when he negotiates with his father. He once said, 'I've gotten thrown out of his office many times,' but he didn't specify whether this was for being a tough negotiator or for failing to fetch his dad's coffee fast enough.

Just how the father-and-son team operates is perhaps best illustrated by the events surrounding the WBA Heavyweight Championship fight on December 12, 1986 between Tim Witherspoon and Bonecrusher Smith at Madison Square Garden, part of the HBO-sponsored Heavyweight Elimination Tournament. Witherspoon had come under managerial and promotional control of the Kings in 1982, when they purchased his contract for $100,000. Owing to several disputes over money in the ensuing years, when Witherspoon felt he was grossly shortchanged by the Kings, the relationship between the promoter/manager twosome and the fighter was strained. Nevertheless, Witherspoon, as WBA Champion, was part of the

Elimination Tournament, and was scheduled to fight another King boxer, former champion Tony Tubbs, in December of 1986. Tubbs, however, claiming he had suffered a training injury, pulled out of the fight. On short notice, the Kings needed a substitute, one who was in condition, ready to fight, and ranked high enough to be a viable contender and acceptable to HBO. In reality, Tubbs was not injured but, like many fighters, was involved in a financial dispute with the Kings.

Bonecrusher Smith was training for a fight down south with Mitch Green, and so was ready to fight. He was approached by the Kings and offered instead what every fighter dreams of, a shot at the title. At the advanced age of 33, Smith knew it would probably be his one and only opportunity to reach for the crown. Not surprisingly, he withdrew from the scheduled fight with Green, left his manager, Alan Kornberg, and signed a contract making Don King his promoter and another making Carl King his new manager. Smith said he knew if he didn't do that he'd probably never get a title shot, since the Kings controlled the division as firmly as the IBC had controlled boxing in the 1950s. Kornberg sued the Kings, who quickly settled with him by bringing him back into the fold as an equal partner with Carl King in the management of Smith. Kornberg, too, knew the reality of life among the heavyweights – and the Kings. It was better to settle than fight.

Next, Carl King went to Witherspoon and told him that Tubbs was out of the fight and instead he would be defending against Smith. Witherspoon did not want to accept Smith as an opponent just days before the fight. He had geared his training to fighting Tubbs, and Smith had a completely different style. Furthermore, he had already fought Smith and beaten him and saw no reason to fight him again. But instead of checking into Witherspoon's allegations of wrongdoing, New York boxing commissioner Jose Torres threatened to suspend Witherspoon if he refused to go through with the bout. Backed to the wall, much as Mitch Green had been, Witherspoon relented. Nicholas Clemente, an attorney for Witherspoon, told Glen Macnow of the Philadelphia *Inquirer*, 'Torres chose to intervene solely on Don King's behalf. It's as if King said, "Jump", and Torres asked, "How far?"' Witherspoon, disgusted with the Kings and all the circumstances requiring him to fight an opponent against his will, went into the ring on December 12 in a lacklustre frame of mind, and was knocked out in the first round by Bonecrusher Smith. Of course, it was a no-lose night for the Kings. Carl King collected his share of Tim Witherspoon's purse as manager. He also collected his 50 per cent share (Kornberg receiving the other half) of the new WBA Champion's purse as co-manager. And Don King collected his fees as promoter of the title match – making it a triple payday for the Kings!

Subsequently, Tim Witherspoon took his turn in line and filed a lawsuit on March 5, 1987, in US District Court in New York. The suit accuses the Kings of restraint of trade, fraud, anti-trust violations, racketeering, unjust enrichment, breach of contract and fraudulent conversion. In it, Witherspoon charges (as have other fighters) that Cart King took 50 per cent of his earnings, even though in all the states where boxing is responsibly governed, including New York, Nevada, New Jersey and California, it is illegal for a manager to receive more than 33 per cent. He also says the Kings forced him to sign blank contracts and to fight when he was injured. He says he was forced to pay Carl King high management fees, even though the promoter's son did not provide him with the services due from a real manager. As an example, Witherspoon said that when he told Carl King he did not want to fight Smith, his 'manager' told him, 'Boy, I don't know if my father will like that. I'll have to ask him.' Instead, Witherspoon contends, Carl King should have taken his side and stood firm against his fighting Smith. But as many, including Witherspoon, ex-champion Alfonzo Ratliff, and New York State Athletic Commission Chairman Randy Gordon, have asked, how can Carl King function effectively as a manager when he is completely beholden to his father, and the fighters he manages are controlled promotionally by his father?

Witherspoon also charges that when he refused to accept Smith, Carl King just crossed Tony Tubbs's name off the contract and substituted Smith's name without Witherspoon's permission, which Carl King denies. In addition, Witherspoon says he was required to train at Don King's Ohio training camp, where the millionaire promoter billed the fighter for everything, including a $113 car rental, a $38 medical test, and new tyres for Witherspoon's car. He also billed Witherspoon $3,500 for travel expenses to a press conference for the fight, which is an expense that should be handled by the promoter, not the fighter. Witherspoon was billed over $14,000 for sparring partners' salaries. But the biggest discrepancy on the itemized expense sheet given to the fighter came under the listing

'Training Camp 28 days @ $100'. That comes to $2,800 for four weeks of training a King's camp. However, in the 'totals' column, an extra zero was added, and Witherspoon ended up being billed $28,000 for 28 days of training! The fighter's total expenses, billed by King, came to over $75-thousand. Such expenses are always supposed to come off the top of the purse, before the fighter and manager divide up their shares. But financial documents from the fight indicate that Carl King first took his cut off the top of the gross purse of $400,000, leaving all the expenses to be charged to Witherspoon's remaining share, which was $200,000 after Carl King had taken his fifty per cent. After expenses were deducted, Witherspoon was left with $125,000. But that was not all. He then had to pay his trainer, Slim Jim Robinson, another expense which is supposed to come off the top of the gross purse. Witherspoon says he finished up with under $100,000, and after paying his taxes, he probably netted $50,000 or $60,000 for losing his WBA Heavyweight title!

Witherspoon's lawsuit contains allegations going further back than the Bonecrusher Smith fight. In 1984, Witherspoon held the WBC version of the title. Don King put him in a fight against Pinklon Thomas, another King fighter, and told Witherspoon his $350-thousand purse would have to be split 50–50 with Carl. Witherspoon went to an attorney, and got his portion of the purse increased from $175-thousand to $250-thousand. In doing so, however, he made the Kings angry. He said Don King told him if the fight went to a decision, he would lose his title. The fight did go to a decision, a very close split decision, and the championship was awarded to Pinklon Thomas.

Witherspoon left the Kings, but had to come crawling back, unable, he says, to get any fights once he walked away from them. Back with the Kings, he got another title opportunity and won the WBA crown. In 1986 he went to London to defend against Frank Bruno, part of the HBO Elimination Tournament. Coming from behind, he rallied to knock Bruno out late in the fight. Mickey Duff, the British co-promoter of the bout, allocated $1.7-million for Witherspoon's end. Then Don King took his fees, Carl King took his cut, expenses were deducted, and Tim Witherspoon ended up with $115,000 out of the $1.7-million that had been allocated to Don King Productions! One of the expenses King deducted from Witherspoon's purse was $250-thousand in 'step aside' money for Tony Tubbs. This is a fairly common occurence in boxing, paying a fighter who is next in line for a fight a fee to step aside temporarily so that a different opponent can fight instead. Tubbs had a contract to fight Witherspoon, which in itself is curious since King controlled Tubbs and presumably could have avoided that situation. Witherspoon says the promoter came to him and told him he would have to pay the $250-thousand out of his end for Tubbs to agree to step aside and allow Witherspoon to fight Bruno. However, Mickey Duff says, he, too, gave King the 'step aside' fee for Tubbs, leaving the distinct impression that King double-dipped for an extra quarter-million dollars. King, of course, denies all allegations. The Witherspoon lawsuit is still pending, and may remain so for quite some time.

Because of the stench that arose from revelations of the shenanigans surrounding the Witherspoon–Tubbs–Smith fight, New York State Governor Mario Cuomo ordered an independent investigation into the circumstances enveloping the fight. Spearheading the investigation was King's old nemesis, Joe Spinelli, who had previously and unsuccessfully tried to nail the promoter when he was with the FBI. Spinelli was now the New York State Inspector General. He found conflicts of interest in that Carl King was the manager of all three fighters involved. Spinelli recommended legislation in New York to prevent a manager from being related to a promoter he was dealing with, to outlaw long-term option contracts between promoters and fighters, and to prevent a manager from having an involvement with both fighters in the same bout.

The New York State Athletic Commission suspended Carl King's licence to manage for one year for failing to notify the Commission he had two fighters on the same card, a violation of a Commission rule. But that suspension did not mean much, because the Kings do most of their boxing business outside New York. Athletic Commission Chairman Torres cried *mea culpa*. He said the Witherspoon–Smith contract was legal because Carl King, acting as manager, had initialled the change from Tubbs to Smith. Torres said he was unaware that Carl King had an involvement with Smith as well as Witherspoon, even though it was common knowledge. Torres had, however, approved the Witherspoon–Tubbs fight, where Carl King also had dual managerial involvement. To make matters worse, the New York Athletic Commission subsequently told the press that Witherspoon had failed a post-fight drug test, only to later recant and say the information was mistaken, but after harm had been done to Witherspoon's reputation. Governor Cuomo was reaching breaking point with Torres. First it was his close, public, unrestrained involvement with Tyson while he was supposed to be an impartial boxing official. Then came his apparent siding with King and compelling Mitch Green and Tim Witherspoon to go ahead with fights they may have had valid reasons to complain about, plus his claimed ignorance of Carl King's triple involvement with Witherspoon–Tubbs–Smith. Finally, reports surfaced that Cuomo found out that Torres had accepted tickets and travel expenses from the Tyson people to attend the Tyson–Tubbs fight in Tokyo. Before he departed, Cuomo made him return them. But Torres's fate was sealed. Shortly thereafter, he resigned from the Athletic Commission, amid widespread reports that Cuomo had forced him to step down.

Because there are few laws governing boxing, Joe Spinelli, while labelling the activities of the Kings a 'blatant conflict of interest', concluded there was no criminality involved. King is simply smart enough to be able to take advantage of the athletes in a sport that is largely unregulated. David Bey, another King-controlled heavyweight contender, said he had to split his purses 50/50 with Carl King, who would not take any action without first checking with his father. 'He was just a front man,' says Bey, 'because Don King couldn't be a manager and a promoter at the same time.' Spinelli says, 'King's contracts are horrible. . .nothing more than legalized extortion. But in the world of boxing, they're legal.'

Don King's oft-repeated slogan is 'Only in America'. On talk shows, in interviews, at news conferences, wherever he can, he is quick to point out what a great land of opportunity the United States is by bellowing 'Only in America!' And he is probably right. Only in America could someone like Don King be allowed to get away with what he has done for the last forty years, starting with his numbers running and manslaughter conviction, and progressing to his octopus-like grip on boxing in general, and the heavyweight division in particular.

12

Wedded Bliss,
Managerial Problems

I think obtaining me was part of Mike's 'game plan' from the very beginning.

– ROBIN GIVENS

NO SOONER HAD Tyson returned from his title defence in Japan than a rift developed between the boxer and his surviving manager. In large part it was because Bill Cayton found himself in a Catch-22 situation. He was perceptive enough to see early on what it would take Tyson, blinded by infatuation, obsession – or love, if you will – months to realize: that the team of Ruth Roper and Robin Givens was not to be trusted. But when he tried to protect Tyson from himself, the fighter took it as an attack on his beloved wife and mother-in-law, and sided with the new women (note the plural) in his life. The trouble began when Cayton learned that Tyson had given Robin power of attorney to sign cheques and financial documents. He had been perturbed enough that Mike had impulsively married without executing a pre-nuptial agreement, and now this new development gave him further cause for concern.

Givens then said there was a problem with Tyson getting access to his money when they wanted to pay for their new mansion in Bernardsville, New Jersey – in cash, over $4-million. There was never an adequate explanation of what exactly the problem was in accessing Tyson's cash. Jacobs and Cayton had $6-million in Tyson's Merrill Lynch account, plus several million more in certificates of deposit and other annuities that would have made him financially secure for the rest of his life even if he never set foot in a boxing ring again. Perhaps the problem was that Givens, as she found out when she went to Merrill Lynch on the day of Jacobs's funeral, did not have access to the money, or that the shrewd Cayton thought it would be more financially prudent of the Tysons to obtain a mortgage rather than plonk down well over $4-million dollars in one lump. Whatever it was, egged on no doubt by her mother, Robin began sending Mike the message that things weren't right in the Tyson financial department, and when Robin spoke, as would be demonstrated many times in the months ahead, Mike listened unquestioningly, time and again turning his back on those who had faithfully served his interests over the years.

The purchase of their home finally completed, the newly-weds moved in and began improvements, renovations and furnishing estimated at a couple of million dollars. It was the house that Mike Tyson wanted, the home of his dreams, where he would live happily ever after with his beautiful wife and lots of children, the first of which was on its way, Robin had told him. Growing up in Catskill, he had gazed at photos of stately homes and castles in Britain and Ireland and vowed he would have something like that someday, and now that day had come. The house was an American castle, named Kenilwood, which had been built in 1897, of stone, in the style of architecture known as Victorian Gothic Revival. It had previously been owned by Sumner Welles, Under-Secretary of State for President Franklin Roosevelt, and other owners had carried the bloodlines of American 'royalty', the Vanderbilts and Astors.

The massive home featured a marble-floored entry hall; a library decorated in all-white, with a white leather sofa (with zebra skin cushions), a baby grand piano, and Louis XV chairs; a formal dining-room with a Baccarat chandelier and a dining-table of mahogany with ebony inlay that seated 16 people for dinner; and gold accents throughout – gilt furniture, and gold leaf on the ceilings.

Mike and Robin had little time to settle in and relax in their castle. She had her TV show and a forthcoming made-for-TV movie that would keep her on a busy shooting schedule in California, and Cayton was busy finalizing plans for the fight Jacobs wanted but did not live to see, the June 27 showdown between Tyson and Michael Spinks, which would mean after April it would be time for Mike to get back to serious training. In the meantime, he and Robin shuttled between Los Angeles and New Jersey, spending what time they could together.

Meanwhile, Don King was getting nervous. He had felt demeaned by his cool treatment in Japan, by the knowledge that the Japanese looked on him as an undesirable in their country. Furthermore, he knew he had no firm deal except on a fight-by-fight basis with Cayton to work on Tyson's bouts. In the coming Spinks fight, he was to have essentially a figure-head role. He would not control the finances or the major decision-making. That would be in Cayton's capable hands, and the big-money worldwide TV, pay-per-view and closed circuit would be run by Shelly Finkel, a firm friend and business associate of the Jacobs/Cayton team. Finkel, a rock music promoter and manager, had bought his way into the lucrative world of championship boxing in recent years, and had relied on Jacobs to lead him by the hand through the unfamiliar world of pugilism. The two had become close, as Finkel, in partnership with Dan and Lou Duva, managed numerous Olympic medal winners, including Tyrell Biggs, Mark Breland, and Evander Holyfield. The selling of TV rights was in Finkel's area of expertise, so there, too, King was superfluous. For the Tyson–Spinks battle, King would be paid a flat fee of $3-million. Out of that, he would have to put together the undercard at a cost of several hundred thousand dollars, and the rest was his to keep. A big payday for very little work. But King chafed at the idea of being just a 'hired hand'. He was uncomfortably aware that he was very expendable in the future, unless he could form an unbreakable bond with Tyson. Recognizing this, and seeing the strained relations developing between the young black fighter and his elderly white manager, King did what he knew would put him on Tyson's side. He decided to ally himself with the women, and set out to win Ruth and Robin's confidence so they could stand united against Bill Cayton.

Kevin Rooney saw what was happening early on. 'All the leeches are out now,' he said, but he had the guts to stand up for what he knew was right. 'I trust Bill Cayton. I knew what we got in Bill Cayton is good.' He remembered Cayton saving him from his own weaknesses. Knowing how Rooney liked to gamble, Cayton had refused to give him his purse money from one of his last fights, held in Atlantic City, until he was safely back in Catskill and away from the temptation of the gaming tables. Over the years, Rooney had seen at first hand the way Cayton negotiated deals for Tyson and the complete fiscal integrity with which he operated; he knew Bill Cayton was operating in the best interests of Mike Tyson. But Rooney was stuck in an awkward position, for to speak on behalf of Cayton meant, by implication, he was coming out against both the women and Don King. By taking Bill Cayton's side, Kevin Rooney effectively sealed his own fate.

In April, before beginning serious training for the Michael Spinks fight, Tyson spent some time at his Los Angeles home with Robin. Coincidentally, Don King also had a home in Los Angeles. Not surprisingly, he spent a good deal of time with Tyson, with Robin and with Ruth. He later claimed he was trying to heal the rift between Tyson and Cayton, but rumours got back to Cayton that what King was actually trying to do was induce Tyson unilaterally to sign an exclusive promotional contract with the wild-haired huckster. Tyson professed suspicion of everyone – except his wife and mother-in-law. He constantly made such statements as: 'People want to be my friend so they can get my money. . . People are trying to steal my fucking money. . . .Do you think I'm gonna trust Don King?. . . .You work all your life, break your fuckin' back, and a guy who doesn't have calluses on his hands wants to take your fuckin' money. . . .I'm gonna wind up rich. . . .They're stealing from me. . .I'm not gonna wind up broke. . . .We all know what Don King is, but if you keep a snake in a room with the lights on, you can control him.'

In May, Tyson and Robin were back east, in their New Jersey home. King, obviously unhappy with his flat-fee arrangement on the Tyson–Spinks bout where he was being paid a mere $3-million on a fight expected to gross as much as $70-million worldwide, let it be known. When he signed the contracts for his participation in the promotion, he added under his signature in his own hand that he was signing under 'economic duress'. Cayton thought this was pretty funny; picking up a quick $3-million for putting together the undercard hardly seemed to constitute any sort of economic duress. For his part, the manager did not want to create any waves. He just wanted all to go as smoothly as possible in the weeks leading up to the biggest-money fight in boxing history. He established a separate corporation, Sports of the Century, Inc., that would receive all revenues pertaining to the big fight, a move he said was made to further ensure protection for all the money due his fighter.

Ruth Roper and Robin Givens, listening to Don King's sweet nothings, continued to nurse a growing suspicion of Bill Cayton. It was obvious they were out of their depth in the unfamiliar and extraordinary world of boxing. They had Tyson retain his own attorney, Michael Winston, who happened to be Ruth Roper's attorney, too. Also working behind the scenes to secure his position in the Tyson picture was Shelly Finkel, who spent a fair amount of time cultivating a relationship with the Ruth-and-Robin team, as well as with Tyson, trying to serve as a conduit between the fighter and Cayton. However, he was also endeavouring to consolidate his own position. He offered to help with his show business contacts in advancing the acting career of Robin, which the family said they interpreted as a 'bribe', and which annoyed Mike, who was well aware of Finkel's financial interest in the TV rights to his fights. With the tug-of-war going on around him the fighter said it was all 'bullshit' and grew increasingly annoyed at the way his wife and mother-in-law were being portrayed in the press as gold-diggers. He constantly said that if his new family wanted all his money they didn't have to steal it, he'd gladly give it to them if they asked.

Despite the love professed between Mike and Robin, things behind the scenes were anything but smooth in the marriage. On the mid-spring afternoon of May 8, 1988, Mike was driving his $150-thousand Bentley down Varick Street in lower Manhattan, near the Holland Tunnel. With him were Robin, in the front seat, as well as the world's most ubiquitous mother-in-law, Ruth Roper. An argument between the young husband and wife developed into a physical confrontation, as Robin started slapping Mike while he was driving. Trying to fend her off, he lost control of the car, and smacked into a parked automobile, damaging both vehicles. Reports later surfaced that the domestic spat erupted when Robin confronted Mike with the fact that she was less than thrilled to find that he was carrying condoms, especially since he wasn't using them in their marital relationship.

Nobody was hurt in the accident, and Tyson made an impulsive gesture of foolhardy generosity that put the incident on the front pages in New York. When two Port Authority police officers who were passing by came over to investigate, Mike flipped them the keys to the Bentley and said, 'I've had nothing but bad luck with this car. You guys keep it.' The stunned cops were delighted with their unexpected windfall. Except for some minor damage to the bumper, the Bentley was in pristine condition. They promptly drove it across the river to New Jersey, and stashed it in a garage. Unfortunately, the next morning word of the incident reached Port Authority Police commanding officers, and all the two cops got instead of a luxury car was a lot of hot water. They were ordered to bring the Bentley back immediately and hand it over to the authorities. At first they refused, saying it was a gift from the heavyweight champion. They were reminded there was the little matter of rules and regulations that did not permit police to accept gifts, which in other circumstances could be construed as bribes. The car was retrieved and impounded, and eventually returned, at the behest of Bill Cayton, to the custody of Mike Tyson's corporation.

The day after the accident, Mike's good friend, Don King, rushed out to buy him a new $175-thousand Rolls Royce to replace the slightly dented Bentley. It was an obviously gratuitous gesture on King's part, designed only to ingratiate himself further with the young fighter, whose trust he was trying desperately to win. When Bill Cayton learned of it, he said Mike would reimburse King for the cost of the new Rolls, making it clear that Tyson could pay his own way and did not need to accept any expensive gifts, especially from Don King.

The fireworks for that week were not yet over. In a telephone interview with sportscaster Bob McNamara of WNYT-TV in Albany, New York, McNamara said Cayton had told him he was fed up with the interference of Don King and the alliance King had formed with Givens and Roper. 'There are three years and eight months to go on the contract. If they try to break it on me I'll take it all the way to the Supreme Court,' McNamara quoted Cayton. 'If, after our contract runs out, Tyson wants me to manage him again, he'll have to beg me. If he doesn't, I'll walk away.' Cayton further said that 'King is winning Tyson with the theory that blacks should stick together. Black trainer, black manager, black promoter, black, black, black.' And he remarked that 'The woman [Mike] is in love with has ideas.' Having spoken perhaps too hastily, Cayton tried to back off from the quotes McNamara attributed to him. He answered inquiries by saying he had been joking, and clarified his remarks to reporter Wally Matthews, telling him he had never said Tyson would have to beg him to continue as his manager in 1992. He had said he might retire at the end of the contract, when he would be nearly 74 years old. If not, and Mike asked – not begged – him to continue, he probably would. As for King, 'He's been making moves all along,' Cayton said. 'I know what King is doing, wining and dining Mike. . . .But I don't think [Mike] can be swayed by it in a business sense. I think Mike has been taught better than that, through countless conversations with Cus D'Amato. Mike knows the way King operates.' What Cayton did not take into account was the remarkable lack of loyalty Tyson was showing toward those who had played the major roles in helping him develop to where he was in his career, and financially, at the tender age of twenty-one. If Cayton had realized this, he would not have been surprised that Tyson was finding it extraordinarily easy to ignore all Cus D'Amato's warnings about Don King. Tyson was angered by Cayton's implications about the motives of his new family members, and called him to express his displeasure. He said it was untrue that Robin had any 'ideas' concerning him or his money, and he did not like his wife and mother-in-law being publicly maligned, since it was upsetting them and turning them into nervous wrecks.

Meanwhile, with Cayton in his New York office putting together all the deals and details that would earn Tyson over $20-million on the Spinks fight, what was Don King doing for his $3-million cut? He was ensconced in an Albany hotel for days, constantly at Tyson's elbow, seeking at every turn to undermine whatever confidence the fighter still retained in Cayton. More and more, Tyson's utterances sounded like the parroting of ideas he was being fed by King. He talked about Cayton and Finkel being 'Jews in three-piece suits', and said that his deal when he fought in Japan had been a bad one. He claimed he had only got $8.7-million and not the talked-of $10-million. Citing the example of the Ali–Foreman bout in Zaire, he said they had earned $5-million each fighting in one of the poorest countries in the world, while he had received less than $9-million fighting in the richest country in the world. Since the Ali–Foreman fight was a Don King promotion, it wasn't hard to figure out who planted that idea with Tyson. What Mike failed, or refused to see, was that Cayton and Jacobs had made a deal on his behalf in Japan so fabulous that the media and boxing people marvelled at it. True, Ali and Foreman split $10-million, but that was for a climactic fight with worldwide interest in which Ali was seeking to regain the championship against Foreman, the reigning undisputed champion and Olympic gold medallist, undefeated and perceived by the public as an indestructible monster, in much the same way as Tyson would later come to be regarded. Each man got $5-million, watershed purses at the time (paid, Tyson failed to realize, by a frivolous dictator bent on self-aggrandizement out of the coffers of his woefully bankrupt nation's resources). Tyson got a purse nearly double that for fighting a fat and out-of-condition opponent who would not even have been accepted by the American public as a viable challenger – hardly a fight comparable with the Ali-Foreman bout.

On May 20, angry with trainer Kevin Rooney for continuing to support Cayton, Tyson moved his training camp from Catskill to Atlantic City. His fight with Michael Spinks was just five weeks away. Two days later, reportedly at the behest of his wife, he summarily fired his friend, confidant, camp coordinator and assistant manager, Steve Lott. He offered no explanation other than to say that although he liked Lott well enough, the man was employed and paid by Cayton, so he couldn't stay. One by one, Mike Tyson was severing all his ties with the past.

On that same day, May 20, on his way to Atlantic City, Tyson and the women met in Manhattan long enough for Mike to close the account at Merrill Lynch which had been established for him by Cayton and Jacobs. He transferred the nearly $5-million in assets to a new, presumably joint, account at US Trust. He also had an additional Wall Street portfolio the two managers had set up worth another $5-million in an annuity plus negotiable securities. Mike had been spending money like water, paying out a fortune on jewellery and expensive gifts for Robin and Ruth, including, for the latter, an $80-thousand BMW automobile.

In an effort to establish a truce, Cayton had dinner with Ruth Roper on Tuesday, May 24. He convinced her that any differences among all the parties concerned should be put on the back burner until after the Spinks fight, especially in order to keep Mike free of worries and on an even keel in his training for what promised to be the most difficult test of his professional career. Apparently he received some assurances from Roper, because he came away from the dinner confident they were all working, at least for the time being, toward the same goal. Cayton succeeded in having Steve Lott reinstated; nearing a momentous showdown with an undefeated champion like Spinks was not the time, he argued persuasively, to make any changes in the people and routines Mike was familiar with.

Meanwhile, Tyson continued to be bothered by the stress which he felt was affecting Robin and Ruth, and himself as well. He talked about leaving the US and becoming a citizen of the tax-haven of Monaco, and reportedly consulted a financial advisor about how much income his nest eggs would provide for the rest of his life if he walked away from boxing there and then.

In an interview with WNYT-TV, his 'hometown' TV station in Albany, Mike stated his confidence in Bill Cayton as his manager, but said he also wanted to work with Don King as his promoter. 'No one can gain control of Mike Tyson, because I'm the boss. Don King is the promoter, Bill Cayton's my manager, and that's as far as it goes. No one's my boss, no one gains control of me. See, that's what people seem to forget. "Control of Mike Tyson", like he doesn't have a brain, he doesn't think for himself. That's totally absurd. . . .Don King has no experience in managing,' Tyson said, somewhat naively. 'He never managed anybody in his life. I don't believe that he's a better manager than Bill Cayton. . . .If Bill Cayton feels like this, perhaps he's paranoid about the situation. No one's going to be my manager but Bill Cayton. As long as Bill Cayton's around, he's my manager, from the beginning to the end. . .to the end of my career, as long as I'm boxing and he's around, he's my manager.'

Tyson professed a personal liking for King, saying, 'He's not a bad guy'. Reminded that Cus had little regard for King, Tyson responded, 'This is business. . .because I don't like you, that don't mean I'm not going to come here and talk to you, do an interview with you. I'd be out of my mind. Business is business. If [King] can come up with the most money, you get him, he's your promoter, [Cayton's] your manager. . . .If they both have my best interests in mind, as they said, then there will be no problem, they can work together. . . .I've been with Bill for a long time and everything's been going quite well, and Don King, he got us into tournaments, got us the fights to get the champions [sic] and everything. . .but the two of them have to become trustworthy towards each other and work together. . . .If they really can't work together with each other for my best interests, then they really don't have my best interests in mind.'

13

Tyson–Spinks: The Making of a Fight

There never were two better men, and none could be more game,
They are both two gallant heroes of honour and of fame.
Then fill a flowing bumper, and jovially drink their health,
May the best man win and conquer, and carry off the belt.

– THE BOLD IRISH YANKEE BENICIA BOY
(regarding the Heenan–Sayers fight)
ANONYMOUS

AFTER STEPPING OUT of the HBO unification tournament early in 1987, Michael Spinks began his preparations for the fight with Gerry Cooney. Despite having failed in his only legitimate test in the ring, when he was stopped by then-champion Larry Holmes on June 11, 1982, Cooney against Spinks would, Butch Lewis knew, be an instant box-office success. In Michael Spinks, promoter Lewis knew he had one of the gamest, most talented fighters in boxing. But he also knew he had a 31-year-old fighter who had been campaigning for ten years as a professional, a fighter whose knees were becoming increasingly feeble with each fight, and, most importantly, a fighter who was never a legitimate heavyweight, whose best moments in the ring as an amateur and professional had come as a middleweight and light-heavyweight. Through a scientifically planned programme of nutrition, strength-conditioning and exercise, Spinks had built himself up to 200 pounds and was fortunate on September 22, 1985, to catch an ageing and fading Larry Holmes on the night Holmes was ready to be taken. He had beaten Holmes closely but convincingly, yet in an April 1986 rematch, seemingly the only people in the world who thought Spinks won the fight were the judges. Everyone else was convinced Holmes had won quite clearly. So Lewis knew there was a good chance a big, legitimate heavyweight like Tucker could upset Spinks, and even if Spinks survived that test, it was an even greater certainly that a devastating puncher like Tyson could end Michael's career. And what if Spinks did stay in the heavyweight unification tournament and met both Tucker and Tyson? At best, he would earn perhaps five million dollars for both fights. Against Cooney he would be guaranteed four million, and Cooney, having been inactive in the five years since his loss to Holmes except for three brief fights lasting a total of barely seven rounds, was beatable. Many in boxing had always questioned whether Gerry really had the heart of a gladiator, and he certainly would come into the fight rusty. Yes, Cooney, though much bigger than Spinks, could be beaten. With his credibility established with a win over a 'name' like Cooney, what would Spinks's services be worth to step into the ring against? As a good businessman, looking out for the best interests of his fighter, Butch Lewis knew there was only one direction to go. Spinks would meet Gerry Cooney in Atlantic City on June 15, 1987. Real estate mogul Donald Trump would put up the money to draw the fight away from Las Vegas and into the gambling capital of the East Coast.

The announcement that Spinks would step outside the HBO tournament to meet Cooney set off a wave of reaction. According to his contract with HBO, Spinks did have the right to fight outside the tournament – provided the winner of such a bout, if Spinks were to be defeated, also agreed subsequently to enter the Unification Tournament. But Cooney's manager, Dennis Rappaport, wanting to keep his options open should his man win, declined to agree to put Gerry in the Tournament. This, combined with his passing on the mandatory challenge of Tony Tucker, led the IBF to strip Spinks of its title. Spinks issued a statement saying he was very disappointed with the action of the IBF; he had always been a good champion for them and had always abided by their rules (except, of course, in this instance). Then, in a jibe at Tyson's claim to the title, won against acknowledged 'cheese champions' Berbick and Smith, Spinks went on to say, 'had it been that I won my title from Tervor Berbick or Tim Witherspoon or James Smith, I and the public may have questioned the validity of my title. However, I beat Larry Holmes, the undefeated, universally-recognized champion, who had beaten Berbick, Witherspoon and Smith, and no one can take that from me by just casting a vote.' *Ring* magazine, for many years considered the bible of boxing, said it would continue to recognize Spinks as the legitimate heavyweight champion. Armed with this, the Spinks–Cooney fight was billed as being for the heavyweight championship. Jacobs and Cayton began posturing in the media that they might now never give Spinks a shot at Tyson, no matter what happened. They criticized Lewis mercilessly, while privately acknowledging to friends that, of course, Tyson would certainly fight the winner, whoever he was.

Spinks entered the ring an 8-to-5 underdog, and even his family was afraid he would be destroyed by the bigger man. His mother, at ringside, was shouting at Butch Lewis that she was going to sue him if Michael got hurt. His six-year-old daughter, Michelle, was lying in her grandmother's lap, crying. Even his older brother Leon, the former heavyweight champion, was crying at ringside as Michael waited for the bell.

The fight itself turned out to be exciting – while it lasted. A sell-out crowd of nearly 16,000 was packed into the Convention Hall on the Boardwalk. Cooney was listed at 6'7", and while he might not have been quite that tall, he certainly towered half a head taller than the 6'2" Spinks. He also outweighed Spinks by 30 pounds – 238 for Cooney, 208 for Spinks. The fight was billed as 'The War on the Shore', but Cooney had little ammunition with which to do battle. His long spells of inactivity, along with the creampuffs he fought when he did step into the ring, had taken their toll. The first couple of rounds were uneventful, Spinks testing to see just what Cooney had to offer, while Cooney did not use his size, his jab, or his once-dangerous left hook to establish his dominance. He seemed cautious, tentative, and couldn't corner the elusive Spinks on the ropes, where a bruiser like Cooney could do the most damage. By the third round, Spinks was beginning to find his mark almost at will, snapping his jab on to Cooney's reddening nose, following occasionally with a right hand to the face. In the fourth round, it was more of the same, as it became clear that Spinks was establishing his dominance. The jab continued to find Cooney's face like a magnet drawn to steel, and the end was inevitable. It came in the fifth round. Cooney threw the left hook that was responsible for so many of his knockout victories, but Spinks countered with an overhand right that landed solidly on Cooney's jaw. It stunned him, and he wobbled, as Spinks swarmed all over him. A left landed to start a flurry in the centre of the ring, and then the punches came rapidly from all directions as the crowd rose to its feet and the shouting became deafening. A left and right to the head ended the flurry as Cooney staggered away. But Spinks would not let his fish off the hook. He followed with a succession of right hands, pounding Cooney's dazed face, until the helpless fighter toppled to the canvas. He climbed to his feet at the count of three, took the mandatory eight-count from referee Frank Cappuccino, and then met the onslaught of the charging Spinks. There was no offence for Cooney to offer, only an attempt at defence, but Spinks was determined to end it here and now. He flurried with combinations too fast to follow – left hooks, overhand rights – every punch seeming to land. Again Cooney fell to the canvas, climbing up slowly to take another eight-count. He nodded at Cappuccino that he was prepared to continue, but he had nothing left. With no control over his legs, he slumped back toward a neutral corner as Spinks hit him with two more overhand rights and another flurry of lefts and rights that caused Cappuccino to jump between the fighters – with Cooney still on his feet but completely helpless – and stop the fight at 2:51 of the fifth round. Michael Spinks had thrown 101 punches in the fifth round of which 84 had landed. Gerry Cooney had thrown 26 punches in the same round and connected with only five. That convincing victory would establish Michael Spinks as a real power in the heavyweight division, the only fighter in the public's eye who could offer Tyson a legitimate challenge.

Jacobs and Cayton, however, adopted an aloof attitude toward Lewis. They felt they had been wronged by the brash young promoter, and now they were in no hurry to do business with him. They would let him squirm while Tyson went ahead and picked up a guaranteed 3-million dollar payday knocking off Tyrell Biggs, 5-million against Larry Holmes, who was staging a come-back, and then a 10-million dollar payday in Tokyo against an out-of-shape Tony Tubbs that ended in two rounds. Spinks, meanwhile, remained inactive. Lewis knew he had a multi-million dollar commodity in Spinks, a commodity that Jacobs, Cayton and Tyson needed. There was no sense in risking overturning the applecart. He was staring the ultimate hustle in the face, and if there was one thing Butch Lewis knew, it was a good hustle.

Ronald Lewis was born on June 26, 1946, and grew up in Philadelphia. His seven-page biography enclosed in the Tyson–Spinks Press Kit says he was an outstanding halfback who 'turned down many college scholarship offers to join his father in the family auto business'. After a stint selling used cars, where (again from his official bio) 'his determination, personality and respect for fairness propelled him to become the business' top producer, surpassing even his dad's output', he began hanging out around Muhammad Ali and his entourage. Using the commonality of race, he was able to convince Ali's manager, Herbert Muhammad, to give him a shot in the

promotion of Ali's forgettable title defence in 1976 against
Richard Dunn in West Germany. Lewis parlayed that into a
job with Bob Arum's Top Rank with the title of vice-president,
Arum needing a street-wise black as his conduit to the fighters he dealt with, who were light-years away culturally and
socially from the Jewish, Harvard-educated attorney Arum.
While with Top Rank, Lewis made the one deal on which
he would eventually build his career and his fortune. He
gained the friendship and confidence of two brothers from
the poorest ghetto of St Louis and, after they both won gold
medals at the 1976 Olympics in Montreal, he beat off all other
promoters and signed them to an exclusive promotional deal
with Top Rank. They were Leon and Michael Spinks. After
just seven professional fights, Leon brought about the upset
of the decade when he dethroned Muhammad Ali to win the
heavyweight title. But seven months later, Ali regained the
title from Leon, and Lewis and Arum parted ways after Arum
discovered about $100-thousand missing from the fight receipts
and accused Lewis – who emphatically denied it – of being the
culprit. Butch was ready to fly on his own, so taking Leon and
Michael with him, he started his own company, Butch Lewis
Productions. Leon quickly faded, and Michael, who had put
his own career on hold during Leon's whirlwind ascent to the
top, fighting just three times in 1978 and 1979, was able to get
back on track. By 1981 he had captured the WBA light-
heavyweight championship, and in 1983, with a victory over
Dwight Braxton, he became undisputed 175-pound champion.
But there was no big money to be made in the light-heavyweight
division, which sent Lewis and Spinks after bigger game in
the heavyweight ranks. When he upset Holmes in 1985, he
became the first light-heavyweight champion in history to win
the heavyweight title.

Jacobs and Cayton maintained their position for a time, saying they didn't need Spinks. On several occasions over the
months, they met with Lewis, but little progress was made.
They were tightening the screws on him, dictating the terms
to him, and, most wounding to Lewis's ego, saying that he
would have no part in the promotion itself, his name would not
appear as part of the promotion, and any money he earned was
a matter between himself and Spinks. After the Tyson–Holmes
fight, Bill Cayton made Lewis a take-it-or-leave-it offer to meet
Tyson in June: $10.8-million guaranteed against 40 per cent of
the profits. Lewis declined. He wanted a $15-million guarantee

for his man. Negotiations broke off. But an unforeseen circumstance now entered the picture. Jim Jacobs's health took a sudden turn for the worse, and although he tried to keep it a secret, Jacobs knew that if this fight-of-fights were to come to fruition in his lifetime, a deal would have to be struck soon with the Spinks camp. Suddenly, Jacobs's threats that 'Mike Tyson will never fight Michael Spinks' were forgotten. Also, there was the perception the Spinks camp was creating in the public mind that Tyson was ducking a showdown against 'The People's Champion'. Everywhere Tyson appeared in public, people would ask him, 'Hey, Mike, when you gonna fight Spinks?' During one encounter in Los Angeles, Tyson almost fought it out with the guy who couldn't let him off the hook about not fighting Spinks. Coincidentally, Butch Lewis was in the same restaurant at the time. More and more, whenever Tyson ventured out, people kept asking him why he was avoiding Spinks, and Tyson grew madder and madder. Was all this orchestrated by Butch Lewis? When asked, Lewis just laughed and said, 'No comment.' Before Jacobs's death in March, Tyson went to his co-managers and demanded that they make peace with Lewis long enough to iron out an agreement and get the showdown with Spinks on track. He was tired of hearing the stage whispers behind his back and the heckling right to his face from fans saying he didn't have the guts to meet Spinks in the ring.

By April an agreement had been reached, and late in the month, Bill Cayton and his attorney, Irving Gruber, and Butch Lewis and his attorney, Milt Chwasky, sat down to finalize details. With Jacobs gone, Tyson was being wooed by Don King, and growing increasingly estranged from Cayton, but the manager held his peace, at least for the time being, in order that the agreement for what promised to be the biggest grossing fight in boxing history, should be settled without a hitch. Lewis had managed to get $13.5-million guaranteed for Spinks – and, along with Don King and the Trump organization, he would be included as one of the promoters of the fight.

When it became certain in March that Tyson and Spinks would fight, bids came in from everywhere to host the event. But from the beginning, it was apparent that only two locales vying for the rights to Tyson/Spinks were seriously in the running: Las Vegas and Atlantic City. In Las Vegas, the Hilton, which had hosted earlier Tyson title fights, thought they had the advantage. But what they didn't know was that the decision

was already a *fait accompli*. Donald Trump had co-opted the
rights to boxing's biggest event more than a year and a half
earlier, before Tyson was champion, when he paid a $100,000
rights fee to bring Tyson vs. Jose Ribalta to his hotel in Atlantic
City. Taking that fight from Las Vegas, though the fight itself
meant nothing to Trump, began a relationship between Trump
and the Jacobs/Cayton team. Then, when Trump got the
Spinks/Cooney 'War on the Shore' and the subsequent Tyson
title defences against Biggs and Holmes, he had extracted first-
refusal rights from both the Spinks and Tyson camps. In the
boxing world of today, one of the main sources of income is the
site fee, a negotiated amount of money paid in order to win the
rights to host a particular fight. In the heyday of Ali's touring
show in the 1970s, Don King had extracted those fees from
individual nations. But now things had shifted to the casinos,
and the big fights were almost inevitably staged in Las Vegas,
until Trump came along. He quickly discovered that bringing
in a big boxing event not only provided worldwide publicity
for the casino hosting the fight, but paid off handsomely at the
tables. On an average Monday in June, the Trump Plaza casino
took in a little over a million dollars. But on the Monday the
hotel hosted the Spinks/Cooney bout, gamblers dropped over
$7-million. They shelled out $8.5-million at Trump's tables on
a cold day in January when Tyson fought Holmes. Trump paid
Don King a site fee of $3.5-million to win the rights to stage
Tyson's October 1987 defence against Tyrell Biggs. He was
overly generous in agreeing to pay that amount, but it won
him the first refusal on Tyson/Spinks. Not that he didn't pay
dearly for it. The Trump Organization paid a record site fee
of $11-million, $4.5-million above the previous record site fee
when Caesar's Palace paid $6.5-million to stage the Sugar Ray
Leonard–Marvellous Marvin Hagler Middleweight Championship fight on April 6, 1987. Some felt he had paid too much,
but as Trump himself modestly said, 'Any fight I've wanted to
get, I've been able to get.' The money didn't matter. One way
or the other, he would make it up. What did matter was that he
had once again taken the play away from Las Vegas. Las Vegas
Hilton chief John Giovenco, furious at what he perceived as a
double-cross by Bill Cayton, could only strike back at Trump
by saying, 'The casino operations in Atlantic City have been an
embarrassment to New Jersey'.

The foot soldier who put the fight together for Trump was
Mark Grossinger Etess, of the famous Grossinger hotel family,

the President of the Trump Plaza. Etess had just four days to add up the numbers, consider the options, and see if the $11-million site fee was viable. If he faltered, Giovenco and the Hilton were more than willing to step in and bring the fight to Las Vegas. With 2,300 ringside seats priced at $1,500 each – the highest ever for a fight ticket – Etess felt the plan could fly. He called Trump to tell him. Trump told him to go ahead and make the deal, but on one condition. He wanted a guarantee that he had the option to stage a future extravaganza between Tyson and boxing's rising young star in 1988, Evander Holyfield.

Home Box Office offered $3.1-million for the rights to show the fight on a tape-delay basis, but in the United States, the world's biggest market for spectacular events, this fight – like Leonard/Hoarns, Hagler/Leonard and the Ali/Frazier fights – was too big to give away on home or cable TV. Instead, it would be offered on an admission-paying basis at 1,600 sites around the country, ranging from large theatres and sports arenas like Madison Square Garden in New York or the Coast Coliseum in Biloxi, Mississippi, to exclusive supper clubs where dinner and the fight telecast could cost as much as $200 per person. Most arenas would charge between $25 and $50 a ticket. If interest in the fight peaked as expected, those closed-circuit locations could produce an estimated $35-million in revenue.

The mastermind behind this huge enterprise was Lou Falcigno, the 50-year-old president of Momentum Enterprises, headquartered in New York City.

While all this planning was going on, the fighters fell into their training routine. At the Concord Hotel in the mountain resort of Kiamesha Lake, New York, Spinks was under the supervision of the legendary trainer Eddie Futch, who looked, acted, and sounded a dozen years younger than his actual age of 77. For more than four decades, Futch had worked with champions and top contenders including Joe Frazier and Larry Holmes. He was a rarity: knowledgeable, intelligent, modest, gentlemanly and universally respected. Working with him was his heir apparent, Hedgemon Lewis, a top welterweight of the 1970s who fought three times for the world title and briefly held New York State recognition as Welterweight Champion. Lewis had retired in 1976 and was now serving his apprenticeship as a trainer. Among Spinks's sparring partners were two men who physically resembled the short, stocky Tyson – Bernard 'Bull' Benton, who had once been Cruiserweight Champion, and Dwight Muhammad Qawi, the former Dwight Braxton, who had been Light-Heavyweight Champion until dethroned by Spinks. The training facility was set up in a large recreation hall behind the Concord's main building, and each day dozens of spectators from among the hotel's guests watched as Spinks went through his routine of rope-jumping, callisthenics, shadow-boxing and sparring. Also in the Spinks camp was 37 year-old Mackie Shilstone, the nutritionist and conditioning coach whose methods and techniques had built Spinks up from a 175-pound light-heavyweight to the 200-pound heavyweight who won the title from Holmes. Shilstone was there to build even more muscle on to Spinks's frame, to see that he stayed away from red meat, and that he took the nutritional supplements and followed the weight-training programme that Shilstone advocated. Shilstone had been a conditioning coach at Tulane University's Athletic Department after playing football (split end) while a student at Tulane (though just 5″8″ and 140 pounds). With a Master's Degree in nutrition and another in physical education, Shilstone had worked his conditioning magic on major leaguers Ozzie Smith, Vince Coleman and Will Clark, on former Middleweight Champion Frank Tate, and on NBA stars Ralph Sampson and Manute Bol, but he gained wider public recognition through his successful association with Spinks, although many traditionalists in the boxing business scoffed at his newfangled methods.

Across the mountains, in Catskill, Tyson went through his daily routine in solitude in the little gym above the police station on the town's main street. Only trainer Kevin Rooney was present, except possibly for a gym assistant, or a friend of Tyson's, or perhaps one of the amateur youngsters who also trained in the gym.

Roughly a month before the fight, both men, as they were contractually obliged to do, moved their equipment, their sparring partners, their trainers and themselves to Atlantic City, where they would be more in the media's eye, and therefore play a bigger role in helping to 'sell' the fight. They did their part. Tyson told the *Boston Globe*, 'I'll break Spinks. I'll break them all. When I fight someone I want to break his will. I want to take his manhood. I want to rip out his heart and show it to him. People say that's primitive, that I'm an animal. But then they pay $500 to see it. . . . I'm a warrior. . . . If I wasn't in boxing, I'd be breaking the law. That's my nature.' Spinks, who came from as tough a ghetto in St Louis as Tyson did in Brooklyn, was less macho: 'I'll carry some fear into the ring, at least I hope I will,' he admitted. 'I think fear is good for a boxer because it makes you respect the individual you're fighting. . .I don't feel I can fight well without it.' He went on to tell how he had fought without fear only once, as an amateur, and how, as a result, he had lost. He described how he had seen his brother, Leon, defeat the Soviet fighter, Rufat Riskiev, and how he had not thought Riskiev much of a fighter. Several months later, he himself had faced Riskiev in Moscow. Overconfident, he underestimated his Russian opponent, was knocked down, and lost the fight. Then, in the Montreal Olympics, he had to fight Riskiev in the finals for the gold medal. He entered the ring with that healthy fear, and used it to his advantage to beat Riskiev by KO and win Olympic gold. It was that same fear that he hoped would carry him through the storm that was Tyson.

Futch felt that Tyson was beatable. He had seen weaknesses in him when Tyson fought Bonecrusher Smith and Tony Tucker. His plan was to have Spinks exploit those weaknesses, but he also acknowledged that if Spinks made 'just one mistake, you can put all of that in the ashcan'.

About four weeks before the fight, Tyson skipped training one day and headed for Manhattan. Bill Cayton had negotiated a $1-million deal for Tyson to be a spokesman for Pepsi-Cola, and the champion was due in the City to film a Pepsi commercial. Tyson turned up at the filming location accompanied by his wife, mother-in-law, and their attorney, Michael Winston. While agency and Pepsi executives, technical crew, producer, director, extras all waited, Tyson balked. Besides his managerial contract with Tyson, Cayton also held a personal services contract with the fighter that covered all outside-the-ring business. Like the standard one-third/two-thirds cut that is traditional in boxing, Cayton's personal services contract also called for him to receive 33 per cent of Tyson's outside business deals (which he, in turn, split 50–50 with Lorraine Jacobs, Jim's widow). But Tyson's wife and mother-in-law persuaded him that this was too much to give up to Cayton. Even though Cayton had a bona fide contract, they decided that with everyone waiting around to film a national TV commercial, this would be a perfect time to put the squeeze on Cayton. Tyson and his entourage walked out. They were going to lunch. Rooney, meanwhile, was seething. The last place he wanted his fighter was 150 miles from Atlantic City, filming a commercial. A day lost in the gym could not be made up. The trainer knew that Spinks was not an opponent to be taken lightly. 'My fighter has the edge in speed and power and smartness,' he declared. 'My fighter will definitely cut the ring off. . .sooner or later Mike Tyson will hit him [and] he's never been hit by Mike Tyson.' But Rooney also acknowledged that Spinks was 'a cutie [who] throws punches from an angle. He's awkward.' Rooney knew that Tyson would need solid preparation if he was to overcome Spinks's 'experience under pressure' and, indeed, cut the ring off and land his bombs on the challenger.

In the past, Tyson had professed no problems with the manner in which Jim Jacobs and Bill Cayton guided his career, negotiated his deals or invested his money to make him independently wealthy by the age of twenty-one. But now, with people whispering in his ear, he sang a different tune. 'I'm throwing those left hooks, I'm taking those punches. For anyone to get one-third of my outside money is totally absurd.'

Cayton was in a difficult position. Unless he gave in, the whole deal would come apart at the seams. By the time the Tyson entourage returned from lunch, he had made his decision. On the spot, he agreed to revise the contract and accept a 25 per cent fee instead of 33 per cent. The cameras rolled, and the next day, Tyson was back to business in Atlantic City.

Tyson's wife and mother-in-law were increasingly becoming the villains in the collective mind of the public. It seemed that they were manipulating the naive fighter, and Tyson was growing more confused, more torn. One night, early in June, needing to get away from it all, he bolted, popping up in New York City, where he went to the local fights at Madison Square Garden and then disappeared without trace. Kevin Rooney was forced to make an unscheduled excursion to the City in order to locate him and bring him back to Atlantic City.

The fear was there. It was coming. And Tyson knew he would have to harness it, control it, in order for it to work to his advantage. He needed the fear, just as Spinks did. Sometimes he worried that he had dominated his 34 opponents so completely that he would become nonchalant and lose that edge the fear provided. He was actually relieved when he dreamed one night that he and Spinks had fought and that Spinks had beaten him. It was a sign the fear was still there.

After a work-out one day, he was answering questions from reporters when one of them asked him about Cus D'Amato, who still casts a long shadow over Tyson. He hesitated, unable to answer, and then suddenly began crying. 'When I was a little boy,' he managed to say, 'I didn't like fighting. But I loved Cus. I wanted to make him happy. He wanted a champ. I didn't want to let him down.'

On other days, he exploded in fits of temper. Assistant manager Steve Lott described the Tyson routine: 'He was just very, very difficult to live with for those five weeks [before a fight]. It's a matter of having to take a lot of shit without allowing your emotions to get involved. . .Kevin would be very vocal. He'd say to Mike, "Fuck you". But I couldn't do that, because I was trained by Jimmy [Jacobs]. . .no matter what Mike said, no matter how he acted, no matter how indifferent he was to what had to be done and how mean he was, or inconsiderate, I just ignored it. I said he's not doing it on purpose, it's the pressure of the fight, and I just had to forget about it.'

Three weeks before the fight, according to Lott, 'Mike was surly. Oh, was he surly. . .It was the pressure. . .I knew it from the first fight, from Catskill, I knew it was his style. I knew that if he didn't go through that, then there was something unusual. . . . He's a very moody person and he's allowed to be moody. He's the fighter. I'm not allowed to be moody. I'm not the fighter.'

Two weeks before the fight, Tyson sat with a half dozen reporters and called them idiots. 'You ruin people's lives. I'm a sucker even to be talking to you guys. I should be ready to rip your heads off, but it's not the right thing to do.' He then launched into a wide-ranging variety of topics, including the perceived attacks on his new family from press and public. 'All my life,' he said, 'This bull never bothered me. I take it all with a grain of salt. But my family, my wife and my mother-in-law, they're being cut to pieces. It's new to them. It hits a nerve. . . . My wife went home, and I can be alone. I'm a loner anyway, and I don't think women should be around fighters in the gym. . . . I'll love her to death after it's over.' Without mentioning any names, he then said that people in the fight business were bigger crooks than the criminals on the streets where he grew up. 'They're not out for my best interests. They tell me they are, but they're not. They say, "I did this for you and that for you," but that's not true. Whatever they did, they did for themselves. Whatever I get, they get a bigger percentage of it. . . . In my situation, it's very hard to find a real friend. The majority of the people have their hands out. . . . I don't want new relationships. That's how these problems occur. Too many friends – excuse me – too many people who say they're friends. I should have known from my background that people are basically not nice, the majority of them.' He said he just wished the fight was today, not two weeks from now. 'When I'm in that ring, I don't have no more problems. It's easy to forget problems when people are throwing punches at your head.'

As his out-of-the-ring problems mounted and his mood swings became known, people began to believe it might affect his performance in the ring. At one point a 6-to-1 betting favourite, Tyson dropped to 4-to-1 by mid-June. Muhammad Ali was picking Spinks to win, but, like Joe Louis before him, Ali's greatness in the ring did not confer any great analytical abilities when it came to picking winners in fights.

A further snag came in May when Robin Givens persuaded Mike to dump Steve Lott, because she did not like him. Only through the intervention of Cayton, who convinced them that things should remain as familiar and stable as possible as Tyson approached the biggest fight of his career, did Givens and her mother relent, and the long-suffering and loyal Lott was reinstated.

Spinks, meanwhile, in a much calmer atmosphere, continued his training at Trump's Castle hotel and casino. But because of fears that Tyson spies were watching the public work-outs, every couple of days he would move to a closed session at a nearby gym. 'Tyson's not invincible,' Spinks told reporters. 'He's not the half man, half beast you read about in the papers. He's very good but, in the end, he's just a fighter.' You couldn't convince Tyson's sparring partners of that, however. On one day, he belted Oliver McCall low, and McCall had to take a rest. He then half-punched, half-wrestled Mike 'The Bounty' Hunter to the canvas, and fired a left hook to Hunter's head while he was down. McCall said Tyson's punches to his biceps sent a numbness through his arms like the kind that follows an electric shock, after which he couldn't lift his arms in the ring to defend himself against Tyson's devastating shots. Tyson was also merciless with his body shots, punches to the sides, the ribs, that were designed, as Tyson bluntly put it, 'to make a man cry like a woman'.

* * *

Another problem arose in the weeks before the fight. The bout was to be sanctioned by all three governing organizations – the WBC, WBA and IBF – because Tyson was recognized as champion by all of them. All three had come to an agreement that each would take turns administering Tyson's fights under its rules and regulations on a rotating basis. The WBA and WBC had had their respective turns earlier in the year when Tyson fought Holmes and Tubbs, and so now it was the IBF's turn, which was even more fitting because the IBF had its headquarters in New Jersey, where the fight was being held. Several years earlier, the WBC, citing questionable medical reasons, shortened its championship fights from the traditional 15 rounds to 12 rounds. Subsequently, the WBC followed suit. The IBF also decided to go to 12 rounds – as from September 1, 1988. The Tyson/Spinks fight would be fought, the IBF announced, under its rules still in effect, meaning a 15-round duration. The WBA and WBC decided to indulge in power play. They insisted that the fight be scheduled for 12 rounds. Bob Lee, President of the IBF, held firm that it would be 15 rounds, or else the IBF would withdraw title recognition from Tyson. The WBA and WBC, once arch-enemies, now presented a united front. Many in boxing felt their real purpose was to undermine and hopefully destroy the IBF, which they saw as a threat to their power and authority, since the IBF was American-based. They said if the fight was 15 rounds, they would strip Tyson of their titles. Cayton sided with the WBC and WBA, and was insistent that the fight be set for 12 rounds.

Tyson continued his gym work-outs but took a week off from sparring because of a small cut over his left eye. He took Sunday June 19 off and spent it with his wife at their home in Bernardsville, New Jersey. He returned to boxing the next day, pounding McCall, Hunter and Melvin Epps in six rounds of work. His fourth sparring partner, Fred Whitaker, was on the sidelines, knocked out of action for three weeks because of the beating Tyson had inflicted on his ribs. Tyson said he didn't give a damn how long the fight was. 'We can go 20 or 25 rounds for all I care. It's a heavyweight championship fight. It should be a fight to the finish.'

In US District Court, Bob Lee sought an injunction on behalf of the IBF enjoining the WBA and WBC from stripping Tyson of their titles if the fight was scheduled for 15 rounds. Cayton and his attorney, Thomas Puccio, met with

Lee to try to persuade him not to withdraw title recognition
from Tyson if the fight were to be 12 rounds. Finally, a week
before the fight, with everyone refusing to budge from their
positions, Larry Hazzard, the Boxing Commissioner of New
Jersey, stepped in. On Monday, June 20, stating that the three
organizations had created an 'embarrassing' situation, Hazzard
declared that the fight would be 12 rounds. Now Lee was faced
with a dilemma. He could stick to his guns, insist that it was
the IBF's 15 rounds or nothing, and strip Tyson, but that
would make the IBF a no-show at the biggest fight of the
year, being held right in their own New Jersey backyard.
Or he could swallow his pride and give in to the WBA, WBC,
Hazzard and Cayton. Three days later, he relented. The fight
would be 12 rounds, the IBF would not strip Tyson of their
title.

Meanwhile, relations between Tyson and Cayton grew increasingly strained, as Don King began to flex his muscles,
aligned as he was with Givens and her mother against the
manager. Anticipating possible trouble, at the beginning of
June Cayton had retained a heavyweight attorney, Thomas
Puccio, who had run the Abscam bribery trials for the federal
government and who had won an acquittal for socialite Claus
von Bulow in the highly-publicized attempted-murder trial
involving his wealthy and comatose wife, Sonny von Bulow.
Cayton announced that he had retained Puccio to prepare for
possible litigation, that Puccio had reviewed Cayton's contract
with Tyson and found it 'fully enforceable' for its duration. The
contract ran until February 1992. Cayton then declared that he
was completely willing to work with Tyson's family on Mike's
behalf, to avoid any unpleasant business such as a court case.
But Robin Givens accused him on a local New York news
programme of trying to sabotage her marriage, charging that
he had offered someone close to the Tysons $50,000 to help
end the marriage. 'He said he'd stop at nothing less than our
getting a divorce. . .It's like something out of *Dynasty*,' she
said. But according to Cayton, 'Once I knew that Mike was in
love with her, and with the Spinks fight coming on, you must
know that there was nobody more zealous in keeping Mike
happily married than Bill Cayton. . . . I always wanted him
to stay married.' Cayton says it was Don King who convinced
Givens that he was trying to end their marriage. 'He was feeding
her all these goddamn lies,' said Cayton, 'and she was believing
them. King is a very convincing scoundrel.'

Givens seemingly grabbed every possible opportunity to speak out against Cayton – accusing him in one TV interview shortly before the Spinks fight of offering someone close to the couple $50-thousand if he could facilitate a divorce between herself and Mike – but something else peculiar started to happen. Stories began appearing in the press about the tumult and turmoil going on in the private life of Mike and Robin, and much of it was attributable to Robin and her family. Two weeks before the fight, Robin said she had suffered a miscarriage. Tyson blamed it on Bill Cayton, saying his estranged manager's statements and actions had caused Robin so much worry she lost the child he had been looking forward to so much.

Barely more than a week before the fight, Robin's sister, Stephanie, a professional tennis player, gave an extraordinary interview to *Newsday*'s Wally Matthews. Speaking from Portugal, where she was playing in a tournament, she told Matthews, 'I've stayed completely out of this so far, but it's just gotten to be too much. . . . I've known about Mike from the first day Robin met him. I've felt it's all been a big mistake from the beginning. Michael's supposed to be the good guy and everybody else is supposed to be abusing him. Nobody knows how abusive Michael is.'

She said that in May, when Tyson was in California with Robin, who was filming a TV movie there, she spent a week with the couple. 'The week was a nightmare,' she said. 'I would call my mom every day to say, "I can't believe what is going on here."' She said Tyson was drinking heavily, and turned up drunk one day on the movie set. Production had to be suspended after Mike 'caused a terrible scene. He started breaking the lights, using foul language, throwing things.' She also gave an account of one evening when Mike and Robin 'had a fight, and he hit Robin on the head, with a closed fist. He knows how to hit her, and where to hit her, without causing any real damage. We had adjoining bedrooms and I was scared, so I made Robin come into my room and closed both doors. I put the latch on, and the deadbolt [lock]. He just kicked the two doors in. I knew he was strong, but I was amazed. . . . You can be so sweet to him and you'll never know what will set him off. He's the type of person who feels, he's Mike Tyson, he can do whatever he wants. He loves to damage things in the house, just for no reason. If he feels like kicking in the TV set, he'll do it. If he feels like punching a hole in the wall, he does it. If he feels like hitting you, he does it. Why? I guess he gets bored. . . . It's just amazing how it's all stayed out of the newspapers. . . . When you're around him, you do live in fear. He's like a bomb, he can just explode. [Robin's] never been alone with him. There's always someone with her, because we're afraid for her. . . . [Robin and Ruth] have tried so hard to make him into a decent human being and they just can't.'

The timing of Stephanie's startling revelations was interesting, because it came shortly after Robin had jetted across the Atlantic to pay her a quick visit. Also, knowing the strong influence Ruth Roper exerted on both her daughters, most observers felt it was unlikely that Stephanie had spoken out independently, without at least the consent, if not the direct instructions, of her mother. Robin, for her part, walked the tightrope, as she had done with her alleged pregnancy, refusing to confirm or deny her sister's charges. She did drop veiled hints, however, telling Wally Matthews, 'We've had four hard months of marriage. He's under a lot of pressure, and it's made him set in ways I'd never seen before. . .I can understand Stephanie's position.' She then said, 'I love Michael dearly. . . . I think we can make a great team. I hope we can have a life together.' Privately, however, another responsible New York boxing writer said Robin had confirmed 'off the record' that Mike did hit her. Why would she do so, and why would Stephanie speak out so strongly, the reporter was asked. 'It's obvious,' he replied. 'They're setting things up for the divorce. These are bad people we're talking about, bad people.'

Bill Cayton, would not speculate, at least publicly, on the timing of Robin's and Stephanie's speaking out to Wally Matthews.The timing could not have been worse, coming less than two weeks before the fight. He denied Robin's allegations that he wanted to break up the marriage. If Mike was happy, he wanted to see the marriage continue, he insisted, reasoning that a contented and domesticated Mike Tyson would have his mind much more focused on his business in ring.

Tyson could not understand why the members of his new family should talk about him like this in print, especially now that he was approaching the critical final days before such a major fight. He denied that he hit Robin, but, as Wally Matthews wrote after speaking with him, he 'seemed to be seething with a cold anger toward the family that claims to love him. "You can't say bad things about a person, call them an asshole, and then say that you love them," Tyson said.

"What they're saying, basically, is that I'm useless. . . . May be [Cayton] is breaking down their wills. . . . I can't worry about it. I'm here training for a fight. . . . It's very difficult when someone's telling you one thing, and the other person's swearing to God he had nothing to do with it. My wife and mother-in-law are telling me differently, but what more can I do for them?. . .Maybe I'm not the man for them. . .I'll get by somehow. I always find a way to get by.'"

Tyson continued, in the days before the fight, to defame Cayton, calling him an 'asshole', 'ruthless', and 'a snake'. It was obvious that Tyson, a simple kid, was being pushed and pulled to the breaking point. 'They all want something from me. They're all making their living off me. Everybody's got their hands out,' he said, echoing his now-familiar lament. He couldn't even turn to his blood relatives, his brother and sister. He and his brother, an ex-serviceman who lived in California, were not close, and his sister, Denise, lived with her husband and two children on the dole, receiving welfare cheques twice a month even after her little brother had earned more than $40-million.

King and Cayton spent Monday, June 20 in court in a dispute over the division of Trump's $11-million site fee. King ended up with $2-million, out of which he had to pay promotional expenses and the purses of the fighters on the undercard. King then launched a verbal attack on Cayton, calling him 'an inveterate liar, a power zealot, a hypocrite of the first order, an evil man, the incarnation of Satan. The kid gloves are off,' said King. He further said that he fully supported Robin and her mother and would help them prove allegations that Cayton was trying to break up the marriage. He then professed fear for Spinks's safety, saying 'Tyson's gonna go in and look at Spinks and see Bill Cayton. I just hope he don't get too brutally beaten.' Cayton barred King from Tyson's work-out six days before the fight, said King's outburst was 'one hundred per cent bull', and vowed that King 'will not, with my approval, be promoting any Mike Tyson fights in the future'. Tyson countered: 'Bill Cayton is through as far as I'm concerned,' but Cayton said, 'I will insist that Mike honour the letter and spirit of his contract to its full duration.' King allegedly told Given's mother that Tyson's people were 'calling Mike a nigger behind his back'. Small wonder that the byplay was beginning to overshadow the fight!

After all of this, the final press conference, the final confrontation between the fighters and their camps, was tame
by comparison. *Ring* magazine, which still recognized Spinks
as champion, used the occasion to present him with a world
championship belt, and Spinks responded: 'It's a great thrill to
be considered a champion.' Kevin Rooney jumped in, asking,
'Who'd Spinks ever fight? Holmes? We knocked him out in
four rounds.' Tyson said, 'I'm the best fighter in the world. No
one can beat me. . . . My objective is to inflict as much pain
as possible, to win and win spectacularly. . .Ever since I was
12 years old, I was groomed to be the heavyweight champion
of the world. I've been prepared to handle the pressure, the
dealing with the press, everything. I think you guys are basically
overbearing sometimes, but none of this bull will affect me in
the ring.' Spinks said, 'I never ran from any man, and I don't
intend to run from Mike Tyson.' Rooney then grew impatient.
'Everybody's being so nice to each other,' he said. 'I just want to
let you know, we're here to kick a little ass.' Rooney had taken
a beating at the craps tables, dropping some $175-thousand over
the previous two weeks, but he was still ready for some more
action. 'Let's get it down,' he challenged Butch Lewis. 'I got
money to bet on Tyson, any amount.' Lewis ignored the offer.

Opinion about the likely outcome of the right was divided.
Ex-champs Tony Zale and Rocky Graziano were looking for
Spinks to outsmart and outpsyche Tyson and pull an upset,
joining Ali in his selection of Spinks. Wally Matthews, an
astute boxing writer for the New York *Newsday*, liked Spinks
to TKO Tyson; veteran boxing announcer Don Dunphy, who
had been broadcasting fights since Louis–Conn in 1941, also
picked Spinks. But Billy Conn, the brash light-heavyweight
champion who had come so close to dethroning Louis in that
classic confrontation before being KO'd by Joe in the 13th
round, liked Tyson by knock-out. 'How soon?' said Conn.
'As soon as he hits Spinks.' Jake LaMotta, the Raging Bull,
was in the Tyson camp, as were former trainer, matchmaker
and TV commentator Gil Clancy, and Larry Holmes's former
trainer, Rich Giachetti. Both liked Tyson by an early knockout. 'Spinks will find out he can't run from Tyson, so he'll
be forced to stand and fight,' said Clancy prophetically. 'That
should make it an exciting fight, but not a long one.' Angelo
Dundee, who had led Ali and Sugar Ray Leonard to world
titles, and had been in the corner of ex-champ Pinklon Thomas
the night Tyson destroyed him, said, 'If Spinks can't hurt Tyson

early, forget about it.' Ex-heavyweight champ George Foreman also picked Tyson, as did two former champs who had felt the power and determination of Tyson in the ring. Bonecrusher Smith chose Tyson by KO. When asked what Spinks would need to win, he said, 'He'd need to take me in the ring with him.' And Larry Holmes, KO'd earlier in the year by Tyson, said, 'Tyson is very hard to hit and he hits very hard, which makes it a bad combination for Spinks.' He picked Tyson to stop Spinks in less than five rounds. Promoter Bob Arum, who had staged some of Tyson's early fights but was now out of favour with Tyson's people because Jim Jacobs believed he had tried to steal Wilfred Benitez from him, hit the nail on the head. He said that when Tyson 'nails Spinks for the first time – and, make no mistake about it, he will nail him – the fight will, in essence, be over. There is no way that Spinks can stand up to the overwhelming power of the champ. . . . Tyson will attack Spinks from the start. . . .will cut the ring off on Spinks and land his devastating body shots. If Spinks survives the first round assault, he will only be postponing the inevitable. Tyson will take him out for good in the second round. . . .Tyson by an early knock-out.'

On Friday, June 24, Tyson dropped a bomb on his manager. An envelope was delivered by hand to Cayton. It contained a letter which read:

Dear Bill:

Starting now, you are to take no action on my behalf as a boxing manager. Any monies you have received for me as a boxing manager must be promptly forwarded to the office of Michael Winston, my attorney. Any monies you are to receive on my behalf as a boxing manager must be forwarded to my attorney Michael R. Winston.

Also, you are directed to advise all persons and companies that owe me money that you are not authorized to receive any monies due me as my boxing manager.

Sincerely,
Mike Tyson

Co: Michael Winston
New York State Boxing Commission
Sports of the Century, Inc.

Tyson had, by virtue of this letter, made the first move to sever his contractual relationship with Bill Cayton. Those who professed to care about him apparently did not mind forcing his hand and taking his mind off the fight just three days before he was due to step into the ring with Spinks. Cayton, in deference to Tyson, had sought to defer any such distractions.

Fighters traditionally weigh in on the day of a fight, because in the divisions below heavyweight they must not exceed the weight limit of that division. However, since a heavyweight weigh-in was essentially superfluous, there being no limit to weight in that division, and because ABC was going to tele-vise it live during its 'Wide World of Sports' programme, the weigh-in was held on Saturday, two days before the fight, in the showroom of Trump Plaza, with the fighters, trainers, officials and aides on stage. Bill Cayton was there. So was Robin Givens and Don King. Givens, either unaware of or unconcerned about a fighter's delicate psyche as a fight approached, spent the time announcing that Cayton was gone after this fight, contract be damned. The fighters themselves did no talking, except in brief interviews with ABC. Spinks was 212¼ pounds, Tyson 218¼. They departed, each to spend the final forty-eight hours resting, waiting secluded from the hundreds of reporters and thousands of fans and camp followers who had gathered in this old seaside resort to witness a fight, or, for those without tickets, just to say they were there.

Sunday was quiet, relatively uneventful, the calm before the Monday night storm. George Foreman, the former Heavy-weight Champion, on the come-back trail at the age of 39 after ending a ten-year retirement, fought in Atlantic City and scored an easy TKO over a journeyman named Carlos Hernandez. The promoter of the fight was the now-retired Gerry Cooney. While Foreman was fighting, down the other end of the boardwalk, at Bally's Casino Hotel, Frank Sinatra was giving an open-air con-cert under the stars. Late in the day, Donald Trump wandered into the Convention Hall that in little more than twenty-four hours would be packed with more than twenty-two thousand people. Now, the Hall was empty except for the HBO televi-sion crew completing its set-up of technical facilities for the fight coverage. Trump sat down in the first row in his VIP section, in the seat he had reserved for Sinatra. He didn't like what he saw. The ring was too high. Looking up from the first row, Sinatra's view would be obstructed. Trump called for HBO's producer, Ross Greenburg, and told him he could not risk an unhappy Sinatra walking out during the fight. The ring would have to be lowered a foot. That meant resetting the ring lights, and repositioning all the cameras. But what Trump wanted, Trump got. Greenburg was in no position to argue. His men began dismantling the ring, and in less than an hour, everything was in place again, and the ring was lower. As it turned out, at least as far as Sinatra was concerned, it really didn't matter. Under contract at Bally's, a rival casino, Sinatra decided it wouldn't be good form to be seen sitting with Trump. He did not turn up for the fight.

The day of the fight began early for Robin Givens and Donald Trump. They were up before dawn to make appearances on ABC's *Good Morning America*, from ringside at Convention Hall. Later, Givens would launch a tirade of verbal abuse at the Trump Plaza front desk manager, incensed that she couldn't get her way and have some relatives stay an extra night at the hotel because the rooms were already booked by other guests. 'Don't you know who I am?' she demanded. Yes, he said, but he couldn't do anything about extending the rooms. At that, Givens threatened to get her husband, who she assured him, would take care of this matter. With that threat, she stormed off. Of course, just hours away from his fight, Tyson never appeared at the front desk to argue his wife's case.

In the afternoon, there was a visitor to Tyson's room. The once-great champion, Roberto Duran, stopped by. Duran had been a boyhood hero of Tyson's, but they had never met. They hugged and began talking. Tyson, intensely interested in boxing history, asked Duran about his ring career, while Duran told Tyson to stay calm, go right to Spinks, who would, he assured him, be nervous. 'You'll catch him,' Duran said. Duran had once been promoted by Don King, who had made millions out of him. After they parted, Duran linked up with King's arch-rival, Bob Arum, as his promoter. Now, most of the fortune that he had earned in the ring was gone, somehow frittered away. He did not have a ticket for Tyson's fight. Apparently, none was forthcoming from King, although it is customary that greats of the past are taken care of in this manner. When Tyson found out, he gave Steve Lott $1,500 to buy a ticket for Duran.

Early in the evening, the doors to the Convention Hall opened and the crowd outside on the boardwalk and inside Trump's casino began to fill the Hall. Fight fans and those who wanted their money's worth after paying out $500, or $1,000, or $1,500, or even a mere $100 for the the cheapest seat in the rafters, filed in early to watch the preliminary fights and keep their eyes open for the celebrities who would arrive as the main event drew closer.

Bill Cayton, his wife, Doris, and Lorraine Jacobs arrived and took their seats at ringside near Donald Trump and his wife and family. At a discreet distance from the Cayton party sat Don King, Robin Givens and Ruth Roper. During one of the preliminaries, Cayton was approached and handed an envelope. He was in for a shock when he opened it. It contained legal papers notifying him that he was being sued by Tyson to break the contract which had been signed just four months earlier.

Tyson bounced from his corner as the echo of the bell faded. He was still annoyed at the intrusion into his pre-fight preparations when Butch Lewis, Spinks's promoter, had entered his dressing room 45 minutes earlier and created a fuss by complaining about a lump under the tape on one of Tyson's gloves. Steve Lott, in the corner with Tyson, recalled, 'I have never seen one fighter attack another fighter like Mike attacked Spinks. Vicious punches, incredible body shots. And that was Butch Lewis, his brilliancy.' Tyson threw the first combination, left jab, a left hook that landed solidly, a right to the body and a right that missed over Spink's head, all the punches coming in the first ten seconds of the round, in rapid succession, as Spinks covered up. Tyson then missed three punches, but kept the pressure on the challenger. Spinks missed a right and then threw another, which missed high. It was his first offensive, launched more in desperation than in any hopes of doing damage, just to try and keep Tyson off him. Tyson threw another flurry, with a right hand, slightly off the mark, the only punch landing, but the power of Tyson's punches was already apparent, even those that didn't land, and Spinks grabbed and held, forcing the first clinch of the fight, his only respite from Tyson's onslaught. Even in the clinch Spinks found no safe haven. Tyson brought up a left elbow into Spinks's face with vicious force. Cappuccino broke them and warned Tyson, 'Hey, Mike, knock it off, man. Knock it off.' A left uppercut inside then drove Spinks back. Tyson was constantly coming forward, and Spinks had nowhere to go but backwards, retreating on legs no longer capable at this stage in his career of taking him safely out of danger. There was another clinch, then two rights by

Tyson. The first landed hard on Spinks's face and drove him back into the ropes. Every punch that landed was hurting, and that right hand was the beginning of the end. Spinks threw a soft right, almost apologetically, but then covered up completely in a peek-a-boo defence, still trying to avoid Tyson's blows. Tyson fired off a rapid six-punch combination, with a right to the ribs doing the most damage. It was obvious at this point that Spinks could not fend off Tyson's fury. Still on the ropes, he slid to the adjoining side of the ring, but was again trapped on the ropes – exactly where he didn't want to be with Tyson. He took a thundering left uppercut-hook to the jaw, followed by a tremendous right to his ribs that collapsed him to one knee.

Just one minute had gone by in the fight, and Michael Spinks was down for the first time in his 12-year professional career. He got up at the count of two, looked to his corner and nodded that he was OK, as Cappuccino tolled the mandatory eight-count and wiped his gloves. He asked him, 'Are you OK, Mike?' and Spinks responded the way all fighters do, acknowledging that he was prepared to continue. He came forward to meet Tyson in the centre of the ring. Tyson took three steps from the neutral corner where he had been sent by the referee. Spinks, in desperation, threw a final right that missed. At the same moment, Tyson threw a left that also missed. But the momentum of Spinks's missed punch turned his body to the left, and for an instant left his head unguarded. Instinctively, Tyson saw the opening and fired a short, pulverizing right hand that landed flush on the jaw of Michael Spinks, finding its way as if guided by some lethal radar between the protection of Spinks's gloves. Perhaps a more perfect, more efficient right hand had not been thrown since the one Rocky Marciano landed on the jaw of Jersey Joe Walcott to win the heavyweight title thirty-six years earlier. Spinks tumbled backwards like a felled tree, his head snapping sharply and bouncing off the canvas. His eyes were open, but his body was paralysed. The medical term is rotational acceleration of the brain, a twisting of the cerebrum as it moves rapidly in the fluid that surrounds it against the inside of the skull. In boxing, it's called a knock-out. At the count of four, Spinks tried to turn and rise off his back, but as the count reached ten, he tumbled face-forward into the ropes, intoxicated by the 100-proof power in Tyson's fists.

Tyson turned to the crowd and extended his arms wide, palms up, as if to say, there, you see, the job is done. Kevin Rooney was in the ring now, hugging Tyson, with the beaming Don King also there, attached to Tyson like a leech. Butch Lewis was supporting the wobbly Spinks, and the ring physician tried to steady the groggy fighter. Tyson moved toward him, and Spinks extended his gloved hand to touch Tyson's and acknowledge the victor. Robin Givens climbed into the ring, assisted by Donald Trump. The fight had taken one minute and 31 seconds. Tyson told Spinks he had watched him since the Olympics, when Tyson was just ten years old. He told Spinks he had admired him for being a great fighter.

Afterwards, in a packed press room, there were the usual post-mortems. 'He was charging in,' Spinks said of Tyson, 'and I was trying to catch him in the process. I tried to take a shot at him, and I came up short. That's when he hit me.' Eddie Futch would later say that Spinks's failure came when he abandoned his game plan, which had been to jab and move, counterpunch, and make Tyson work, miss punches, and slow down. Futch also said Spinks wasn't scared, no matter what anyone said. But Richie Giachetti, who had been in the corner with Holmes the night Tyson stopped him, said Spinks had the same look on his face that Larry had just before the bell, a look he had never seen on Larry's face in any of his other fights. It was the look of fear.

Tyson, meanwhile, with his wife at his side, stood at the podium and continued his battle with the press. 'I wasn't very appreciative of what you guys, you reporters, did to me,' he said. 'You tried to embarrass me. You tried to embarrass my family. You tried to disgrace us, and as far as I know this might be my last fight.' He concluded by offering the opinion that 'There's no fighter like me. I can beat any man in the world.' Robin took Mike's hand in hers and kissed it, looking out at the press and smiling. In the background, on the podium, stood his estranged manager, Bill Cayton. Tyson ignored him.

For all concerned, the fight was a tremendous financial success. The crowd at Convention Hall paid a live-gate record of $12.3-million. Gross receipts, counting theatre, foreign, pay-per-view and merchandising would reach an estimated $70-million, making this the largest grossing fight in boxing history, a record previously held by the Leonard–Hagler fight in 1987, which grossed an estimated $60-million. The Trump Plaza casino had a drop – the amount of chips purchased by gamblers – of $11.5-million on the day of the fight, which was a record. The four-day weekend drop at the casino came to $30-million.

The house profit margin on a drop of $30-million would be about $5-million, to perhaps $7-million. Tyson's purse would approach $22-million, of which Kevin Rooney would receive $2.2-million off the top. The manager's share would be some $6.5-million. Michael Spinks, for whom this would be a farewell to boxing, would probably net for himself, after taking care of trainer Eddie Futch, promoter Butch Lewis, and Uncle Sam, a nest egg of about $5-million to retire on. Michael Spinks had always been a gentle man. He had said it was painful for him to watch the vultures pick away at his manchild brother, Leon. He had called boxing 'a dirty business' and so now he could leave it as he had graced it, with dignity.

Tyson talked of retirement. He told Mike Marley of the *New York Post* the day after the fight that it had definitely been his last appearance in a ring. 'Don King was laughing, but when he finds out I'm serious, he won't be laughing,' he said. 'I don't want to deal with this bullshit anymore. . . . I had fun. Boxing was good to me, but nothing lasts forever. . . . I decided it's time to move on. It's time to call it a day. . . . I don't like reading that my wife is a whore, that my mother-in-law is a sneaky conniver. And then I read that I'm an idiot. I know it goes with the territory, but it's difficult.'

Tyson, of course, would fight again. It was all he knew. That night in Atlantic City he had shown the world that he truly was invincible in the ring. But outside the squared circle, his familiar world was crumbling around him.

14

The Summer of Discontent

No one's going to be my manager but Bill Cayton. As long as Bill Cayton's around, he's my manager, from the beginning to the end of my career.

– MIKE TYSON
May, 1988

HAPPY FOR HIM in victory, Tyson's friends were at the same time concerned for him. Over and over, he had vowed he would not end up like Joe Louis, or Muhammad Ali. He would quit with all his money, he said, but things continued to point in a different direction. Tyson indicated he was considering a move to California, where Robin worked and spent most of her time. Those around Mike knew if he established residence in California, he could be hit harder than any opponent had ever hit him if (and it was obvious to all that it was more a question of when rather than if) he and Robin were to divorce. California is a 'community property law' state, meaning all property in a divorce is divided 50/50, right down the middle between the two parties involved. Concern for Mike's welfare grow, but no one could point things out to him without seeming to come down against Ruth and Robin.

Cayton, meanwhile, turned his attention to the legal papers he had been served with at ringside himself. He charged that Don King was behind it, stirring things up in an attempt to 'steal' Tyson from him. He labelled King 'stupidly greedy', and pointed out that it was he, Cayton, who had been working steadily on Mike's behalf. It was he who had negotiated the compromise with the WBC, WBA and IBF over the duration of the bout. Maintaining Tyson as undisputed champion was worth potentially millions of dollars in terms of commercial endorsements. Cayton had, on that front, negotiated lucrative deals not only with Japanese breweries but with Kodak and Pepsi-Cola in the USA for TV commercials that added considerably to Tyson's income. Another deal had been arranged with Nintendo, the most popular home video game in the country, for a video game called 'Mike Tyson's Punch Out', and Tyson had filmed a TV commercial for Nintendo as well.

Cayton pointed out that, far from working in Tyson's best

interests, King had acted in several ways that might have cost Mike perhaps millions of dollars. Without Cayton's knowledge, prior to the Spinks fight, King had made a deal with a company in California to set up a telephone number which people could call for a fee during the fight and which would provide them with a running account of the bout. This might have kept thousands of people from buying the fight on pay-per-view home TV, or from going to theatres to see it closed circuit, cutting sharply into California revenues. When Cayton got wind of it, he forced King to cancel the deal. And in May, when King had bought his Rolls-Royce gift for Tyson, he had arranged only a $15-thousand insurance policy on it, leaving Tyson incredibly vulnerable to a potential lawsuit. If he had had an accident involving any type of injury to another party and been at fault, he could have been sued for millions of dollars once it was learned he was Mike Tyson, and it would have come out of his pocket since King's insurance policy would have covered only $15-thousand. Cayton had quickly straightened this out. (*Note*: King, after making much public fuss over his Rolls-Royce 'gift' to Tyson, had quietly informed Cayton that although he'd laid out the funds for the purchase, he did expect Mike to repay him.)

On the day after the Spinks fight, which was also the day after the filing of Tyson's lawsuit against Cayton, the manager, along with Lorraine Jacobs, the widow of his partner, appeared at a news conference to respond to the allegations. Tyson's suit, filed in New York State Supreme Court, charged that Jacobs and Cayton fraudulently induced him to sign new contracts with them in February of 1988, a month before Jacobs died, without his being informed that Jacobs had a terminal illness. Tyson maintained he would never have signed something that would allow Bill Cayton to become his sole manager if he had known Jim Jacobs was fatally ill. He further charged that he did not read the contracts, nor did Jacobs read them to him or explain the conditions of the contracts to him. The truth of the matter was that Tyson was willing and happy to sign the new contracts at the time, that they were explained to him by an Athletic Commission Attorney, and his close friend and confidant, Jose Torres, was there to look after Mike as well, and, in his capacity as Chairman of the State Athletic Commission, he signed and approved all the new contracts.

At the news conference, held at the offices of Milbank Tweed Hadley & McCloy, the firm in which Cayton's attorney, Thomas

Puccio, was a partner, Cayton said, 'I'm very disappointed in Mike. I thought Mike had far greater respect for Jim's memory. I'm outraged at this lawsuit.' Tyson stated in his legal papers that, 'Cayton has not been, is not now and will not be [my] boxing manager.' To this Cayton responded, 'Mike Tyson knew all along that Jimmy and I were truly co-managers. . . .[that] most of the negotiations were conducted by and large by me.' Tyson's lawsuit said Cayton was not entitled to any portion of the proceeds from the Spinks fight, even though the contract between him and Cayton was in effect and Cayton had handled the negotiations for the entire fight.

Lorraine Jacobs broke down in tears as she expressed her disappointment in Tyson. 'It's very difficult,' she managed to say. 'We love Mike. We've known him since he was thirteen. Both Jim and Bill treated him as they would have treated a son. I just can't believe Mike would do this. It's distressing.'

Attorney Puccio was the strongest in his denunciation of Tyson's charges. 'Tyson maligns and does dishonour to the memory of his close friend and mentor Jim Jacobs who, with Bill Cayton and Cus D'Amato, guided his career, which has now reached this crowning moment. Jim is no longer with us and cannot defend himself. More than anything else, that is what makes this suit a low blow. . . .Mike Tyson may have been in top form in the ring, but the allegations he made in the lawsuit are not worthy of a champion,' said Puccio, who further labelled the charges by Tyson 'a sham and totally unsupportable'. Although it was obviously apparent that the idea for the lawsuit did not jump full blown out of the head of Mike Tyson, Puccio was accurate when he said, 'It's almost beyond belief that Mike Tyson would put his signature to these charges. . . .Let's put the hat squarely on who it belongs – Mike Tyson. He brought the charges. He's responsible for them.'

Don King, meanwhile, who had been inseparable from Ruth and Robin in the days leading up to the Spinks fight, and had labelled Cayton 'Satan in disguise' and 'the devil incarnate', took an uncharacteristically humble stance. Not wanting to seem too pushy or aggressive in the eyes of Ruth Roper or Robin, he said, 'Mike Tyson is my boss. When Mike speaks, I listen.' Boxing people wondered how long it would take until that situation was reversed. One day, he said Tyson was 'the hottest property in the world', and talked of marketing Tyson around the globe, a Tyson 'Ambassadorial tour of fighting in the grand style with a lot of flair and excitement', as Mike went from country to country, taking on national champions. And who better but to promote such a tour than the 'Only In America' man himself? 'It would be extremely difficult for an ordinary promoter to do something with a fighter who has beaten everybody, but I'm an extraordinary promoter. I have imagination. My only hope is that I have the opportunity to earn Mike's trust.' Tyson's next fight was scheduled in two months' time, in London against number-one challenger Frank Bruno, but already there were ominous rumblings that Tyson would not be at Wembley Stadium on September 3. Tyson said he was tired, he might retire. King said Tyson just needed a rest when he spoke of retirement, and if Mike didn't want to fight, 'Bruno could be put on hold', no matter that a contract had been signed by Tyson. Of course, King had no interest in seeing Tyson fight Bruno in England, because he was not involved in the promotion, which belonged to Jarvis Astaire and Mickey Duff. Privately, Tyson told friends if he was going to fight Bruno, King was going to be part of the promotion. The battle lines were drawn.

Also entering this three-ring circus was the 'boy billionaire', Donald Trump. He suddenly surfaced alongside Ruth and Robin, all smiles, saying he had joined the Tyson family as an advisor to the champion, giving as his altruistic reasons, '[Mike] happens to be one hell of a good guy, that's why I'm here to help him. . . .I'm a friend and advisor.' He also said he was motivated by the affection he had developed for Ruth and Robin, who he said, had been treated 'unfairly' by the media and the public, given treatment 'they don't deserve'. Two days after coming on the scene, Trump's high-powered public relations man, Howard Rubenstein, called a news conference. It was held on July 11 at Trump's Plaza Hotel in Manhattan, in the Grand Ballroom. Tyson stepped to the podium and said, 'I'm calling the shots. I will manage my own self. Anyone who goes against me can no longer be associated with me,' and he made it clear that that included his trainer, Kevin Rooney, who had continued to insist in interviews that 'Bill Cayton is an honest man. . .he's careful about his fight-er's money.' Tyson continued, 'I did the sweating inside the ring. . . .Without me, [Cayton] wouldn't have had a chance of even putting his foot in the door at HBO.' (Subsequently, Seth Abraham, HBO's executive in charge of sports, pointed out that Cayton had been negotiating deals and fights with HBO

long before Tyson came on the scene.) Tyson announced he
had set up a company called Mike Tyson Enterprises, which
would include Ruth Roper, attorney Michael Winston, and
new friend Donald Trump, among others, to advise him on
his business and boxing careers.

Attorney Winston said that Jacobs and Cayton had taken
advantage of Tyson by not advising him to be represented by an
independent attorney when signing contracts with them. 'Here
was a young man,' Winston said, 'with no legal experience,
dealing with two very shrewd businessmen. That was not fair,
it was simply not fair.'

Trump had worked closely with Cayton and Jacobs, not only
on the Spinks fight, but on the Biggs and Holmes bouts as well,
along with other deals not involving Tyson, but now he too said
that for Tyson not to have had his own counsel when dealing
with the managers was 'quite unfair. . . .this isn't a question of
taking sides. I'm doing what I think is right.' The media was
highly suspicious of Trump's motives. The youthful entrepreneur had established a pattern over the years of seeking the
spotlight. He was considered a publicity hound, someone who
craved public attention as much as he did making money. And
really, how much of a 'good guy' could he really have felt Tyson
was, who had once responded to his greeting and proffered
handshake before the start of a news conference by glaring at
him and saying 'Get the fuck outta here'? Perhaps Trump liked
to be at the centre of the storm, on TV and in the newspaper
at the side of the Heavyweight Champion. No doubt he also
liked the numbers with $-signs in front of them that he saw
following the Spinks fight. It was certainly to his advantage to
keep Mike Tyson in the fold and therefore fighting for Trump
in Atlantic City.

The usually cynical media were almost universal in their praise
for Cayton's abilities as a manager. Mike Katz, writing in the
New York *Daily News*, said, '[Cayton]turned the books over
weeks ago and so far, there has not been one instance cited
by Winston of dishonesty. No one has accused Cayton of
dishonesty before, a remarkable claim in boxing.' Ira Berkow,
in *The New York Times*, wrote, 'Cayton, now 70, and in boxing for some 40 years, has before this been known as a tough
businessman but an honest one, and never a rip-off artist.'
Columnist Mike Lupica, in the *Daily News*, said, 'Robin Givens
has worked it out so that Mike Tyson doesn't trust Bill Cayton
anymore. . . .Mike Tyson is not being smart. Tyson probably

should be worried about his wife, who showed up on their first date with her mother and three publicists. Bill Cayton is an honest boxing manager, something as rare as a day in June when two boxers make $35-million between them. . . .But Robin Givens and Ruth Roper, her mother, have begun to move Cayton out. . . .The wife, and her mother, have become friendly with the shark, Don King. . . .Cayton may have been slow to see what was happening to him, and he may not give Tyson the hugs Jimmy Jacobs did, but Cayton deserves better at age 70 than this. . . .Bill Cayton has a contract. Robin Givens has a bedroom. Somebody stop this fight.'

The bottom line was, Cayton's contract was solid and enforceable. Cayton knew it, but wanted to avoid the acrimony that would grow out of a full-scale courtroom battle. Michael Winston knew it, and said he wanted 'to see if we can work together to resolve this without litigation'. Trump knew it, and was advising the Tyson side to settle the dispute with Cayton. And meanwhile, the British promoters Jarvis Astaire and Mickey Duff were growing nervous. They had a contract but no firm commitment from Tyson as to his intentions concerning the September 3 fight at Wembley with Frank Bruno. They were pushing the deadline by which they had to sign an agreement for leasing the massive stadium. The Wembley people wanted an answer soon, because if they didn't have a heavyweight fight there on that date, Bruce Springsteen and U-2 both wanted it for concerts.

Robin Givens, meanwhile, continued trying to stir up the situation rather than settle it. She said her husband should have stood up to Cayton in a stronger manner, that he should have told him to stop talking to the press about her or 'I'm going to punch your face in'. In interviews she would teasingly say Michael didn't hit her, but he did throw things, he had tantrums, but she would never stay in the relationship if she were being abused. Then later, in other statements, she would admit that Tyson was dangerous to the point where her mother hired bodyguards.

Certainly things were not all sweetness and light at the big mansion in New Jersey. The Tyson's live-in butler/chauffeur and cook/maid were fired after just three months. They spoke to Mike McAlary of the NY *Daily News* of fights, arguments, a strained relationship and a controlling, interfering mother-in-law. They had been hired by Ruth Roper's assistant, and told, 'You work for Ruth Roper. Anything you see this guy

do, you report back to us confidentially. And if you ever cross
her, you're finished.' The husband-and-wife team of caretakers
recalled the first breakfast they cooked for the newly-weds,
bacon and eggs. Tyson sat down, said, 'I don't like pork,'
picked up the bacon with his hands and dumped it on Robin's
plate. 'I thought to myself right then,' said the butler, 'this is
not such a good relationship.'

Arguments were constantly overheard, and Mike often slept
alone on the couch in his den, the room where he spent most
of his time. One night there was an especially loud argument.
The next morning, according to the butler, Robin came into
the kitchen and asked for an ice pack for her face, which he
remembered being 'not so good' when he looked at it.

The couple had another disagreement one night when he
drove them to the theatre in their Rolls-Royce to see a play,
at Robin's insistence. Afterwards, as the butler/chauffeur
drove them home, the argument heated up. Robin shouted
at Mike, 'You embarrassed me in front of everybody. I'm sick
and tired of you. You're a lowlife. You're a nobody, a no-class
nobody.' Tyson ordered the chauffeur to 'drop this bitch' off at
her mother's house, then take him home to New Jersey, but
Robin insisted the mansion was her house, and that was where
she was going. Tyson then jumped out of the car on a deserted
Manhattan street corner, and disappeared for four days.

Ruth and Robin invited their friends out to the estate, people Mike didn't much care for and quickly grew bored with,
but they didn't like it when he had his buddies out to visit.
Finally, the end came for the butler and cook. Mike began
to like them, began confiding in them, told him that he loved
Robin but she didn't love him. 'Ruth Roper gets scared when
Mike Tyson starts liking people,' said the butler. He and his
wife were fired.

Tyson's attorney, Michael Winston, who had charged that
Cayton had some of Tyson's money in accounts under his own
name, had obtained a temporary restraining order on June 30
which prevented Cayton or the corporation he had established,
Sports of the Century, from receiving any of the proceeds from
the Spinks fight. That money would be frozen until the parties
involved reached some sort of agreement.

On July 14, Tyson indicated he would indeed fight Frank
Bruno in London on September 3, and a meeting was set for the
next day between Cayton's attorney, Tom Puccio, and Michael
Winston to work out the arrangements. Although Cayton had

requested and been granted an extension by the WBC until January for the mandatory defence against Bruno, he, Astaire and Duff were concerned that if the fight didn't take place in September, it would have to be moved from Wembley Stadium, which would seat forty thousand for the bout, to an indoor arena once the autumn weather set in, where perhaps only eight or ten thousand spectators could be accommodated. This could cost Tyson a million dollars or more in purse money.

Mike, meanwhile, continued to make absurd statements. He said Cayton and Jacobs had actually held him back, that he should have been fighting for the championship a year before he finally did. Considering it was he – not Cayton or Jacobs – who lost twice in the Olympic trials in the summer of 1984 and that in 1985 he had just turned pro and was still fighting largely unknown powder-puffs, and that Cayton and Jacobs were bringing him along according to the game plan his own mentor, Cus D'Amato, had laid out, his statement had absolutely no foundation.

Kevin Rooney continued to support Cayton, despite the warnings from Tyson to button his lip. He said Bill Cayton had never done anything except help Tyson. He called Cayton a 'square shooter', and said all of Tyson's money had been well invested by the two managerial partners. He said perhaps the smartest thing when he suggested that if Tyson and Cayton didn't sit down and work things out themselves, the lawyers involved were the ones who would be making all the money.

Speaking of lawyers, another was added to Tyson's team. With a courtroom battle looming, Ruth and Robin felt they needed a big name to bolster the efforts of Michael Winston, so they retained Peter Parcher to be their trial attorney. Parcher, whose clients included Mick Jagger, Billy Joel, Paul Simon and Bruce Springsteen, said Jacobs and Cayton were derelict not only legally but morally in not seeing to it that Tyson had independent legal representation when he signed contracts with them. 'This lawsuit isn't just about money,' Parcher claimed. 'Since Mike Tyson doesn't get along with Cayton, doesn't he have the right to say "You're fired"?' he asked. The attorney, whose clients were from the world of show business, mistakenly compared the practices in the entertainment field to those in boxing. 'As a performer becomes a star, on the level of a Tyson, his manager is not entitled to take 33 per cent of his earnings. That's not the way it works in the entertainment business.' But one-third has always been the standard purse cut due a manager in boxing, where an effective manager performs many functions for a fighter not required of a show-business manager.

On Tuesday, July 19, all parties gathered in the chambers of Justice David Edwards, Jr., in the State Supreme Court Building on Centre Street in Manhattan. Well, almost all parties. The plaintiff himself – Michael Tyson – did not appear. He was not required to by law, since he was represented by counsel, and no doubt he did not relish the prospect of a direct confrontation with the man at whom he'd been hurling so many accusations. Yet this was the Heavyweight Champion of the World who had announced he was the boss, he was running things, he was taking charge.

During the preliminary hearing, Justice Edwards later announced, some progress was made on two issues: working toward an arrangement that would allow the Bruno fight to take place with all those involved in the dispute participating, even though the larger Tyson–Cayton contractual issue might still remain to be resolved in court at a later date; and disposition of the more than $21-million in Tyson revenues from the Spinks fight, which had been frozen by court injunction.

Thursday, July 21, was spent by the various parties in meetings in the judge's chambers and in private rooms, but it was a day of progress. On hand were Tyson, Robin Givens, Ruth Roper, Bill Cayton, Lorraine Jacobs, Donald Trump, plus attorneys Puccio, Winston, Parcher and various associates, and this time Tyson himself. For nearly seven hours they talked and negotiated, and at the end of the day an agreement had been worked out to distribute $16.5-million from the Spinks fight. Justice Edwards vacated the temporary restraining order he had issued on June 29. Mike Tyson was issued a cheque for $10-million. Cayton and Mrs Jacobs received $5-million, and Kevin Rooney $1.5-million. Several million dollars more in revenue were still to come in from the US and around the world. Still unresolved was the matter of whether, when, and how matters would proceed toward making the Tyson–Bruno fight for September, less than two months off. Jarvis Astaire was on his way to New York from London at that very moment to meet with everyone involved in a last-ditch effort to try and salvage the September 3 date.

Following the all-day session in court, and the resolution of the Spinks fight money impasse, Thomas Puccio said he had no doubt that Bill Cayton and Mike Tyson would be able to work together in the future. 'We're basically down to one issue:

money, how much Tyson will get and how much Cayton will get. Bill can advise him on fights, but Mike Tyson will decide where and when he fights,' said Puccio.

Michael Winston said, 'The two main issues are money and the term of the contract. I think they can build toward a working relationship again if certain issues are resolved.' Tyson's attorney was realistic enough, however, to offer the observation that he didn't think the two would ever be buddies who could sit down and share a beer or two. But that night, attending an amateur boxing show at Madison Square Garden, Tyson told Bill Gallo of the *Daily News* that he doubted he could get along with Cayton in the future because the manager 'took advantage of me'. He said Steve Lott was now out as his assistant manager, but he had not reached a decision about Kevin Rooney's future, although he made it clear he was angered because Rooney 'went out of his way to go against me'. He said he credited only Cus D'Amato for his success, 'because he laid down the plans which he handed over to Jacobs. Every step I took was the original idea of Cus and nobody else.' Over the course of the hearings, Tyson continually referred to Cayton as 'crude', 'despicable' and someone who made him 'sick to my stomach'. A misinformed Tyson said that Wilfred Benitez, who had been managed by Jacobs and Cayton, was broken, and that the other world champion handled by Cayton, lightweight Edwin Rosario, had recently declared bankruptcy. In fact, the nutty Benitez and his equally irresponsible father were the ones who had themselves raped the Puerto Rican fighter's finances, despite the best efforts of Cayton and Jacobs to try to avert such a situation. When they established a money market fund containing hundreds of thousands of dollars to provide for Benitez's future, the fighter depleted it within 60 days, and would accept no financial advice from his managers. As for Rosario, at a Madison Square Garden press conference on July 28 to announce a forthcoming Rosario fight, a smiling Rosario stood next to Bill Cayton at the podium as Cayton, uncharacteristically blunt, labelled Tyson's statement 'bullshit', and said, 'Edwin Rosario is in fine financial condition. He has a six-figure trust fund here in New York.'

On Monday, July 25, fresh from a weekend respite, the parties reconvened at Justice Edwards's chambers at the State Supreme Court Building, and behind closed doors the dispute was finally resolved. In a compromise agreement that avoided a protracted court battle, Bill Cayton retained his role as Mike Tyson's manager for the full duration of the contract, which ran to February 11, 1992. But in a major concession by Cayton (which Donald Trump took full credit for imposing on the manager on Tyson's behalf), he agreed to reduce his percentage from 33 per cent to 20 per cent. As far as the personal services contract between Tyson and Cayton, which covered such out-of-the-ring income as commercials and endorsements, Cayton's percentage was reduced from 33 per cent to 16 ⅔ per cent on existing deals and 10 per cent on any future deals negotiated by Cayton. Tyson retained the right of refusal on any such deals. Cayton won a major point when it was agreed that his company, Big Fights, Inc., would have the exclusive right to license all television foreign rights agreements for Tyson fights and receive a 20 per cent commission for doing so, a concession providing tremendous financial potential to Cayton, because the 20 per cent commission on foreign rights negotiations was in addition to the 20 per cent he would receive from all gross fight revenues. The agreement further stated that Tyson had the right to have his own attorney review all fight contracts, that he could turn down any fight he did not want to take part in (somewhat meaningless in that the WBC, WBA and IBF all had mandatory challengers that Tyson had to face or else risk being stripped of his title, so the only fights he could turn down were the voluntary defences), and that he was entitled to have his own accountant receive a full accounting of all revenues. Finally, it was agreed that 'The fraud claim against Jacob [sic] and Cayton is withdrawn.'

The next day, a news conference was called at Trump's Plaza Hotel to announce the terms of the settlement. Along with the parties involved in the litigation, two other pleased parties were on hand – Jarvis Astaire, British promoter of the Bruno fight, and Seth Abraham, whose HBO network would televise it in the United States. They were anxious to sit down and finalize the match as soon as the press conference ended. Cayton said, 'I'm pleased this matter is resolved and that Mike and I can work together as we did in the past. We might have gone to court and won, but a court settlement would have led to bitterness. My attorneys decided this was the wisest thing to do and I agreed.' He said he hoped Tyson would 'enlighten' him as to the specifics of how he had been kept in the dark financially. 'The fact is,' Cayton said, 'before any fight was made, Jim and I would bring Mike into the office and discuss the fight with him. We never made a decision without Mike getting at least the right to know what was going to happen. Of course, he always had the right to refuse. . . .I'm absolutely confident that history will decide he is the greatest heavyweight champion of all time. I'm pleased to be continuing my career with him,' he concluded, even though Tyson had refused to stand with him at the podium. Thomas Puccio said Tyson had always had the right to turn down fights or opponents, so adding those points in writing was just 'window dressing'. When Donald Trump outlined the terms of the settlement, smirking Robin Givens applauded wildly. Michael Winston said, 'I think we accomplished everything we wanted. Mike's calling the shots, controlling his own destiny, and he still respects Bill's ability as a businessman.' Lorraine Jacobs said she was pleased it was all over, but when asked if she could forgive Tyson for accusing her late husband of fraud, she said, 'I'd really rather not comment on anything.'

Then it was Mike Tyson's turn. Stepping to the podium, dressed, for a change, in a tailored suit and tie, he said, 'I'm running my show. That contract I was in was like a servant contract. I fought who, when and where they said I should. Cayton did a good job financially, but he didn't inform me of certain things. If I hadn't been married to Robin, my eyes might never have been opened. We had to go through ridicule and scandal. I personally don't get embarrassed myself, but my wife and mother-in-law were embarrassed and might have left me if they weren't so strong.' Tyson said he would have liked to have gone to trial because 'Deep down inside, I wanted to see my lawyer Peter Parcher work in court.' He said Cayton 'is employed by me; I'm not employed by him. . . .The main thing is, if I don't agree to anything, it doesn't have to happen. . . .He's good at what he does, and as long as he abides by all the terms of the agreement, everything will work out. We don't have to get along. . . .As for winning or losing, I'm walking away with a better deal than I had when I started.'

Tyson wasn't quite finished, however. As a stunned Jarvis Astaire and Seth Abraham listened, he said, 'I think I'm going to pass on the Bruno fight and take six or eight weeks off to relax. I just don't feel like fighting right now. Please, by no means am I scared of Bruno. I just don't want to get on a plane and fly five hours, or three hours, or whatever. I want to stay in the United States.' Astaire offered the opinion that Tyson's first decision on his own was a bad one, 'commercial suicide'. He said perhaps Tyson didn't care about a mere $2-million, but moving the bout from the stadium indoors to Wembley Arena later in the year would cost him at least that, from a projected $8-million to perhaps $5- or $6-million. But Don King, quiet during the court proceedings and conspicuously absent, was spending time with Tyson at the fighter's New Jersey home, and it was a safe bet he wasn't encouraging Tyson to go to England and fight Bruno for his promotional rivals, Astaire and Duff.

Later, when he intensified his attacks on Cayton, King would single out the deal Cayton made for the Bruno fight in London as having been a terrible one for Tyson; in fact, the opposite was true. It was in fact a deal which Cayton's negotiations began with securing $4-million from HBO, which Cayton arranged would remain in the US and therefore would not be subject to British taxes. Next, all foreign TV money outside Britain would be paid to Tyson in the United States – over $2-million – and therefore would also not be subject to British taxes. There was $1.5-million allocated for all expenses, which included (and was quite unusual in this respect) all sanctioning fees, some $350-thousand. Out of the $1.5-million would also come Bruno's sanctioning fees, the promoter's sanctioning fees, the rental for Wembley, advertising costs, plus $100,000 'pocket money' in cash to Tyson for his own personal expenses. Bruno was to get a purse of $1.8-million.

Cayton arranged separate deals with Toyota for $500-thousand for which the Japanese auto manufacturer would receive advertising and promotional consideration such as having their logo on the ring canvas, the ring posts, and in the stadium, plus being identified as the fight's 'sponsor'. He also negotiated a $500-thousand deal with the BBC for delayed broadcast rights in Great Britain, plus an additional estimated half-million dollars that would accrue from concessions, souvenirs and the like. The gross purse would have come to about $9-million, out of which would come the $1.5-million for expenses and Bruno's purse of $1.8-million, leaving Tyson just about $6-million or slightly under. In addition, Cayton bargained for an extraordinary assortment of 'perks' worth perhaps another $400-thousand. These included 16 round-trip Concorde tickets, 40 additional tickets on regularly-scheduled jetliners, suites for Robin and Ruth in one of London's finest hotels, along with suites in a beautiful training facility Tyson would use outside London.

Mike Tyson was unmoved and apparently unimpressed. At

a meeting that month in the HBO offices attended by Cayton, Tyson, and HBO senior executives Michael Fuchs and Seth Abraham, Tyson said point-blank, 'I don't want to go to London.' Cayton was aware that pulling out of an agreed fight against the mandatory challenger meant risking being stripped of the title by WBC. And make no mistake, it was Mickey Duff's intention to pressure the WBC to do just that, and then move Bruno into an elimination bout for the vacant title as the number one contender, meaning Bruno could win a portion of the title without having to fight Tyson, and making an eventual meeting between the two worth much more to Bruno. 'Mike,' Cayton said, 'you've signed a contract, you must honour it.' 'I don't want to honour it. I don't want to go to London,' he reiterated. 'You're my manager. Get me out of it. I don't care what it costs.' And that was that.

As August came, the winds shifted dramatically on two fronts. In the hope that Tyson would relent and fight Bruno in London, as he was contractually obliged to, the fight date was moved back to October 8, when it might still be just possible to squeeze it in outdoors at Wembley. During the second week of August, Jarvis Astaire announced in London the fight would take place, and on Monday, August 15, at a Wembley news conference, Bruno said, 'People are making Tyson sound like a monster, but no man is unbeatable and I am a stone [14 pounds] heavier than him. This fight is all about power. . . .I have been watching videos of Tyson and I have spotted quite a few weaknesses. . . .He's going to get murdered, not me. . . .He doesn't scare me.' Wembley was scaled for a live gate of $7.65-million with a sell-out, which the promoters said they expected. That would make it the biggest financial windfall in British sporting history. John Morris, Secretary of the British Boxing Board of Control expressed his faith in Bruno's forthcoming effort. 'In no way will Frank Bruno be a lamb led to the slaughter,' he said. 'We could have the biggest boxing upset of all time here.' Terry Lawless, Bruno's manager, said Frank's aim more than just going in to grab the $1.7-million purse. 'Frank has desperately wanted to fight Tyson since they first met. I have never known anyone so desperate to fight someone. It's a pride fight for Frank,' said Lawless.

On that same Monday, August 15, some 3,500 miles away, in Cleveland, Ohio, Tyson was hedging. 'We really haven't decided if we're fighting him or not,' the champion told the press who had gathered for a Don King-arranged ceremony in which Tyson was being presented with the ceremonial key to the city. Tyson was staying with King at the promoter's home outside the city; as a matter of fact, the two had of late been virtually inseparable, and the suspicion was that King was up to no good, with the malleable young champion in his grasp. But in an effort to subvert the Bruno fight, Don King was overplaying his hand and was in the process of making a major blunder.

The previous week, King had been with Tyson in Los Angeles. Jose Ribalta and his manager, Luis DeCubas, were summoned from their homes in Miami and the four met to negotiate a fight. King told Ribalta and DeCubas that Tyson would fight the Cuban-born heavyweight in October, not Frank Bruno, and had them sign an agreement to that effect which offered a purse of $700-thousand to Ribalta. When Cayton, Astaire, Duff, got wind of it, along with Ruth, Robin and attorney Winston, the shit hit the fan. Tyson had listened to Don King singing him the 'You're The Boss, You're Calling The Shots' song and had acted, as usual, impulsively, jumping right in to dance to the tune without being properly informed. A month earlier, Tyson had complained in his legal papers that he had never been represented by his own attorney when dealing with Jacobs and Cayton. Now that he had an attorney, he didn't consult him. But it did not take Winston, Ruth Roper and Robin Givens very long to come to the conclusion that King had been working behind their backs to deal independently and directly with Tyson and that Tyson was now heading for legal trouble. Just three weeks earlier, a legal war had been averted when a new agreement was reached with Bill Cayton. This stated that Cayton remained Tyson's manager, and one of the key points in the contract with Cayton stipulated that Tyson could not engage in any fights except those specifically approved by his manager, despite all the rhetoric that Tyson was 'the boss'.

King then announced he had Tyson's signature on a contract to promote his next fight. 'I have a written contract,' he declared, looking like the cat who had just eaten the canary. 'Rest assured, I've got paper. I don't do nothing just oral,' and he said he had done what he had done with no other intention except 'love', insisting it was not a desperate act of disruption on his part. Thomas Puccio advised Bill Cayton to sue King for tortuous interference with his contract with Tyson. 'The contract King purports to have isn't worth the paper it's written on,' declared Cayton. Astaire and Duff saw King's move as a direct attempt to sabotage the fight at Wembley, and were also contemplating legal action. So, suddenly, in one move, Don King had alienated the two women he had spent months smooth-talking in an effort to win their confidence, had put Tyson in potential legal hot water, and was facing a possible lawsuit from the champion's manager, as well as another from the British promoters. But one week later, a single punch thrown not in the ring but in the middle of the night on a steamy Harlem street would turn everything topsy-turvy, the first in a series of events that would generate more newspaper copy, magazine stories and TV reports than any of Tyson's 35 fights, as his life began more and more to resemble, at one and the same time, a television soap opera, a slapstick comedy, and a Greek tragedy.

15

Those Lazy, Hazy, Crazy Days of Summer

If anger is not restrained, it is frequently more hurtful to us than the injury that provokes it.

– SENECA

ON TUESDAY, August 23, Tyson was due in Catskill, where Kevin Rooney expected him to put in his first day of training for the Bruno fight. However, at about 4 am on August 23, Tyson and two friends pulled up in his Rolls-Royce to 43 East 125th Street, the heart of Harlem, just off the corner of Madison Avenue. Tyson's two companions were Walter Berry, the former St John's University basketball star then playing with San Antonio in the National Basketball Association, and Berry's cousin, Tom Smalls. At that address was a clothing store called Dapper Dan's, frequented by customers ranging from fancy Harlem dandies and rap music stars to pimps and drug dealers. (Also at that address, according to police, was an unlicensed 'after-hours' club in the basement.) Owing to the nocturnal nature of much of its clientele, Dapper Dan's was open when Tyson arrived to pick up a custom-made $800 white leather jacket.

Mitch Green lived on 160th Street in the Jamaica section of the borough of Queens, but he considered Harlem his turf and it just so happened that he was hanging around with some friends nearby. Word quickly filtered to him that Tyson had just arrived at Dapper Dan's, and he made an instant decision to go and confront the heavyweight champion.

A former street gang leader who had spent time in juvenile detention centre, Green had turned to boxing and – after a solid amateur career – became a professional in 1980, when he was 24 years old. Standing 6'5" and possessing considerable talent, he had the potential to go far, and after racking up a string of wins under the management of Shelly Finkel and Lou Duva, NBC Television included him a group they called 'Tomorrow Champions' in a televised boxing series of the same name. Green lost a 12-round decision to former champion Trevor Berbick, his only loss until he dropped the 10-round decision to Tyson in May of 1986, by which time he had switched management to the Don and Carl King team. Despite lots of big talk, Green, who still faced a bright future as a fighter, never fought again. He developed a pattern of erratic behaviour that made him too unstable to fight. His driver's licence had been suspended or revoked a remarkable 54 times, and charges against him from 1983 to 1988 included driving without insurance, driving under the influence of drugs, plus five accidents involving personal injuries to others. After one arrest, a urine test performed on him came back positive for 'angel dust', and his behaviour at Gleason's Gym on the one or two days he turned up there in 1988 to make an attempt at training led those present to conclude he was functioning under the influence of some foreign substance in his body. He was also arrested for robbery when he commandeered a gasoline station, chased the attendant away, and began pumping the gasoline himself for customers and pocketing the cash. He provoked a highly publicized confrontation with Don King at a 1986 news conference when he arrived uninvited and threatened King's life, and he had previously invaded a Larry Holmes news conference, challenging the then champion to a fight and pointing his finger directly into Holmes's face until one of Larry's bodyguards bit it! This, then, was the Mitch Green who decided to drop in on Mike Tyson at Dapper Dan's.

According to various accounts, Green went inside the clothing store and began egging Tyson on. 'I was telling him,' Green himself said, '"You know I didn't really fight you. You really didn't beat me, 'cause Don King done took my money."' He then began yelling, 'Don King robbed me,' to which Tyson allegedly responded, 'Don King robbed me too. He robs everybody.' 'You're with Don King,' Green said to Tyson. 'You both owe me money.' Tyson said he left the store and headed for his car to end the showdown with Green, but Green followed him on to the street and grabbed him, ripping his shirt. 'It happened so fast,' Tyson later said, 'I was very upset that he ripped my shirt, and I was upset that he came back again. I was getting paranoid because he was close to me so I defended myself. I had no choice but to defend myself. I wasn't planning to punch him. I was fighting because I was scared. I hadn't had a street fight in seven years, I was getting scared.'

Tyson apparently told Green that he was talking bullshit. 'You're going to tell me I didn't beat you?' Tyson asked. 'I won that fight. I beat you.' According to Green, Tyson said, 'We can do it again now.' Green said he saw Tyson adjusting the gold rings on his hand as if he was getting ready to punch. Now out on the sidewalk, Green said Tyson 'sucker punched me and ran, and his boys held me, like they were breaking up a fight, while I was trying to get to him. They hit me cheap shots, too. . . .Mike Tyson, Heavyweight Champion of the World, a cheap shot like that.' Tyson and witnesses, however, say it was Green who threw the first punch, striking the champion in the chest. In an instant, Tyson fired one right hand, gold rings and all, right between Green's eyes, inflicting a wound that required five stitches to close it. In the ensuing scuffle, Green broke the rear view mirror off Tyson's Rolls-Royce. Both men then went off to hospital, Green to North General to be stitched up, and Tyson to Manhattan's Mount Sinai to have his hand looked at. He arrived at the emergency room at 5.30 am complaining of a bruised hand, was treated and released 45 minutes later. Green proceeded from the hospital to the 25th New York City Police Department precinct house to file assault charges against Tyson, which Tyson later termed 'ludicrous. . . .I'm a victim and then he presses charges on me'. Tyson said he did not plan to file counter charges.

Later in the day, the hand still bothering him, Tyson went to an orthopaedic hand specialist, and x-rays revealed his one-punch fight with Mitch Green had cost him dearly. He had suffered a hairline fracture of the third metacarpal bone, the bone on the back of the hand running from the middle knuckle back toward the wrist. His hand was set in a protective cast for three weeks; now the October 8 date in London which was still being worked on was in danger of cancellation before it was even set.

In the days following the incident, the TV newscasts and newspapers had a field day, questioning Tyson's motives and judgment in being out and about at 4 am, especially on the day he was to begin training, and reporting Mitch Green as he ranted and raved at a news conference he called, and on TV talk shows. 'He was acting like a sissy. . .he's scared of me,' said Green. 'He's a homo, ho-mo. He may go both ways, but he's a homo. . . .He's a half-retarded, henpecked little sissy. . . .Where's Michelle. I want Michelle. . . .' What Green was trying to do was parlay the highly-publicized incident

into a million-dollar rematch with Tyson, and for several weeks
thereafter he actually succeeded in creating enough interest to
make a future showdown – in the ring – a distinct possibility.
Green challenged Tyson, Bill Cayton liked the idea of a 'grudge
match', saying Tyson–Green was 'absolutely a very attractive
fight now', and the hype was on, even as the British promoters of Tyson–Bruno secured an October 22 back-up date at
Wembley, anticipating that the injury to Tyson's hand might
push their bout back two more weeks.

There was just one obstacle to a Tyson–Green fight, a little
matter of rules. No sanctioning group would permit a fight for
the title unless the challenger, that is Mitch Green, was ranked
in the top ten, and because of his more than two years of
complete ring idleness, he was unranked. In order to become
ranked, he would have to defeat someone in the top ten first.
Such disparate figures as Seth Abraham of HBO, Green's former manager, Shelly Finkel, and his former promoter and current arch-enemy, Don King, made a concerted effort to get him
a fight, but Green really wasn't interested. He kept insisting he
didn't need to fight anyone first, just Tyson. Even his current
managers acknowledged their man didn't really want to fight.
He turned down several fights his managers had been trying to
make since his 1986 loss to Tyson, one for $40,000 and another
for $25,000, plus an easy one for $7,500, saying he wouldn't
take them because it was beneath his dignity to fight for such
low purses.

Finally, in exchange for dropping his charges against Tyson,
which he did two days after filing them, Bill Cayton gave Green
a letter of agreement saying he could have a fight with Tyson,
if he got himself in shape and back in the rankings. 'How do
you like that? I'm a hot item right now,' said Green, with an
inflated opinion of his own worth. Tyson issued a statement
which said, in part, 'I can beat this guy anytime, anywhere,
anyplace. I will teach him a lesson in the ring that he should
have learned already.' Calling Green's attack on him a 'cheap
publicity stunt', he called on Green to 'be a man for once. . .get
into shape, get his act together with some good tough prelim
fights so that he's ranked again, [and] I'll definitely teach him
such a lesson in the ring that he'll never forget.'

Despite all the publicity and interest generated by this
apparently chance encounter of two heavyweight ships passing (and colliding) in the night, Mitch Green made no effort to
follow through on any of the things being done on his behalf to

help him get in shape, and before long all talk of a Tyson–Green bout was dropped and forgotten. The next time Mitch Green was heard of was four weeks later, when he was arrested on a Harlem street for disorderly conduct after stopping his car and causing a traffic jam while he raved and cursed about Mike Tyson. Officers from the Emergency Services unit had to use electric stun guns to subdue the crazed fighter. Two days later, he was arrested once again, this time for third-degree assault after his girlfriend called the police and said the boxer, who was the father of her child, had beaten her.

One footnote: the inscription meticulously sewn on to the back of the white leather jacket that Tyson had stopped by Dapper Dan's to collect, read in large letters, 'Don't Believe The Hype'.

On September 1st, earlier than expected, the cast was removed from Tyson's right hand, and he was given the go-ahead to resume serious training in Catskill for the Bruno fight. He would return to Catskill for a week, before accompanying his wife to the Soviet Union where she was scheduled to tape two special episodes of her TV sitcom. While in Moscow, Kevin Rooney was to join him and Tyson would train there for a week, come back to the United States for several days, then move his training base to London on September 25. He left his doctor's office in midtown Manhattan with a protective, removable plastic support on his hand, and although he could resume training, he would not use the right hand until it was no longer sore.

On September 2, he worked out in the gym, then stayed out late at the Albany-area nightclub he frequents, Septembers, in the town of Colonie. The next morning, he arrived at the gym alone at 10 am in his BMW, removed his hand brace, and went through a light work-out with the bags and in the ring, although there was no sparring. He was supervised by Rooney. He showed a visitor his hand, which was clearly still swollen across the back, where the break had occurred. After the work-out, he returned to the house with John Etheridge, a reporter on the London *Sun* newspaper, and Etheridge's photographer, in tow. The weather was beautiful, and after climbing to his pigeon loft and letting his birds out to fly, he sat down on the porch and gave Etheridge a relaxed interview. He talked about how he was finding himself as a person, how he was no longer into jewellery, into buying cars, how he was discovering that money was not really important. He reminisced about when he had little money, and was happy to buy used leather jackets at rummage sales for $30 around the Catskill area; about how he would beg his friends to buy him a Whopper at Burger King, and how they tried to talk their way into the local movie theatre at two-for-one prices. He seemed nostalgic about the old days, perhaps thinking life was simpler before fame, success and money complicated it.

Shortly after noon he ended the interview. He wanted to shower, change and drive to Atlantic City, a good 3½ to 4 hours from Catskill, to see Buddy McGirt defend his Junior Welterweight title against Meldrick Taylor. But after the newspapermen departed, he felt groggy, and could hardly keep his eyes open, tired from his late night at Septembers. Jay Bright strongly advised him not to attempt the long drive to Atlantic City and back in his fatigue condition, and Tyson saw the wisdom of this. He rested, watched on TV as McGirt lost his title to Taylor, and then drove the 40 miles to Colonie where he once again spent the night at Septembers.

On Sunday morning, September 4, the entire United States eastern seaboard, from Florida to New England, was blanketed in bad weather. Torrential rains had fallen all night in New York, and it was still pouring in the morning when Mike woke up, watched a movie on his VCR, and then sat in the living-room reading a magazine. Around eleven o'clock he told Camille Ewald he had nothing to read and he was going to drove two miles into town to buy some magazines. She told him to be careful because of the terrible weather. Mike then went outside and got behind the wheel of the $71-thousand BMW 750iL, a 12-cylinder powerhouse he had purchased as a gift for Robin.

Many of Tyson's friends will joke that Mike Tyson behind the wheel of a car is more dangerous than Mike Tyson in the ring. Teddy Atlas recalls Mike mounting the sidewalk and hitting a mailbox while trying to drive the first used car Cus D'Amato bought for the teenage fighter. Jay Bright laughingly said he hides behind trees when Mike gets in the car to drive. D'Amato once told his young fighter, after taking a drive with him, 'Mike, I'll never have to use a laxative again.' Tyson had no luck with cars, even when he wasn't driving. Before he and Robin were married, following an argument, she got into his Mercedes 560SL and slammed it into the rear of his Rolls-Royce, damaging both vehicles. On this rainy morning in Catskill, the BMW was parked on the grass. Tyson turned on the ignition, hit the gas pedal, and the wheels began spinning in the wet grass and mud. Camille came out on the porch to try to tell him there was a telephone call for him. At that moment, the wheels suddenly grabbed and the car shot forward out of control. It lurched about thirty feet, and the right front bumper slammed into a chestnut tree at the edge of the property. It bounced off the tree, sustaining heavy damage to the front end, then came up to a stop in some shrubs a short distance away. When Camille got to the car, Tyson appeared to be unconscious. His head was slumped back, his eyes closed. She slapped him a few times, and he came to, asking her, 'Camille, what happened?' 'You hit a tree,' she told him, and then he drifted off into unconsciousness again. Jay Bright phoned for an ambulance, which came from Catskill in about ten minutes. Tyson, according to one of the attendants, was still unconscious, although his pulse, breathing and blood pressure were normal. They rushed him to the small Catskill Hospital, but a short time later it was decided to move him to the larger Columbia-Greene Medical Center about fifteen minutes away in Hudson, New York, where a CAT scan could be performed.

Meanwhile, Ruth Roper and Robin Givens were notified in New York City about the accident, and immediately began the two-hour drive to Catskill. Tyson had wanted Robin to spend a few days with him there while he trained and before they both left for the Soviet Union, but she had opted to stay in the City to attend the US Open Tennis Championships, which were under way. Before starting out for Catskill, Roper had told Camille they would want to transfer Mike to Columbia-Presbyterian Medical Center in Manhattan, where they felt he would receive better diagnostic treatment.

When Camille went to see Mike at the hospital in Hudson, around one o'clock in the afternoon, the fighter was fully conscious and in good spirits, though rather embarrassed by the mishap and the fuss. Camille told him that Ruth and Robin wanted him transferred to New York City, but Mike said he wasn't going anywhere until he had something to eat. He was starving, and food was his major concern at that moment. Jay Bright went to a Chinese restaurant and brought him a large quantity of fried rice and beef with broccoli, which the champion ravenously consumed. Mike joked with Camille about what a 'nice Labor Day weekend' it had turned out to be, with him in the hospital, and the two laughed about it.

His spirits brightened further when Robin arrived later in the afternoon, along with her mother and their public relations representative. By then, Tyson had undergone a CAT brain scan, and EEG and EKG, and Bill Cayton had been informed by Columbia-Greene doctors that Mike was 'absolutely okay'. Shortly after 7 pm, with local newspaper and TV cameramen waiting outside, Mike was brought out, strapped to a stretcher, looking bewildered and embarrassed, and placed in an ambulance for the trip to Manhattan. In response to a question, he nodded and quietly acknowledged that he was feeling fine. Robin got in the back of the ambulance with him, and as photographers jockeyed for position to take pictures through the ambulance window, she blocked their view with her hand until a towel was placed across the window to curtain-off the view. Earlier in the afternoon, there had been an unpleasant shouting match between Robin and trainer Kevin Rooney, when he arrived at the hospital to visit Tyson. Robin had tried to prevent him from getting into Mike's room, but he had brushed past her and gone in to see his young charge.

Shortly after 9 pm, Tyson's ambulance arrived at Columbia-Presbyterian Medical Center in Northern Manhattan, where reporters, photographers and TV cameras were waiting. As Tyson's stretcher was taken out of the ambulance, Givens became involved in another scene, shouting at the newspeople to 'leave him alone, nothing's the matter, give the guy a break'. No one was bothering Mike, just taking his picture, but Givens suddenly jumped right over her husband's stretcher, which was momentarily on the ground, and lunged at a TV cameraman, pushing him until he admonished her to 'Take it easy, lady': thus she became the focal point of the next day's TV newscasts and newspaper photos.

In the hospital, Tyson was once again subjected to a battery of even more sophisticated tests. Late that night, the Assistant Professor of Neurology at the hospital told the media that Mike had 'suffered minor trauma to the head and the chest wall' as the result of banging into the steering wheel when he hit the tree. She said he would remain in the hospital to undergo further observation and diagnostic testing, but his condition was 'quite stable' and he was 'neurologically normal'.

The next day, Monday morning, Roper and Givens made another calculated move typical of them. Mike was isolated in a private room on the ninth floor, with security guards posted to protect his privacy. Two women compiled a list of approved visitors to Mike's room. Bill Cayton and Kevin Rooney were not on it. They had made it clear many times that the people who had been with Mike all along, from the beginning, were not part of their group. Even Cus D'Amato, who, despite some errors in judgment, had done more for Mike Tyson than anyone else, was no longer in favour with the two women. Robin had said in the past she was 'tired of constantly hearing about an old dead man I never knew', that she didn't want her life infringed upon by the 'ghost' of Cus D'Amato. The past meant nothing to these women. They were calling the shots now. Bill Cayton tried as gracefully as possible to accept the fact that he was turned away when he tried to visit Mike, but Rooney was enraged. So were others, including Broadway and film star Danny Aiello and photographer Brian Hamill, who were also unceremoniously rejected when they arrived at the hospital. Aiello and Hamill were personally turned away by Robin, who gave them a curt 'no', with no explanation or even cursory thanks for dropping by.

The list of who could enter the inner sanctum and visit Mike was bizarre. It included, besides Roper and Givens, Roper's assistant and henchwoman, Olga Rosario, Peter Parcher and Steven Hayes, the two attorneys retained by Roper to represent Tyson, Donald Trump and his wife, Ivana, and Howard Rubenstein, Trump's public relations man, who had been retained by Roper and Givens to represent them as well as Mike. 'Mrs Trump!' exclaimed Danny Aiello. 'We've known Mike since he was a kid. Trump knows him for half an hour,' he told Pete Hamill.

Roper spoke touchingly of her daughter's loyalty. 'Robin is hanging in there with her man, as usual,' she said. 'When he gets bruised, she hurts.' Don King, on the outside looking in, offered his opinion that something was evidently wrong with Mike, he was confused. Those around him, suggested the benevolent promoter, shouldn't be so concerned about Mike fighting and making money; instead they should be interested in his welfare as a human being, said King. Sugar Ray Leonard put forth the opinion that 'there is something bothering Mike, probably something that stems back to when he was a kid.' Larry Holmes said Tyson needed some guidance and good advice, and sent Mike a telegram offering to help if Mike wanted to talk to him. Muhammad Ali said he had never got into trouble while champion, but said Mike was 'still young and he's got a few little faults and habits, which we all have, that have got to be corrected. He's in a position now where the world is watching him and I think after a few mistakes, he'll realize that. . . .If he wasn't famous and he wasn't where he was, he wouldn't make the news. But he's popular.'

On Tuesday, Tyson underwent further testing. It was determined he could be released within a day or two, but Dr Britton then pronounced the words that Jarvis Astaire and Mickey Duff didn't want to hear. She said that since Mike had been unconscious for about twenty minutes following the accident, he had suffered some temporary amnesia, his doctors recommended that he should not train for 30 to 60 days, making an October date at Wembley an impossibility. In London, Jarvis Astaire acknowledged that both October 8 and the back-up date of October 22 were now out of the question. He said there was no choice but to implement the contingency plan of moving the fight indoors to a much smaller venue, the Wembley Arena, and a tentative date of December 16 was set. Astaire made it clear there would be no stepping aside by Bruno to allow Tyson to fight an interim challenger. 'Bruno is the nominated next challenger,' he said. 'We have a contract for Tyson to fight him and that is what will happen. . . .If anything, this should give Frank encouragement. The invincibility of Tyson has taken a bit of a blow. Once he gets over his initial disappointment Frank is going to fancy his chances even more. Psychologically, what's happened must worry the champion.'

Back at the hospital, Tyson was getting petulant and restless. The security guards assigned to him described him as a 'big baby', complaining all the time and watching television constantly, throwing the white hospital gowns at nurses and attendants and telling them he only wore black.

The front page headlines all week had riveted people to the Tyson story 'Iron Mike KO'd In Crash', 'Car Skid KOs Tyson', 'Iron Mike Faces Brain Scan', 'Tyson's Bout (vs. Bruno) KOd', 'Alone At the Top, Tortured Tyson Has Nowhere To Turn', 'Tyson–Bruno Off, Doctor Says Champ Needs Time To Recover'. But the *New York Daily News* headline on the morning of Wednesday, September 7, set off more reaction, controversy, claims and counter-claims than any Tyson had previously had in the three years since he first hit the news. 'EXCLUSIVE: TYSON TRIED TO KILL SELF,' said the paper's front page in two-inch bold black letters. The sub-heading said, 'Friends reveal suicide threat.' The story, written by columnist Mike McAlary, was, to say the least, sensational. It claimed that on Sunday morning, Tyson, whose mind 'was racing and tortured', called Givens in Manhattan and told her 'I'm going to go out and kill myself. . . .I'm going to crash my car.' He then went to the BMW and hit the gas pedal without putting on his seat belt, and 'aimed the car into a tree'. McAlary then presented an entire dossier of allegations, among them that the previous Thursday Tyson 'had threatened to kill Givens', and that the next day, 'according to. . .friends', two shotguns were delivered to Tyson. 'I'll kill you and then me,' McAlary reported Tyson as saying to Robin.

When Givens arrived at the hospital upstate on Sunday afternoon, according to McAlary, Tyson said to her, 'I told you I'd do it. . .and as soon as I get out of here, I'll do it again.' McAlary said for several weeks Roper and Givens had tried unsuccessfully to get Mike to see a New York psychiatrist, Dr Henry McCurtis, who was the Director of Psychiatry at Harlem Hospital, and who specialized in the treatment of athletes suffering from stress. While in hospital, Tyson had at last spoken with McCurtis. Although the psychiatrist would not discuss Tyson with him, McAlary's sources told him McCurtis believed 'Mike Tyson should be committed for psychiatric evaluation'. He went on to reveal that 'Only a small circle of people know what is said to be Tyson's real problem, that he has a chemical imbalance that prods him to violent behaviour. . . .As a child, the champ reportedly took medication for this affliction. But then he became a boxer and quit the medication. His old trainer, Cus D'Amato, believed that he could control Tyson by keeping him in the ring. But. . .evidently there is no controlling his demons. . . .The people with knowledge of Tyson's problems include Donald Trump and public relations man Howard Rubenstein. Tyson's lawyers – Peter Parcher and Steven Hayes – also understand the situation. . . .They are more interested in the fighter's future than his next fight.' He included Givens and Roper among those truly concerned for Tyson's well-being, painting Cayton and Rooney as money-grubbing and only interested in milking every last dollar from Tyson: 'The nonfight people were trying to help the heavyweight champion of the world save his life. The second set – the fight people, Cayton and Rooney – were trying to save a meal ticket.'

The writer further portrayed Givens as the long-suffering wife, saying she was 'distraught' when she entered Mike's hospital room, and depicting Tyson as a monster. 'The Tyson

marriage that you see on television – the smiling pictures you
see on gossip pages – is a lie. Mike Tyson, his friends and
relatives say, is a wife-beater. They say he has learned to hit
his wife with the bottom of his hand, boasting that this is a blow
that when delivered correctly, leaves no mark.

'The champion is also said to be big on choking. He grabs
Givens by the neck, friends say, and shakes her. . . .Mostly,
Tyson curses his young wife. He does this in public. He also
takes phone calls from girl-friends in front of his wife.' McAlary
then added, that two months earlier, Tyson and Givens had
vacationed at Donald Trump's hotel on Paradise Island in the
Bahamas, and while there Tyson got into a fight with both his
wife and her friend, Lori McNeil, one of the premier professional women's tennis players, who was also at the hotel.
'Tyson is reported to have smacked both women,' according
to the sensational *Daily News* story. 'According to friends of
the couple,' wrote McAlary, 'Givens suffered a black eye and
a swollen jaw. She spent most of her vacation waiting for the
bruises to clear.'

Those who bought the *Daily News* that morning certainly got
their money's worth. Tyson could not believe it when he saw
the paper. He called Camille in Catskill and rhetorically asked
her, 'Who the hell said I was committing suicide?' Reaction
was swift. Respected columnist and author Pete Hamill wrote:
'I have only one response to this story. Bull.' Pat Putnam, of
Sports Illustrated magazine, wrote, 'The story made for juicy
reading, but there was a problem: It was a plant, and an
artless, bubble-headed one at that.' One by one, those who
really knew Tyson reacted. Bobby Stewart said, 'I dispensed
the medication [at the Tryon school], probably most of them
[the boys] were on medication at the time, something to slow
them down. Mike was not on anything.' Teddy Atlas said
Mike was not on any medication while at Catskill, something he certainly would have known about as the fighter's
trainer, friend, and housemate. Kevin Rooney also confirmed
this, and called the story 'bullshit'. Bill Cayton termed the
Daily News story 'obviously a plant. . .outrageous. . .a pack
of falsehoods and untruths. . .despicable lies. . . .' All those
who knew Tyson treated the allegations of attempted suicide
as a joke, pointing out that you don't run your car thirty feet
across a wet lawn into a tree if you're trying to kill yourself,
and as for McAlary's charge that Tyson wasn't wearing his
seatbelt, it wasn't necessary in the BMW, which, as Mike well

knew, was equipped with an inflatable bag safety feature in the front seat. The collision into the tree wasn't even of sufficient force to release the air bag!

Award-winning sports columnist Jerry Izenberg wrote in the *New York Post* that the McAlary piece was 'a calculatedly leaked story – apparently from one of the attorneys his wife's family chose for [Tyson]', and he described the entire situation as 'an emotional tug of war over [Tyson] in which the participants are engaged in a deadly game of media roulette with a bullet in every chamber. . . .with no place to hide, no place to think things out and no place for Mike Tyson to catch his breath. . . .unless the heavyweight champion gets the one-on-one help he so desperately needs with absolutely nobody else involved, it is a story with a frighteningly predictable ending.'

Tyson's sister went to visit him at the hospital the day the story appeared. She said Mike laughed about the suicide report, and told her 'I wouldn't even know how to do it.' In a telephone interview with sports reporter Carl White, Tyson said the story was 'ridiculous. . . .They're trying to make a freak show out of my life, to say I would try to kill myself. Nobody has more, better reasons to live than I do. . . .No one loves living more than I do. . .I have way too much butt to kick in the ring to try to kill myself out of the ring. . . .Why does my wife have to be a bad person? We're both basically good people. We're high strung but we're basically good people.' He added, 'I love my wife. I don't beat on my wife. I'm never going to leave my wife. My wife's never going to leave me.'

16

To Russia. . .With Love?

The unfortunate thing about public misfortunes is that everyone regards himself as
qualified to talk about them.

– E. M. CIORAN

ON WEDNESDAY EVENING, unannounced and undetected,
Tyson was released and slipped quietly out of the hospital
into a waiting limousine with his wife and mother-in-law. All
week it had been said he would go to Catskill to get some rest
under the care of Camille Ewald, but instead Ruth and Robin
took him to the New Jersey mansion. A final barrage of ultra-
sound tests, electrocardiograms, radioisotope scans and blood
tests showed that there had been no damage done to his heart
despite the bruising to his chest from the impact with the BMW's
steering wheel.

Tyson's true friends believed that most of what was going on,
from the 'revelation' by Robin's sister that Mike beat his wife,
to the story of his suicide attempt, his emotional instability,
and, again, his violent behaviour toward Robin, was nothing
less than a carefully orchestrated plot to establish grounds for
a divorce that would allow Givens to walk away with a big
settlement of cash and property.

Lori McNeil, Givens's tennis player friend, issued a statement
concerning McAlary's allegations that Tyson hit her along with
Robin during their vacation in the Bahamas: 'The player
they made reference to is not me, nor do I know who they are
referring to. I have never even been to Paradise Island.'

But accounts of a wild scene in the Bahamas did emerge
independently from hotel employees. Apparently Givens left
their $2-thousand-a-night suite to go out for the day, and Mike
heard that her old flame, Eddie Murphy, was also vacationing
somewhere on the Island. According to those at the hotel,
he confronted her in the lobby when she returned late in
the afternoon, accusing her of sneaking off to visit Murphy.
Givens denied she even knew where Murphy was staying. That
night, a sulking Tyson drank heavily at the hotel bar while

Givens sat with him. From his early days in boxing, when he wouldn't touch alcohol, Tyson had become a heavy drinker. Shortly before 11 pm, hotel security said a woman staying with the Tysons reported a disturbance in their suite.

When two security guards arrived and entered, they say they saw Tyson hitting Givens, while she screamed for him to stop. Seeing the security guards, Tyson became more enraged, punching one of them and chasing them into the hallway as they begged him to cool down. They were not anxious for a confrontation with the formidable Tyson. Givens told the guards they were useless. 'You think they're going to protect you against me?' Mike asked her, and then started to strip off his shirt as if he was getting ready for more action. The guards retreated, and while Tyson's temper was momentarily defused, Givens reportedly packed a bag and left for the night. The next day, however, after Tyson calmed down, the two were back together. Tyson was billed for nearly $400 in damages, which included a door kicked off its hinges and splintered during the previous night's outburst.

It was painfully obvious there were serious problems in the Tyson–Givens marriage, a union of two people who were quite ill-suited for one another. Too many friends of both talked about constant fighting and arguing. Even before they married there was the incident in Steve Lott's apartment, one of many. Tyson told Colin Hart of the London *Sun* newspaper that he and Givens, then just his fiancée, fought all the time. 'She knows she can't hurt me if she kicks me in the head,' he said, 'so she tries to kick me in the groin.'

On Thursday, September 8, against doctors' orders and quite unexpectedly, Tyson showed up at Kennedy Airport and boarded a plane to Moscow with Robin, their time at the airport having been spent in a VIP lounge, away from reporters, photographers, and a crowd of about 200 people waiting to catch a glimpse of the couple. They were then taken through a security entrance and escorted on to the first class section of the Scandinavian Airlines plane, bound for Moscow via a stop in Copenhagen. His right hand was once again in a full cast, just a precaution according to Bill Cayton, since Mike had been neglecting to wear the removable protective brace he'd been provided with. Givens said Tyson had decided to accompany her to get away from all the commotion. She denied the suicide report was accurate, saying her husband had too much to live for – including her – to want to kill himself, although Mike McAlary had reported in his story – which was completely pro-Givens and Roper – that the young actress had been calling people from her car phone all the way to Catskill the previous Sunday, telling them 'Michael just tried to kill himself'.

On Friday, September 9, Tyson and Givens arrived at Sheremetyevo Airport in Moscow, still denying the suicide reports. In New York that same Friday, sports writers on two separate newspapers speculated that Tyson's massive muscle build-up over the previous three or four years, his mood swings from euphoria to depression, his violent temper tantrums could be attributed to steroid use, since all of these symptoms can be side effects of the artificial-hormone muscle-building drug.

In Moscow, Mike spent the first few days visiting Soviet amateur boxers, sightseeing at Lenin's Tomb, becoming annoyed that the Soviets knew the visiting soccer star Pele very well but had little idea who he was, greeting his mother-in-law, who joined the couple a few days after their arrival, and pining to get back to the USA and back into the ring. He told reporter Barry Levine he was ready to go back to New York just three days after he got to Moscow, a trip it was believed Givens forced him to make against doctor's orders because she didn't trust him alone while she was away for two weeks. Mike was unhappy that his mother-in-law had joined them in Moscow, unhappy with what he described as their cockroach-infested room in the famous Rossiya Hotel, unhappy with the quality of Soviet food.

On their final night in Moscow, he finally blew. He became completely irrational. He climbed out along a railing in the hotel and hung from it for ten minutes. He also terrorized Robin, Ruth, and Phyllis Polaner, whom Roper had recently hired to work as an assistant to Robin and Mike. Tyson reportedly stabbed at Polaner with a fork and kicked at her. He then chased the three women, in their nightclothes, out of their suite. They ran to the lobby for safety, but Mike followed them. They tried to calm him as hotel security guards watched, but then Tyson confronted the guards, asking them what they were looking at and making threats. Roper was so concerned for their safety that she hired several former New York City detectives to provide private security at the Tyson mansion in New Jersey when they returned home. She was finally convinced that she and her daughter had to get away from Tyson before he did something drastic to them in one of his rages.

* * *

While Tyson was in the Soviet Union, the various parties concerned with his boxing future were meeting in New York, trying to resolve their differences. Tyson's continuing troubles outside the ring had cost him several major endorsements, including Pepsi Cola, which did not renew the deal it had with Tyson for TV commercials leading up to and following the Spinks fight. Several meetings were arranged between Cayton and Howard Rubenstein, the PR man retained by Ruth Roper to represent Tyson, and between Cayton and the Parcher and Hayes legal team, also retained by Roper, in an effort to bury the hatchet and work in the common interest of advancing Tyson's career. Cayton said he was willing to be reconciled even with Donald Trump, who had forced him to accept a reduction in his managerial cut from 33 per cent to 20 per cent.

Dan Klores, the Rubenstein PR man who was with Tyson constantly in the hospital, privy to all the Tyson–Roper–Givens conversations and therefore a prime suspect in Cayton's eyes in the plant of the suicide story, called the manager to say he was innocent. So did attorney Parcher. Trump said he was being falsely accused of being the story's source by Cayton because 'I killed [Cayton] on the contract' renegotiation. Ever the diplomat, and concerned as always to act in Tyson's best interests, Cayton simply said, 'We're ready to work for Mike Tyson instead of against each other.'

On Tuesday night, September 20, Mike and Robin returned from Moscow. When Tyson spotted the security guards hired by Ruth at his home, he was not pleased. He told Robin to get rid of them, then he and his friend, Rory Holloway, drove off in the middle of the night shouting at the security men to 'fuck off'. Shortly after 3 am he arrived at Camille Ewald's home in Catskill, but left there a little after 8 am and drove back to his New Jersey home. He then went out for a midday jog. While running, he spotted a WNBC-TV news crew taping him on the quiet street outside his house. He responded to their presence by throwing his Walkman radio at them, then running over and grabbing the camera. The taped incident, of course, made the TV newscasts around the country, but neither Tyson nor the television station had any further comment regarding it.

The next day was an emotionally draining one for the champion. He sat down for a marathon therapy session with Dr Henry McCurtis, the psychiatrist Roper and Givens had been encouraging him to consult. Also present were the two women. Afterwards, Tyson and Givens spoke with Mark Dionno of the *New York Post*, and Tyson said he was a manic-depressive. 'I was born with this disease. I can't help it. . . .This is the way I was all my life,' he said. He talked of going through three- and four-day periods without sleeping, of being extremely depressed and 'very, very high-strung'. Givens was quick to apportion blame, saying, 'He's been [like this] for many years and they've been ignoring it.' Givens vowed to stand by her man, saying she and Mike were in tears during the session with Dr McCurtis, whom two weeks earlier Tyson had ordered out of his hospital room, threatening to kill him. Now Mike said he would make the effort to work with Dr McCurtis to understand his illness. 'How can you turn your back on someone who is making a commitment to try?' asked Givens.

Dr Gene Brody, who had been Tyson's personal physician until Givens and Roper came on the scene, and who had also been Jim Jacobs's doctor, discounted the manic-depressive story. He said most doctors could tell when a person was a manic-depressive, and that Mike had seemed perfectly normal to him.

On Friday night, September 30, much of the country sat transfixed as Mike Tyson, Robin Givens, and Ruth Roper allowed the ABC News programme '20/20' to come into their New Jersey mansion and put the young couple's personal life under the microscope of the television camera's lens. The interviewer was Barbara Walters, who had carved out a reputation for being able to secure hard-to-get interviews and often make people reveal things about themselves they would not tell other interviewers. In this instance, Walters's skills at eliciting information were hardly necessary. Givens was ready and willing to air the dirty laundry for everyone to see. Walters, good friends with Donald Trump and thus able to get access to the Tyson family, was willing to provide Givens with the forum to discuss the family's personal problems. Speaking with Walters individually, Ruth Roper said she had become a 'surrogate mother' to Mike, that she loved him like a son, that she wasn't trying to control him or his money, but that 'people who earn a living through Michael' found her close relationship with him intimidating. Walters then asked, 'Like Bill Cayton?', to which Roper replied, 'Yeah, like Bill Cayton, to be very direct.' Don King's involvement as an instigator in the whole Tyson mess was never explored by Walters. In a separate interview taped with Cayton at his office and inserted in the programme,

Walters asked him whether he was concerned that if Tyson had to take psychiatric medication to control his emotions he might not be able to box. 'If Mike Tyson needs medication,' replied the manager, 'I want him to take medication. Whether he boxes or not is of no great interest to me.' 'You make money from him,' shot back Walters. 'I have money,' the millionaire Cayton pointed out to her. 'I don't need Mike's money.'

Walters did a one-to-one interview with Tyson, during which he told her, 'I'm not a psychopath or a maniac or anything. . .I've seen some doctors and I have a very slight illness that I had all my life, just being extremely hyper. . . .I'm a moody person by nature. . . .At times I raise hell, yeah, and I like to raise hell because that's basically my nature, coming from my background.' Tyson denied the reports that he hit Robin. 'My wife and I have arguments,' he said. 'I grab my wife and hold my wife, I shake my wife up, but I never struck my wife.'

The interview with Tyson, which was taped several days before broadcast, had concluded when Givens, who did not participate, approached Barbara Walters and said to her, 'You're not getting the story straight.' She volunteered to tell the truth, and so the cameras rolled again, and with Mike at her side, without speaking up once to contradict her, Robin Givens said of their marriage, 'It's been torture. It's been pure hell. It's been worse than anything I could possibly imagine. . .every day has been some kind of battle, some kind of fight, with managers, with members of family. . . .The fights with [Mike] make me wonder why I'm going through the other fights, the other battles. . . .He's got a side to him that's scary. Michael is intimidating, to say the least. . . .He gets out of control, throwing, screaming, he shakes, he pushes, he swings. . .and just recently I've become afraid, very very much afraid. . . .Michael is a manic-depressive. He is. That's just a fact. . . .The type of disease Michael has. . .it's something he's had for a very long time. It went untreated, therefore it got worse.' Givens insisted, though, that she loved him, that he wasn't a bad guy, he had a sense of humour, he was smart and gentle.

Walters asked Givens about the lack of a pre-nuptial agreement. 'Why should there be?' replied the actress. 'There's a certain sense of idealism that comes with being young that I wouldn't trade for anything in the world. We got married to be together forever, not to plan for divorce.' At this point, Mike jumped in and said, 'I do have many millions. My wife would just have to ask for it and she has everything I have. If she wants it right now, she could leave right now, take everything I have. Just leave. . .she has the power to do that. She's still here, she tolerates my shit, and I love my wife.' Mike said he was aware his illness had to be 'taken care of', but he said he was not taking the Lithium his doctor had prescribed because 'I'm handling myself very well'. Givens concluded her remarks by giving credit to her always-present mother. 'I don't know what Mike Tyson would be without my mother, what we would be. She's been the glue that's kept us together. . . .and I do come with a package, that's how I am. My mom, my sister.' Robin expressed her concern that if she and her mother left Mike he would be alone: 'He would have gotten so bad that I think maybe one day he would have been more deliberate [than the car accident of two weeks earlier] and killed himself, or hurt somebody else.'

Privately, Tyson had told Camille Ewald while staying in Catskill the previous weekend he was not taking the Lithium because he didn't like what the pills did to him, how they made him feel sluggish and dopey. 'I like the way I am, the way I used to feel,' he told her, and ignored persistent calls from his doctor reminding him to take the mind-controlling drug. Dr Gene Brody, Mike's physician, had said repeated blood tests he'd given Mike had never revealed any 'chemical imbalance' in Tyson's system.

Both Tyson's friends and impartial observers were shocked in the wake of the televised interview. Bill Cayton said he did not believe Mike was a manic-depressive, but was turned down by Ruth Roper when he asked if Mike could be seen by an independent doctor – alone. 'I feel it's imperative that Mike have at least one other psychiatrist examine him,' said Cayton. 'What are they [Ruth and Robin] afraid of? That they'll be contradicted?' Tyson's friends said there was a concentrated effort on the part of the two women to cut Mike off from all those previously close to him. They said the women constantly changed the phone number at the house so no one could reach him. Camille Ewald said Mike was 'an emotional captive' who had confided to her the previous weekend at her house that he was very unhappy with his marriage. Jose Torres said Mike was not a manic-depressive, but a confused young man who had been manipulated and brainwashed. 'Ruth Roper is a danger-ous woman,' he said. 'She has complete control over Tyson.' Other friends termed the entire affair a 'diabolical plot' against Mike, and were shocked that he could sit quietly stroking his wife's neck while she aired all their private business, true or untrue, on national TV. They said Mike appeared to have been drugged, perhaps with a dose of Lithium, before the interview. They felt he had been humiliated by his wife and mother-in-law for their own self-serving ends.

Slowly, as the feedback filtered to him over the weekend and it dawned on him just what had taken place, Tyson grew enraged. He knew he had taken a prescribed combination of Thorazine and Lithium before Barbara Walters and her TV crew arrived at the house. On Sunday morning, Tyson's rage erupted. In an argument with Robin he picked up a sugar bowl and threw it across the room, smashing it. He then allegedly threw some chairs through the windows, while Givens ran to phone Dr McCurtis. While Mike continued his rampage, she and Ruth escaped from the house and drove to a nearby gas station, where they called their friend, Shelly Finkel, who had been at the house with Mike and the women the previous day, Roper's birthday. They then telephoned the Bernardsville police, asking them to come to the house. When they arrived, Givens and Roper returned. Dr McCurtis phoned back, and told the women to leave the house as soon as possible, advising them to arrange for emergency psychiatric evaluation for Mike. He also spoke to the police at the house, and told them he was worried about the safety of Givens and Roper.

Tyson was calm when the police arrived, but became agitated again when Givens brought them into the house to show them the damage. He began to yell that he owned the house and everything in it, and it was none of anybody's business if he wanted to break his own things. Givens and Roper packed their bags preparing to leave for Roper's apartment in Manhattan. When they left the house, Tyson came outside and began to confront them once again, and another shouting match developed. Tyson then turned his attention to the police, telling them in the language of the streets that he did not want them on his property. 'Fuck you all,' he shouted, 'Fuck you cops, you scum. Get the fuck off the property, and fuck off.' With that, he got into his Mercedes and drove off.

Givens did not file a formal complaint, so no arrest was made, but she did go to the Bernardsville police station and give a detailed seven-page statement about what had transpired, thus establishing an 'on the record' account of the incident.

Tyson arrived in Manhattan, trying to meet up with his fellow boxer and friend Mark Breland, who was managed by Finkel.

He missed their rendezvous. Mike had telephoned his sister, Denise, and made her promise him that he would be buried next to their mother. She became concerned, and called Bernardsville police, asking them to return to the house and break in if they got no answer. When they got back to the house, however, Tyson's friend, Rory Holloway, answered the door and said that Mike had left. Tyson's brother, Rodney, speaking from Los Angeles, also expressed concern to Mike Katz of the *Daily News* about Mike, describing Ruth and Robin as 'manipulative'. On Monday morning, Givens flew to Hollywood to resume taping her TV show. That same morning, October 3, something very unexpected happened. Mike Tyson paid a visit to his estranged manager, Bill Cayton, and his estranged friend, Steve Lott. He ran up the stairs to Cayton's private office and embraced his manager, the first thaw in their relationship since the death of Jim Jacobs nearly seven months earlier. He hugged Steve Lott as well, and they all sat down to talk. Mike was warm and outgoing. He told Cayton he was anxious to get back into the ring and fight. He didn't mention the previous day's incident at his home. Cayton said he would go ahead with plans to have Mike meet Frank Bruno in London on December 17. First, however, he wanted Mike to undergo complete neurological and psychiatric evaluations, just to be sure.

The next day, Tyson was examined by Dr Abraham Halpern, Clinical Professor of Psychiatry at New York Medical College, who gave him a clean bill of mental health. 'I saw Mr Tyson and, from a clinical standpoint, he showed no signs of a major mental disorder. Certainly there's no sign of a manic-depressive condition or psychosis,' he said, adding that he had spoken with Dr McCurtis, and that McCurtis had said he had never diagnosed Mike as being manic-depressive. 'Dr McCurtis spoke of a mood-regulatory disturbance,' reported Dr Halpern, 'and that's a far cry from a major mental illness such as manic-depression.' He said Dr McCurtis had examined Mike once, but got most of the information about his behaviour from Ruth Roper and Robin Givens. Mike had been put on Lithium by Dr McCurtis on 'a trial basis' to 'stabilize' his moods, a treatment Dr Halpern termed 'not unreasonable', although not necessary. 'He needs to be goal-oriented again,' he said. 'He wants to box, and the training would be most therapeutic right now.' He did suggest Mike should see a psychotherapist, 'somebody to talk to that he trusts to relieve his pressures', and added that Mike 'misses his wife terribly and he loves her'. If, indeed, Dr McCurtis had never diagnosed Mike as manic-depressive, then it was others who decided to use that term to describe Mike's condition. When the neurological experts confirmed Mike was showing no signs of injury from the car accident, Bill Cayton said 'All systems are go' for the Bruno fight in December. Tyson was flying to Detroit for the weekend to see Mark Breland fight. Then he would head for Catskill to begin training.

By now, although Mike was still obsessively attached to Robin, the people closest to him could hold their peace no longer. Jay Bright said the people 'who know Michael and who genuinely care about him are disgusted by what they saw on that show. To see his wife emasculate him on national TV like that was offensive and vile.' Camille Ewald said, 'If that was my wife sitting next to me saying those things I would have choked her.' And Ewald now had much more to say. Roper and Givens were angry with her because, like Cayton, she had wanted Mike to be examined by other doctors besides Dr McCurtis. She now revealed that when Mike began earning large purses, Jim Jacobs had arranged for Camille to be paid house expenses by Mike, such as phone, electricity, repairs, taxes, an amount coming to thousands of dollars a year, nothing to Tyson, nor did Mike have any objections about taking care of the woman who had cared for him (and silently put up with, as he termed it, 'my shit'). When Ruth Roper came on the scene, everything was paid through the company she formed, Mike Tyson Enterprises. Roper and Givens told Ewald they thought it was only fitting, since she was an old woman and Mike was paying the bills, that she should leave the house in Catskill to Mike in her will. To tighten the vice on Ewald, they stopped sending her expense cheques. At one point, Kevin Rooney had to bail her out when her telephone was about to be disconnected for nonpayment by the phone company. 'I don't think we should pay the bills,' Roper told Ewald over the phone in September, 'unless Mike will be inheriting the property.' Ewald became angered with Roper when Tyson's mother-in-law asked her why Mike was paying for the house upkeep and not Cus's other fighters, Jose Torres and Floyd Patterson. Ewald told her it was because Torres and Patterson had never lived in that house. When he learned what was happening, Bill Cayton took over payment of the house bills.

Ewald also said Roper had refused to pay thousands of dollars in outstanding bills to the private limousine company that chauffeured Tyson, because the company refused to report back to her every place they drove Mike, every stop he made, who he went to see.

With Tyson willing and anxious to fight, Bill Cayton outlined a plan for him that in the space of twelve months would earn him $50-million gross. It would start in December with the scaled-down (due to the move indoors) purse of $6-million against Bruno in London. In Rio, during Carnival in February, there would be $9-million for an easy defence against Brazil's Adilson Rodriguez, in April, $5- or $6-million for a mandatory defence in the United States against number one IBF challenger Carl Williams, followed by a bout for perhaps $10-million in Milan's soccer stadium against Italian challenger Francesco Damiani in June. Then would come the big one, the next 'super-fight', late in the year, a closed-circuit and pay-per-view $20-million payday for Tyson against undefeated World Cruiserweight Champion Evander Holyfield. Tyson would then finish the year in Japan, which desperately wanted him for another performance, against 41-year-old former Heavyweight Champion George Foreman. The only thing Bill Cayton had not taken into consideration, the one thing that would rend all these plans asunder, was the sudden re-entry into Mike Tyson's life of Don King.

17

Divorce. . .and Don King

The devil can quote scripture for his purpose.

– SHAKESPEARE

DON KING had been waiting patiently, quietly, biding his time. Better than anyone, he knew how to exploit a weakness, and when he saw the opening left by the rift between Mike and the Roper–Givens team, it was the opportunity he had been waiting for. He moved quickly to fill the void and renew his relationship with Tyson. With Ruth and Robin in Hollywood, King quickly re-established contact with Tyson, offering to help him protect his assets, most of which had been transferred into Mike Tyson Enterprises, which was Tyson's company, and of which he was President, but which Ruth Roper actually controlled. King and Tyson went to the offices of Tyson Enterprises to check on Mike's financial records, but found the office locked. The key was with Ruth Roper – in California.

King proceeded to take Tyson from financial institution to financial institution, changing his accounts. Since his marriage and the formation of Tyson Enterprises, all Tyson's accounts had become joint, meaning Robin had complete access to them as well as Mike. King quickly saw to it that this was changed. Mike transferred all his assets into new accounts, with only his name on them, making it impossible for Robin to use any of his funds. Only Tyson now had the authority to write cheques, and, with King's help, he cancelled all his joint credit cards.

In Los Angeles, meanwhile, Robin Givens retained the noted celebrity divorce lawyer, Marvin Mitchelson, almost as soon as her plane touched down, and on Friday, October 7, in Los Angeles County Superior Court, she filed divorce papers against Mike. The grounds were cited as 'irreconcilable differences', and, in part, her divorce papers said, 'My husband has been violent and physically abusive and prone to unprovoked rages of violence and destruction.' She specifically mentioned the hotel incident in Moscow, saying Mike began to 'lose control over his emotions. . .[and] started throwing champagne bottles around our room. At the peak of his manic state,

Michael went down to the bar and started drinking vodka, glass after glass, like it was water. He then returned to our room, grabbed a handful of Lithium and locked himself in the bathroom, saying he was going to kill himself.' After recounting his alleged chasing of her, her mother, and their assistant to the lobby, his threats to a Soviet security man, and his hanging from a hotel balcony for ten minutes, threatening to kill himself, she went on to claim, 'On the plane [returning from Moscow] Michael swore at me, called me a "whore" and a "slut", and said he was going to kill me, that he had guns at home. He told me, "The world will forgive me because I have succeeded in making everyone think you are the bad one."' She also recounted the previous weekend's outburst in New Jersey, saying Mike had awakened her when he was drunk by jumping on her in bed and punching her in the body and head. 'He started throwing dishes and liquor bottles at me and hit me with one dish that shattered all over me.'

In New York, Raoul Felder, one of the most successful and high-powered divorce attorneys in the United States, was sought out by the press for his opinion on what promised to be the most publicized divorce in recent years. Felder came down firmly on Mike Tyson's side. 'The woman's married eight months,' he said, 'and this poor guy got his money by getting beaten up and she's going to seek half of it, and she expresses her love rather peculiarly by suing him for divorce.' Felder termed Givens's action 'a very obvious and, I must say, a rather shabby ploy'. Knowing that Mitchelson had filed the divorce action in Los Angeles because California had a 50/50 community property divorce law, where Givens stood to collect half of Tyson's estimated $40-million in assets, Felder suggested that Tyson seek to have the divorce action moved to New Jersey or New York, where his assets would not be in nearly as much jeopardy.

After covering his assets in New York, Tyson had flown off with Don King to isolate himself at the promoter's home out-side Cleveland. Before departing, he, King, Bill Cayton and other Tyson advisors, met at HBO's offices, and King and Cayton made peace, uniting to protect Mike and work in the common interest against Roper and Givens. They considered a counter-attack: filing to have the marriage annulled on the grounds that Givens had tricked Tyson into marrying her. According to Cayton and others, on January 15, about three weeks before the marriage, Ruth Roper had called Jim Jacobs and told him Robin was three and a half months pregnant. Jacobs felt they had to get Tyson married to Robin, for a very practical reason: Tyson's endorsement contracts contained moral clauses, and he and Cayton felt Mike's lucrative outside-the-ring income might be jeopardized by an out-of-wedlock pregnancy, especially if things got nasty. Still, the elopement on February 7, *sans* pre-nuptial agreement, had taken the managers by surprise. Givens never appeared to be pregnant, gave conflicting stories herself, though certainly Mike believed she was. He had even mentioned that she was pregnant while they were in Japan in March. Further information surfaced when Givens's gynaecologist, Dr Sheldon Cherry, confirmed that she did indeed have a 'spontaneous miscarriage' on June 3, three weeks before the Spinks fight. However, Dr Cherry said the actress was about six or seven weeks pregnant at the time, which meant she had conceived well into April, and so, barring an earlier pregnancy, which she never claimed, she could not have been three and a half months pregnant in January.

Don King had retained Howard Weitzman to handle Tyson's divorce litigation. Before leaving New York for Los Angeles on Monday, October 3, following the rampage at their New Jersey home, Givens had written a cheque against an account of Mike Tyson Enterprises, Inc. By the time the cheque reached the Chase Manhattan Bank, on which it was drawn, for collection later in the week, Tyson's accounts had been transferred, and it bounced. Givens was furious privately, but denied writing the cheque. Unfortunately for her, it turned up in the hands of Tyson's attorney. It was written for $581,812, payable to Robin Givens Productions, and noted in her handwriting 'Reimbursement on expenses'.

On Sunday, October 9, while Don King took Tyson to services at Cleveland's Holy Baptist Church – certainly a new environment for the champion, who was presented with a bible and told by Pastor Henry Payden, 'Mike, you have a way of knocking men down, but Jesus has a way of picking people up' – Ruth Roper and Robin Givens were busy in Los Angeles. Four days after retaining him, the women dropped Marvin Mitchelson as Robin's lawyer. Over the years, Mitchelson had become one of the highest of high-profile divorce attorneys, representing Joan Collins, Bianca Jagger and Soraya Kashoggi, but had fallen on difficult times in recent years, beset by numerous legal problems himself, involving a variety of serious charges. Clearly, Roper and Givens had had second thoughts about retaining Mitchelson. They then hired none other than Raoul Felder to represent Robin, the same Raoul Felder who just days earlier had publicly sided with Tyson and called Givens's divorce action a 'shabby ploy'. Now that he had reviewed the case more thoroughly, Felder told the press that Robin 'was beaten, abused and so forth, and apparently it's undenied [by Tyson]'. There was no doubt that Felder knew his business. *Forbes* magazine said of him: 'Raoul Felder is the divorce lawyer of choice for many of the power set. He's represented dozens of the rich and famous during the thirty years he's been practising. Felder's divorce practice is now the nation's largest, grossing him some $15-million per annum.'

Felder announced that Robin loved Mike, that he hoped to negotiate a settlement to avoid a dirty public trial, that he would meet with Howard Weitzman, Tyson's lawyer, 'to try to resolve this quickly, equitably and civilly', that Robin said she would settle it quickly 'if Michael apologizes to me', and, he maintained, she had never said she was pregnant prior to the couple's marriage. 'The pregnancy came after the marriage,' he said. Neal Hirsch, a West Coast associate of Felder's, would have direct responsibility for handling the case for Givens.

Tennis star Lori McNeil then re-surfaced to lend documentary support to her friend Robin. Having denied Mike McAlary's story in the *New York Daily News* about Tyson's rampage in the Bahamas in July 1988, she now told McAlary she had lied in doing so because she was 'very afraid of the whole situation'. Now, she said, she was really telling the truth: 'I'm still afraid, but I think that it's something that should be told. It's something I've seen and it's the truth. People don't really know the other side of Mike Tyson.' McNeil said the threesome had dinner, and they were all drinking, especially Tyson. 'He drinks a lot anyway,' she said. Back in their suite, Robin complained Mike had been flirting with another woman at the bar. A few minutes later, with Givens and McNeil apparently in a room separate from Mike, 'He kicked in the door, and then he came into my room after Robin. He dragged her back to his room,' said McNeil. 'I went in there and he was hitting Robin and dragging her and saying he was going to kill her. He was choking her. . . .She was screaming. So I called security. . . .Security came in and he was hitting Robin and choking her. And they chased him out into the hall. He made a big scene in the hall with security. He was totally out of control. . . .He hit me in the mouth. . .and busted my lip. I was trying to stop him from

hitting Robin. . . .He was swinging with his fist. I saw him
kick her.' McAlary also reported Givens as saying, 'The time
in the Bahamas was the first time Michael ever hit me in the
face. . . .He was choking me and I went into the bathroom to
vomit. I was leaning over the toilet and Michael kicked me in
my rear end.'

One week after Givens had filed for divorce in Los Angeles,
Mike Tyson came back punching with a counter-suit. In a
ten-page document filed in New Jersey State Superior Court
on October 14, the World Heavyweight Champion charged in
his own divorce petition extreme cruelty on the part of Robin
Givens, alleging his wife of eight months had 'tricked' him into
marriage with a false claim of pregnancy, and that he was 'the
hapless victim of intentional fraud'. His papers further charged
that when she married him, Givens was 'motivated solely by
personal aggrandizement and a need to enhance her level
of public recognition and personal wealth. . . .Having been
tricked into marriage by the defendant, the plaintiff found
himself constantly manipulated by her and her family to the
point of personal distraction regarding his own welfare and
career. . .[then began] a campaign to publicly humiliate him,
strip him of his manhood and his dignity and to destroy his
credibility as a public figure,' after which she left him 'with
as much notoriety as possible and [sought] whatever personal
gain might be available to her both in terms of media notoriety
and asset acquisition.'

The same night, October 14, Givens was back on *20/20* on
ABC-TV with Barbara Walters. A tear trickled down her cheek
as she maintained 'Nobody can love Michael more than I love
Michael. . . .I didn't get married to get divorced. I'm 23. I'm
idealistic.' She said she had filed for divorce in California simply
because that was where she lived, not because she stood to get
half of Tyson's fortune under California's divorce laws. 'If I
offended his fans, I apologize. If I offended him, I apologize.'

Tyson, needless to say, would have no part of a second
appearance on the programme. Instead, at the home of Don
King, he gave an interview to the Chicago *Sun-Times* charging
that Roper and Givens 'don't like black people. . . .They use
them, but they don't like or respect black people. They want
to be white so bad. The way they talk about black people,
you'd think you were living with the Ku Klux Klan. . . .They
thought they were royalty. She and her mother want so much
to be white, it's a shame. And they were trying to take me away

from the people I grew up with and throw me into their kind of high-class world. . . .The issue really is not money. I don't blame anybody for trying to get money. It's just the idea that they played the scheme on me. It was like a sting game. They drew me in. They worked on my emotions because I was in love. . . .She just tried to ruin me and destroy me. Not only did she want to take my money, but she wanted to ruin me, embarrass me, take away my manhood and humiliate me on television so that no woman would ever want me again. And that was evil.' Tyson concluded by saying, 'She had her chance and she blew it. She blew the opportunity of a lifetime. Nobody is going to ever want her. She just missed out on the train.'

Things took yet another unexpected turn a few days later when Raoul Felder read a statement to the press from Robin saying she would grant Tyson a divorce and that 'I will not seek nor accept any money for myself. . . .I never wanted anything but what was best for Michael. I never wanted anything for myself and I never sought anything for myself.' The statement went on to say, 'I never married Michael for his money. . . .I represented a threat to many other people and that threat was engendered by my love for Michael. I have never said one bad word about Michael or done anything to hurt him personally.' Then the woman who had chosen to go on national television and talk about her marriage said, 'We were not permitted the dignity of dealing with our private problems,' concluding 'I wish him well.'

'I interpret this to mean they give up all claim to money and property that belongs to Mike and we have achieved a knockout here,' said Tyson's attorney, Howard Weitzman, who speculated that Givens may have been concerned about her deteriorating public image and her fear over what might have been divulged had the divorce case gone to trial. He said that the day before Robin issued her public statement that she did not want any money from Mike, Raoul Felder had called him and asked for an $8-million settlement, then, after consulting with Robin, had lowered the demand to $2-million, the money she said she had in her possession, but she had refused Weitzman's demand that her accounts be subject to an audit.

On November 7, Tyson said in the *New York Post* that Givens was trying to 'steal' his money: 'It turns out she was lying when she said she didn't want anything from me.' He said she wanted to keep the New Jersey mansion, now worth about $8-million with its furnishings and improvements, plus more than

$1-million in jewellery. She also wanted him to forget about having his lawyers check into the disappearance of $5-million which occurred, according to Tyson, during her shifting from one bank account to another. 'The nature of those two women,' Tyson told the *Post*, 'is to be mean and vindictive. She said she wants nothing but she refused to sign a release. . . .Those two are the slime of the slime. And anyone associated with them is slime. . . .She stole from me and she said I beat her up. If it was such a living hell, how come she wants to get back together?' He said Givens had been sending signals she was interested in a reconciliation. 'They tried to turn me into an imbecile. They got enough already from me. Everybody could see it, everybody but Mike.'

On Saturday, November 5, Mike Tyson was in Las Vegas to attend the Sugar Ray Leonard–Donny Lalonde fight. Also in Las Vegas was Robin Givens. At a meeting that day in the Alexis Park Hotel, the battling couple sat down face to face for the first time since Givens and Roper had bolted from the New Jersey mansion six weeks earlier. Tyson and his attorney, Howard Weitzman, were in the room, along with Don King, when Givens arrived with her attorney, Neal Hirsch. She walked straight to Mike, embraced him, and tilted her face up to kiss him, but he pulled away and only let her kiss him on the cheek. She sat next to Mike and kept easing her chair closer and closer to his, and even tried to stroke his leg, which he wouldn't let her do. Then, taking his chin in her hand, she turned his face towards hers and said, 'Mike, isn't it true you still love me? Isn't that why you call me all the time? Let's go into another room alone and talk. I need to talk with you alone.' Tyson refused to take the bait. 'You're a conniving bitch. I don't trust you,' he told her. 'It's over between us. I want you out of my life. You were my dream once, now you're my nightmare.' The meeting ended at that point, as Givens stormed out, saying, 'You haven't heard the last of Robin Givens.'

Eleven days later she struck back with a vengeance when her attorney, Raoul Felder, filed a libel against Tyson in Manhattan Federal Court for $125-million. The suit asked for $25-million for damages and injury to Robin's 'good name, professional reputation and social standing', plus $100-million in punitive and compensatory damages. It accused her estranged husband of holding her up to 'public contempt, ridicule, embarrassment, disgrace and prejudice' by libelling her with his statements in the November 7 *New York Post* article, and described the allegations that she was trying to steal his money as 'false, defamatory, malicious and libellous'.

Howard Weitzman called the lawsuit 'outrageous and ludicrous', saying, 'This young lady once again is attempting to shift blame from her conduct to someone else and blame them for any problems she perceives she's having. . . .What you have once again is Robin Givens bickering in public with her estranged husband and attempting to generate publicity for herself.' Besides, added Weitzman, 'Truth is the best defence against libel.'

At least Robin and Mike were reunited in one sense. They were named as co-defendants in a lawsuit filed by Jack/Paul Waltzer, Inc., a Manhattan furrier, for non-payment of a $91,000 bill. It seems that the furrier had sold Mike and Robin a Russian golden sable coat that was to be a birthday present for Ruth Roper on October 1. The couple gave it to Ruth on her birthday, but unfortunately the next morning came the big blow-up, followed by the women's departure for Los Angeles and the filing of divorce papers. When the bill subsequently arrived, Mike understandably refused to pay it and said he wanted his mother-in-law to return the coat, which she, infuriated, did not wish to do.

Robin and Mike kept talking to the press, she in a *People* magazine story where she said, 'If I had to do it all over again, I'd let him do whatever he wanted to do. . . .I would not say a word if Michael stayed out for three or four nights, which is what he did.' She also said about herself, 'I'm one of the nicest, most fair people I know. . . .I think [Mike] is probably going to turn out to be the all-American tragedy,' she predicted. At a Chicago news conference on December 13 (where he was dressed in a full-length white mink coat, with jewelled gold bracelets on both wrists), Mike fired back, saying, 'In Hollywood you make money by being either the best person or the worst person. She's making the most money on being the bitch of Hollywood.' He denied her allegation in the *People* that he admitted his weight was up to 255 pounds. He said he weighed 240, and would be back in training in a few days for his fight with Frank Bruno. He again claimed Robin had stolen 'millions of dollars' from him.

Yet, incredibly, Tyson was still irresistibly drawn to her. On Sunday, December 4, she was in New York City, staying at her mother's apartment. She phoned Mike, who had apparently been phoning her constantly since their breakup, and told him, sobbing, that everyone hated her and she was going to lose her role in her TV sitcom. Mike took the bait, and came running. He picked her up in front of her mother's building, and the two went for a drive. She tried to get him to abandon his personal and business relationship with Don King. A bit of sexual teasing went on in Tyson's Rolls-Royce as well, and then she told Mike she had to go to the airport to catch a flight back to LA, jumped in a cab, and was gone. Tyson later said he was a 'sucker' for meeting her and thinking they could get back together, but three weeks later he was in California and the estranged couple were together again, on a movie date. Don King, at home with his family for the Christmas holiday, was not pleased when he learned of the Tyson–Givens rendezvous. In the meantime, attorney Weitzman discovered another cheque – this one for $2-million – signed by Robin Givens four months earlier and transferred into the account of Robin Givens Productions. The word 'gift' was written on the cheque.

During all of this marital intrigue and turmoil, Mike Tyson and Don King were virtually inseparable. Tyson spent a great deal of time sequestered at King's home outside Cleveland, where virtually no one, including Bill Cayton, could reach him. Cayton adopted a conciliatory attitude toward King, saying publicly that the promoter had worked in Mike's best interests by helping him transfer his assets into accounts safe from Robin Givens and Ruth Roper. But ominous rumours began to filter from Ohio to New York in October: King was trying to subvert the December 17 date for Tyson to meet Bruno in London by working to move the fight to Las Vegas; King was trying to influence Tyson to fire his trainer, Kevin Rooney; Tyson was seriously considering buying a home in Cleveland to be close to King.

Many people were at a loss to explain Tyson's attraction to King, which they likened to that of a moth to a flame, but Kevin Rooney told columnist Denis Hamill in *Newsday*, 'It's because of [King's] black ghetto, jive jailhouse background. It's the black thing. King is literally putting the con on him with his flash and black talk. See, Mike was in reform schools but King went to the big house for murder. And the only reason Mike never went to the big house is because of Cus D'Amato. But growing up, Mike looked up to hoods. Now he's looking up to an ex-hood with a legal licence. If he falls into that trap it will be sad. See, King is trying to make him cut all his ties to Cus the same way Ruth and Robin did. . . .I work in a jail [coaching boxing] so I know what's going through Mike's head right now. He wants to be with one of his own, a ghetto ex-con.'

Meanwhile, word reached Cayton that Tyson had re-injured his broken hand. The original break was not a serious one, but Tyson, ignoring doctor's orders, did not allow it to heal properly. He failed to wear his removable brace regularly after the cast was removed late in August, which kept the injury aggravated, and he was not wearing it the morning of his car accident. A cast was put back on the hand while Mike was confined in hospital. When he departed for Moscow with Robin, the cast was in place. But photos taken of him in Red Square just a couple of days later showed no cast on his hand. He had removed it himself. Now, a month later, amid reports he might have been fooling around in King's gym, possibly punching a heavy bag, the hand had swelled again and there were fears it might have been re-fractured. However, Dr Richard Rhodes, who examined the fighter in Cleveland, said it was not a break, just swelling because it had never properly healed.

Tyson, no doubt encouraged by Don King, was now insisting that the Bruno fight be moved to the United States, just as he had originally told Cayton in the summer, even as public talk of the fight being held in Wembley continued. The December 17 date was also looking unlikely, since the Vegas casinos considered the week before Christmas 'dead' time, when their business dropped off too much to warrant the expense of investing millions of dollars to bring the fight to Las Vegas. Jarvis Astaire, Mickey Duff, Bill Cayton and HBO executives huddled in New York for two days to try to work things out in mid-October, while Tyson remained in Cleveland. Frank Bruno said he wanted the fight in Britain, where Tyson had agreed to fight him. It wasn't a question of money, said the challenger, 'I want to win the title in front of my own fans.' King had no involvement in the London fight, which is why many suspected he was working hard behind-the-scenes, with Tyson's cooperation, to shoot it down. In Las Vegas, his power base, he might somehow worm his way in to the promotion. But King continued to maintain he was working to put Team Tyson back on track, including Bill Cayton–manager, Kevin Rooney–trainer, and, of course, Don King–promoter.

Tyson now insisted he could not travel to England to fight because his divorce litigation and negotiations made it necessary for him to remain close to home. Astaire and Duff had

Bruno fly to New York to argue his case in public. At a news
conference, Bruno said he'd had just about enough with the
constant delays and uncertainty. 'The promoters don't know
what's going on, Tyson's manager doesn't know what's going
on, I'm the number one contender and I don't know what's
going on,' he complained. 'The only one who knows what's
going on is Tyson, and he's nowhere to be found. First it was
his legal fight with his manager, then he broke his hand, then he
smashed up the car, now he's getting divorced. Every day you
pick up the paper, there's something new. Frankly, I'm getting
ticked off about it. His problems are not my problems, but I'm
being affected by them. I would like to win the title in front of
my countrymen. I owe my countrymen a lot.'

However, after continued meetings with Cayton, convinced
it was Tyson's intention to bypass a trip to London, contract or
no contract, Astaire and Duff relented and agreed to move the
fight to the United States. As a result of the concession, Tyson
would take a reduced purse, and Bruno and company would
have theirs doubled, from $1.8-million to some $3.6-million.
Meanwhile, Tyson, who had said he couldn't leave the United
States because of his pending divorce, turned up with Don King
in Venezuela, where they attended the annual convention of
the WBA.

Tyson's father, Jimmy Kirkpatrick, who had abandoned his
family twenty years earlier, and who hadn't seen Mike since
the funeral of the champion's mother six years earlier, now
turned up again. The 64-year-old disabled veteran was living
on a small government pension in a public housing project
in Brooklyn. In a television interview he said he was now a
born-again Christian, a very changed man from the one who
had abandoned his family, and he would like the opportunity
to sit down with Mike and talk to his famous son. Even though
he had no contact with Mike, he said it made him very proud
when he walked down the street in his poor neighbourhood
and heard people say, 'That's Mike Tyson's father.' Tyson
learned of these public overtures, but he was not yet ready
for a reconciliation. Perhaps he did not yet have it in his
heart to forgive him, or perhaps he was suspicious of his
father's motives. Back in the Catskill days, Bobby Stewart
had once asked him, 'If you ever make any money, which
you probably won't, what if your dad surfaced and you had
something?' Tyson had replied, 'I'd have nothing to do with
the scumbag.' Stewart said, 'Your mother died probably in

part as the result of him leaving her, so just remember that.'
And maybe Mike did.

Any delusion on Bill Cayton's part that he could somehow
work cooperatively with Don King ended on October 21,
when, without consulting anyone, Tyson signed a four-year
contract granting King sole and exclusive rights to promote
his fights. The nine-page document makes for fascinating reading, because the contract, signed willingly and voluntarily by
the Heavyweight Champion, is almost totally in Don King's
favour. Legal experts termed it 'a promoter's contract, not a
fighter's contract'. It was almost as if Tyson signed it to spite Bill
Cayton. The day before it was actually signed, King telephoned
Cayton and told him he had a four-year exclusive promotional
deal with Tyson. 'Mike has given me power of attorney,' said
King, 'and I'm taking over everything.' The call was made from
the Chicago offices of King's attorney, Charles Lomax, and
Tyson was also on the line. Cayton told them he found it all
totally unacceptable, but Tyson jumped in and said, 'Yes, I've
given him power of attorney,' with Lomax clarifying for Cayton
that it was a limited power of attorney. Jacobs and Cayton
had never had that power; Mike signed exclusively in matters
concerning his own money. Tyson then got back on the line and
began cursing Cayton in vulgar gutter language, at which point
Cayton told him, 'I will not accept that language from you.'
Tyson replied, 'You're threatening me.' Several days earlier,
at the WBA convention, in Venezuela, Tyson had used similar
abusive language about Cayton, referring to him as 'that white
motherfucker who stole my money'.

The day after the phone conversation, Tyson signed the
agreement. It said, 'Whereas, Tyson wishes to grant to Don
King Productions the sole and exclusive right to secure, arrange
and promote all professional boxing bouts requiring Tyson's
services. . . .for a term of four years commencing on the date
hereof (Oct 21, 1988). . . .DKP shall promote not less than
three bouts requiring Tyson's services during each year of
the term hereof. Such bouts shall be on dates and at sites to
be designated by DKP and shall be against opponents to be
designated by DKP with Tyson's consent, such consent not to
be unreasonably withheld.'

The financial arrangements were thus: King would pay
Tyson $1-million for each fight, plus $200-thousand for training expenses. In addition, Tyson would get two-thirds of the net

receipts, 80 per cent in the case of closed-circuit/pay-per-view bouts. King defined net receipts as total gross receipts from all sources 'less DKP's out-of-pocket expenses, including without limitation all applicable taxes and the amount paid to Tyson, (i.e., the $1,200,000 guarantee per fight).

The contract further provided that if 'any court in any jurisdiction' declares the exclusivity of the contract to be illegal, King would still have the right to promote three Tyson fights a year on a non-exclusive basis. It stated that 'Tyson represents and warrants to DKP that he is free to enter into this Agreement. . . .and agrees to indemnify and hold DKP harmless against any and all liability, cost or expense, including reasonable attorneys' fees, that DKP may incur as a result of any breach or inaccuracy of any of the foregoing representations and warranties.' It also gave King the right to have Tyson examined by a doctor of the promoter's choosing in case the fighter claimed he could not perform due to injury, and that if Tyson retired during the term of the agreement, it would be suspended and then would remain in effect if Tyson came out of retirement at any point in the future to fight again.

Promoter and attorney Dan Duva said it was ludicrous that Tyson should sign a contract like that, especially since he and King had no legal right to enter into a contract with each other without Bill Cayton's consent, according to the contract between Cayton and Tyson. Duva termed it a 'blatant breach of contract by Mike Tyson and a blatant interference with a contract by Don King', and said it was foolhardy of Tyson, the most valuable athlete in the world, to sign an exclusive contract with anyone. He could make the most money by putting his services up for bidding on the free market among promoters on a fight-by-fight basis. If Cayton and Tyson were interested in an exclusive contract, however, with King or any other promoter, Duva estimated it would be worth a $5-million up-front signing bonus to Tyson, plus a guaranteed $100-million over the four year term. King paid Tyson no bonus, guaranteed him a mere $12-million for the four years, an amount Tyson could earn in one fight, and King, doubtless realizing that the contract would be answered by a lawsuit from Cayton, put in a provision for his own protection making Tyson liable for all legal fees arising from any litigation!

Lee Pollock, a noted attorney from White Plains, New York, who was familiar with contracts, agreed with Duva. What bothered him most was the failure of the contract to make any provisions for an independent accounting of expenses. He said, a 'very troublesome aspect of the agreement is its failure to define the term "net receipts", from which Mike's 66⅔ per cent would be derived. To prevent Mike's share of the receipts from being siphoned off, it is essential to specify the "out-of-pocket" expenses which may be deducted from the gross receipts before application of Mike's 66⅔ per cent. . . .and since information concerning the expenses is in Don King Production's control, I would urge that there be a specifically imposed obligation to account for all expenses prior to DKP's receiving its share, and that there be an obligation to place all receipts in a trust or escrow arrangement until there has been a satisfactory accounting.' None of those protective clauses appeared in the agreement Tyson signed.

The contract, on its final page, did recognize that Tyson had a manager's contract with William Cayton 'whereby Cayton's approval of any bout is required'. The contract was forwarded to Cayton for his signature. Naturally, he refused to sign it, and without his signature it was not valid. Instead, Cayton and his long-time attorney, Irving Gruber, went straight to the New York State Athletic Commission and sat down with new Chairman Randy Gordon (who had replaced Jose Torres) to discuss the situation. Cayton made it clear he was optimistic he could have a settlement without litigation and work out a deal with King in the best interests of Tyson. 'But obviously,' said Cayton, 'an exclusive four-year promotional contract is not in the best interests of Mike Tyson.' He felt he held a trump card, in that his boxer-manager contract with Tyson contained a provision for 'specific performance', which Cayton said left the decision on who Mike fights, where he fights, when he fights and for how much money, in the manager's hands, although Tyson did retain the power of veto. The bottom line was, however, that if Cayton did not approve a fight, contractually Tyson could not fight. And Cayton made it clear that unless King and Tyson reached some agreement with him he would file a complaint with the Athletic Commission that could lead to King's losing his promoter's licence. What Cayton did was exactly the right thing, according to attorney Lee Pollock. 'Bill Cayton's refusal to sign the agreement,' he said, 'is not only justified, but necessary for Cayton to fulfil his obligations [to work in his fighter's best interests] as Mike's manager.'

Tyson and King were angry that Cayton would not concede defeat and sign. Tyson termed it a 'low blow' and said Cayton was 'against us'. King said he and Tyson were inseparable and nothing or no one was going to break them up. Late in October, King and Tyson headed for Las Vegas, where King was promoting the lightweight title fight between Julio Caesar Chavez and Jose Luis Ramirez, which HBO was televising. Two days before the fight, King and Tyson announced that the champion would become a promotional partner of King's, and his first venture as a co-promoter was the Chavez–Ramirez fight. 'Me and Don King have made a deal,' said the naive Tyson. 'He'll be working as my associate and partner,' said King. 'We love each other, so we're partners. He's working with me in every fight.'

On the day of the fight, Bill Cayton and Lorraine Jacobs met King and Tyson to try to reach a compromise. The parties were actually close to reaching an agreement for King to promote Tyson on a fight-by-fight basis, when Tyson reversed himself and insisted King be given the four-year exclusive. The meeting broke up, and everyone proceeded to the arena at the Las Vegas Hilton to watch Chavez defeat Ramirez. Kevin Rooney was at ringside, acting as a commentator for HBO. When he spotted 'promoter' Tyson in the ring before the main event began, he shouted up to him, 'You look fat. When are you getting back in the gym?' Tyson looked down at his trainer from the ring and said, 'Fuck you.' And so, the impasse remained. Cayton had a valid contract, but an unwilling fighter whom he couldn't force to fight against his will. King had an invalid contract, but, as he was boasting, 'I can deliver the fighter. Cayton can't.' Tyson, who had claimed that one-third was too much to pay Cayton and had renegotiated his manager's share down to 20 per cent the previous summer, now found one-third an acceptable amount to pay Don King, according to the contract he had just signed with the promoter. King further protected himself in the limited power-of-attorney agreement he had with Tyson, which said King was liable only for 'wilful default, and not errors of judgment'. That meant if King made a mistake of some sort while acting on Tyson's behalf, Tyson would have to prove that King had done it intentionally and fraudulently in order to recoup damages in court.

Bill Cayton received an unexpected phone call that week. It was from Robin Givens. She called to apologize to the manager, saying how sorry she was for all the things she had said about him which she now knew were untrue, and which she said had been fed to her by Don King. 'I think she was sorry,' Cayton said, 'because she knows that I was always on her side, because I was in favour of the marriage.'

Another voice surfaced: that of Donald Trump, Tyson's erstwhile advisor. Trump wanted to collect an overdue bill. It seems that when he stepped in to 'advise' Tyson in his dispute with Bill Cayton before and after the Spinks fight, he had what he termed 'a verbal agreement made in front of witnesses' with Tyson to receive a fee for his services. The fee was $2-million for helping Mike renegotiate his contract with Cayton. 'When Cayton saw me come down the pike with my killer lawyers, he did a total el foldo,' boasted Trump. 'I proceeded to beat the hell out of his manager to get the ridiculous fees reduced. Now that it's all settled, it's time for Mike to pay. Mike would still be in that contract mess if it wasn't for me.' Now, he wrote to Mike: 'As per our conversation, I know that you now feel it is time to live up to your promise of making a $2 million contribution to various charities as selected by me. . . .Over the course of your career, I have probably saved you substantially in excess of $50-million, and therefore the $2-million contribution, all of which will go to worthy charities, is very reasonable. . . .It is great getting your phone calls and I am always here to give you advice.'

At the end of October, King and Tyson jetted off once again, this time to Mexico City to attend the WBC's annual convention, where Tyson was presented with a solid gold and jewelled championship belt by Jose Sulaiman, and where he joined arm-in-arm with King and Sulaiman after Sulaiman was re-elected WBC President.

As mid-November came, the impasse remained between Cayton and King, and Tyson said he didn't want to fight Bruno on January 14, the new date which had been set, because he wanted to take it easy and not train during the holiday season. Cayton continued to threaten lawsuit if things could not be resolved out-of-court with King and Tyson. He was determined to stand his ground, although he hoped for some agreement that would allow the Bruno fight to be staged, even while the larger issues remained unresolved, so that Tyson, who was getting as fat as a pig from inactivity, could get back into training. He said he would not sign the exclusive promotional contract despite an offer from Howard

Weitzman that Cayton's attorney should draft a letter, which
Tyson would sign, absolving the manager from any responsibility should Tyson come to the realization that the promotional
contract was indeed a bad deal for him.

King, attached to Tyson like a Siamese twin, continued to
keep Mike on the move. They distributed Thanksgiving turkeys to poor families in Tyson's old neighbourhood and in
Harlem, then it was on to Chicago, where they gave out more
turkeys, visited the Reverend Jesse Jackson at his Operation
Push headquarters, attended a memorial service for the late
Mayor Harold Washington, went to a fund-raiser for a black
priest who was a friend of theirs (he had actually performed the
Tyson–Givens nuptials) and whose church had burned down,
and then they went on to Hyannis, Massachusetts, where
they taped a segment for a Special Olympics TV show with
the Kennedy family at their compound on Cape Cod. Tyson's
attorney told Jarvis Astaire that Tyson would be reporting
to Catskill on November 28 to begin training with Kevin
Rooney and it looked for a while as though the January
14 date would be met. But no breakthrough came in the
contract dispute, and on November 22, the date was cancelled, as Cayton held firm. 'I wouldn't let a stranger sign
that contract,' he said. 'If Don King gets control of Mike
Tyson he controls boxing. I'm not going to let that happen.'
Howard Weitzman blamed Cayton for the latest postponement, writing to Jarvis Astaire that Cayton 'is determined
to prevent Mike from fighting except upon the unreasonable
terms which he has attempted to dictate to Mike.' Responded
Cayton, 'Don King hates me because I'm the one guy keeping him from taking over Mike Tyson and boxing. Tyson
hates me because I wouldn't let him commit economic suicide.'

The next day, November 23, Tyson filed a lawsuit in Manhattan federal court, seeking once again to break his contract with
Cayton. Weitzman maintained this action was strictly Mike's
doing, that King and his attorney, Charles Lomax, wanted to
try to settle the dispute with Cayton. Four days later, with Jesse
Jackson and Don King in attendance, Mike Tyson was baptized
at the Holy Trinity Baptist Church in Cleveland. Clad in a white
robe, Tyson was immersed in a baptismal pool in the church as
700 parishioners watched, then he sang and clapped his hands
along with everyone else to the sounds of gospel music. 'I felt
so clean, so pure and reborn,' said the champion, 'and I think it

is going to change my life. . .baptism is an unbelievable experience.'

On November 30, Kevin Rooney telephoned Camille Ewald from the gym in Catskill. He was very surprised when a familiar but unexpected voice answered the phone. It was Mike. Rooney had heard rumours that Tyson was planning to get back into the gym, but he had no idea the heavyweight champion was two miles away, at Camille's. Tyson said he would be in the next day, and indeed, on December 1, Tyson walked into the little gym above the police station for the first time in three months. Rooney put him through a moderate work-out of floor and bag exercises, but all was not well. Tyson became annoyed at Rooney's loose lips. The trainer appeared on the Madison Square Garden Network with sportscaster Dave Sims and offered Mike unsolicited marital advice. He said he thought it would be good for him to date Robin again, since he knew the two had had a Manhattan rendezvous a few days earlier. He also said he thought Tyson's baptism had been 'orchestrated', presumably by King and Jesse Jackson. Mike felt Kevin was interfering in his personal business, and he responded by doing what it had been rumoured for weeks he intended to do. He fired Rooney, who had been his friend for eight years and his trainer for six. Unable to do it to his face, or over the phone, instead, he announced it in the newspaper, saying Rooney had 'fired himself' by not heeding Tyson's warnings not to discuss his personal affairs publicly. As far as he was concerned, Rooney said, he was still Tyson's trainer until Mike told him otherwise 'to my face, like a man'. He said King was behind it. Like Cayton, he felt King was poisoning Tyson's mind. All things considered, it was not a good holiday season for Rooney. In the midst of a divorce himself, he was sentenced to three years' probation for assaulting the boyfriend of his estranged wife a year earlier. The sentence came just two weeks before Tyson let him go. Tyson continued to confirm that his decision on Rooney was final, and that if need be he would train himself until he secured a replacement.

On December 15, at a Los Angeles news conference with all parties present, the long-awaited and five-times-in-five-months postponed fight between Mike Tyson and Frank Bruno was officially announced. It would be promoted by the Las Vegas Hilton, which would pay a $7-million site fee to stage the fight which by now had built strong worldwide interest due to Tyson's out-of-the-ring tragi-comic life. 'I'm happy to be back,' said the Heavyweight Champion. 'I've been channelling all my energy and vision into this fight,' said Bruno. 'I've got the power to do what needs to be done.' The fight would take place on February 25, 1989, the 25th anniversary, coincidentally, of Muhammad Ali's victory over Sonny Liston, which gave him the Heavyweight Championship. Although King was not the promoter of the fight itself, he was the promoter of the undercard, which he loaded up with fighters controlled by Don King Productions. In order to have the fight go forward, Bill Cayton had compromised a great deal. Because certain safeguards he had always insisted on to protect Tyson were not in this fight contract, Cayton did not sign it. Cayton would be allowed to attend all press conferences and the weigh-in, but he really had no say over what Tyson did. It had clearly become King's ballgame. Howard Weitzman was quick to point out that although Cayton had this level of participation, and although he would be listed as Tyson's manager, it did not mean that Tyson recognized Cayton as his manager, and the lawsuit the champion had filed to try to break his managerial ties with Cayton still stood. As regards Donald Trump's claim for $2-million for services rendered, Weitzman said, 'Mike Tyson doesn't owe Donald Trump anything.'

Tyson set up his training camp in Las Vegas, ensconced in promoter Don King's Vegas home, with a guard dog, Terminator, stationed nearby to keep unwanted guests away. The year came to an end with his former attorney, Michael Winston – dismissed by Ruth Roper several months earlier, then retained by King to handle Tyson's affairs, only to be dismissed again in favour of Howard Weitzman – refusing to hand over files in his possession pertaining to Tyson until the champ paid $17-thousand in legal fees he said was still owed to him.

18

The Bruno Fight. . .
At Last

I have known the time when a pugilistic encounter between two noted champions was almost considered in the light of a national affair; when tens of thousands of individuals, high and low, meditated and brooded upon it, the first thing in the morning and the last at night, until the great event was decided. . . .in the days of pugilism it was no vain boast to say, that one Englishman was a match for two of t'other race; at present it would be a vain boast to say so, for these are not the days of pugilism.

– LAVENGRO
GEORGE BORROW

THERE WAS MUCH speculation as to who would get the plum assignment to replace Kevin Rooney as Mike Tyson's trainer. Angelo Dundee, an excellent in-the-ring motivator, and Joey Fariello, a disciple of Cus D'Amato who handled Mark Breland, were talked about, but they were white, and it was widely believed that King was persuading Tyson to replace his all-white corner of Rooney, Lott and Baranski, with black cornermen. Among the black trainers whose names were mentioned were men like George Benton and the master, Eddie Futch, who had handled Joe Frazier, Larry Holmes and Spinks. Futch had once been secretly approached by Jim Jacobs early in Tyson's career, not necessarily about replacing Rooney, since a promise had been made to D'Amato that Rooney would always be with Tyson, but certainly about joining with Rooney. When word of the approach leaked out, Jacobs vehemently denied ever talking to the great trainer, but Futch and Tyson both eventually confirmed that such a meeting had indeed taken place. One drawback to anyone on a level with Futch was money. King and Tyson were certainly not going to pay a new trainer anything approaching the ten per cent Rooney received as the standard trainer's fee.

Eventually, early in January, Tyson settled on an unknown young black man named Aaron Snowell from Pennsylvania. Snowell had never fought, and although he claimed he had trained Tim Witherspoon, he had actually just hung around the gym and helped out according to Witherspoon himself, whose

trainer had been Slim Jim Robinson. Boxing people regarded
Snowell as nothing more than a 'gym rat', someone who hangs
around at fight gyms. But Snowell had three key qualifications:
he was black, he would work cheap for the opportunity, and
when Witherspoon had split with King, Snowell had remained
loyal to the promoter. When Tyson began sparring at Johnny
Tocco's Ringside Gym in Las Vegas early in January, Snowell
was in place, supervising the work-outs. Joining him in handling
Tyson's training was the champ's buddy from Albany, Rory
Holloway, who had assumed the title of assistant manager
formerly held by Steve Lott, although he was in no way as
competent to deal with camp duties and coordination as Lott
had been. Holloway was simply a young guy who was in the
right place at the right time, having met Tyson when the teenage future champion was competing as an amateur in the (NY)
Empire State Games, in which Holloway was playing basketball. The two became friends. One Tyson insider who knew
Holloway quite well described him as 'a puppy, completely
dependent on Mike.' *Newsday* reporter Tim Layden described
Holloway as 'a very odd guy who fell into a situation and
has taken advantage of it. He's completely infatuated and
misguided as to his own worth on the face of the earth.' And
so, the corner for the champion was being put in place.

'It's ridiculous for me to pay someone like Kevin Rooney ten
per cent of my purse when there's no loyalty on his part,' said
Tyson, with Don King at his side, during a small press gathering
at the Hilton on January 7. Tyson said the turmoil that had
surrounded him was because 'When I have these long lay-offs
I get in trouble. The way I am is the way I am: high-spirited,
energetic and wild. I'm going to live the way I want to live
anyway. I have to live my life. Once I start to change, that's
the first sign of failure.' He added that 'My friend Frank Bruno
is in real trouble.' Tyson said he was down to 230 pounds, from
a reported high of 255, and he would be 'perfectly comfortable'
going into the fight without any trainer in his corner if need be.
King just beamed and reiterated his oft-repeated 'Tyson is the
boss. When Mike speaks, I listen,' nonsense, while continuing
to control Tyson and not let him out of his sight.

Tyson and King were due to give depositions to Thomas
Puccio in the champion's lawsuit to break his contract with
Cayton. The deposition, a pre-trial questioning procedure conducted under oath but outside the courtroom, was to be held
in Las Vegas according to a ruling by a Federal judge in New

York, so as not to disrupt Tyson's training. Tyson's questioning by Puccio took place on Monday, January 9, and Tuesday, the 10th. King watched the procedure on a closed-circuit TV monitor in another room, while in a separate room sat Cayton, his wife, Doris, and Lorraine Jacobs, also viewing the proceedings on a television monitor. They heard Tyson revile the man who had helped guide his career to its present peak, saying, 'I want to terminate him. I don't like him. I don't want him around. He gets me sick to my stomach. I just want Don King as my promoter. No one's going to dictate my life when I generate the capital.' He called Cayton 'crude and diabolical and a funny old man', and one could hear the words of Don King every time Tyson opened his mouth. Every time there was recess, King dashed in to consult with Tyson.

'Regardless of the price, my intention is to terminate him,' said Tyson of his manager when the questioning resumed. 'He's a horrible, wretched guy, a liar, a hypocrite, not a very nice man.' However, he offered little in the way of substance in his testimony, admitting he knew very little about his finances and business, despite accusing Cayton of stealing from him. 'I didn't know nothing. Basically, I was a space cadet,' he said.

Puccio asked Tyson about a $10-million cheque he had received following the disbursement of funds from the Spinks fight. Tyson said he did not know where the money was or if it had been deposited. 'I handed you the cheque in court,' said Puccio. 'What did you do with it?' Tyson said he had put it in the bank. No, he had given it to his accountant. That is, he had given it to his lawyer to give to his accountant. 'Do you know where the money is deposited?' asked Puccio. Tyson replied, 'No.' 'You don't know where this $10-million went?' he was again asked. 'No,' came the answer. Tyson also said he had no idea how much money he had before the Spinks fight, and denied he had ever been shown any post-fight financial statements by his managers. At another point, Tyson told Puccio, 'I'm the boss.' Puccio asked him, 'Where does it say in the contract you're the boss?' Replied Tyson, 'Let Bill Cayton fight.'

During the questioning, Puccio got Tyson to admit under oath that he had signed several agreements with Don King without the knowledge or consent of Cayton, which was a violation of Cayton's contract with the fighter, and when Puccio asked whether Tyson was a silent partner in putting together the undercard of the Bruno fight, attorney Weitzman told Tyson not to answer. Tyson complained that the questioning was 'pissing me off' and 'stressing me out'. Unbelievably, during the deposition he made vulgar sexual gestures of Joann Crispi, an attractive attorney who was an associate of Puccio. Then, after defending King as the person 'who helped me to blossom into a man' and calling Cayton a man 'with a slavemaster mentality', he had the audacity during a recess to walk right up to Ms Crispi and tell her, 'I want to fuck you'.

Puccio was extremely pleased following the two days of depositions. He felt Tyson had demonstrated he had no substantial case against Cayton, and that he was unable to substantiate claims Cayton had misappropriated his money. He described the information he had obtained on the secret contracts signed between King and Tyson as 'devastating'.

The day following the depositions, Tyson, no doubt still feeling 'stressed out', broke training and disappeared from Las Vegas without bothering to inform either King or his 'trainers' that he was leaving. Several hours later, he stepped off a plane in Vancouver, Canada, where Robin Givens was on location filming an ABC-TV movie. It seems Tyson had phoned her to say he missed her, and she suggested he fly up. He caught the next plane out of Vegas, not even taking a change of clothes or a toothbrush. When he arrived at the hotel, he found reporters, photographers and TV cameras waiting for him. Since the trip was completely spontaneous, someone must have tipped them off that he was arriving. Someone in Vancouver. Someone who knew he was coming. That narrowed the choices considerably. As Tyson stalked the Hotel Vancouver lobby, trying to find out where Robin was, the cameras were on him, and he blew a fuse. He grabbed a $1,200 Nikon F3 camera out of the hands of a photographer for the *Vancouver Sun*, and hurled it against a wall. Mike Timbrell, a cameraman for Canada's BCTV, was taping the incident when Tyson lunged at his $70-thousand TV camera and tore the viewfinder off it, smashing it to the ground, then tried to grab the camera. Timbrell broke free from Tyson and escaped onto the street through the hotel's revolving door. He suffered minor injuries to his hand in the scuffle with the heavyweight champion, but said he did not plan to file assault charges. The *Vancouver Sun* said it would bill Tyson for damages to the Nikon.

Once upstairs, Tyson found a gift Robin had left for him in her suite and a note telling him to come on up to where the filming was taking place. He dashed up, and Robin greeted him warmly, introducing him to the cast and crew. He watched her work for about two hours, until 8 pm, and when the filming was finished for the day, she walked over to Mike and gave him a big kiss. Hand in hand, they returned to her suite, and did not leave it until the next morning. They ordered dinner from room service, including two dozen raw oysters, and put the 'Do Not Disturb' sign on the door.

In Las Vegas, King was furious when he learned where Mike was. The one person he wanted to keep Tyson away from, even more than Cayton, was Givens – and her bed. If Mike became reconciled with her, King knew he risked being dumped once again. However, at midday Thursday, Tyson jumped on a plane at Vancouver airport and arrived back in Las Vegas late in the afternoon, his whirlwind twenty-four-hour excursion to Canada over. Givens told reporters that she and Mike were continuing to see each other as often as they could, even as their divorce proceedings went ahead. 'We're happily estranged,' she said. She revealed there were many show business offers coming in to her now, and acknowledged 'Certainly all that's happened has raised my recognition factor.'

On Friday, January 13, with the Bruno fight six weeks off, Tyson returned to Tocco's Gym and boxed nine rounds, pounding his three sparring partners hard. The sessions were closed to the press, and Tyson's bullying security guards got into several scuffles and shouting matches outside the gym with newsmen.

On Wednesday, January 18, it was Don King's turn to give depositions in the Tyson–Cayton lawsuit, which were conducted in New York City at the offices of Puccio's law firm. Puccio questioned him about his son's involvement in his business, suggesting that King had acted as both a promoter and manager, a violation of boxing commission rules. King's attorney, Bob Hirth, an associate of Charles Lomax, said Bill Cayton was the only person he knew who acted as both a manager and promoter. Puccio also questioned King about the involvement of Rory Holloway and John Horne with Tyson. Both were constantly at the fighter's side, and Horne was reputed to be 'King's man,' there to keep tabs on the champion and report back to King. In response to Puccio's questions, King denied that he or his company had paid either man any money. Puccio sought to establish that Holloway and Horne might also have interfered with Cayton's contract with Tyson. King testified that he had gone from New York to California in April of 1988 in response to a phone call from Tyson, who had asked him for help in dealing with Cayton. King said

Tyson told him Cayton 'was no good, that he hated him, that he wasn't going to fight for him, that he was the worst man he ever met. . . .[Mike] said, "I want to know the business side of boxing. I'm tired of [Cayton] messing with my life."' When asked what his relationship was with the champion, King said, 'He's a friend of mine', and added, 'The fact is Mike Tyson always called me. I've never called Mr Tyson.' King said that far from interfering with Tyson and his managers, he had even encouraged Mike to remain loyal to them when Mike wanted to leave Cayton and Jacobs. '[Mike's] brother came to me earlier, I think before the Berbick fight, and asked me what I would do for him [Tyson]. I ran right to Jim and Bill, just like I always did.' This may well have been true – when Jacobs was alive. It was only after Jacobs's death that King began his seduction of the heavyweight champion. He also testified concerning what Puccio termed the two 'illegal' contracts he had signed with Tyson. At one point the promoter said he actually took fewer years in the four-year exclusive promotional deal signed on October 21 than Tyson wanted to give him. 'Mike said he wanted me to be his promoter for life, but I said let's just make it for four years,' said King, who acknowledged that he had never informed Cayton about the deal. When Puccio pressed him and asked if it was not customary for the promoter to deal with the manager and not directly with the fighter in boxing, King replied, 'You can't ask a normal question when dealing with an abnormal situation.'

Bill Cayton was in the room, along with Lorraine Jacobs, during the questioning of King, but that didn't stop the promoter from defaming the manager while under oath. 'You are representing Satan,' he told Puccio, and went on to label Cayton 'a hypocrite, an inveterate liar, a tyrant, a power zealot. . .When I said he was Satan in disguise, the disguise is gone, he's just Satan. . .The man is an egotistical maniac. No one likes Bill Cayton. He's never been liked by anybody. No sooner did Jim Jacobs die, the man went completely berserk.' He termed Cayton's contract with Tyson 'an ownership. This is a slave contract, an unbridled contract over this human being.'

King said Tyson called him in May of 1988 and asked him to come to Albany, where the fighter negotiated a contract (never put into effect) with King to promote his first fight following the Spinks bout, even though Tyson knew full well that he had a signed contract with Astaire and Duff to fight Bruno in London. Then King said, 'You have to understand one thing,

I am the best promoter in the world. My record substantiates that. . .despite a few allegations by dissidents. My record is irrefutable.' When Puccio told him 'You're not here to make speeches,' King replied 'You subpoenaed me, now you've got to deal with me.'

When the formal portion of the deposition was over, King launched another tirade, aimed directly at Cayton sitting just a few feet away. 'You are a lying hypocrite,' he screamed. 'Jimmy Jacobs was the most loved man in boxing. You are the most hated.' Cayton called King a liar, and King responded by calling him a 'despicable liar'. Then, in the presence of Lorraine Jacobs, King became abusive. 'You're a liar, Bill Cayton, you're a lying motherfucker. You desecrate Jim's memory.' 'You're a lowlife', Cayton told King, who replied, 'I certainly am, when I look at a despicable motherfucker like you. . . .You never were loyal to Jim.' King stomped out of the room. Puccio wasn't flustered, saying, 'It's all part of his act, which you have to listen to if you want to hear him. . .[it's] the price you have to pay in order to get him to testify.' Lorraine Jacobs was upset for Cayton, but the manager just called King 'one hundred per cent bluff and bluster'.

While all this was going on, Frank Bruno was quietly training in the Arizona desert, having arrived in the United States on January 5. The fight had caught the imagination of the British public, with whom Bruno was extremely popular, and was the biggest sporting event involving Great Britain since the winning of the World Cup soccer championship in 1966. The fight would be televised in as many as 40 closed-circuit locations throughout England and Ireland, even though it would begin there at 3 o'clock in the morning of Sunday, February 26, local time. Those with satellite dishes would see the fight live at home on Sky Television, and the BBC would replay it on tape on Sunday afternoon. Jonathan Martin, the BBC's Director of Sports, said a 'massive audience' was anticipated. The intense interest was a tribute to the 27-year-old Briton, who would make the thirteenth attempt in this century by an Englishman to win the Heavyweight Championship of the world, the previous twelve having been unsuccessful, and despite their affection for him, even his countrymen knew Bruno was a long shot to fare any better.

Franklyn Roy Bruno was the youngest of five children of Jamaican immigrants to England. His father was a baker, and

Bruno's neighbours in Barmouth Road, Wandsworth, where he grew up, remember young Frank as a quiet, polite, and well-mannered boy. However, at the age of 11, the big lad hit a schoolteacher during an argument, and was packed off to reform school. It was the only trouble he was ever in, unlike Tyson. Even in reform school he was known as a gentle boy who worked at weekends at a home for the elderly, often taking wheelchair-bound residents out for walks. When he returned to Wandsworth at the age of 16, he was over 6 feet tall and weighed more than 200 pounds. He began working out in amateur boxing gyms, and at the age of 18 he became the youngest British amateur heavyweight champion in history. It was around this time that he met Laura Mooney, a white girl who had grown up in the London borough of Hammersmith and who worked at a children's nursery. The couple began living together, a relationship that continues to this day, and which has produced two beautiful young daughters.

Bruno turned pro in 1982, and won his first 21 fights by knockout, against generally mediocre opposition, his biggest wins coming against veteran Americans Scott Ledoux, Barry Funches, and Jumbo Cummings. On May 13, 1984, at Wembley, he was matched against future champion James 'Bonecrusher' Smith, and was leading in the fight when he was KO'd by Smith in the tenth round. After rebuilding with wins over Phil Brown, Anders Eklund, Lucien Rodriguez, and over-the-hill former champion Gerrie Coetzee, he was matched for the heavyweight championship against Tim Witherspoon at Wembley. Again, he was leading on the scorecards going into the eleventh round, but was KO'd by Witherspoon, coming so close, but failing in the end to win the WBA title. Four victories in 1987, all by KO, against trialhorses Chuck Gardner and Reggie Gross, and faded names James 'Quick' Tillis, who was no longer quick, and Joe Bugner, whose glory was more than a decade behind him, somehow catapulted Bruno back into the number-one challenger's position. The combination of his not wanting to risk that top ranking, which meant another title opportunity, and the five months of delays due to Tyson's star-crossed life, meant that Bruno would step into the ring against Tyson on February 25 after 16 months of inactivity.

Tyson's inexperienced handlers continued to wield a heavy hand. Rory Holloway warned reporters who were allowed into the gym one day that 'Anyone asking questions about

Mike's personal life will be escorted out of here.' Tyson told the newsmen he was considering bringing Kevin Rooney back into the fold, but not for the Bruno fight. He did make another addition to his corner. Jay Bright, his long-time housemate in Catskill, was brought in to assist with his training and work his corner. Bright knew the D'Amato philosophy from living in the house with Cus and Camille for ten years, but he was even less experienced than Aaron Snowell. Bright had never fought (although he liked to say he'd had a few amateur fights) and had never worked with a fighter before. But he was familiar with Mike, which would give the champion a certain element of comfort, and as Steve Lott said, Mike would do whatever he wanted to anyway once the fight started. Bright said he was just happy to be able to help out Mike and that he wasn't concerned what the champion, whom he looked upon as a 'brother', paid him.

Both the British and American press were upset at being unable to reach Tyson. Only one journalist, from a New York tabloid, had unrestricted access to both King and Tyson, but he was known as 'King's designated writer'. Anyone who wrote impartially – journalists like Mike Katz, Phil Berger, Wally Matthews – were kept as far away from Tyson as possible. Several moonlighting Cleveland police officers served as bodyguards, keeping the press at arm's length. The new Tyson entourage, sporting purple and gold jackets supplied by King that said on the back 'It's a Family Affair – Team Tyson', had little knowledge of, or regard for, a journalist's right to ask questions in an unrestricted format. King had claimed he cut Randy 'Tex' Cobb's purse in the Holmes fight because Cobb did not come to Houston early enough to help promote the fight, yet he was apparently not interested in letting Tyson help promote the Bruno fight by talking to reporters, even though many seats remained, and would remain, unsold at the Hilton. Without access to Tyson, some newspapermen had to rely on their own imaginations to come up with story angles. Britain's the *News of the World* carried a story that Tyson and King were approached by two characters who offered an incredible $80-million if Tyson would throw the fight to Bruno. The source of this story was not revealed but the paper reported that Tyson furiously ordered the 'bums' out of his sight 'before I kill them'. The British press also made quite a fuss about Bruno employing a hypnotherapist, Dr David Silverman of Las Vegas, to help put him at ease and build his confidence. 'When I wake up [from the hypnotic trances],' said Bruno, 'I feel as if I could fight King Kong, let alone Mike Tyson.' The champion, as usual, had his hypnotist, John Halpin of New York, in camp with him. Along with watching movies and listening to rap music, Tyson spent some of his relaxation time racing around the desert in his new white 4-wheel drive, $170–thousand Lamborghini LM002 off-road vehicle, for which he paid cash, and which he had no trouble getting up to 120 mph on his joy-rides, since it had a 450 horsepower engine.

In November, a drunk and loud Tyson had made a fuss at the Las Vegas Hilton gambling tables, shooting dice, cursing, and 'causing a whole lot of commotion' according to one witness. Then he had been asked to leave by hotel security. But now, in training, Tyson kept more to himself, out of the public eye, and, according to Hilton Hotel security personnel, the champion was this time staying out of trouble.

Bruno shifted his training camp to Las Vegas from Arizona and went about his business in his usual no-nonsense, dignified manner. Colin Hart of the London *Sun* newspaper, said Bruno was 'easily the most popular sportsman in Britain', a phenomenon he found somewhat curious since 'he hasn't won anything'. BBC boxing commentator Harry Carpenter said the British were a people who preferred 'a good loser to a flashy winner'. Another reason for his popularity might well have been that the British people (and many Americans as well who were rooting for Bruno) felt that he conducted himself with the demeanour of a champion, while Tyson had demonstrated time and again that his personal conduct left much to be desired.

The usually placid Bruno did become annoyed at the poor treatment he said he and his party were receiving at the Hilton, saying the hotel was 'treating me like a dog. . .This is the worst [hotel] I have been in for looking after a fighter,' complaining he even had to purchase a Tyson-Bruno souvenir T-shirt, since the Hilton wouldn't give him one. However, from his purse as well as from his share of closed-circuit TV revenues in Great Britain, Bruno stood to net $2-million for himself, to add to his personal worth that was already estimated at $5-million, so he was willing to put with the Hilton's behaviour towards him.

While keeping Tyson away from the boxing journalists, King engineered a series of appearances on TV talk shows, where Tyson would not be pressed very hard on controversial issues such as his relationship with King. On most of these shows, King appeared as a guest alongside Tyson. On the *Phil Donahue Show*, Tyson said he still loved Robin, 'but it's an unhealthy situation. I can't live with her. . . .We both made a mistake. We were young and got married.' Of his mother-in-law, whom just a few months earlier he had defended, saying that he loved her, considered her part of his family, he simply said, 'I have no relationship with the woman.' On a satellite interview with David Frost in London for 'TV-am', he said he was not interested in a reconciliation with Givens, and that his new-found Christianity gave him comfort in times of trouble. In several interviews on ESPN, the cable sports TV network, Tyson said he didn't think he'd end up broke when his career was over, but acknowledged that 'smarter businessmen than me has [*sic*] been tricked out of all their money'. About his preparations for the fight, he said he would be completely ready, because he was aware that if you go into a fight only halfway prepared, 'you're going to be pickin' your butt off the canvas'. He said he was ready to get back into action. 'I just want to fight. I'm very hostile at this particular moment in my life.' The low point came on the *Arsenio Hall Show*, a late night variety programme. Hall, a black comedian, seemed both incapable and unwilling to ask King and Tyson any hard questions, and Tyson used the appearance to slander Bill Cayton shamelessly once again, saying, 'When I was with the opposite people, when I was with Bill Cayton. . .people that was [*sic*] actually stealing my money and had the complexion for the protection.' This was an allusion to Muhammad Ali's remark about white people that they had 'the complexion and the connection to get the protection'. Thus, Tyson injected race as an issue, which in fact it never had been in all his years with D'Amato, Jacobs, Cayton, Ewald, Atlas and Rooney. But when Hall gave him the opportunity to tell how Cayton had stolen from him, Tyson could offer no specifics beyond saying, 'it's very simple, then again it's very complex, because I had no experience'. He gave King credit because 'he showed me God'. 'Now I'm with Don,' he said, 'and we're two black people, and we're generatin' power.'

King, for his part, termed his association with Tyson 'a wonderful relationship. . . .demonstrating to America, to friend and foe alike, that two people of colour can come together and do just as any other people would do. . . .we understand who we are and we love ourselves.' He praised Tyson as a champion who in the future would show he was the greatest of all time, saying, 'I'm like John the Baptist, a voice crying in the wilderness, talking about one that's coming greater than I,' and, gesturing toward Tyson, concluded his speech: 'This is a bad nigger, babe.'

While in Los Angeles with King early in February taping several TV appearances, Mike unexpectedly turned up at Robin's house carrying six dozen red roses. He spent the night with her, and the next day the couple were out strolling and embracing on fashionable Rodeo Drive in Beverly Hills. Several days later, Robin signed, at last, the divorce decree, and King wasted no time getting Mike legally apart from Givens, once and for all. Although Tyson had won the right several weeks earlier to have his deposition with Cayton's attorney Tom Puccio conducted in Las Vegas so as not to interrupt his training routine, now with the fight just eleven days away, King hustled Tyson on to the promoter's private jet and flew with him to the Dominican Republic, a five-hour flight, where a divorce could be obtained in twenty-four hours. All that was required was an overnight stay. On February 14, a mutual divorce was granted to Mike Tyson and Robin Givens, after which the promoter and his charge returned to Las Vegas, with King chanting 'Free at last, free at last', as they were met by reporters at the airport.

The specific terms of the divorce, by mutual agreement, were not announced. Raoul Felder said his client, Givens, 'will keep what was hers, including all of her jewellery, and he will keep what is his.' But, of course, it wasn't quite that simple. Felder acknowledged there would be an audit at a later date, that would set 'a floor to what she receives'. She would not get the New Jersey mansion, but she would keep the couple's luxury cars, and the house in the Hollywood Hills that was in her name, but which Tyson had purchased and furnished at a cost of more than $1,250,000. This, along with the jewellery Mike had lavished on her, plus several hundred thousand dollars' worth of clothing, mean that Robin would come out of the marriage with millions of dollars in assets. And still unanswered was the question raised by Tyson of what had happened to millions of dollars of cash he said was transferred from Mike Tyson Enterprises accounts to accounts controlled by Robin Givens Productions. One thing she had to give up was his name: a stipulation of the divorce said she could no longer use the name Tyson.

Back in New York things were also happening. Kevin Rooney's attorney arrived in US District Court in Albany, New York, and slapped Mike Tyson with a $10-million lawsuit on Rooney's behalf, claiming breech of contract. It was based on what he said was an oral agreement that he had to be Mike's trainer for life, with a set fee of ten per cent. Coming when it did, the lawsuit was impetuous and ill-advised. Tyson had been saying 'Kevin is my man', and making it clear he intended to reconcile himself with his trainer following the Bruno fight, which he was making Kevin sit out as a sort of punishment. Now he was furious. He said Kevin 'just did something unprofessional' by speaking out on matters involving Mike's personal life, but now, by suing the champion, Rooney had gone 'out of his way to make it personal. Now he'll never be involved with me again, never.' Rooney fired back that Tyson had never even called to discuss the matter with him, that he only read about it in the newspapers. 'What was I supposed to do, sit around like a jerk?' asked Rooney. 'Fuck him. He's a jerk,' said the dismissed trainer.

With the fight now just a few days off, grizzled old gymkeeper Johnny Tocco said Tyson seemed ready. 'I've seen him train for five fights now. I've never seen him let up on any sparring partners. He's an animal. He's got seven sparring partners now and he needs them because he keeps hurting them. He gets them hurt and he wants to finish them off whether it's gym work or a fight.' Tocco said Snowell and Bright seemed to be a bit disorganized. 'They both are yelling instructions to him, which isn't too good, but I don't think he listens to anyone in there, anyway. All he needs is someone to tie the gloves on, and anything in front of him he goes after. Anything in front of him, once that bell rings, you're gone.' Michael Spinks, who was in Las Vegas, said, 'Boxing is the best job in the world to let off steam, and people are in trouble when Tyson wants to let off steam.'

At the final pre-fight news conference, Tyson said he liked 'the single life', that he was 'very happy at this particular moment in my life and Don King put a big hand in it'. 'Thank you, champ,' answered King. About his topsy-turvy year, Tyson said, 'I'm a human being, I'm bound to slip on a banana peel,' but he said people shouldn't feel sorry for him. 'That insults me,' said Tyson. 'I ask for no sympathy. I despise sympathy. I hear people say, "Poor Mike Tyson." There is nothing poor about me.'

'I don't think people respect him,' said Bruno of the champion. 'He's done too many crazy things. He's young and he's got to do some serious, serious learning to bring him off his pedestal. I'm the one to do it.' Responded Tyson: 'He's a good fighter, believe it or not. He didn't get to be number one by laying on his butt. When you look at him, he's very threatening-looking, but I give him no chance. I'm basically not a hostile person, but I'd say he's in some trouble.' With King and his new triumvirate of camp coordinator John Horne, plus cornermen Snowell and Bright, surrounding him, Tyson said, 'I'm glad to be back in the ring, because this is where I dominate.'

When King began to insult absent manager, Bill Cayton, Jarvis Astaire walked off the dais. Cayton was resting in New York, on doctor's orders, following several days of hospitalization. He had just returned from testifying as a defendant in London in a lawsuit precipitated by King, who, according to Cayton, had made an unauthorized deal for ITV to televise the fight in Britain. The suit was decided against ITV by the High Court and in favour of Sky TV, and the court also issued a financial judgment against ITV for $700-thousand, but following his successful testimony, Cayton returned to New York suffering from exhaustion. At the Las Vegas news conference, King accused Cayton of entering the hospital to avoid giving a deposition in the Tyson lawsuit.

In New York, both prior to and following his trip to London, Cayton had been working quietly behind the scenes to see if some compromise could be worked out with King to avoid disruptive litigation. In the waning days of January, Cayton spoke by phone with James Binns of Pennsylvania, an attorney who was the WBA's legal advisor and a major power broker in that organization. Binns was an ally of King, but had also helped Cayton and Jacobs on various matters, and Cayton felt he was an honourable man who could be trusted. In that phone conversation, Cayton advised Binns confidentially that he and his attorneys were on the verge of filing a formal complaint against King with the New York State Athletic Commission for interfering with Tyson. Binns said, 'Bill, I hate to see it come to that because if it does, the chances of a settlement are remote.' Binns went on to explain that once the Commission took over jurisdiction of the matter, a private deal between the parties involved would then be out of their hands. Cayton explained, 'I have no choice in the matter. You know what's been said, you know what Don's done.' Binns interjected. 'Let me talk to Don,' he suggested. 'Maybe there's a way of settling this.' Cayton said he'd prefer Binns not to intercede with King, reminding the attorney that he had been close to a settlement several times – most recently at the meeting in Las Vegas prior to the Chavez–Ramirez fight – but that each time things had collapsed. (In Vegas, Cayton had offered a settlement based on King working with them on a fight-by-fight basis, or a group of fights: he had offered King the opportunity to promote the final four fights of the seven-fight HBO contract with Tyson, but King and Tyson were insisting on the four-year exclusive contract.)

Binns asked Cayton if he could talk to Tom Puccio, and Cayton reluctantly agreed. Puccio agreed with Binns, and convinced Cayton to give Binns a shot at dealing with King. 'If he can do it,' said Puccio, 'Why not let him?' Before long, Binns notified Cayton that he had spoken with the promoter, and King was ready to sit down and try to hammer out some arrangement. Cayton consequently agreed to hold off on the filing of his formal complaint against King. It was agreed King would come to New York to meet sometime during the first half of February, before Cayton's trip to testify in London, but that meeting was never arranged, although the attorneys for both sides did begin talks. During Cayton's absence, however, things fell apart; as he was to learn once again, accommodation was not in King's vocabulary. Even King's ally James Binns apparently threw in the towel in exasperation. During the week preceeding the Bruno fight, Binns said, 'Bill Cayton has been very reasonable. He made King a very good offer.' Larry Holmes, from afar, still issued warnings to Tyson about King. 'You don't get off the horse that brought you over the bridge to get on another horse,' said the ex-champion, 'Especially not that horse. I know that horse too well.'

The weigh-in was held on Friday, February 24, the day before the fight, on the stage of the Hilton's Showroom Theatre. Several thousand British fans were in Las Vegas for the fight, among them former European and Commonwealth Heavyweight Champion Henry Cooper, still much beloved by his countrymen for his two game but unsuccessful efforts against Muhammad Ali a generation earlier. Most of the Brits sported T-shirts with a picture of Bruno superimposed over the Union Jack, and a rowdy group was among the hundreds of people who jammed in to watch the weigh-in. When Bruno entered, wearing an aqua-blue sweatsuit and a red baseball cap, his fans began chanting 'Bru-no, Bru-no, Bru-no.' Tyson indicated Bruno should step on the scale first, which he did.

His weight was announced at '228 pounds – 16 stone, 4 pounds.'
Tyson came in at a trim '218 pounds – 15 stone, 8 pounds.' When
he stepped down, he tried to engage Bruno in a stare-down
match, but Bruno was having none of it. He avoided Tyson's
eyes, looking down, at which point the champion pulled his
red-and-black bikini underwear shorts down to give Bruno a
look at the 'family jewels'. It was a primitive, crude gesture
on Tyson's part, but George Francis, Bruno's trainer, said it
did not bother his man, although it did prompt a headline in
the next day's *Mirror* in London that said, 'Tyson Flashes A
Warning'. There was little betting on the outcome of the fight,
since the Las Vegas line had Bruno a solid 7½-to-1 underdog.
Most of the betting centred on whether Bruno would last more
than one round, or more than four rounds, or whatever. Back
in Catskill, Kevin Rooney said he would be rooting for Tyson,
who he thought would stop Bruno, although he did say the
fight could be tougher and go on longer than many expected.
He himself would be spending Saturday night coaching several
amateur fighters he was training in an amateur tournament in
Schenectady, New York.

Frank Bruno was the first to enter the Hilton's indoor arena,
wearing a bright red robe trimmed in shiny gold lamé. Moments
later came Tyson, who tossed a terrycloth towel off his shoulders halfway down the aisle to enter the ring traditionally
barechested. During the instructions at centre ring from referee
Richard Steele, it was Bruno who stared directly at Tyson, and
the champion who averted his glance.
    At the opening bell, both men advanced strongly toward
each other, and after barely seven or eight seconds, the crowd,
hardly settled in, was stunned when Tyson hurt the towering
Brit with a right hand. Bruno's knees wobbled, and he stumbled
backwards. Another right caught him, mostly with forearm, but
the force of the inaccurate punch, with Bruno already hurt,
sent him to the canvas after just 11 seconds had expired in
the round, and many thought they might be witnessing the
fastest heavyweight title fight in history. Tyson, who often
used dirty tactics in his fight, fouled Bruno by punching the
challenger after he was clearly down, but referee Richard
Steele chose not to penalize, or even warn, the champion.
Bruno rose to his feet immediately, and Tyson later recalled
telling himself when he saw Bruno get up, 'Oh, man, this guy
means business.' Bruno then held Tyson behind the head with

his left arm, and clubbed the champion repeatedly with rights to the head. Tyson, in turn, replied with his own dirty tactics, banging Bruno in the face with his elbow. Bruno was bleeding from the nose. Bruno then spun Tyson into the ropes, and with the champion's back to him, whacked Tyson with several rabbit punches. Steele stepped in and called a halt to the action, waved Tyson to a neutral corner, and informed the judges at ringside he was deducting a point from Bruno's score for the challenger's tactics. Moments later the crowd was electrified when Bruno connected with a right hand which clearly hurt Tyson. He followed with a solid left, and Tyson's legs turned wobbly for an instant, the champion losing his footing but not going down. It was, however, the worst Tyson had ever been hurt in any of his 36 fights, and Bruno was coming back very impressively and strongly. With 35 seconds to go in a thrilling first round, Bruno again hurt the champion with a hard left hand, and Tyson responded by clubbing Bruno with another illegal elbow to the head. The bell ended the round and the crowd responded with cheers, having witnessed much more than they had expected at the start of the evening. In the corner, Lawless told Bruno, 'You hurt him.'

In round two, Bruno continued to hold Tyson behind the head with his left hand, despite warnings from referee Steele. He landed two solid lefts to Tyson's body, bringing chants of 'Bruno, Bruno' from the two thousand British fans among the nine thousand in attendance. Frank responded with a good left hook-left uppercut combination, but a sharp right hand to the jaw by Tyson hurt him. Tyson then subjected his opponent to a flurry of punches as the round came to an end. In the corner, Jay Bright encouraged Tyson to 'throw those punches with bad intentions, mean', while in Bruno's corner, Lawless urged his man, 'Frank, get yourself together now. . . .you took his best shots.'

In the third round, Tyson attacked Bruno's body, while Bruno started by continuing to land his left effectively. Bruno forced a clinch, and Tyson dug a brutal hand to his ribs. Mike then lunged and missed several punches, but landed a good right to Bruno's head in the final minute. The Londoner responded with a solid right to Tyson's head, and dug several lefts to Tyson's body just before the bell. Tyson then shot a left to Bruno's face clearly after the bell ending the round, another one of his customary dirty tactics. It brought boos from the crowd, but no penalty from referee Steele. Aaron Snowell admonished his man during the rest period to use 'body shots, a lot of those "sevens", stay inside'.

Tyson opened round four with big right to Bruno's head, while the challenger pawed with an ineffective, slow jab. The two men exchanged solid lefts, and Tyson nailed Bruno with a good right to the body. Tyson's body shots were beginning to take their toll, knocking some of the starch out of Bruno and slowing him down. Inside the one-minute mark, Bruno was stunned by a right to the head, followed quickly by two lefts and then two sharp left jabs. Tyson ended the round strongly, with a left uppercut and another left elbow.

Round five was the challenger's last stand. During the first minute there were several mauling clinches, with Bruno clutching behind Tyson's head once again, prompting Steele to shout, 'Last warning – you're holding, Frank.' Just past the halfway mark, Tyson hurt Bruno badly with a left hook, followed by a right uppercut. Bruno was forced to clinch to try to clear his head. Tyson then came out of the clinch with a pulverizing right hand, the first in a ten-punch combination that came from all angles, punctuated by several damaging left uppercuts. With 20 seconds to go in the round, Tyson backed Bruno to the ropes and fired a damaging right hand to Frank's ribs, two right uppercuts, and a left hook to the head. Bruno was nearly helpless. Seeing this, Terry Lawless jumped on to the ring apron to try to stop the fight. Ringside officials tried to stop him, but Richard Steele had also seen enough. He jumped between the fighters as Tyson got one final right-hand punch off, landing it on Bruno's bloodied face. It was all over as Lawless made it into the ring, the stoppage coming at 2:55 of the fifth round. Tyson quickly moved back toward Bruno to embrace his beaten challenger. Once again, as he had demonstrated against Spinks, adversity outside the ring – this time a broken hand, mood-altering drugs, a car crash, and a divorce – did not affect his performances inside the squared circle, which was his domain. True, he did show signs of rust, but he also showed he was, far and away, the best heavyweight in the world. Speaking of Bruno and the rest of his opponents after the fight, Tyson said, arrogantly but accurately, 'How dare they challenge me with their primitive skills. They're as good as dead.' 'He beat me fair and square,' acknowledged Bruno. 'I have no excuses.' Bruno's performances was praised in the American press, which labelled him 'the gallant Briton' with 'a stout heart' who 'fought with valour.' When he returned to England three days later, he was met by a crush of fans and reporters at Heathrow Airport. Bruno managed to say he was sorry he hadn't brought the title home and hoped to meet Tyson again in the ring, in London, when 'I reckon I would stop him next time. . . .I proved he's only human, he can be hurt.' After that, fans and reporters broke through police security barriers and the scene turned to chaos. It was as if Bruno had brought home the belt. Scuffles erupted, cameras were knocked over as well as people, and Bruno, along with his girlfriend were quickly escorted by police to a waiting car. Clearly, Bruno had done Great Britain proud. 'If he had not been up against such a great fighter,' said John Morris, secretary of the British Boxing Board of Control, 'we might now have our first heavyweight world champion this century. He showed all the knockers who said he had no right in the ring with Tyson that they were utterly wrong. . . .he hit Tyson harder than anybody ever has, and I am proud of him,' an opinion that was generally reflected throughout the country.

Back in the United States, King and Tyson appeared on the *Arsenio Hall Show* again, where they apparently had a free platform, and King said he was proud because 'We made history. This was the first time Mike had blacks in his corner.' King, ever injecting race although constantly denying he was a racist, seemingly had no concern for the competency of the corner, just that three black men – Snowell, Holloway and Horne – were in it, along with Jay Bright, who was white. Others had more concern. Jerry Izenberg wrote in the *New York Post*, 'As the fight wore on. . .Tyson's corner looked and operated as if it had just stepped out of the Inter-City Golden Gloves semifinals. . . .Collectively, they provided no answers. . . .beyond lifting the stool into and out of the ring, they contributed little. . . .On another night, with another opponent, it could have been a disaster.' And Michael Katz, in the New York *Daily News*, wrote that Tyson was 'filled with arrogance, pumped up with poison. He does not need a trainer, he said after a performance that could have embarrassed a Golden Gloves novice. . . .Mike Tyson should get down on his knees and beg Kevin Rooney to take him back.'

With the fight behind them, Cayton and his attorneys, Puccio and Gruber, no longer had a need to keep the lid on, and Cayton was finished with trying to work out an accommodation with the stubborn King. Barely thirty-six hours after the fight, at the opening of business on Monday morning, Cayton filed his official complaint against King with the New York State Athletic

Commission. The 24-page document charged the promoter with 'deliberate disregard of the Tyson–Cayton boxer–manager contracts, commission rules and established boxing practices.' The Cayton complaint asked that the Athletic Commission fine Don King and his company and revoke King's promotional licence if it was determined he had violated Cayton's contract and Commission regulations. Letters were also sent to both Tyson and King by Puccio warning them that if they attempted to arrange any fight without the participation and approval of Cayton they would be in violation of Tyson's contract with his manager. Puccio said anyone interested in arranging a Tyson fight would be informed they must deal only through Bill Cayton. 'We allege that Don King has in effect attempted to steal Mike Tyson,' said Puccio, who also said Tyson might have misappropriated between $800-thousand and $1-million which the Hilton paid to him directly (a rules violation by the Las Vegas hotel) in order to reduce the amount due to be paid to Cayton. The manager said, 'I truly believe that if Mike could get out from under the influence of Don King, he would come back to me. Really, he loved me when he was younger.' On the wall of Cayton's office, in fact, was a photo Tyson had inscribed 'To my dear friend and the man I love greatly, From your boy, Mike.' Cayton said the problem was, 'I haven't been able to get to him. They have an iron curtain around him that I can't break through. . . .[but] I will not ignore my responsibilities by surrendering to the extortionist demands of Don King. As long as I am Mike Tyson's manager, I will not allow him to be added to the scores of boxers over the years who claim to have been raped and pillaged by Don King. . .I will do everything in my power to keep him from committing economic suicide with Don King.'

One week later, on March 7, Cayton and Puccio dropped their other bomb, and it was a big one. They filed a giant lawsuit against King in US District Court in New York, alleging no fewer than 38 charges of federal anti-trust violations, racketeering, defamation, extortion, mail and wire fraud, and interference with contractual relations. The lawsuit charged that through a 'pattern of racketeering' King had monopolized heavyweight championship boxing and that a desire to continue this control of the heavyweight division was King's motivation for undermining Cayton's contract with Tyson. The suit alleged: 'King maintains this monopoly by, among other things, signing champions to long-term,

exclusive promotional contracts. Potential contenders are in
turn told that to fight King fighters in championship fights,
they must sign with King themselves. . . .King generally waits
until a manager, or promoter, has developed a fighter to
the point where he is of commercial appeal. . . .King falsely
convinces the fighter to trust him. . .that he can make more
money for the fighter and that, unlike the current advisers
he acts out of love and racial unity. . . .Should the fighter
subsequently tire of withering purses and diminishing bank
accounts and seek to break free, King threatens to have the
fighter disciplined, or barred from competition by sanctioning
bodies. . . .when King realized that Tyson would be able to
dominate the heavyweight division, it became imperative to
sign Tyson to a long-term deal. . . .Should King succeed in
forcing Cayton to ratify an exclusive promotional contract with
King. . .King will eliminate competition among promoters in
the relevant market.' Cayton asked for an injunction to prevent
King from negotiating deals or signing contracts with, or for,
Tyson.

Late in March, Howard Weitzman questioned Bill Cayton
for four hours in a deposition related to Tyson's lawsuit to
break his contract with his manager. Weitzman pursued a line
of questioning aimed at trying to establish that Cayton had
violated Athletic Commission rules, which allows only one
manager for a fighter. Weiztman questioned how Cayton could
have been Tyson's co-manager while Jacobs was alive. However, there was no violation of rules. It is common for fighters to
have a manager and a co-manager in New York State. As a matter of fact, when Carl King moved in on Bonecrusher Smith in
1986, he became co-manager with Smith's true manager, Alan
Kornberg. Co-manager is simply a common usage term, the
second party involved with a fighter actually being an assignee
for a specific percentage, designated by the manager.

Then Weitzman 'revealed' he had determined in the course
of the deposition that Cayton did not have a valid manager's licence when he signed his new contract with Tyson in
July of 1988, making the contract voidable. However, this
revelation (a 'big bombshell' according to Don King), had a
very short life. Four days later, Athletic Commission Chairman Randy Gordon said Bill Cayton did indeed have a valid
manager's licence all along. Tyson's attorney then charged
Cayton with double-dipping into Tyson's foreign-rights earnings, since Cayton's company which marketed Tyson fights

overseas received a 20 per cent commission, this in addition to the 20 per cent managerial fee Cayton received. The only problem here was that the 20 per cent marketing commission was clearly defined in the July 1988 contract which Tyson had signed and which had been reviewed and approved by the champion's attorney.

During the first week of April, King struck back by filing a counter-complaint against Cayton with the Athletic Commission. King charged that Cayton had 'financially abused' Tyson 'through fraud, the use of unlicensed sham corporations and blatant conflicts of interest'. It seemed to be the ultimate example of the pot calling the kettle black.

19

Defeat!

Humpty Dumpty sat on the wall,
Humpty Dumpty had a great fall,
All Don King's horses,
And all Don King's men,
Couldn't put Humpty together again.

– GEORGE FOREMAN
former Heavyweight Champion
February 12, 1990, following Tyson's defeat

FOLLOWING HIS VICTORY over Frank Bruno came an offer for Tyson to defend his crown in, of all places, China. The Chinese government agreed to back the fight with $25-million, with a target date of November. The opponent was to be the former champion, George Foreman, now making a comeback. Estranged manager Cayton said Tyson's share would be $20-million. But shortly afterwards came the student rebellion and in the wake of the Chinese government's brutal repression of the pro-democracy demonstrators, the fight deal dissolved.

About the same time, Cayton, who had already paid Thomas Puccio $1.7-million in legal fees in his ongoing litigation with King and Tyson, ended his relationship with Puccio and retained a new – and presumably less pricey – attorney, David Branson of Washington, DC.

Also around this time, Tyson was granted a final divorce from Robin Givens in the state of New Jersey, his legal place of residence. This was necessary because New Jersey did not recognize the legality of the divorce granted four months earlier in the Dominican Republic. Givens, meanwhile, in an interview in *TV Guide*, said the thrill and the danger of the relationship was what had drawn her to Tyson. 'It was so dangerous, I loved it,' she said. 'He was exciting. I can't describe it – I mean, bad. He was a turn-on...I think that what people don't realize with a certain type of woman is that there are times when she wants the man she is with to be a man.' Givens also said Tyson had recently been to her house several times, once to say he loved her, but once, according to another source, to slap her around. The article described Givens as living in 'semi-seclusion, groping to make sense of her life...She hardly sees anyone, she's isolated...Her

337

future is unclear, her personal life is torn.' And an executive who worked with her said, 'This girl has serious problems. She is looking for danger...What she needs to do is go immediately to a psychiatrist.'

Cable TV giant HBO, the primary presenter of Tyson's fights under an exclusive contract, was angling to sign Tyson to a lifetime deal. Meanwhile, Tyson's next fight, to be carried by HBO from Atlantic City, was scheduled for July 21, against the IBF's No. 1-ranked contender, Carl 'The Truth' Williams. Although top-ranked, Williams had a suspect jaw. As a relative novice, he had put up an outstanding effort four years earlier in a title challenge against Larry Holmes, losing a very close decision. But in 1986, he was knocked out by Mike Weaver. Overall, his record stood at 22-2, with 17 KOs, and he was an imposing physical specimen at 6'4", 225 pounds, and with the longest reach among any of the top heavyweights.

The fight itself did little more than earn Tyson a quick $4-million ($1.2-million for Williams) and enhance his already unbeatable reputation. A little beyond the one-minute mark of the opening round, the champion nailed Williams with a left hook on the right side of the head, sending the challenger down hard. Williams attempted to rise from the seat of his pants, but slumped back. His second effort succeeded, and he got to his feet at the count of eight. But his eyes were glazed, and when referee Randy Neumann, himself a former heavyweight fighter, asked Williams if he was all right, there was no response. Neumann signalled the bout over 1:33 into round one. At that point Williams protested, saying he was ready to continue, but it was too late. It was victory number 37 and KO number 33 for Tyson.

Interest was now building more than ever for a showdown with Cruiserweight Champion Evander Holyfield. Since moving into the heavyweight division, Holyfield had established himself as the legitimate top contender, with KOs over James Tillis, Pinklon Thomas, Michael Dokes, Adilson Rodrigues, and Alex Stewart. After his victory over Williams, Tyson had moved to the side of the ring where Holyfield was seated and shook his gloved fist in Holyfield's direction, and had said he'd fight Holyfield for free in the basement of the Convention Center in Atlantic City. 'Whoever comes back upstairs will be the champion,' sneered Tyson, but what the management of both fighters had in mind were purses totalling $30 or $35 million.

Next up for Tyson, however, was top-ten contender Donovan 'Razor' Ruddock, the Canadian Heavyweight Champion. With the two one-round blowouts of Spinks and Williams, and the financial shellacking the Las Vegas Hilton took in promoting the Tyson–Bruno fight, the hotel/casinos in Vegas and Atlantic City were not lining up to pay huge site fees to buy the fight. The Convention Center, which can seat 16,000 had only 11,000 on hand for the Williams fight, and 5,000 of those seats had been given away for free by the casinos to their best customers. After scrambling around, Don King found a financial backer in Canada, and the fight was set for the Northlands Coliseum in Edmonton, Alberta, in November.

Meanwhile, in Albany, New York, a judge ordered Tyson to conduct three clinics at youth centres and fined him $300 after the champion pleaded guilty to two speeding charges, including the one in which he had drag-raced his Lamborghini at 71mph in a residential neighbourhood. The $300 didn't really put a dent in Tyson's wallet, and he was able to turn down an offer from London-based Winners Worldwide, Ltd, a sports promotions firm, of $100-million to go on a one-year worldwide tour, facing a different opponent each month in a different country.

During the summer, Bill Cayton and Don King became embroiled in yet another battle as hearings began at the New York State Athletic Commission on Cayton's charges that King should have his promoter's licence revoked for interfering in Cayton's contract with Tyson, and King's counter-charges that Cayton had duped Tyson into signing a new contract just a month before Jim Jacobs died. After a month of hearings, however, State Athletic Commission Chairman Randy Gordon dropped the investigation of King, saying he was not interested in driving potential fights away from New York, but welcomed the chance that King would, in the future, promote fights in the state. Cayton, meanwhile, was honoured as Manager of the Year by the World Boxing Association, the International Veteran Boxers Association, and the American Association for the Improvement of Boxing.

On October 9, before leaving for Canada to complete his training for the Ruddock fight, Tyson went to Albany, where he conducted a sparring session and signed autographs at St Joseph's Youth Center. Later in the day, he gave an anti-drug talk at a community centre, thus fulfilling his court-assigned obligation. He then headed to Edmonton, where 5,600 seats for the Ruddock fight were sold in the first 48 hours they were on sale. Tickets in the 18,000-seat Coliseum were priced at 50 to 1,500 Canadian dollars apiece.

Three weeks before the fight, Tyson began complaining of

pains in his chest that were hampering his ability to train. Two doctors, including Tyson's personal physician, Dr Elias Ghanem, who flew up from Las Vegas, examined the champion. (Ghanem, who had served in Las Vegas as Elvis Presley's personal physician, was also an official of the World Boxing Council.) They diagnosed Tyson as having a viral infection, known as costochondritis, which is similar to pleurisy. They said he had to rest for at least a month to recover, and the local promoters had no choice but to cancel the fight. They hoped for a rescheduling early in 1990, since they had already advanced King and Tyson $800,000 in expense money, but King had other ideas.

A week later, after staging an apparently remarkable recovery, Tyson was seen partying with half a dozen women until 2:30 at the China Club, a trendy New York night spot. How sick had he really been? Estranged manager Cayton offered the opinion that if you have a serious lung inflammation, 'you don't go into restaurants and then disco till three in the morning. You should be in bed.' The same week, Tyson also popped up in Washington, DC, where he spent a lot of time at the equally trendy Chicago Bar and Grill, this time bouncing around town with seven women.

Tyson did take the time, in a grandstand move obviously orchestrated by someone more devious than him, to send a letter to New York Governor Mario Cuomo, asking the governor to appoint a panel to investigate how 'I was deliberately tricked by my late manager, Jim Jacobs, and Bill Cayton, my current manager, and Jose Torres, former chairman of the State Athletic Commission, into signing a slave contract that fraudulently willed Tyson, myself, to my current manager, Cayton'. Tyson again showed incredible ingratitude by linking the name of his late and close friend, Jacobs, to charges of fraud. Not surprisingly, Don King immediately made the letter available to the press. The letter went on to imply that Jacobs and Cayton were 'gangsters and shady characters' who had conspired to see to it that Tyson was 'being ripped off and … robbed of my money'. One can only say thank goodness that a saviour like Don King came along in the nick of time to save Tyson from the Jacobs-Cayton plot!

In a letter to the *New York Times*, Cayton struck back, saying, 'There's never been a more calculating, blatant and ruthless slave master than Don King. Ask any fighter King has taken over …Tyson, as all who have tried to reach him during his "takeover" have learned, was held incommunicado. He may or may not know it, but no calls were permitted to be put through to him; no letters reached him; he was effectively put behind an iron curtain to all those who had his real interests at heart ... I welcome having an investigation. There is a great deal to be revealed.'

Tyson, who publicly admitted he had had a drinking problem, was unknowingly, through his lifestyle, sowing the seeds of his own boxing downfall. In the meantime, while Tyson partied in nightclubs a week after cancelling the fight in Canada, Ruddock and his promoter, realizing there would be no Tyson fight, filed a lawsuit against Don King for breach of contract, saying King had cancelled the fight because he had a more lucrative offer for Tyson to fight in Japan on February 11. The opponent was to be an undistinguished journeyman heavyweight who would offer Tyson little resistance. Certainly he would be easier for Tyson than Ruddock. His name was James 'Buster' Douglas.

As the new year dawned, two pieces of news interested fans of the heavyweight division. On January 15, in Atlantic City, huge (253 pounds) and ancient (41 years old) George Foreman became, along with Evander Holyfield, the fighter most likely to generate more money than anyone else in a fight with Tyson. He did it by demolishing Gerry Cooney, ending Cooney's misguided comeback hopes with a devastating knockout in the second round. Even though Cooney was not ranked, had not fought since being KO'd by Michael Spinks two and a half years earlier, the victory, the 20th in his comeback, coming over a 'name' opponent, gave Foreman instant credibility, and the former Heavyweight Champion immediately began lobbying in the media for a crack at Tyson, although he said he was insulted by a paltry offer of $5-million from Don King to face Tyson.

The other exciting news was that an agreement was finally reached for the fight everyone wanted to see – Tyson versus Holyfield. Donald Trump, paying the largest site fee in the history of boxing ($12.5 million), secured the rights to the fight. It would be held on June 18, 1990, in Atlantic City. Tyson would be guaranteed $22 million! Holyfield's guarantee was $12 million. Both would share in the pay-per-view TV profits, and important to King's arch rivals, the Duvas, who were Holyfield's promoters, if their man won, King would not have any options on future Holyfield promotions ending King's stranglehold on the heavyweight division.

Over in Tokyo, meanwhile, ticket sales were sluggish for Tyson's defence on February 11. Douglas was perceived as a hapless victim, and the 60,000-seat Tokyo Dome would not even come close to selling out. Around the rest of the world, the fight evoked little interest. After all, who was Buster Douglas?

James 'Buster' Douglas was a 29-year-old heavyweight from Columbus, Ohio. His father, Billy 'Dynamite' Douglas, had been a top middleweight contender in the early 1970s, a man who had fought, and defeated, heavyweights. His son, who had turned pro in 1981, had once wanted to be a professional basketball player. He was a star in junior college in Kansas, but his grades were not good enough to allow him to play when he transferred to a four-year college, and he dropped out. Among his 29 victories were wins over Randall 'Tex' Cobb, Greg Page, and Trevor Berbick, but those wins were lacklustre, and three of his four losses were by KOs. The most notable came in Las Vegas on May 30, 1987. Fighting for the vacant IBF World Heavyweight Championship against Tony Tucker, Douglas, using all his talent, was beating Tucker fairly easily for nine rounds. Suddenly, however, in the 10th, Douglas, the title seemingly within his grasp, ran out of gas and, by his own admission, just gave up. He stood against the ropes while Tucker pounded him until the referee stopped the fight. Tucker, the new champion, went on to earn a big payday and give a good account of himself when losing a decision three months later to Tyson. Billy 'Dynamite' Douglas, who had been his son's trainer, walked away from his son's corner, so disgusted with Buster's quit job that he never worked his son's corner again, or attended any of his fights.

Douglas was managed by John Johnson, a feisty, 45-year-old former high school football coach with a master's degree in psychology. Douglas was one of the many heavyweights under Don King's promotional control, and so when King needed a safe, handy opponent for Tyson, Douglas got the call – and the opportunity to earn a $1.3-million purse to play his role as the sacrificial lamb. Until recently Douglas had been working on a truck unloading and delivering carpets, so the money, and the chance to fight Tyson, looked very good to him and Johnson, who was also a man of very modest means. They prepared to leave for Japan – and then disaster struck. On January 18, 1990, at the age of 46, Buster's mother, to whom he was very close, died suddenly of a stroke. Douglas was devastated, and considered cancelling the fight, but in the end he decided to go on with it, because his mother was one of the few people who had believed in him, and believed he was going to beat Tyson. When a reporter in Tokyo asked him if he was dedicating the fight to his mother, Buster replied, 'I'm dedicating my life to my mother'. His uncle,

J. D. McCauley , the brother of Buster's mother, was now training him. McCauley said he thought Buster would turn the tragedy into a positive. 'I really believe that,' McCauley said. Douglas, whose wife had left him several months earlier, said of himself, 'Something great must be about to happen to James Douglas, because something out there is definitely trying to deter me.' On the heavy bag Buster would pound in the gym were written the words: 'The Road to Tokyo and the World Championship. Kick Mike Tyson's Ass! The Greatest: James Douglas.' Also in the gym were the words of the late Ohio State University football coach Woody Hayes: 'Honesty Plus Hard Work Equals Success. All Things Being Equal, the Athlete in the Greatest Condition Will Win.' The caps Douglas and his entourage wore on their heads were embroidered with the simple words: 'James Douglas Only My Best.'

In Tokyo, Tyson's sparring sessions were erratic. He reportedly skipped a week of boxing, some of his other sessions were described as sluggish, he was said to be overweight, and his trainer, Aaron Snowell, even admitted Tyson was eating just one meal a day – soup and salad – to take the weight off. This is not the way for a 220-pound heavyweight to maintain his strength, but the professional discipline instilled by Kevin Rooney and Steve Lott was obviously missing from the training camp. Sports headlines were made a few weeks before the fight when former champion Greg Page, working as a Tyson sparring partner, dropped Tyson with a solid shot to the head.

Only 40,000 seats were sold for the fight, compared to 52,000 two years earlier when Tyson had fought in Tokyo. Tyson, earning a purse of $6-million, weighed in at 220½ pounds, while Douglas, a strapping 6'4", tipped the scales at 231½ pounds. In Las Vegas, most casinos were not even accepting bets on the fight. At the Mirage, which was, the odds opened at a remarkable 35-1 against Douglas, and then, even more amazingly, dropped even further, to 42-1 on fight day. If all that wasn't enough to discourage the challenger, he had been suffering from a cold and was taking antibiotics. Summing things up at the final pre-fight press conference, a confident Tyson, no doubt with Douglas in mind, said, 'If you can't fight, you're fucked.' John Johnson said he told his fighter to 'get Tyson down. I don't care how you do it. Run over his ass but get him down.' Johnson said that in his job with the Department of Youth Services in Columbus, Ohio, he'd worked with many young men like Tyson. 'Mike Tyson is a bully,' said Johnson. 'If you hit a bully, you get his respect. Every time Tyson gets hit, he freezes. "I'm the baddest of the bad". that's how they feel until you hit them upside the head.'

The only journalist who gave Douglas a shot was Tim May, and he was a writer for the challenger's hometown paper, the *Columbus Dispatch*. May predicted a Douglas victory because he would be inspired by the memory of his mother and because he disliked the bully Tyson was. 'Who knows where those combined forces will take James Douglas tonight?' wrote May on the morning of the fight. 'To the boxing upset of all time, a win over undisputed Heavyweight Champion Mike Tyson?'

Douglas entered the ring amid little fanfare. Tyson, a towel draped over his shoulders, climbed through the ropes a few minutes later. The referee, Octavio Meyran Sanchez of Mexico, an experienced official who had been the third man in the ring for the infamous Sugar Ray Leonard–Roberto Duran 'No Mas' fight, called the boxers and their seconds to the centre of the ring for their final instructions. Douglas appeared calm and confident. Unlike many of Tyson's previous 37 opponents, he did not seem to be frightened, although he was just seconds away from facing the onslaught of the most feared fighter of modern times.

What was about to unfold had been hinted at six days earlier by the perceptive, Pulitzer Prize-winning columnist for the *New York Times*, Dave Anderson, who wrote: 'The undisputed, undefeated and undignified World Heavyweight Champion had emerged as his own most dangerous opponent. Considering his competition, the only person who can beat Tyson is Tyson himself. By not training. By not caring. By not surrounding himself with experienced cornermen...Reports from Tokyo of Tyson's training are enough to question if the champion is sabotaging his own reign...If Tyson were to need advice in a prolonged brawl, he might miss [Kevin] Rooney's experience.' Rooney himself said, '[Mike] doesn't respect [cornermen] Bright or Snowell or Don King. He just wants to be paid. He's slowly been slipping. He's losing his interest.'

At the bell for round one, Douglas came out with confidence and smothered Tyson's customary opening burst of energy. Moving quickly, staying away from Tyson's power while throwing punches constantly to keep Tyson from launching his own attack, Douglas was masterful. He snapped quick left jabs, and behind it threw crisp right hands, landing enough to win the round handily. In round two, Douglas fired five- and six-punch combinations, blasting a solid right off Tyson's head in the first minute. He tied Tyson up inside, nullifying Tyson's usually effective uppercuts. Another strong right hand found Tyson's head, and Douglas followed up with a barrage of punches, keeping Tyson on the defensive. He finished strongly with a five-punch combination that ended with a good left hook in the final half-minute of the round.

The challenger used the same tactics in rounds three and four, the beautifully timed left jab keeping Tyson off, aided by lateral movement. By now Sugar Ray Leonard, expert commentator on the HBO telecast, observed that Tyson was 'not on...he doesn't have it'. A concerned corner, led by Aaron Snowell, was unable to get Tyson to snap out of his lethargy. '6-4-1 inside,' they told him, going back to the D'Amato numbered-punch system. 'Just don't stand there...work...do it...let it go, you're too flat-footed...don't be so cautious with the punches...you got to use that 'seven' to back this guy up,' Snowell and Bright told Tyson between rounds. But unlike the attention Teddy Atlas and then Kevin Rooney demanded of Tyson, he did not once look in the eyes of his cornermen during this fight to acknowledge that he comprehended what they were telling him.

In round five, jabbing and moving, shooting the right hand behind it, Douglas began to inflict serious damage. Tyson's left eye began to swell, and midway through the round, a right-left combination rocked Tyson. Taking a chapter from Tyson's book of intimidating tactics, Douglas had the temerity to whack Tyson with a good punch after the bell. At last Tyson was getting a taste of his own medicine. Incredibly, with a swelling eye and the Heavyweight Championship of the World on the line, Tyson's corner had no Enswell with them, the flat piece of stainless steel kept ice cold for the application on swellings. It was standard equipment in all competent corners, but instead Tyson's cornermen – who also didn't even have the second-best tool with them, an icebag – applied cold water to Tyson's eye. What was the cold water contained in? A condom!

In rounds six and seven, the trouble the Heavyweight Champion was in became more apparent. A relaxed, confident Douglas, sticking to his game plan, staying off the ropes, where Tyson can inflict heavy damage, continued to double his jab and bang the stiff right hands off Tyson's face. While a desperate Snowell told Tyson in the corner, 'You gotta punch, Mike...gotta back this guy up,' Douglas's cornermen advised him, 'Stay alert...it's your fight, your show...beautiful jab...The fuckin' guy is scared to death.'

The first 2:55 of round eight was a carbon copy of the seven previous rounds. Douglas was in command, winning the round quite comfortably, forcing Tyson, for the first time in his career, to back up. Then, suddenly, unexpectedly, coming off the ropes, the puffy-eyed, tired champion fired a right upper-cut between Douglas's gloves, catching him flush on the chin, and sending him down on his back. Annoyed at his lapse of concentration, Douglas rolled to his side and pounded his glove in frustration on the canvas.The referee jumped in immediately to start the count. Douglas listened, and at 'eight' began to rise, getting to his feet as Meyran reached 'nine'. Douglas, obviously in command of his senses, stepped toward Tyson to resume the fight, but the bell sounded to end the round.

Don King immediately jumped out of his chair, where he was seated next to Donald Trump, and launched a verbal tirade at WBC President Jose Sulaiman, supervising at ringside. 'Look at what you've done!' screamed King. 'What kind of ref did you bring me from Mexico? You're going to get my man beat.' King maintained that Meyran's count was too slow, that Douglas should have been counted out. 'Stop the fight,' insisted King. 'The fight's over,' he screamed as an embarrassed Sulaiman sat silently. Then, shouting up at Meyran, King directed another verbal torrent at him: 'What were you looking at? You should have known the man was out. You should have counted him out.' Meanwhile, in the corner, Douglas's handlers made sure their man wasn't seriously hurt. Then manager Johnson reminded Douglas about his mother and her hopes for him to win the title. As Douglas would later say, 'I came back. I sucked it up . . . I went out and fought my fight.'

At the bell for round nine, Tyson did not follow up on his advantage. Instead, Douglas came on strong, throwing a six-punch, rapid-fire combination, landing three of those punches solidly, forcing Tyson to back up. The champion responded with a booming right off Douglas's skull, forcing the challenger momentarily to stumble. But then, remarkably, another onslaught by Douglas wobbled Tyson, who drifted back looking for refuge along the ropes, where Douglas pursued him, snapping Tyson's head back with vicious punches. Tyson looked ready to go, but the round ended.

The champion fired his last burst of ammunition at the bell opening the tenth round, which would be the final round of his 39-month reign as titleholder. He landed a strong right hand, but Douglas didn't budge. Tyson looked beaten, his left eye a swollen mess, his legs gone, his body weary. Just past the one-minute mark, Douglas launched the final attack that would bring about the unbelievable. He shot a devastating right uppercut off Tyson's jaw. The rock-solid head of the champion bounced like it had been struck by the San Francisco earthquake.Tyson's eyes rolled in their sockets. Douglas followed with a four-punch combination – a right, left, right, and then the final, crushing left hand, thrown with the force of all his bodyweight behind it. Tyson toppled onto his back; his mouthpiece went flying in the air. He rolled over onto all fours and, oblivious to the count, crawled to recover the mouthpiece, awkwardly stuffing it back into his mouth as Meyran kneeled over him, counting to ten. Tyson's eyes were glazed. At 'nine' he was stumbling into his feet, but Meyran waved the fight over. Mike Tyson had been knocked out! By Buster Douglas!

Moments later, as Tyson was led to his dressing-room, the ring announcer proclaimed, 'The winner, by knockout, at one-minute, 23-seconds of the tenth round, and new Heavyweight Champion of the World...James Buster Douglas!' In an emotional TV interview in the ring, all Douglas could say was, 'My mother, God bless her heart,' before breaking down in tears. He regained his composure to say, 'I was mediocre, I did leave a lot in doubt, but it was time for James Douglas to come out of the closet... That's just what I did, whip his ass...I fear no man, I believe in God.' When the championship belt was placed around his waist, all he could say was, 'This is a dream, truly a dream. So many times I watched this happen to other fighters, I said one day it's gonna be me.' Of his strategy, which he had discussed by phone with his father, who then watched the fight on TV in Columbus, Ohio, the new champion said, 'I let him run into the jab...let him be a tough guy. You want to take it? O.K. He was flat on his ass.'

The now infamous aftermath was, if possible, even more incredible that the fight. King, trying to salvage his meal ticket, grabbed the referee, Meyran, and Sulaiman, and took them into a room. When they emerged and called a press conference, Sulaiman announced that a protest had been filed by one of Tyson's cornermen, and that the result of the fight was being suspended because the tape seemed to show that Douglas was down for more than ten seconds in round eight, and that Meyran made a mistake in the count. The WBA, represented by its president, Gilberto Mendoza, concurred. Both organizations said they were withholding recognition of Douglas until they could meet ten days to two weeks later to review the situation. Only Bob Lee, president of the IBF, remained sane and announced back in the United States that, having won the fight fair and square in the ring, the IBF would recognize Buster Douglas as champion. Sulaiman, remarkably, defended his misguided actions by saying, 'It is our obligation to fight for justice.' And, even more incredibly, King, playing the role of the impartial promoter, had the audacity to claim of the protest, 'I'd have done the same thing for Buster Douglas. If I see something wrong, I'm a stickler for the rules.' Tyson, echoing the party line, said, 'I can handle a loss, but I want to lose fairly . . . Greater fighters than I have lost.' But Tyson, a student of ring history, did not sound convincing. In his heart he knew that titles were won and lost in the ring, and that Douglas had indeed beaten him fair and square. Douglas's manager, John Johnson, said, 'It's a disgrace. What they're doing shows a total lack of character and respect for the game by those people who are doing it . . . the hell with them.'

The outcry against the WBC, the WBA, and King for their power play aimed at depriving Douglas of his title, was immediate and worldwide. 'If they don't honour me, it's ludicrous. They have no ground to stand on,' said the new champion. John Saraceno, in *USA Today*, wrote that boxing, 'with a history of severe image and credibility problems, is left with the aroma of week-old sushi'. Promoter Bob Arum said, 'This could have have been a Cinderella story, a great, great night for boxing, but these two Noriegas have to inject their sleazy, slimy politics and do the most ludicrous, preposterous thing . . . This is the last straw. The organizations [WBA and WBC] have to be banned.' Highly regarded columnist Mike Lupica, in the *National Sports Daily*, wrote that 'Don King [is] a bedbug of the first rank in a sport filled with them.' Mark Dilonno, in the *New York Post,* wrote, 'This "controversy" is nothing more than Don King calling in his political markers. His store-bought organizations [the WBA and WBC] don't want to lose the King-sized perks, so they're trying to keep Tyson and the mega-million paydays, which translate into lucrative sanctioning fees.' And Dave Anderson in the *New York Times* commented, 'If either organization were to rule a "no decision", or, worse, were to reverse the outcome in Tyson's favour, the action would be boxing's most memorable miscarriage of justice. Also at its most aromatic, Don King's personal brand of controversial cologne permeated the scene. In boxing, a promoter is supposed to be neutral, but in sitting at Tyson's side during Tyson's complaint, King resembled the "manager" he is accused of being.' Promoter Don Elbaum, who had once been a partner of King's, said, 'All the credibility of boxing has gone down the drain. If Don King has Jose Sulaiman and those WBA guys so bought, these guys should absolutely be thrown in jail.'

Over the next forty-eight hours, things once again took a dramatic turn. In Japan, referee Octavio Meyran, an obvious scapegoat, had told the press, 'I recognize my mistake.' But once back in Mexico City, Meyran changed his tune. He said he had not made any mistake, that he was not obligated to look at the ringside timekeeper to pick up the count, that Douglas was clearheaded and obviously able to continue, and that Douglas 'won the championship fair and square'. Realizing their mistake, the WBA announced two days after the fight that they were recognizing Douglas as champion. Within hours the WBC made a similar announcement. Jose Sulaiman said he was wrong in ever announcing he would withhold recognition from Douglas. 'I feel embarrassed for putting doubt on a situation that had no doubt. It was a big mistake to have waited this long.' Although it was widely believed the King-inspired protest was a ploy to force Douglas at the very least into an immediate rematch with Tyson, the WBA and WBC did not order any such rematch, leaving Douglas free to do whatever he decided.

After their return to New York, King and Tyson held a news conference on February 13, at which time they too backed off. King said he had never intended to deprive Douglas of the title, and said Team Tyson was withdrawing all protests. Said Tyson: 'The new champion won the title. I wouldn't want the title on a changed decision. The only thing I ask is for a rematch. Once I get a rematch, I'll take care of everything.' King had the audacity to suggest that his protest had served a positive purpose, that Buster Douglas was now a bigger name and thus able to command more money, thanks, of course, to King and the controversy he generated!

As for the facts, yes, Douglas was down for 13 seconds. However, Meyran began his count immediately. If anyone was at fault, it was the ringside timekeeper, who can clearly be seen raising one finger at the instant Douglas hit the canvas, when in reality he should not have indicated 'one' until a full second after Douglas went down.

Second, in no rule book does it say a fighter must be counted out after ten *seconds*, but rather after a ten *count*. And that count is administered not by a machine, but by a human being, and so it can vary and, in fact, often does. Many ten-counts in fights take longer than ten seconds on a clock. It is the referee who is in charge of that count. When Tyson went down in round ten, he, in fact, was given 14 seconds to regain his feet by Meyran. That is just the cadence of how Meyran, an experienced official, counts.

Lost in the artificial long count controversy were two other important pieces of information. First, Douglas thoroughly dominated the fight from beginning to end: he landed more punches (230) than Tyson threw (214)! And, second, if anything deserved investigation, it was not the length of the count, but the manner in which the WBC judges scored the fight. While Larry Rozadilla had an accurate card through nine rounds, with Douglas ahead 88-82, judge Masakazu Uchida had the fight dead even at 86-86, and judge Ken Morita, incredibly, had Tyson ahead 87-86! James Sterngold, in the *New York Times*, summed it up by writing of the scorecards, '[it] suggested to some fight people that politics were already at play to keep Tyson champion [had the fight gone to a decision]. "In Japan and Korea," said the IBF spokesman, Sy Roseman, "they have a history of promoters buying judges and some of the most ludicrous decisions."'

Just a few years before, Buster Douglas stood anonymously on a street corner in Columbus, Ohio, during a parade for hometown hero Jerry Page, who had just captured an Olympic gold medal. He was handing out flyers for a forthcoming fight card on which he would be featured. Now, on a cold, windy February day, it was Buster Douglas's parade. Along with his eleven-year-old son, his girlfriend, and the manager who believed in him when few others did, the new champion was honoured by his city, and the governor declared it James Douglas Day in the state of Ohio. Every national TV programme wanted Douglas as a guest. He and Johnson criss-crossed the country during the following few weeks, appearing on shows and talking to promoters, who were lining up for Douglas's services. Don King claimed he had, of course, options to promote Douglas's future fights in his contract with the new champion, but Johnson said King's behaviour in trying to overturn the fight result showed that he was not acting in the best interest of Douglas, and so had violated the contract. And anyway, Johnson said, the state of Nevada did not recognize the legality of option contracts, so he would have Douglas fight in Las Vegas. Steve Wynn, owner of the newly opened Mirage Hotel, made Douglas an offer that dwarfed even Tyson's deals. He said he would pay Douglas $25 million to fight Evander Holyfield, and if he was successful against Holyfield, he would give Douglas a purse of $35-million to meet Tyson in a rematch.

That was a staggering $60-million for two fights. No offer in the history of sport had come close to it.

Wynn's hotel corporation filed a lawsuit in Nevada seeking to have King's contract with Douglas declared null and void. King, who had of course encouraged Tyson to challenge the fighter's contract with Bill Cayton, struck back. Now that the shoe was on the other foot, King was righteous in his opinion that a fighter had to fulfil his contractual obligations. King filed a counter-suit in US District Court, desperately trying to maintain his loosening grip on the heavyweight division. After all, if Douglas was successful in his attempt to avoid fighting for King, or if Douglas fought and lost to Evander Holyfield, over whom King had no control, the Heavyweight Championship would be out of his control. King charged Wynn and his Golden Nugget corporation with interfering with his contract with Douglas and asked for an injunction to prevent Douglas from fighting if King was not involved in the promotion. The only thing that was clear was that when Douglas did fight again, win or lose, he would be set for life financially. The soft spoken, gentlemanly new champion would never have deliver carpets from the back of a truck again.

20

The Inevitable End

He is a role model for our youth, an American Hero for us all ... He represents America ...
He is our ambassador of goodwill to all peoples of the world. Indeed, he is one of our national
treasures. Boxing needs a hero ... and God sent Mike Tyson.

– DON KING

FOUR MONTHS AFTER his shocking loss to Buster Douglas, Tyson returned to the ring. There were persistent rumours he was not in the best condition and had been drinking heavily, but even if the stories were true, he was not expected to receive much of a test. His opponent for the June 16, 1990, bout at Caesar's Palace in Las Vegas would be Henry Tillman. In 1984, as amateurs, Tillman had won both decisions, keeping Tyson off the Olympic team. Tillman had medalled in the 1984 Games, but his pro career fizzled after he was KO'd by Evander Holyfield. That loss was followed by a succession of knockout losses, and Tillman had virtually disappeared from boxing when he was plucked from the sidelines to be fed to Tyson. The fight was part of a double-header. The other bout featured 42-year-old George Foreman, continuing his successful comeback, against Brazilian Adilson Rodrigues. The fights were laughable. Both Tillman and Rodrigues had already been knocked out by Holyfield. (Meanwhile, up in Catskill, New York, Tyson's former friend and trainer, Kevin Rooney, was having his home seized by the IRS, and he was forced to file for Chapter 11 protection in US Bankruptcy Court in Albany. Rooney had earned upwards of $4 million with Tyson, but a divorce, bad loans to fair-weather friends, naive and ill-informed investments in racehorses, and a big gambling habit had eroded all those earnings. He was in debt for $1.3-million, owed the IRS over $700-thousand in unpaid taxes, and was in debt for a half million dollars to three casinos in Atlantic City.)

On June 16, Tyson knocked Tillman out cold with the first solid punch he landed, late in the first round. Foreman flattened Rodrigues in a couple of rounds. Much more interesting than the fights was the team that promoted the show: bitter rivals Bob Arum and Don King. What had forced these two enemies to bury the hatchet – at least temporarily – and work together in a promotion? It was a new threat from the outside, from Steve Wynn, owner of the new Las Vegas showplace, the Mirage. Wynn had decided to muscle in big time on the boxing scene. And, God forbid, he decided he could do it without middlemen promoters like King and Arum. Wynn felt he could do it with his chequebook alone, and if he was successful, he could put King and Arum on the sidelines and run big-money boxing spectaculars on his own.

King (promoter for Tyson) and Arum (promoter for Foreman) felt they could grab the public's interest with a pairing of Tyson vs. Foreman. (Tillman and Rodrigues got $250,000 each to serve as punching bags in the June 16 show. Foreman got $1-million and Tyson was paid $3-million. But, then again, Mike did have a new mouth to feed. He acknowledged that he had recently fathered a baby boy with a Los Angeles woman named Natalie Fears. Tyson named his son D'Amato, in tribute to his late mentor.) King, meanwhile, counter-sued Douglas and the Mirage for $75-million for infringing on his contract to promote Douglas's future fights. And, trying to protect his meal ticket, King saw to it that there was a new trainer running things in the Tyson camp after the incompetent performance of Aaron Snowell and Jay Bright in Tokyo. King brought in his man, Richie Giachetti, Larry Holmes's former trainer and managerial front man for King. Giachetti would run things from now on, and Snowell and Bright were allowed to stay on as window dressing. Veteran expert cutman Eddie Aliano also came on board, replacing someone named Taylor Smith, who had come to Tyson's corner in the Douglas fight and forgot to bring an Easwell, which would have helped ease the bad swelling around Tyson's left eye during the fight.

King's lawsuit against Douglas/Johnson and Wynn/Mirage went to federal court in New York. Developer Donald Trump testified on behalf of King. He said that he was sitting with King at ringside in Tokyo, and that by the fifth round of the Tyson–Douglas fight he and King had already reached a handshake agreement to stage a rematch at Trump's casino in Atlantic City. At this point, Trump's financial empire was crumbling around him, and he was fighting a desperate battle to keep creditors and bond holders at bay. Three of his top executives were killed late in 1989 in a helicopter crash, and many of his senior management people had left, either fired or, fed up with Trump's arrogant, overbearing and egotistical style, had resigned. Among the victims was Trump's own brother, Robert, top man at the Taj Mahal. Highly regarded and with a much more respected style than his brother, Robert quit after Donald humiliated him publicly in a loud argument. Trump's debt was said to be $2 billion, and lawsuits were beginning to pile up. Of course, getting hold of the highly desired rematch would be a financial and publicity windfall for his casinos. Wynn's deal with Douglas would keep Trump from even having a chance to get the Douglas–Holyfield match and potential Douglas–Tyson rematch, so it was obvious why he was eager to see King win the lawsuit. As King put it when asked why he and arch enemy Arum were working together, 'We find Steve Wynn's acts more despicable than anything we could have done to each other.'

By mid-July, there were reports that King and Wynn were willing to settle their differences out of court, and the case was officially dropped on July 17. Under terms of the settlement, Wynn was free to proceed with his promotion of Douglas's defence against Holyfield. Douglas would get a purse of $24-million, with $8-million for challenger Holyfield. The door was left open for King to be co-promoter of an eventual Tyson–Douglas rematch. For dropping the suit, King and Trump were given a payoff settlement of $7-million to divide. (Trump had also sued Wynn over his 'handshake' deal with King, which he claimed Wynn had violated.) And the jury in the trial, which had endured listening to nine days of testimony, was invited by King to be his guests at Tyson's second comeback fight, against Alex Stewart, in Atlantic City. One juror, after being dismissed, summed things up by saying, 'Don King may be a bad guy, but [Trump and Wynn are] not exactly pillars of integrity.' King, ever the master of hyperbole, said regarding the settlement, 'We have the ability to put away the acrimony, the hostility that had existed, and come together at the table of brotherhood.' In other words, Money Talks, Nobody Walks.

At the press conference to announce his fight with Alex Stewart, Tyson was his usual charming self. Asked if he felt confident, he replied, 'I'm confident Alex Stewart is dead.' Just how sure was he of victory? 'I'm going to kill him, otherwise it doesn't count,' said Tyson. A few weeks before the Stewart fight, a jury in New York City ruled that Tyson had committed battery on Sandra Miller, one of the women who had accused Tyson of grabbing and fondling her breasts and buttocks at Bentley's disco. However, the jury awarded her a mere $100 in damages, ruling that Tyson's behaviour was 'not outrageous'. Tyson laughed as he peeled a $100 bill off the wad in his pocket.

When Tyson fought Alex Stewart, the outcome was no surprise. Stewart, previously KO'd by Holyfield, completely froze in the ring, and Tyson destroyed him in less than one round. But the fight that would have a profound effect on the future fortunes of Tyson and King had taken place two months earlier. In October, at the Mirage, Evander Holyfield met Buster Douglas for the title. Douglas came into the bout embarrassingly out of shape, especially for a man being paid $24-million to put on a competitive show for the paying public. It didn't take long for the clock to strike midnight on Douglas's Cinderella story. He was knocked out early, losing the crown he had won so impressively just eight months earlier. With Holyfield the new Heavyweight Champion of the World, Steve Wynn's deal to promote a Tyson–Douglas rematch evaporated, and suddenly King and Tyson were on the outside looking in. The Holyfield team of Dan Duva and Shelly Finkel were now calling the shots. King and Tyson had put them off, made them wait, and now they would be in no rush to give Tyson a crack at winning back the title from their man. Bypassing Tyson, they signed for Holyfield to make an April 1991 defence against George Foreman in Atlantic City. That fight itself was exciting and more competitive than many expected it to be. Foreman finished on his feet, losing a unanimous decision, but his strong stand against Holyfield kept him alive and viable in the heavyweight division.

Waiting in the wings, Tyson took a March 18 fight at the Mirage against Canada's Donovan 'Razor' Ruddock, considered one of the best contenders in the world by most observers. Their fight was tough and competitive, with Ruddock landing hurtful blows and Tyson, who led on the scorecards, doing the same. But Ruddock again demonstrated what Douglas had proven: that Tyson was certainly no longer invincible. In the seventh round, however, Tyson stunned Ruddock, who staggered into the ropes. Without so much as looking at him, much less checking to see if he could continue, referee Richard Steele, a once excellent third man whose skills and judgment were becoming increasingly questionable, jumped in and stopped the fight, giving Tyson a TKO victory and setting off a storm of controversy.

Several days later, in an unrelated matter, Tyson, in another paternity suit, acknowledged that he had fathered a baby girl the previous year with a Manhattan woman named Kimberly Scarborough.

The controversial ending to the Ruddock fight generated interest in a rematch, and a press conference was called in May to announce the June 28 fight. Tyson's behaviour at that news conference shocked many, and had even veteran reporters and boxing people raising their eyebrows. Tyson launched a monologue that went beyond the normal 'I'm-gonna-kick-your-ass' fight hype. He promised Ruddock that when they fought, 'I'm gonna make you my girlfriend.' He called Ruddock 'a transvestite' and said, 'I can't wait for you to kiss me with those big lips of yours.' Ruddock took the high road, saying he wouldn't dignify Tyson's remarks with a response. He told Tyson that one thing money can't buy is class, and that Tyson would never have any class. But many were left wondering if Tyson did not have deep-rooted psychological and sexual dysfunction problems. King didn't seem to mind the remarks. After all, it would help create interest in the rematch, and although Tyson, in private, was increasingly angered at King's failure to get him a title fight, it benefited King more to keep Mike fighting the Ruddocks, Stewarts and Tillmans, in fights King promoted, than to get Mike a title fight that might be promoted by a Wynn or a Duva.

In the rematch, fought in Las Vegas with the temperature near 90°, Ruddock had his jaw broken early by a Tyson punch. Tyson used what were his normal dirty tactics. He was penalized twice by ref Mills Lane for low blows, and once for hitting after the bell. Ruddock was knocked down twice, but was not seriously hurt either time. Tyson's eroded skills were apparent. He no longer used the jab effectively, no longer threw the lightning-fast combinations and the body punches taught him by D'Amato, Atlas and Rooney. His bob-and-weave defence was all but gone, and he initiated clinches, a sign of lack of desire. Ruddock, perhaps bothered by the broken jaw, did not fight with the fury he had demonstrated in the first fight. At the end, Tyson won a unanimous 12-round decision, raising his record to 41-1. The stage was now set for the big one, Tyson vs. Holyfield, a fight that promised to be the richest in boxing history. When the deal was made, Holyfield was guaranteed $30-million and Tyson $15-million. Organizers predicted that when all revenues were added up – live gate, foreign rights, closed circuit and pay-per-view, merchandising and delayed-broadcast rights – the fight would be the first $100-million attraction in boxing history. Caesar's Palace in Las Vegas won the rights to stage the fight, which was set for November 8, 1991. The only problem was that a November fight would leave Mike Tyson with three months of idle time before he'd have to start training, all summer with nothing to do. And history had shown that when Mike Tyson had free time, he got into trouble.

Indiana Black Expo was scheduled to be held in Indianapolis in mid-July. The annual exposition would also feature the Miss Black America pageant, as well as an appearance by Jesse Jackson and a concert by singer Johnny Gill. Rev. Charles Williams, organizer of Indiana Black Expo, decided to extend an invitation to Mike Tyson to attend, and Tyson arrived late in the afternoon of July 17. He was mobbed by fans as he walked through the airport. Dennis Hayes, Tyson's guide and bodyguard, moved the ex-champ along into a limo for the ride into the city. Tyson first detoured to a Holiday Inn, where he hooked up with rap singer Angela Boyd. Known professionally as B Angie B, she is sometimes Tyson's girlfriend. They spent a few hours together. (Boyd would later testify that she and Tyson had sex several times during his thirty-seven-hour stay in Indianapolis.) At mid-evening, Tyson and his entourage headed to Seville's, a nightclub on the outskirts of the city. They were treated royally, given free drinks, and Tyson consumed several beers. And again, Tyson was mobbed by fans. About four hours later, at 1pm, the Tyson party arrived at Mirage, another club. Tyson halted traffic outside the club when he stopped to sign autographs. Around two o'clock on July 18, about nine hours after he had arrived in Indianapolis, Tyson checked into the Canterbury Hotel for the night.

Around noontime the next day, Tyson met Rev. Williams and Johnny Gill in the lobby, and the group moved on to the Omni Severin Hotel, where a rehearsal was underway for the twenty-fourth annual Miss Black America Pageant, and where Tyson and Gill had agreed to tape some promotional spots with the contestants. Tyson interacted with the contestants, and was later accused by several of being very free with his hands, especially around their breasts and buttocks. Among those Tyson talked to at the rehearsal was an 18-year-old contestant representing Rhode Island named Desiree Washington, who was apparently asked out by Tyson and who gave him her hotel phone number.

At five, at the Convention Center, Tyson was on hand for the opening ceremonies of the pageant, and numerous contestants would charge that he fondled their buttocks and breasts, even during an opening speech by the Rev. Jesse Jackson. Three weeks after the pageant, the previous year's Miss Black America, Rosie Jones of Connecticut, filed a $100-million lawsuit against Tyson, saying he grabbed her buttocks during the pageant and whispered suggestive and perverted sexual remarks in her ear. Jones said she told Tyson, 'Don't disrespect me and I won't disrespect you', but that Tyson just laughed at her. Jones's boyfriend, who was present, then approached. Seeing him, Tyson said, 'Is this your woman? What are you going to do, beat me up?' Jones, a well-spoken and well-educated 27-year-old computer coordinator for an aerospace company, said she was filing the civil assault-and-battery lawsuit because she felt Tyson 'has to be taught a lesson that he can't treat women any way he wants to...Assaulting women seems to be common behaviour for Mr Tyson.' While fondling her buttocks, Jones said Tyson told her, 'You're so fine.' When she told him to stop, he said, 'What's the matter, don't you want to help a black man out?' She said she told him he didn't need her help.

Another contestant, Artavia Edwards of California, said Tyson 'grabbed my butt', then approached her later on, asking if she had a boyfriend. She said yes, and Tyson said, 'Does that mean I don't have a chance with you?' She said she didn't answer him, but put her hands behind her buttocks to shield them. When the ceremony ended, Tyson, along with Williams and Jesse Jackson, headed to a restaurant called the Black Orchid. With them was Donna Thompson, a student intern from Butler University working at the pageant. Thompson said Jesse Jackson's bodyguards told her they would look out for her because 'Mike Tyson is a dangerous person'. After dinner, Tyson headed back to his room at the Canterbury to change clothes, then left for the Johnny Gill concert at the Hoosier Dome, which he watched from the wings backstage.

At about one-thirty on the morning of July 19, following the conclusion of the concert, as Tyson was being driven in his limo, he used the car phone to call Desiree Washington, the pageant contestant he had met the previous afternoon. Tyson asked the girl to get dressed and meet him. She agreed. What transpired in the next hour and a half led to one of the most highly publicized trials involving a well-known celebrity that the world has ever seen.

On July 20, shortly before 3am, Desiree Washington went to the Methodist Hospital emergency room and reported to the Indianapolis police department that she had been raped by Mike Tyson in his hotel room during the early hours of July 19. Tyson was long gone from Indianapolis by then. As a matter of fact, he had checked out of the Canterbury unexpectedly at about 4:45am, about two and a half hours after Ms Washington alleged she was raped, even though he had prepaid for two more nights at the hotel, and even though he was committed to make several personal appearances in the city later that day. At six, Tyson boarded a flight for Cleveland, where he owned a house near Don King. His departure from his room was so hasty that he left a Do Not Disturb sign on the door. Therefore, maids did not clean the room, and police were able to recover the bedsheets and blanket, a T-shirt and other pieces of evidence that had not been removed or laundered.

On Tuesday, August 13, a six-member grand jury was empanelled in Marion County, Indiana, to investigate the rape allegations, which had been formalized on July 22. Tyson was among those subpoenaed to testify before the grand jury, whose proceedings were held in secret, but he was not obligated to appear. One of those who did was Virginia Foster, the female limo driver who had chauffeured Tyson and Ms Washington to the Canterbury Hotel. A guidance counsellor at a local junior high school, who also ran the small Solid Gold Limousine Service with her husband, she was regarded as a key witness.

On Friday, August 30, Tyson's legal team took a big gamble. They allowed Tyson to testify. It was a move that most accused do not take, but the theory was that Tyson's story might be convincing enough to help him avoid an indictment. The grand jury had already heard from his accuser. Under Indiana law, if just two of the six voted not to indict, the charges would be thrown out. Tyson's legal team hoped he could convince at least two jurors he was not guilty. Tyson testified for three hours, while Don King waited in a nearby room. The strategy failed. On Monday, September 9, Mike Tyson, by a vote of 5 to 1, was indicted by the grand jury on charges of rape, confinement and two counts of criminally deviate conduct, the latter charges specifically relating to allegations that Tyson also penetrated Ms Washington with his fingers and performed oral sex on her. Tyson was in Las Vegas, preparing for the November 8 fight with Holyfield, when the indictment was handed down. For Tyson it must have been a shock, since King had assured him all along he would never be indicted. Marion County Prosecutor Jeffrey Modisett, who was in charge of the case, said he expected Tyson to surrender on his own. An arrest warrant was issued, and bail was set at $30,000. In meeting the press, Modisett, speaking of Tyson's accuser, said, 'She expected to have a platonic date, she didn't expect to have sex with him. When she refused his advances, he forced her to have sex with him.'

Two days after the indictment was handed down, Tyson,

accompanied by King, flew from Las Vegas and surrendered to
authorities in Indianapolis. He was booked and released after
posting the $30,000 bond, and being fingerprinted and
photographed. Tyson entered a plea of not guilty during a ten-
minute court proceeding with Superior Court Judge Patricia
Gifford. Tyson and King then held a news conference, where
Tyson stated, 'I didn't hurt no one...she knows what happened
in that room. I know what happened, and I know I'm
innocent...I'm extremely worried about the situation, but I know
I'm innocent.' When Tyson was asked if he still planned to
proceed with his fight against Holyfield, he replied, 'Why
shouldn't I be able to fight? This is the way I make my living. The
fight comes first. After the fight, I can take care of this.' Back in
New Jersey, promoter Dan Duva, himself an attorney, said the
fight would go on as scheduled, because Tyson was innocent until
proven guilty.

As if Tyson did not have enough trouble – the rape charge, the
$100-million civil suit filed by Rosie Jones – more was on the
way. A 28-year-old woman named Robin Young, an NYU
graduate and aspiring model, filed a $2-million personal-injury
suit against him, charging that Tyson 'forcefully grabbed
(her)...in a sexually suggestive and embarrassing fashion' at
Manhattan's trendy China Club the previous November, ten
months earlier. She said she waited so long because she didn't
have the courage to make the accusation until Rosie Jones filed
her suit. Then Natalie Fears, the woman he had already
acknowledged fathering a son with and who he was paying
support to, according to his lawyer, filed an $11-million paternity
and palimony suit. Responding to all this, King said it was all
'black-on-black crime', with Tyson the victim of opportunistic
women. In addition, J. Morris Anderson, founder of the Miss
Black America Pageant, filed a $21-million lawsuit against
Tyson, saying Tyson's behaviour ruined his pageant's reputation,
that the fighter molested ten contestants, and Anderson also
named Expo president Rev. Charles Williams, who invited Tyson
to Indianapolis, in the suit. Anderson charged that as a friend of
Tyson's, Williams should have known 'of Tyson's history as a
serial buttocks fondler of black women, and a perpetuator of lude
[sic] and disrespectful acts against black women of the most
vulgar type'. However, someone might have had a heart-to-heart
talk with Mr Anderson, because four months after filing his suit,
he did a complete turnaround. He not only dropped the lawsuit,
but said the women who said Tyson fondled them were liars, that

it would be 'detrimental to black people to drag this matter out any further', and that he was having 'second thoughts about participating in the crucifixion of a black role model'. At this point, though, how many responsible people in the black or white communities still clung to any shred of belief that Mike Tyson was any kind of a role model?

In mid-October, the moral question of whether or not the Holyfield fight should be held under the cloud of Tyson's indictment and pending trial (a date of January 27, 1992, had been set for the start of jury selection) became moot. Tyson suffered a rib injury in training, and it was legitimately severe enough to force a postponement, despite reports that King, fearing loss of his substantial cut of Tyson's purse, insisted that Mike go ahead with the fight. Tyson's doctor said it would be six to eight weeks before Tyson could resume heavy training. The promoters, huddled with King, the TV people, and Caesar's Palace representatives to find a date that would enable them to salvage the mega-money fight before Tyson's trial, and possible incarceration should he be convicted, made the fight disappear forever. They looked at several dates in January, even though the Nevada desert air was often near freezing at night at that time of year and the outdoor fight would subject both the fighters and 15,000 spectators to possibly severe weather. That factor, and a variety of other logistical and scheduling problems, caused a stalemate, and everyone was resigned to the reality that it was impossible for the fight to occur before the trial got underway.

Desiree Washington, despite the misguided attempts by Tyson's supporters to question her motives, was no gold digger, no floozy, no Jezebel. As a matter of fact, she was the ideal All-American girl. She was beautiful, intelligent, talented, and her resumé was extraordinary. She had just finished high school, and had won a full scholarship to Providence College while working sixteen hours a week at K-mart. While in high school, she had been a member of the National Junior Honor Society, freshman class president, a member of Pep Club, Lettermen's Club, sophomore class social committee, captain of the JV cheerleaders, a varsity cheerleader, member of the National Junior Olympic All-Star Softball team, member of the varsity track team, and winner of the Good Citizens Award. In addition, she was one of 33 US high school students selected to travel to the Soviet Union in 1990 as a goodwill ambassador. Outside school, she was a Big Sister who volunteered time working with mentally retarded people, and she was an active member of her

Baptist church as an usher and Sunday school teacher. She was a strong individual, and she would need that strength to get her through a trial with world attention focused on it, and especially to get her through a cross-examination by Tyson's formidable defence attorney.

Sixty-year-old Vincent Fuller was senior partner in the Washington, DC, law firm of Williams & Connelly, founded by the late Edward Bennett Williams, who had been considered by many legal experts to be the best trial lawyer since Clarence Darrow. Fuller's fee was five thousand dollars a day, and his track record showed he was worth it. In 1982, defending John Hinckley for the attempted assassination of President Reagan, he had gained a not guilty verdict by reason of insanity. Fuller was also the attorney for junk bond king Michael Milken, and did a masterful job as attorney for Don King when he was tried for tax fraud in 1985. Fuller was so skilful in shifting blame to bookkeeping errors he attributed to King's accountants that he virtually destroyed the government's case and won an acquital for King without having to put even one of his own defence witnesses on the stand.

Opposing the high-powered attorney, Marion County Prosecutor Jeffrey Modisett had an ace up his own sleeve. He hired 44-year-old Indiana native Greg Garrison to try the case for the prosecution. Garrison was considered as dynamic, as spellbinding in the courtroom as Fuller, and the trial rapidly shaped up into a Heavyweight Championship showdown of trial attorneys. Garrison would try to establish to the jury a pattern in Tyson's behaviour. He would try to introduce as much evidence as he was allowed of Tyson's past behaviour involving women. Fuller, on the other hand, would try to establish reasonable doubt in the jury's minds on his client's behalf. Early on, the Tyson team suffered a setback when the presiding judge, Patricia Gifford, allowed evidence gathered by the FBI investigation into the alleged rape to be used. On the other hand, Fuller gained a victory when the judge ruled that a videotape made by a local TV station at a news conference attended by Tyson could not be admitted as evidence. On the tape, Tyson, apparently unaware he was being recorded, was heard uttering to a crony, 'I should have killed the bitch.'

The trial opened as scheduled on Monday, January 27, and the first three days were devoted primarily to jury selection. Each day, as Tyson arrived at the City-County Building, where the trial was being held, crowds of supporters outside and in the lobby shouted words of encouragement: 'We know you didn't do it, Mike'. 'Hang in there, Mike'. 'They got you guilty, but this ain't Mississippi'. In fact, many of these so-called supporters were brought in by Tyson's people to put on a show of support. None shouted out on behalf of the victim. It was a travesty and a disgrace. Equally disgraceful was the behaviour of some black leaders and clergymen who tried to make the trial out to be a racial persecution of a black hero, although nothing could have been further from the truth. State Representative William Crawford, speaking for himself and a group that included Expo organizer Rev. Charles Williams, said, 'An American of African-American ancestry shall once again be Marion County's victim of injustice.' New York activist and rabble rouser Al Sharpton, a long-time supporter of King and Tyson, sped to Indianapolis, where he termed Tyson's trial a legal lynching. All these pillars of the community quick to rush to Tyson's support conveniently forgot that it was a young black woman with a quality upbringing and intelligence who had possibly been violated by Tyson, and that Tyson had a long history pointing to the fact that he was an unrepentant thug. But then again, Desiree Washington had no power and no bankroll, whereas Tyson and King did and were big contributors to the Cleveland Baptist Church.

There were also allegations that the jury-selection process was unfair because it did not accurately reflect the black population in Marion County. That population was 21 per cent black, but jury selection was done from voter registration lists, and for some reason, only 8 per cent of the blacks in Marion County had taken the time to register to vote. As it turned out, of the twelve jury members selected (eight men, four women), three were black, and so the jury wound up being a quarter black. The four alternates selected for the jury were white. 'All we want is a level playing field so justice can prevail,' Don King told reporters. A group of prominent black clergymen and civic leaders said they had 'grave concern that this country's legal system may be on the brink of historical injustice'.

It didn't take long for the drama to explode. On Thursday, January 30, the lawyers delivered their opening arguments. Pointing to Tyson, Garrison said, 'This person is guilty of pinning that eighteen-year-old girl to a bed and confining her...callously and maliciously raping her even though she cried out in pain.' Fuller then delivered his opening remarks. He sought to portray Desiree Washington as a calculating gold digger, mature beyond her years. He said she was educated and sophisticated, and Tyson, who never finished high school, was, basically, her victim. Fuller said Ms Washington had told other contestants of Tyson, 'He's rich. Did you see what Robin Givens got out of him? Besides, he's dumb.' Fuller said her scheme was to spend time with Tyson, hoping it would 'lead to some long-term relationship'. Fuller said the two had consensual sex in Tyson's room, and when an exhausted Tyson refused to escort her back downstairs to the waiting limo, she became upset and angry at him because, 'she found herself treated as a one-night stand, and she has a compelling desire for money'.

Then, after hearing briefly from the first witness – another contestant in the pageant – Greg Garrison went in with his big gun. He called to the stand the alleged victim, Desiree Washington. The courtroom, packed with spectators and reporters, was hushed, the jury completely riveted for nearly three and a half hours as she told her story. She related how she had met Tyson on the afternoon of July 18 at the pageant rehearsal. 'He pointed to me and said, "You're a nice Christian girl, right?" I smiled and said, "Yeah." ...He stopped in front of me and hugged me and asked if I wanted to go on a date with him. I said sure.' She was excited to have a date with Tyson, because her father, brother and grandfather watched all his fights and idolized him, and because she hoped they would go to parties where she could meet other celebrities on hand for the Black Expo. She testified that she even brought her camera along when Tyson picked her up late that night. She said she trusted Tyson because she saw he was wearing a button that said, 'Together in Christ', and that she saw him at the pageant opening later that day praying with Jesse Jackson.

She said Tyson phoned her from his limo shortly after one-thirty and said, 'Just come down. I want to talk to you. We can go around Indianapolis.' She told him it was late, that she was in her pyjamas, and suggested they get together the next day, but Tyson said he would be leaving town. Her friends encouraged her to get dressed and meet him, so she agreed. When she got downstairs and into the limo, 'He hugged me, and went to kiss me. I kind of jumped back because I was surprised that, being who he was, he acted like that and, besides, his breath smelled kind of bad.' After that, she testified, Tyson was well behaved, but a few minutes later said he had to make a brief stop at his Canterbury Hotel suite, and invited her up while the limo, driven by Virginia Forster, waited for them. Once in the hotel room, she continued, Tyson insisted on talking to her, asking about her family, whether they liked him ('They don't know you,' she told him), her feelings for him, talked about pigeons he kept as pets in Catskill.

She continued, 'He said, "Do you like me?" I said, "I don't know you." ... He had been really pleasant, and his voice changed and he said, "You're turning me on." I said, "I don't know what you think I came here for. I'm not like those other girls." He said "You're a good Christian girl." I just got really nervous. I said, "I want to go out and see Indianapolis like you said." He said okay, and I went to the bathroom.' When she emerged, she said she saw Tyson sitting on the bed in just his underwear. 'What was your reaction?' Garrison asked her. 'I was terrified,' replied Ms Washington. 'What did you say?' Garrison asked. 'It's time for me to leave,' she said she told Tyson. 'He said, "Come here." ... He pulled me fast. He said,"Don't fight me", and he stuck his tongue in my mouth. It was disgusting ... He started taking off my jacket, and I was saying, "Stop, get off me, stop, stop, get off." ... He kept saying, "Don't fight me, relax, don't fight me!" ... I was punching him on the arm and he didn't feel that ... I said, "Ow, please, you're hurting me." My eyes were filling with tears. He started laughing, like it was a game, like it was funny ... He pulled out his penis, and I just freaked out. I started saying anything ... I said, "I have a future ... I can't have a baby. Please put a condom on." I just said anything that I could think of. He said, "I don't have a disease, and I know you don't either." ... He said, "We'll have a baby." And he jammed himself into my vagina. It was excruciating. It just felt like something was ripping me apart. I was trying to punch him and stuff like that. I was trying to back up. I was trying a lot of things. Nothing worked. He said, "Don't fight me, Mommy." He was slamming really hard ... I tried to get away and he grabbed me. "I told you not to fight me," and he rolled me over again.' She said Tyson then withdrew his penis and ejaculated. 'He said, "Don't you love me now?" I just looked at him like I was disgusted.'

After making her way downstairs and back to her hotel in the limo, Ms Washington said, 'I went into the shower and stayed there for a while ... I felt like I couldn't get clean.' When Garrison asked her how she managed to get through the rest of the pageant, she said she played softball for twelve years, often with bruised or broken bones. 'I always make the game and finish the play,' she said. 'I just never quit. I'm not a quitter. If I was a quitter I wouldn't be here today. I finish what I start.' She said she initially wasn't sure what she was going to do about the attack, but when her family arrived in Indianapolis from their home in Rhode Island, she spoke with them. 'They said, "If this happens to someone else, how are you going to live with yourself?"' That's when she decided to report the incident to police and file charges. Tyson sat expressionless during her testimony. The rest of the courtroom was mesmerized.

The next day, all were prepared for the onslaught of Fuller's cross-examination, but for the most part, it never came, and when it did, Desiree Washington refused to be rattled. For three and a half hours, Fuller questioned her, asked about her motives. 'Did you have some hopes of establishing a relationship with Mr Tyson?' Fuller asked her. 'I would never see him again. How could I hope to have any relationship with him?' was her reply. 'After the encounter,' continued Fuller, 'didn't you say, "Aren't you even going to walk me downstairs?"' 'No, I didn't want him to,' answered Ms Washington. 'I didn't want him near me.' She said she was 'fooled' by Tyson, but went to his room because she trusted him. 'Anybody can be fooled. I look back on it now and say, yeah, it was stupid. But that didn't leave any reason for him to do what he did,' she said. Fuller asked her about Tyson's remark that she was a nice Christian girl and what she felt Tyson meant about that. 'That I was a believer in God,' she replied. 'So is Mr Tyson, isn't he?' asked Fuller. 'So he says,' she answered, making no effort to disguise her sarcasm. 'You willingly drove to his hotel? You willingly went to his suite? You willingly sat on the bed?' Fuller asked in questioning her motives. But she did not get flustered. She said her only expectation was that they would make the rounds of parties still underway, and that's why she even brought her camera. 'He said we'd go around Indianapolis and talk. I thought that meant those parties, that we'd see people, take their pictures ... That's what I most wanted.' When she stepped down from the stand, her testimony over, Tyson's team must have sensed they were in trouble. Desiree Washington had more than held her own with the mighty Vincent Fuller.

Next on the witness stand was Christopher Low, a bellman at the hotel, who was delivering food to Tyson's guide and bodyguard, Dale Edwards, in the room next to Tyson's when Ms Washington was leaving. He said she appeared to be dazed and disoriented, and was wandering down the hallway in the wrong direction. When she was on the stand, Desiree had said Edwards was in the hallway as she left Tyson's room, and that he appeared to smirk at her. In his testimony, bellman Low confirmed that he saw Edwards smirk when he saw the young girl leaving Tyson's room.

The next day, Tyson arrived at court accompanied by his usual entourage of flunkies, headed by John Horne and Rory Holloway, the fighter's $250-thousand-a-year friend. Also with him, arm in arm, was 86-year-old Camille Ewald, still a defender of Mike's. King, never missing a trick, had flown in Mike's 'white mother' to be seen at his side, day in, day out. Following his daily early-morning three- or four-mile run at the suburban house where he was staying as a guest, Tyson arrived at court each day in a suit and tie. King, keeping a low profile, did not come to the courtroom, or arrive with the entourage.

On the stand that Friday, the fifth day of the trial, was Virginia Foster, the school guidance counsellor and limo driver. She testified that Desiree Washington, who looked normal, with her hair fixed up, when she entered the limo, returned to the car from her visit to Tyson's room looking 'like she may have been in a state of shock . . . dazed, disoriented. She seemed scared.' Foster said the girl got into the car and said, 'I don't believe him. I don't believe him. Who does he think he is?' When Tyson had made his original call from the car to persuade Ms Washington to join him, Foster said, 'I heard him pleading . . . "Please come down, I just want to talk to you." . . . It was like he was begging for someone to come down and talk to him. He said it several times, like men do when they're trying to get a woman to do something for them. So they beg and beg for it.'

What was more remarkable, but what the jury was never allowed to hear, was Foster's account of what had happened to her the night Tyson arrived in Indianapolis. Foster, who was 44 years old, said Tyson asked her into a room, saying he just wanted to talk, then grabbed her, started kissing her, then opened his pants and exposed himself to her. Foster, who was helping carry luggage into the suite at the Canterbury, was streetwise enough to get Tyson to drop his act. Seeking to have her account admitted into evidence, Garrison had appealed to Judge Gifford, without the jury present, saying Tyson's behaviour with the limo driver was 'almost a fingerprint' of the crime he was accused of. But ruling for the defence, the judge would not allow Foster to tell this story to the jury, since it was not evidence of 'sexually depraved instinct', which under Indiana law meant homosexuality, bestiality or child molestation.

Next, Dr Thomas Richardson, an emergency-room physician at Methodist Hospital who examined Ms Washington about twenty-six hours after her encounter with Tyson, said he found two vaginal abrasions. He said in over two thousand pelvic examinations he'd performed on women, he'd seen those abrasions only twice, and that they were consistent with forced or very hard intercourse. He said that during his examination, Ms

Washington was worried that she might have become pregnant or contracted a sexually transmitted disease from Tyson. The day's testimony concluded with an appearance by Dr James Akin of the Indiana University School of Medicine, who said he had conducted more than twenty thousand pelvic examinations in his career. He said the abrasions found by Dr Richardson were 'incredibly unlikely to happen in consensual sex'.

The trial recessed for the weekend, but that Friday night, an embarrassing spectacle took place, run by people who should have known better. The National Baptist Convention, USA, Inc., the largest black religious organization in the country, along with Louis Farrakhan's Nation of Islam (strange bedfellows?) sponsored a rally, along with local churches, in support of Mike Tyson. He sat in the pulpit of a packed Christ Missionary Baptist church as songs, speeches and prayers were offered on his behalf. National Baptist Convention President, Rev. Dr Theodore Jemison, said, 'Our brother needs us.' Rev. Henry Payden, who described himself as Tyson's 'personal pastor', was also there, complete with gold pendant and diamond ring. Earlier, he had told *New York Post* columnist Mark Kriegel, 'I don't see Mike as a rapist...My gut instinct tells me that Mike was acting as a man.' Little surprise that Tyson is a heavy contributor to Payden's church in the fighter's adopted home city of Cleveland. No one from the National Baptist Convention bothered to organize a prayer rally for Desiree Washington, member of the Baptist church, church usher, Sunday school teacher, companion to the mentally retarded. But she couldn't write big cheques like Don King and Mike Tyson did, could she? And it was curious how Farrakhan, who had been quick to jump to the support of Tawana Brawley and her fictionalized story of how a group of white men raped her in an upstate New York town several years earlier, now came out in support of an accused rapist, a career thug, and turned his back on a black woman with a much more credible account than Brawley.

As the trial continued, Tyson's legal team was successful in having the judge dismiss the charge of confinement, the least serious of the charges against him. But they failed in an effort to have three new defence witnesses testify, women who had suddenly come forward to say they saw Tyson and Desiree Washington kissing in the limo prior to the alleged rape. Prosecutor Greg Garrison argued that the women had had months to come forward, but waiting until the trial was underway and the prosecution was about to rest its case cast doubt on their credibility. Judge Gifford agreed.

On February 4, the prosecution rested its case with a dramatic testimony from its final witness, the mother of Desiree Washington. In a tear-filled appearance on the stand, she said of her daughter, 'She's just not the same any more, and she hasn't been since she came home...She has nightmares because she sees his face. She's scared.' Did her daughter ever become street smart? asked Garrison. 'No,' replied Mrs Washington, 'unfortunately, she didn't. She's not street smart at all.' She went on to testify that when she and the rest of the family arrived in Indianapolis and saw Desiree, 'she looked terrible. She didn't look like the same daughter I sent to Indianapolis. I just hugged her. She was pale and upset. She wasn't wearing any makeup. I just grabbed her and hugged her', and with that, the mother who carried the pain of her daughter broke down and cried, as did many in the courtroom, including one of the alternate jurors. 'It's not her any more. She secludes herself in her bedroom.' She said her daughter told her, 'Mom, I'm not your daughter any more...She's gone. She's not going to come back!...I just want my daughter back,' said the distraught mother. Amid the emotional impact of such testimony, Fuller barely mounted a cross-examination, asking just two brief questions.

Later that day, over objections by the defence, the jury was allowed to hear the recording of the call Desiree made to the police emergency 911 number the morning after her visit to Tyson's room. In part, although never using Tyson's name, she told the 911 operator, 'You know, thinking this was a nice person ...we went in [to his hotel room] and the person started attacking. By attacking me, he became very aggressive, trying to take my clothes off and I was like, well, I have to leave. See, I'm not like that and so the person agreed..."You are a nice girl, you are a Christian girl", and things like that. And so, I was like, well, you know, "I just want to get that straight that I don't want to do anything", and I kept saying that over and over again, and this person went on to say that that's what made him want me more because I didn't want to do anything, basically. He kissed me and, "Oh, you are turning me on because you are not like the rest of these girls. You are not a city girl." And then the person tried to take my clothes off again, and succeeded and then just basically forced himself upon me.' The police operator was then heard saying, 'Okay, you did tell him no, you said?' And she responded, 'Yes, I said no.' 'Do you know this person?' she was asked, and her response was yes. 'Do you know him well or is this somebody you just now met?' 'It's someone that's like famous.' 'Somebody famous?' 'Uh-huh,' she responded, and then went on to explain, 'I came out of the bathroom and this person was in his underwear and just basically kind of did what he wanted to do and kept saying, "Don't fight me. Don't fight me." And I was saying, "No, no. Get off of me please. Get off of me." And he was like, "Don't fight me. Don't fight me." And the person is a lot stronger than I was and he just did what he wanted and I was saying, "Stop, please stop." And he just didn't stop.' The complete call lasted thirteen minutes, and then the prosecution rested.

That same night, a fire broke out in the hotel where the jurors were sequestered. They were evacuated onto the street while firemen fought the blaze. Three people, including two firefighters, were killed. None of the jurors was harmed, but the trial was postponed for a day. There were, of course, rumours that the fire might have been deliberately set in an effort to intimidate the jurors. Although the evidence pointed to the fire having been accidental, Judge Gifford, along with lawyers from both sides, interviewed each juror before the trial resumed. One member of the jury, a black male, did ask to be excused. He was replaced by a white alternate juror, so the makeup of the jury was now ten whites and two blacks.

When the trial resumed later in the day on Thursday, February 6, the defence opened its case. First on the stand were four pageant contestants. Madelyn Whittington said she had heard Ms Washington say she'd go out with Tyson because he was rich and dumb. 'She seemed very determined to go out with him,' Ms Whittington said, but she and the defence witnesses who followed her all painted a picture of Tyson being a sexual predator who was on the prowl. Whittington said Tyson made sexual advances to her, and when she turned him down, he was heard to say, 'Who does she think she is, that little Catholic school motherfucker?' Cecilia Alexander testified that she saw Tyson and his accuser 'cuddling' during the afternoon pageant rehearsal. Parquita Nassau, another contestant, testified that Tyson grabbed her buttocks on July 18, and said to her, 'I could have any one of those bitches out here. I know you want me.' Under cross-examination, Nassau did agree that Desiree Washington appeared to be 'naive in regards to her date with Mr Tyson'. Even Tyson's friend, singer Johnny Gill, appearing embarrassed on the witness stand, admitted, 'Mike was basically being Mike...He was putting the moves on some of the contestants.' Gill said he did see Tyson fondling some of the contestants.

What was emerging from this testimony was a surprising, to say the least, defence strategy. Tyson's lawyers were trying to build a defence based on the fact that their client was a known, dangerous, nearly out-of-control sexual predator, and so Ms Washington should have known better than to go to his room with him! In other words, help destroy Tyson's reputation in an effort to beat the rap. A defence medical expert, Dr Margaret Watanabe, testified that the vaginal abrasions found on Ms Washington could have occurred from consensual sex, but under cross-examination said she respected Dr Jack Akin's opinion expressed during his testimony that it was 'highly unlikely'. Then the defence did what it had not originally planned to do, but what the overwhelming case built by the prosecution had forced it to do. The defence put Mike Tyson on the witness stand.

Tyson was questioned by Vincent Fuller for more than an hour and fifteen minutes. Fuller asked him if anything 'sexually explicit' was said during his initial meeting with Desiree Washington. 'Ummmm...yeah,' said Tyson, who continued that when he asked her out and she suggested dinner or a movie, he told her, '"I don't have that in mind," I said, "I want to be with you. I want you."' Tyson then turned to Judge Gifford and said, 'It's kind of crass. I'd rather not say it. If Your Honour will give me permission...' and Judge Gifford nodded. Then Tyson told the jury, 'I explained to her that I wanted to fuck her.' He continued, 'She said, "Sure. Just give me a call." She said, "That's kind of bold." I said, "That's the way I am. I like to know what I'm getting into before I get into it."' He said that he called her from his car phone that night, asking her to come down and meet him. He told her, 'Wash your face. Put some water on your face. Comb your hair and put on something loose.' He said that while in the limo, 'I kissed her, she kissed me.' He said they went to his room, sat on the bed, talked, that he began kissing her while she was taking off her clothes and he was removing his. Then 'I was having oral sex with her,' he testified, until she told him to stop and told him 'she wanted me to insert my penis'. Tyson said they had intercourse for fifteen or twenty minutes, and when they finished, Ms Washington appeared happy, only becoming annoyed when he refused to take her downstairs, telling her 'that was the way it was'. I said, 'The limousine is downstairs. If you don't want to use the limousine, you can walk.'

Fuller asked his client if he had forced the young woman to have sex. 'No, I didn't. I didn't violate her in any way, sir.' He continued, 'She never told me to stop. She never said I was hurting her. Nothing. No.' But under Garrison's cross-examination, Tyson was caught in a lie. Garrison asked him why he had never told the grand jury that he propositioned Ms Washington by telling her, 'I wanna fuck you.' Tyson said, 'They cut me off.' But when the tape of his grand jury testimony was played for the court, it was clear that Tyson was never cut off, that he was asked several times if he said anything to her besides, 'I just want to be with you', and his answer to the grand jury was no.

Two more pageant contestants testified following Tyson. Tanya St Clair said she heard Desiree Washington talking about Tyson's 'butt, saying, "Oh, it's really something to hold onto."' and hearing her speculate about the size of the ex-champion's penis. But Sharmell Sullivan, winner of the Miss Black America crown, said she never heard any such remarks and, 'I would definitely recollect a statement of that nature because it's very blunt and I'm not used to hearing things of that nature at a beauty pageant.'

All that remained were the closing arguments. Garrison approached Desiree Washington and her mother, who were back in the courtroom for the first time since giving their testimony. Garrison knew that Tyson had been his own worst witness, awkward, unsure of himself, his story filled with contradictions. Garrison took Desiree's hand and said, 'The fight is over, just loosen up. We kicked his ass.' Tyson sat across the courtroom, staring at her, trying to have her make eye contact with him, trying to intimidate her. She didn't give in.

First to address the jury was Vincent Fuller. He said his client 'doesn't possess the intelligence or analytical skills that others who are more fortunate have achieved'. He hammered away at his theory that Tyson's accuser was a Jezebel, worldly wise and out for money, or else someone 'so mature for her age' would never have accepted Tyson's blunt invitation for sex 'unless she knew what was coming...I submit that she was comparing herself to Robin Givens...[with] the hope and expectation that something might develop between herself and Mr Tyson.' If she did not intend to have sex with him, then why, said Fuller, did she remove a panty liner when she went to the bathroom in Tyson's suite? Fuller told the jury that only when she realized there would be no relationship with Tyson, that she was a one-night stand, did she become 'embarrassed and humiliated by her own conduct. She understood that she had no business in that room at two o'clock in the morning with a man she did not know,' so she fabricated a story of rape.

Barbara Trathen, a prosecutor working with Garrison, gave the first part of their final argument. She called Tyson 'a wolf in sheep's clothing' who used 'the cloak of Christianity' to get 'an excited teenager' up to his hotel room. Ms Trathen told the jury, 'That defendant, Mike Tyson, used his fame and his reputation the same identical way that a thug in an alley uses a knife or a gun ...Rape is rape.'

Then it was Garrison's turn. He said the contention that the victim was a calculating gold digger was 'a ridiculous fairy tale'. He pointed out that if she really had been after Tyson, she could have spent the night with him in his room, which the fighter had invited her to do. 'That would have been a home run,' said Garrison. 'If you're the little weasel here who wants his life and his money, you sleep with him. You spend the night.' Instead, he reminded the jury, she rushed back to her hotel and stayed in the shower because she felt she couldn't wash the dirt off herself. Pointing to Tyson and his legal team, Garrison said, 'Her sole crime, aside from being eighteen years old, was to have the gall to stand up to his resources and his defence team.' Garrison continued, 'We need to open the doors and turn on a big fan and blow away all of Mr Fuller's smoke. Then take a hose and wash the mud off these people,' pointing to Desiree and her mother. Garrison reminded the jury that two expert medical witnesses had said the vaginal bruises observed on Ms Washington were virtually never seen after consensual sex, just six times in all their combined years of practice. 'If that's a reasonable doubt,' he said, 'I'll eat your hat. I'll eat all your hats.' At mid-afternoon on Monday, February 10, the jury retired to begin its deliberations.

It took the jury less than ten hours to reach its verdict. Everyone was summoned back to Courtroom 4 of the Marion County Superior Court shortly after 10pm. Don King accompanied Tyson. He sat in the front row of the spectators' section, holding a Bible. Camille Ewald, Tyson's elderly surrogate mother, was not present. Tyson sat impassively as the bailiff handed the jury's verdicts to Judge Gifford. 'We the jury,' she read out loud, 'find the defendant, Michael G. Tyson, guilty of the crime of rape', and Tyson's head moved back in response to hearing the words. Judge Gifford then read two additional guilty verdicts, on both counts of deviate sexual conduct. In response to Fuller's plea, the judge allowed Tyson to remain free on bond pending his sentencing, but requested his passport be surrendered. After King handed over Tyson's passport, the fighter, his lawyers and entourage left the courtroom.

A short while later, speaking with the press, the jury foreman said 'a chain of events that accumulated' convinced the jury of Tyson's guilt. 'We felt that clearly consent was not given.' A black woman member of the jury said the issue of the racial makeup of the jury was a tempest in a teapot, saying it had no bearing on the deliberations. She said it was not a black-white issue, only 'the accumulation of the evidence' that mattered.

Tyson's defence team issued a statement saying, 'We are greatly disappointed in the verdict returned last night. We remain convinced of Mr Tyson's innocence and will take appropriate steps to pursue all appellate review available to him. The trial is but the first step in the process of arriving at the truth. When that process is completed, a new trial had, and all the evidence heard, we have faith that Mr Tyson's vindication will be complete,' thus setting in motion the expected next move, an appeal of the conviction. Within days of the verdict, it was announced that Harvard University law professor Alan Dershowitz, who has made a speciality of handling the appeals of unsympathetic clients such as real estate mogul Leona Helmsley (on tax fraud charges) and socialite Claus von Bulow (on attempted murder charges) would handle Tyson's appeal.

Tyson, said to be dejected and upset with the way he was portrayed by his defence team, flew back home to Cleveland with Don King. He never called elderly Camille Ewald, who sat in her hotel room before returning to her home in Catskill, and said, 'Evidently [Mike] didn't want to see me.' Desiree Washington returned to Rhode Island to resume her college studies. Near Cleveland, a few days later, Tyson was pulled over while driving his Red BMW at 73 miles an hour in a 55 mph zone. He was ticketed on his Ohio licence. He apparently still held a New York driver's licence as well, although it's illegal to have driver's licence from more than one state.

As for the aftermath: developer Donald Trump, in a tremendously ill-advised PR blunder, went public with a suggestion that since, in his opinion, it would be 'beneficial to no one' if Tyson went to jail, he should be allowed to remain free and fight so that proceeds from his bouts could be used to set up a fund for Desiree Washington and other rape victims. Of course, Trump conveniently failed to mention that it was his fervent hope that Tyson would fight at his casinos, which would help bail Trump out of his own serious financial problems. A storm of criticism rained down on Trump from all quarters, and Marion County

Prosecutor Jeffrey Modisett said, 'We don't take Mr Trump's offer seriously ... An offer to buy someone's way out of prison or out of a sentence is not appropriate.' A spokeswoman for Indianapolis Mayor Stephen Goldsmith said, 'How offensive. We have a judicial process for these matters, and it's not for sale.'

Desiree Washington, whose anonymity had been protected during the investigation and trial, decided to go public. She said she wasn't doing it for the publicity, but because it was the 'right thing to do'. She said in an ABC-TV interview that she was offered a million dollars to drop her case against Tyson, but refused the offer and reported it to her attorney, who went to the authorities. She refused to say who approached her with the offer, but the *New York Daily News* reported that 'a high-ranking federal law enforcement official' said the FBI was investigating the Rev. T. J. Jemison, President of the National Baptist Convention USA, Inc., in connection with the bribe offer. Jemison (whose organization had bestowed its 1990 Humanitarian Award on – guess who – Don King!) denied the charge and acknowledged that he had called Washington at her home simply to ask her why she was pursuing her case against Tyson, and for no other reason. The final irony was that Washington said in her ABC interview that she would have dropped her charges if only Tyson had admitted he was wrong, that he had a problem, and that he needed some help. 'I pity him,' said the young college student.

Some so-called black leaders continued to pursue their attempts to keep Tyson out of prison, charging blindly that his conviction was in some way racist. Columnist and author Pete Hamill best summed things up when he wrote, 'The people who spend Tyson's money are crying racism, implying what the Klan would never state: black women are there to be raped and discarded. The fact remains that in Tyson's short life, some of the best things that happened to him came from white people, some of the worst from black people.'

The conviction meant that the Tyson–Holyfield fight would never take place. It was likely that when the appeal process was played out, Tyson would go to prison, realistically for three to five years with time off for good behaviour. He would be free, if that happened, when he was only thirty-one or thirty-two years old, certainly young enough to resume boxing. But it was likely that he would never shake off the rust that would accumulate in prison. He might fight again because it was all that he knew, but he might never be the formidable presence he once was. (There were two fascinating coincidences surrounding the Tyson case: his conviction came on the second anniversary of his title loss to Buster Douglas, and, without the fanfare of a circus, in a virtually empty courtroom in Miami, former Heavyweight Champion Trevor Berbick, the man whom Tyson beat for the title, was also convicted of rape. His victim, a former baby-sitter for his children, said Berbick, a self-styled Christian preacher, told her, 'He hadn't had sex in a long time and that God would understand and that I should, too.' After Berbick raped her, he challenged her to 'Go ahead and report it. No one will believe you.' Berbick was wrong.)

For Tyson, the possibility of prison was just one of his problems. Profligate spending, and an appalling lack of knowledge about his own finances and where his money was or who had it, had helped reduce his fortune considerably. When Cayton and Jacobs were guiding his career with a strategy to make Tyson the richest athlete in the history of sports, it may have seemed inconceivable that Tyson would one day wind up broke. Tyson's personal fortune had dwindled in 1991 to $15-million. While that was more than most people could spend in a lifetime, it was a fraction of what he should have been worth. He spent millions on shopping for himself and for his hangers-on, as well as on legal fees for the constant lawsuits he has been besieged with. Shortly before his trial began, Natalie Fear's paternity suit was dismissed when a court-ordered blood test showed that Tyson was not, after all, the father of the little boy he named D'Amato after his late trainer. But Bill Cayton did win a summary judgment in his case against Tyson and King to recover the 20 per cent of Tyson's purses he was legally entitled to as Tyson's manager, but had never been paid. Tyson owes Fuller's law firm an estimated $2 million for his defence in the rape trial. And there was the Rosie Jones lawsuit hovering over him, as well as the possibility that Desiree Washington would win a major civil judgment against Tyson. All of this could reduce his net worth to very little. It was remarkable, considering his fights and endorsement deals grossed perhaps $100-million. But it is equally remarkable that a fighter, schooled by D'Amato, Cayton and Jacobs, could waste money on a fleet of thirty exotic sports cars, and could take such little interest in his own money that he would say he had no idea where a $10-million cheque from the Spinks fight was deposited; that after seeing two cheques for $100,000 each issued by Don King Productions to his aides Horne and Holloway, Tyson would say he had no idea how much they were paid, even though they were paid from his money; that when asked during a deposition in 1991 about the multi-million dollar worldwide TV fees for his fights, all he could reply was, 'I don't understand anything about the foreign affairs...I just go out and fight and hopefully get the fee.' The handwriting is on the wall. He is troubled, he needs help, and he is destined to get into trouble again. If, when his fighting days are over, he winds up broke, now a likely scenario, he will once again be swallowed up by the mean streets from which he emerged. It was F. Scott Fitzgerald who said, 'Show me a hero, and I'll show you a tragedy.'

21

In Prison, and Out

No matter what anyone says, no matter the excuse or explanation, whatever a person does in
the end is what he intended to do all along.

– CUS D'AMATO

TYSON'S APPEAL TEAM, led by prominent attorney Alan
Dershowitz, was not successful in its attempts to keep Mike out
of prison. In March 1992, he was incarcerated to serve his six-
year sentence. Automatic time off for good behaviour would cut
that sentence in half. However, early in his term, Tyson got into
trouble several times, once for threatening a guard. As a result,
his release date became May 1995 instead of March.

While in prison, Tyson eventually settled into the routine. He
began to take instruction in the Islamic faith from a teacher named
Muhammad Siddeeq. Meanwhile, Dershowitz tried several
additional appeals, claiming there were important witnesses who
hadn't been heard at Tyson's trial. But the Indiana courts once
again denied those appeals. Tyson was in for the duration.

The boxing world forged ahead even with its star attraction 'on
ice'. Evander Holyfield, who had become champion with his
knockout of Buster Douglas, lost the title on a decision to Tyson's
old Brownsville chum, Riddick Bowe, in November 1992. In a
rematch a year later, the smaller Holyfield regained the crown in
a gutsy effort by outpointing Bowe. In the interim, while
champion, Bowe had rejected the WBC title belt, actually
dumping it in a garbage can in a highly publicized staged photo-
op. Bowe and his manager, Rock Newman, did not like the
WBC's politics. So, when Holyfield regained the title, it did not
include WBC recognition. Once again, the title was divided. The
WBC version eventually landed in the lap of the undistinguished,
but Don King-controlled, Oliver McCall.

Holyfield, however, was generally regarded as the true and
rightful champion. That was until early in 1994, when Michael
Moorer lifted the crown from Evander by a narrow 12-round
decision. Ironically, Moorer's trainer was Teddy Atlas. The man
who had on principle walked away from Mike Tyson a dozen

378

years earlier at last had his own Heavyweight Champion. And it was widely acknowledged that the only reason Moorer won the title from Holyfield was the magnificent job done in his corner that night by Atlas. Many times during the bout, Moorer seemed to lose his resolve, the between-rounds tongue-lashings from Atlas appeared to revive his courage when he left his stool. At one memorable moment in the fight, as Moorer came back to the corner after a lacklustre round, Atlas sat down on the stool instead of the fighter and told Moorer that if he didn't want to win the title, he – Atlas – would go out and fight him. Moorer got the message, and did enough to win, although barely. A short time after the fight, following medical tests, it was revealed that Holyfield had fought while impaired by a serious, previously undetected, heart condition. Cardiologists told him his career was over, and Holyfield retired.

Moorer's reign lasted only a few brief months. In his first defence, he signed to fight the venerable former champ George Foreman, now 20 years removed from the last time he had held the belt. Moorer seemed to be having little trouble with Foreman. He won round after round, and was in control of the fight well into the second half of the bout. Then the wily Foreman set Moorer up with a perfect combination, and knocked him out to make history.

Foreman was nearly 46 years old, the oldest man ever to win a boxing championship in any weight division in the history of the sport. Foreman, who had transformed himself into a media darling during his second incarnation in the ring, became an instant superstar. His victory revived interest in the moribund heavyweight division. And with his win coming just months before Tyson's scheduled release, the speculation immediately began about the potential of a 'dream match' between Tyson and the ageing champion who won his first crown when Tyson was just seven years old.

Back home in Indiana, prison officials announced that the extra time which had been added to Tyson's sentence would not be applied after all. That meant his original release date was restored – March 25, 1995. By now, the sharks were in a feeding frenzy. Everyone wanted a piece of the action, everyone wanted to get on the Tyson bandwagon before it took off, especially amid constant rumours that Tyson had smartened up and realized that perhaps he shouldn't hook up with King once he resumed his career. There were reports that Tyson would be handled by a variety of people and, in particular, that he would probably look to the Muslims for his new management team.

Suddenly, Evander Holyfield announced that he was returning to the ring. A deeply religious man, Holyfield claimed his heart ailment had been cured by a faith healer. Late in 1994, Holyfield went to the Mayo Clinic, and the famed hospital's heart specialists, after a battery of tests, proclaimed his heart to be in perfect condition! In February 1995, presented with the evidence, the Nevada Athletic Commission lifted its medical suspension of the former champion and restored Holyfield's licence to fight. Even more remarkable, Buster Douglas, who had not been seen near a boxing ring since he lost the title to Holyfield in 1991, announced that he would make a return to the ring. Douglas weighed 285 pounds, hadn't fought in four years, and the previous year had gone into a diabetic coma. But, since he was the only man to defeat Tyson as a professional, he felt he deserved to get in line for a payday.

In the meantime, Riddick Bowe and Rock Newman were having their own problems with the internal politics of the various and sundry world boxing organizations. Despite Bowe being recognized as one of the two or three best heavyweights in the world, the WBC, WBA and IBF refused to give him his deserved ranking. Newman said it was because he wouldn't pay bribe money to those who ruled those various groups. Bob Lee, President of the IBF, countered by calling Newman's charges 'sour grapes from ... one of the world's worst managers ... a guy unable to move his fighter'. But it was curious that mediocre fighters like Tony Tucker and Bruce Seldon, controlled by Don King, were ranked above Bowe.

A fourth boxing organization, the WBO, had emerged. Its champion was an African-born British fighter named Herbie Hide. Newman and Bowe decided to chart their own course. They signed to fight Hide, figuring a victory by Bowe would give credibility to the WBO belt, and make Bowe once again a force to be reckoned with. On March 11, 1995, in Las Vegas, Bowe – with a 27-pound weight advantage and 3-inch height advantage – knocked Hide down seven times and stopped him in the sixth round to become the WBO Heavyweight Champion. At ringside that night was none other than the Rev. Charles Williams, the very same man who had Mike Tyson in Indianapolis as the guest of his Black Expo in 1991. Rev. Williams arranged a meeting between Newman, Bowe and Tyson at the Indiana prison where Mike was serving the final two weeks of his sentence. Newman began to pitch for a Tyson–Bowe showdown.

In the meantime, Foreman signed to make an April defence against the hardly known and lightly regarded Axel Schulz of Germany. It was apparent Big George didn't want to risk losing his crown while he awaited a possible fight with Tyson that his promoter, Bob Arum, said would be the biggest grossing fight in history. Foreman, starting the hope, said it would be 'the greatest show on earth'. He added, however, that if Don King was involved, 'I'm out, I'm gone. I'm not going to be around.'

And so, as he emerged from prison with a king's ransom in boxing offers at his feet, it was apparent that Mike Tyson, if he was dedicated enough and strong-minded enough, would have ample opportunity to restore his badly depleted financial assets. More importantly, he'd had much time to think and contemplate during his three years in prison about the direction he wanted his life to take as he turned 29 years old. Were his new religious convictions sincere, or would he put them aside as he apparently did after Don King arranged for his earlier baptism in the Baptist Church? Would he learn to respect women and treat them with dignity, despite his past record? Would he take more direct involvement in handling his own financial affairs or be willing once again to risk financial ruin? Would he emerge as a dominant force in the heavyweight division, or would more than three years of inactivity have eroded his skills too much for him to be able to regain them? There were many unanswered questions, but Mike Tyson, still not 30 years old as he prepared to resume his boxing career, would have many years to answer them.

Some of the answers became all too apparent very quickly. Tyson's release from prison was set for March 25, 1995. Several hundred journalists and technicians from around the world were on hand outside the prison in the freezing pre-dawn hours. Dozens of satellite trucks were on site. Shortly after 6, three Lincoln limos pulled up. Promoter Don King emerged from one, followed by a group of burly bodyguards, along with King and Tyson cronies John Morne and Rory Holloway. Reporters also spotted a 30-ish, attractive woman entering the prison. It turned out she was the new love of Mike Tyson's life. Her name was Monica Turner. She was a medical student at Georgetown University, where it was said she drove around campus in a Mercedes-Benz. Tyson had met her in 1991 at a party at the home of actor Eddie Murphy. Turner had a bit of a past. She had a five-year-old daughter fathered by a much older man, a 57-year-old who was currently serving a ten-year prison sentence for cocaine trafficking.

About 20 minutes after entering the prison, the group emerged, the bodyguards forming a flying wedge around Tyson. The ex-heavyweight champ was dressed in Muslim clothing, including an Islamic skullcap. King's men tried to block the photographers' view of Tyson. As it turned out, the reason for this (unknown at the time to Tyson) was that King had cut a deal with the Showtime cable TV network for the first TV interview and pictures of Tyson. As Tyson and the King group were leaving the prison, an entourage arrived representing Louis Farrakhan's militant Muslim faction. They tried to take charge and block the photographers, but the Indiana prison police regained control of the situation.

King was anxious to whisk Tyson away. He had a plane waiting at the airport to fly them back to the King/Tyson compound in Ohio. King had a surprise party planned, and he wanted to get Tyson away from the Muslims. But Mike asserted himself. He wanted to go to the Islamic Society of North America's mosque for a prayer service, and that's where the convoy of limos headed. Among those waiting there for Tyson was Muhammad Ali, who joined the others in prayer with Tyson. While the impatient King cooled his heels, a breakfast followed.

Eventually, way behind King's schedule, the group headed to the airport. The limos reportedly reached speeds exceeding 100 mph, escorted by off-duty Indianapolis policemen using police department squad cars. As a result, the Indianapolis Police Department launched an internal investigation into this unauthorized use of police cars being driven at dangerously high speeds just to get King and Tyson to their plane. Despite all this, prison officials were very happy to be rid of Tyson, according to investigative reporter Bob Michals. A journalist covering the Tyson story for *The Globe* tabloid, Michals was told by several prison officials that Tyson had been getting away with so many things during his three years in the slammer that they were glad to see him gone once and for all. Michals broke a story in *The Globe* that several prison guards were under investigation for allowing Tyson special privileges during the three years, including choice food brought in from the outside, extra phone calls and virtually unlimited visitation. Several of the guards, who earn very modest salaries, suddenly popped up driving brand new $30,000 automobiles.

Michals also learned that Tyson had been having sexual relations regularly while in prison with a female drug counsellor – right in her office! 'Tyson was in her office two or three hours a day, every day, alone, in a locked, private office.' According to reports, Tyson had promised her a car. The aftermath, said Michals, after officials learned of the hanky-panky, is that the woman 'no longer does individual counselling. She lost her office. They investigated her, but they couldn't make anything stick.'

When King, Tyson and the entourage arrived back in Ohio on the day of Mike's release, it didn't take long for the ex-champ to become very angry. He'd known nothing about the Showtime deal. He wasn't in the mood for a surprise party, especially one where alcohol and pork products – both forbidden by Islamic law – were being served by King. Tyson ordered everyone except Horne, Holloway and his girlfriend out of his home. Meanwhile, King had had enough of the tug of war with the Muslims. He ordered them to leave, telling them, 'This boy [Tyson] ain't goin' to Mecca, he's goin' to Las Vegas.' King was flexing his muscles, confident that despite all the rumours, whatever deal he'd cut with Tyson was airtight.

Five days later, Tyson answered a lot of the questions, ending the speculation about his future. He called a news conference in Cleveland to announce his plans. Several high-profile Muslims from the boxing world were there, among them boxing promoters Akbar Muhammad and Bilal Muhammad. Also there was promoter Harold Smith, as well as former World Light-Heavyweight Champion Matthew Saad Muhammad. Tyson had idolized Saad as a youngster, watching him fight on TV. Saad had grown close to Tyson, visiting him during his imprisonment. King was not in attendance, but there was no doubt his presence was felt. Moments before Tyson was to appear, his bodyguards swept through the room, ordering the three promoters and Saad Muhammad to leave. The promoters had offers to counter King's deal, offers they hoped Tyson would at least listen to. King wanted them nowhere near Tyson. Saad Muhammad was not a promoter, but he was a pious, practising Muslim, sincere in his beliefs, and he wanted Mike to listen to him before jumping back into bed with King. He didn't want to leave. Horne and Holloway made it clear to the bodyguards that Tyson would not appear until they got Saad Muhammad out. Anthony Pitts, Tyson's thug-for-hire, had to grab Saad by the arm and threaten him to make him leave with the other three. Saad was shocked and disappointed by Tyson.

When Tyson finally appeared, no longer wearing Muslim clothing, it became immediately apparent that after three years away, it was once again going to be business as usual. In a brief statement, Tyson said, 'There's been a lot of speculation about my plans. Here they are: I will fight again. I want to confirm John Horne and Rory Holloway as my co-managers. I also want to confirm that Don King continues to be my promoter. Don is the greatest promoter in the world. John and Rory have given me great advice on my professional career.' Much to the disappointment of rival WBO, Tyson said he would continue his association with Showtime TV and also announced a deal with the MGM Grand Hotel in Las Vegas to stage his fights.

The deal King had cut with the MGM Grand was a six-fight package that would run through 1997. No dollar figures were announced, but it was known King had been seeking $200-million from the MGM Grand, and he probably wound up with a package worth about $150-million. Tyson took no questions from the scores of reporters. He concluded his statement by saying, 'May Allah bless you all', and he was gone. So much for leaving King and hooking up with the Muslims. As Tyson departed, he laughed and said to Horne and Holloway, 'I really fucked them up.'

The following week, on April 8, King had a double-header heavyweight bill he was promoting in Las Vegas, and that's where Tyson headed. In one fight, Oliver McCall was defending his WBC heavyweight title against 45-year-old Larry Holmes, who took short money – just $350-thousand – and was forced, against his better judgment, to deal with King once again, just to have one final chance to win a title. In the other bout, Bruce Seldon was fighting Tony Tucker for the vacant WBA title, which that organization had taken away from George Foreman when Foreman decided to defend his title against the unranked German fighter Axel Schulz. On the night of April 8, McCall won a decision against Holmes, while Seldon scored an upset TKO against the over-the-hill Tucker. (Two weeks later, on April 22, Foreman's years caught up with him. Schulz, just 26 years old, appeared to dominate the fight, but when the decision was announced, Foreman was the recipient of a 'gift' majority decision by the infamous Las Vegas judges. He thereby retained his IBF Championship.)

Tyson did not attend the McCall–Holmes fight, wanting to avoid the crush of attention he knew he'd receive if he showed up at ringside. But Tyson wasted little time while in Vegas, spending a good chunk of the money King no doubt advanced him from the $150-million MGM Grand deal. He purchased a $3-million estate in Las Vegas, reportedly purchased five BMWs at Chaisson's Motor Cars, and then dropped $200,000 on clothing for himself and his buddies at the Versace store in the MGM Grand.

Some of the most respected boxing writers in the country had the situation sized up pretty quickly. Wallace Matthews, in the *New York Post,* wrote that Tyson was 'a man whose only contribution to society over the past four years was an uncontrolled sexual rampage at a beauty pageant he was attending as a so-called black role model.' Matthews wrote of 'the emptiness of Tyson's words, the sham of his purported "conversion" to Islam and the ludicrousness of his claim of having "developed his mind" during three years in prison...Tyson has never asked King for an explanation, even though during their first association something like $30-million of his money somehow went south.' Greg Logan, in *New York Newsday*, wrote, 'Tyson came out of prison...as the most valuable free agent in the world and signed a six-fight deal with King without ever listening to bids from other promoters...Everyone says King is far and away the smartest man in boxing. Words like "devious" and "Machiavellian" and "evil" also got a lot of play from King's rivals. Tyson was no match for King.' Michael Katz, in the *New York Daily News,* wrote, '...it would seem Mike Tyson has no character. He left prison and went back to Don King, the man who "managed" his money almost comically.' George Foreman told Katz he didn't believe Tyson had changed while in prison, and said he did not think Tyson's embrace of Islam was sincere.

Those Muslims who had been spurned by Tyson also voiced their views. Matthew Saad Muhammad said, 'Don [King] must have offered him a deal he couldn't refuse. But he's gonna find out the truth eventually in a hard way. It happened to all of us. I fought for Don King. I know.' Promoter Harold Smith said, 'I'm sad because I know what's going to happen to him. Nothing's changed. As far as I'm concerned, that kid is still doing time.'

The astute and highly regarded veteran journalist, Jack Newfield, summed it up best. In a column directed straight at Tyson, he wrote: 'You could have revolutionized all of boxing by declaring yourself a free agent, which was the way Muhammad Ali and Sugar Ray Leonard maximized their opportunities...But you decided to go back to Don King...It was tragic...Don King, as a promoter, always makes more money than the fighter...You had a chance to change all that. If you had learned anything in your three years in prison, you would have realized that promoters should work for you. You should not work for any promoter...If you had declared yourself a free agent, letting King and all other bidders come to you, it would have changed the economics of the cruellest game for ever. All the talk about a new Tyson, a wiser Tyson, a religious Tyson, a free-thinking Tyson turned out to be wishful thinking. There is no new Tyson, just a weaker self that caved in to King's brilliant con at the last minute...But Don King did not cause your downfall. You're responsible for your own actions. You have only yourself to blame...You could have become a leader who liberated fighters all over from a system of exploitation. Mike, you blew it. And I feel very sad for you.'

22

Return to the Ring

ON THE NIGHT of August 19, 1995, just a few miles from his new multi-million dollar home in Las Vegas, Mike Tyson waited to make his first entrance into a boxing arena in four years and two months. He was behind closed doors. No TV cameras had been allowed into his dressing-room so millions of viewers around the world could peek in on his pre-fight preparations.

First into the ring was 26-year-old journeyman opponent Peter McNeeley, wearing a green satin robe to accentuate his Irish heritage. McNeeley came through the ropes and skipped around the ring, playing to the crowd, enjoying what was to be his all too brief moments in the spotlight. Then, with the lights still dim and an angry rap-music song blaring from the arena speakers, Mike Tyson, surrounded by his entourage and followed closely by Don King, began his walk down the aisle and towards the ring. His attire was the same as it always had been – Spartan, black boxing shoes, no socks, no robe, just a white towel with a hole cut in the centre pulled over his head, and draped over his shoulders. The cheers of the crowd built as Tyson climbed the stairs and entered the familiar confines of the squared circle.

Ring announcer Jimmy Lennon Jr, introduced first McNeeley, and then Tyson, a trim 220 pounds, and still being billed as 'fighting out of Catskill, New York'. Referee Mills Lane brought both men to the centre of the ring for the instructions, Tyson staring at McNeeley, while the man everyone referred to as 'the challenger', even though this was not a title fight, just smiled to hide his nervousness. And then the bell rang.

McNeeley, deciding his best chance was to try to overwhelm Tyson and nail him quickly with a haymaker, charged across the ring and swarmed all over Tyson along the far ropes. In an instant it happened. Tyson lashed out with one punch and McNeeley was down. A mere seven seconds had elapsed since the opening bell. McNeeley bounced up immediately, unhurt, and literally jogged around the ring, so pumped up was he with adrenalin. Mills Lane gave him the mandatory 8-count. McNeeley then charged right back at Tyson. The crowd was loving it. However long it lasted – and no one expected it to last very long – they'd at least see some

387

action. McNeeley was nothing if not game. He certainly wasn't trying to run and hide from Tyson, who seemed rather befuddled by McNeeley's aggression. McNeeley caught Tyson with one fair shot, and then Tyson, gathering himself, lashed out with two lefts and connected with a right uppercut. McNeeley hit the canvas for the second time. He was up quickly, a bit more stunned this time than on the first knockdown. Lane waved Tyson to a neutral corner. McNeeley staggered slightly into the ropes as Lane began another 8-count. He was game to continue. His eyes were clear. And then, suddenly, McNeeley's manager, Vinny Vecchione, was in the ring and, just as suddenly, the fight was over. The rules clearly state that if a cornerman enters the ring, his fighter is automatically disqualified. And that's what happened. Mills Lane declared Tyson the winner by disqualification, not knockout, at one minute and 29-seconds of the first round.

The crowd was stunned. McNeeley had been prepared to go on. The spectators wanted to see the bout come to its rightful conclusion. They began to chant, 'Bullshit, bullshit', but that did not change the result. McNeeley went across the now crowded ring and got Tyson's ear. He whispered his congratulations, telling Tyson he was a man, a great fighter, and that he was one of McNeeley's heroes. McNeeley did not appear terribly upset at the controversial actions of his manager, but other champions were quick to express their opinions. Michael Spinks said if his corner had done that to him, 'I'd be kickin' their butts.' Bobby Czyz said if his corner had stopped one of his fights that quickly, 'They'd have a fight with me right there on the spot.' Joe Frazier said, 'You're a gladiator. When you sign the contract, you're supposed to be carried out on a shield.' Sugar Ray Leonard said he'd fire his corner for doing something like that. Leonard added, 'People are not here to see a bizarre ending. Mike Tyson is supposed to be the saviour of boxing. This type of fight hurts boxing.'

Tyson said he thought he'd hit McNeeley hard, but not hard enough to knock him down. But Tyson had no complaints about the way it ended. 'Eventually, he would have gotten hurt,' said Tyson. 'I'm a blood man. I like to finish it.' King said, 'Don't take it out on Mike Tyson and don't take it out on Peter McNeeley. If you want to jump on Vinnie Vecchione, be my guest. He got his fighter disqualified.' Vecchione simply said, 'I made a judgment. I have to live with that. As far as I'm concerned, I did the right thing for my fighter.' It was apparent what had happened. Vecchione had hinted at it broadly the week preceding the fight, when he told the *New York Daily News,* 'If it comes to [McNeeley taking a vicious beating], I'm going to be in that ring in a split second...I love that kid. He ain't gonna get hurt.' And that's just what Vecchione did. After all, the $540,000 payday was in the bank. What was the point, Vecchione figured, of letting his fighter get cold-cocked by Tyson? Take the money and run! There was obviously a tacit understanding between Vecchione and McNeeley's dad, Tom, the ex-heavyweight who had fought Floyd Patterson 34 years earlier and who was, on this night, in his son's corner, that young Peter would take no unnecessary punishment. Just hours after the fight, in the early hours of Sunday morning, Peter McNeeley was in the Betty Boop lounge of the MGM Grand Hotel, smoking a cigar, celebrating, buying beer for his hometown pals.

The newspapers came down fast and hard. The headlines read: 'Rip Off In The Ring', 'Utter Disgrace', 'What a Joke!', 'Pay TV Viewers Want Their Money Back'. Wallace Matthews, writing in the *New York Post,* said, 'The entire show was a discredit to Tyson, to King, to Showtime and to the MGM Grand, if such a thing is possible.' Associated Press TV writer Steve Wilstein wrote in his column, 'Boxing fans wasted $49 for 89 seconds of pay-for-view buffoonery, chicanery and outright fraud...The 49 bucks it cost to watch Tyson's comeback might as well been tossed in the garbage...This so-called fight smelled worse than the garbage. It had the aroma of a scam, a swindle, a theft.' King, of course, didn't give a damn. He and Tyson had their $25-million payday, with more of the same guaranteed from the six-fight package deal he had put together with the MGM Grand and Showtime TV. His justification: 'They all fought bums, Ali, Tyson, Joe Louis. For Larry Holmes, we would find guys in the morgue...This ain't nothing bad I'm doing here. It really don't matter who you put in with Tyson, the people want to see him. If I'd have put a black guy in there, it wouldn't be nearly as good,' said King, always the pragmatist. 'If I had a black kid, he'd be calling me a dirty motherfucker before long. Of course, I wouldn't be making as much cash with a black guy, but it ain't about cash. I make the cash, the cash don't make me. If I can do this with a Peter McNeeley, then imagine what I could do with a live body.'

The second fight in Tyson's comeback was scheduled for November 4, 1995 in Las Vegas. The opponent was another untested heavyweight who appeared soft and overweight. His name was Buster Mathis, Jr. And, as with McNeeley, there was a connection with Cus D'Amato. Mathis's father had been a top ranked heavyweight in the 1960s. D'Amato had trained Buster Mathis, Sr. Eventually, they split. Joey Fariello, a protégé of D'Amato, took over as Mathis's trainer. Ultimately, Mathis was knocked out by Joe Frazier in a fight for the vacant heavyweight title. Buster, Sr., eventually became the trainer of his son. He died during the summer of 1995 as he was getting Junior ready for the Tyson fight. And it was Joey Fariello who stepped in and became the trainer of Buster Mathis, Jr.

Mathis was to earn 800-thousand dollars for the fight. Tyson was getting 10-million. Four weeks before the fight, Tyson suffered a fracture on the thumb of his right hand. The injury was not made public. His doctors felt it would heal in time for the fight. But, on the Monday before the bout, Tyson threw a punch during a sparring session and re-fractured the thumb. This time, there was too much pain. On November 1, just four days before the bout, it was cancelled. Tyson headed home for the holidays. His career, at least temporarily, was on hold again. He would not set foot in the ring again until 1996.

For now, it was time for Tyson to replenish his greatly diminished bank accounts. His profligate spending, his divorce from Robin Givens, his legal expenses incurred during the rape trial and subsequent appeals, his out-of-court civil settlement with Desiree Washington, and, of course, his management at the hands of Don King and cronies, had all served to drain his supply of cash. And there had been quite a supply. Along with the fight deals Bill Cayton and Jim Jacobs had negotiated for him, Cayton's brilliant financial management had also put in place for Tyson a variety of endorsement deals aimed at making him the richest athlete in sports history. Eastman Kodak, Nintendo, Suntory Beer, Toyota, Pesi-Cola had all lined up to use Tyson as a spokesman. Cayton had also lined up deals with Nabisco and the 3M Corporation. But then Tyson chose to dump Cayton and self-destruct.

There are things that appeared to be a certainty as Mike Tyson resumed his boxing career and approached his 30th birthday: he certainly would earn a second fortune; he almost certainly would become a champion again in the boxing ring; he certainly would be idolized again by many, and vilified by many more. What was less certain was what would happen to Tyson as a man. Was his conversion to Islam sincere? Several years earlier, he had been baptized as a Christian in a highly publicized ceremony orchestrated by Don King. His professed belief in Christianity did not temper his behaviour towards women nor his overall arrogance. Would he now, finally, learn from his mistakes, remember the lessons Jacobs and D'Amato and Atlas and others tried to teach him? Would he become a worthy citizen when his boxing days were finished, or would he and trouble continue to find each other? After the McNeeley fight, *New York Times* columnist Harvey Araton made this observation: 'As much as Ali transcended boxing for his classic ingenuity, Tyson is a global phenomenon for his naked brutality. Nothing more, nothing less ... Tyson is a fearsome creation of a Brooklyn ghetto ... Undoubtedly, his appeal in some corners is the hope that he and all he stands for will be vanquished for ever. If he's getting rich on that primal conception, he's also being set up for a fall.'

PROFESSIONAL RING RECORD

Michael Gerard Tyson
'Iron Mike' 'Catskill Thunder'

Born June 30, 1966, Brooklyn, NY

Year	Date		
1985	6 March	Hector Mercedes, Albany, NY	KO-1
	10 April	Trent Singleton, Albany, NY	KO-1
	23 May	Don Halpin, Albany, NY	KO-4
	20 June	Rick Spain, Atlantic City, NJ	KO-1
	11 July	John Alderson, Atlantic City, NJ	KO-3
	19 July	Larry Sims, Poughkeepsie, NY	KO-3
	15 August	Lorenzo Canaday, Atlantic City, NJ	KO-1
	5 September	Michael Jack Johnson, Atlantic City, NJ	KO-1
	9 October	Donnie Long, Atlantic City, NJ	KO-1
	25 October	Robert Colay, Atlantic City, NJ	KO-1
	1 November	Sterling Benjamin, Latham, NJ	KO-1
	13 November	Eddie Richardson, Houston, Texas	KO-1
	22 November	Conroy Nelson, Latham, NJ	KO-2
	6 December	Sammy Scaff, Madison Square Garden, NY	KO-1
	27 December	Mark Young, Latham, NY	KO-1
1986	11 January	David Jaco, Albany, NY	KO-1
	24 January	Mike Jameson, Atlantic City, NJ	KO-5
	16 February	Jesse Ferguson, Troy, NY	KO-6
	10 March	Steve Zouski, Uniondale, NY	KO-3
	3 May	James 'Quick' Tillis, Glens Falls, NY	W-10
	20 May	Mitch 'Blood' Green, Madison Square Garden, NY	W-10
	13 June	Reggie Gross, Madison Square Garden, NY	KO-1
	28 June	William Hosea, Troy, NY	KO-1
	11 July	Lorenzo Boyd, Swan Lake, NY	KO-2
	26 July	Marvis Frazer, Troy, NY	KO-1
	17 August	Jose Ribalta, Atlantic City, NJ	KO-10
	6 September	Alfonzo Ratliff, Las Vegas, Nevada	KO-2
	22 November	Trevor Berbick, Las Vegas, Nevada (Won WBC World Heavyweight Championship)	KO-2

PROFESSIONAL RING RECORD

1987	7 March	James 'Bonecrusher' Smith, Las Vegas, Nevada (Won WBA World Heavyweight Championship)	W-12
	30 May	Pinklon Thomas, Las Vegas, Nevada (Retained WBC/WBA Heavyweight Championship)	KO-6
	1 August	Tony Tucker, Las Vegas, Nevada (Won IBF World Heavyweight Championship)	W-12
	16 October	Tyrell Biggs, Atlantic City, NJ (Retained undisputed World Heavyweight Championship)	KO-7
1988	22 January	Larry Holmes, Atlantic City, NJ (Retained undisputed World Heavyweight Championship)	KO-4
	21 March	Tony Tubbs, Tokyo, Japan (Retained undisputed World Heavyweight Championship)	KO-2
	27 June	Michael Spinks, Atlantic City, NJ (Retained undisputed World Heavyweight Championship)	KO-1
1989	25 February	Frank Bruno, Las Vegas, Nevada (Retained undisputed World Heavyweight Championship)	KO-5
	21 July	Carl Williams, Atlantic City, NJ (Retained undisputed World Heavyweight Championship)	KO-1
1990	11 February	Buster Douglas, Tokyo, Japan (Lost undisputed World Heavyweight Championship)	KO by 10
	16 June	Henry Tillman, Las Vegas, Nevada	KO-1
	8 December	Alex Stewart, Atlantic City, NJ	KO-1
1991	18 March	Razor Ruddock, Las Vegas, Nevada	KO-7
	28 June	Razor Ruddock, Las Vegas, Nevada	W-12
Imprisoned – March 1992–March 1995			
1995	19 August	Peter McNeeley, Las Vegas, Nevada	W-1

TOTAL BOUTS	*WON*	*LOST*	*KO's*
43	*42*	*1*	*36*

Appendix: Documents

$5000 00/xxx .   August 1   1956

On demand   after date I promise to pay
to the order of International Boxing Club
Five thousand _____ 100 Dollars
Payable at _____
Value received
No ____ Due ____   Floyd Patterson — Constantine D'Amato
U.S. Bond.

$15000 00/xxx .   June 7   1956

On demand   after date I promise to pay
to the order of International Boxing Club
Fifteen thousand 00/xxx _____ 100 Dollars
Payable at _____
Value received
No ____ Due ____   Constantine D'Amato for Floyd Patterson
U.S. Bond.

IOUs for $20,000 in unsecured cash loans from the IBC to Cus
D'Amato. The loans were taken shortly before Patterson won the
heavyweight title, when D'Amato knew that he intended to sever his
relations with the IBC. Despite frequent demands, D'Amato
steadfastly refused to ever repay these loans.

STATE OF NEW YORK
DEPARTMENT OF STATE

DIVISION OF
STATE ATHLETIC COMMISSION

Chapter 714, Laws of 1921

APPLICATION FOR
BOXER'S LICENSE

THIS SPACE FOR
COMMISSION USE ONLY

Deputy's interview
Fingerprint record
Preliminary screening
Pending number ___ 902
Fee received ___ $10 ___ 4/5/84
Amount
Medical ~~NOT~~ APPROVED 2/26/85
Final screening
License number # 321

The undersigned having paid the legal fee as provided in Chapter 714 of the Laws of 1921, hereby makes application for a License as a Boxer.

899-99-1014

Date __ 11-5-84 __

Social Security Number [ ] Phone Number __ 518- _____

Name __ MICHAEL GERARD TYSON __

Ring Name __ SAME __

Address __ R.D. 3 BOX 242 __ City __ CATSKILL __ State __ N.Y. __ Zip __ 12414 __

Age __ 18 __ Date of Birth __ JUNE 30, 1966 __ Perm. Residence last 5 years __ IN CATSKILL __

PROOF OF AGE

Birth Certificate _____ School Record _____ Baptismal Certificate _____ Passport __ ✓ __

Any Official Document Showing Birth Date _____

Normal Weight __ 210 LBS __ Ring Weight __ 206 __ Marital Status __ SINGLE __ Citizen __ U.S.A. __

Height __ 5' 11½" __ Color of Eyes __ BROWN __ Color of Hair __ BLACK __

Distinguishing Marks __ NONE __

Occupation __ FIGHTER __

Employer Name and Address __ NONE __

Manager's Name __ Jim JACOBS + BILL CAYTON __ Phone Number __ 212-532-17N __

Address __ 9 E 40TH ST __ City __ N.Y. __ State __ N.Y. __ Zip __ 10016 __

Is manager authorized to contract for your appearance or services? __ YES __

References: __ CUS D'AMATO __ Address __ RD 3 BOX 242 CATSKILL 12414 __

__ STEVE LOTT __ Address __ 2450 E. 40TH ST. N.Y. 10016 __

~~JOSE TORRES~~ PETE HAMILL __ Address __ N.Y. STATE ATHLETIC COMM __

Have you ever been convicted of a crime? _____

If so, when and where? Give full particulars _____

Where do you train __ CATSKILL __ Trainer's Name __ CUS D'AMATO __ Address __ RD 3 BOX 242 CATSKILL N.Y. 12414 __

I subscribe and affirm under the penalties of perjury, that the statements made in this application have been examined by me and to the best of my knowledge and belief are true and correct.

Mike Tyson
Applicant's Signature

APPROVED __ 3/8/85 __ 19___

DIVISION OF STATE ATHLETIC COMMISSION

____ Jose Torres ____ CHAIRMAN

The very first application for a professional boxer's license, signed by 18-year-old Mike Tyson in 1984. It was approved by the then New York Athletic Commissioner, Jose Torres, who was a friend of Tyson, Jacobs and D'Amato. Tyson mistakenly entered Torres's name as a reference. That was crossed out, and the name of writer Pete Hamill substituted.

NEW YORK STATE ATHLETIC COMMISSION
BOXER-MANAGER CONTRACT

AGREEMENT made this ....5th..................................... day of ....November.., 19 84 .,
between ....Michael Gerard Tyson... (hereinafter referred to as the "Boxer") residing at
RD 3 Box 242 Catskill N.Y. 12414 .... and ....Jim Jacobs..
(hereinafter referred to as the "Manager") residing at ....9 East 40th St. New York, N.Y. 10016....................

In consideration of the covenants, conditions, and mutual promises contained herein, the parties hereto agree as follows:

FIRST: This agreement shall be binding on all parties for a period of .4 1.... years (not to exceed four years) from the date
hereof.

SIXTH: Any and all purses, prizes, fees, or other remuneration earned by, or in behalf of, the Boxer for, or in direct re-
lation to, boxing, sparring or training services rendered, or to be rendered, by the Boxer shall be divided and distributed as follows:

   (a) payment or repayment for all reasonable and necessary training and transportation expenses incurred by, or on
       behalf of, the Boxer; and, of the remaining sum,

   (b) ....33 1/3.... % (not to exceed 33⅓%) to the Manager;

   (c) ....66 2/3.... % to the Boxer; and

   (d) .... % to ....(Name)............................., the Trainer, pursuant to a separate agreement
       filed herewith. (Note: It is not necessary that a Boxer have an agreement with a Trainer.)

All distributions shall be made within 10 days of the receipt of same by the Boxer or Manager.

The Manager guarantees that in *no contract year* shall the monies paid to the Boxer, pursuant to clause (c) above, be less
than ....$30,000.00....................... Dollars.

ELEVENTH: In the event of an unresolved dispute between the aforestated boxer-manager, the Commission may, at its
discretion and option intercede in said dispute by notifying both aggrieved parties in writing as to its intention to mediate the dispute and that the decision rendered by said Commission shall be binding on both parties.

The parties further specifically certify, warrant, agree, and understand that no such agreement, whether oral or written,
shall be binding unless specifically approved by and filed with the Athletic Commission.

The undersigned have read and understand this agreement, and have received a copy of it.

Witnessed by:

....
A Representative of the Commission

Approved by:

....
Chairman

....
Boxer

....
Manager

A portion of the first contract between Jim Jacobs and Mike Tyson,
executed in November 1984. Four months later, the 18-year-old
Tyson had his first pro fight.

June 24, 1988
By Hand and By
Certified Mail, Return Receipt Requested

Mr. William Cayton
9 East 40th Street
New York, New York 10017

Dear Bill:

    Starting now, you are to take no action on my behalf as a
boxing manager. Any monies you have received for me as a boxing
manager must be promptly forwarded to the office of Michael
Winston, my attorney. Any monies you are to receive on my behalf
as a boxing manager must be forwarded to my attorney Michael R.
Winston.

    Also, you are directed to advise all persons and companies
that owe me money that you are not authorized to receive any
monies due me as my boxing manager.

Sincerely,

Mike Tyson

c.c. Michael Winston
      New York State Boxing Commission
      Sports of the Century, Inc.

RECEIVED

∴ / 1988

RECEIVED Commission
..... .ork Office

JUN 27 1988

Athletic Commission
New York Office

Tyson's letter to Bill Cayton, delivered to the manager three days
before the Spinks fight. Michael Winston eventually fell out of favour
with Ruth Roper and was replaced as Tyson's attorney.

25 July 1988

Michael Tyson (hereinafter Tyson) c/o Winston &
Bonner, 730 Fifth Avenue, New York and William Cayton
(hereinafter Cayton) 9 East 40th Street, New York
have reached the following agreement in principal to
be later entered into full contract form.

1.   With respect to the New York State Athletic
Commission Boxer-Manager contract signed on February
12, 1988 and now in effect, Cayton will continue
to act as manager under the terms therein
provided until February 11, 1992 except as follows:

    (a) Cayton will receive 20% and Tyson 80% of the
        net remuneration earned by Tyson from his
        boxing activities.

    (b) Tyson has the right to have his attorney
        review all fight contracts and to veto any
        fight that he does not want to engage in.

    (c) Tyson has a right to veto the hiring of a
        trainer and any assistants.

    (d) Tyson has an absolute right to a full and
        complete accounting of all revenues past, present
        and future by an accountant of his choice.

11. This understanding is subject to the approval of
the New York State Athletic Commission.

12. The fraud claim against Jacob and Cayton is withdrawn.

13. Neither party shall issue any press release or
any other public statements regarding the subject
matter of this Settlement Agreement other than a
joint press release agreed upon by the parties.

_____
Michael Gerald Tyson

_____
William Cayton

_____
Sports of the Century Inc.

by _____
William Cayton, President

WE 7/27/88   MT 7/27/88

A portion of the agreement reached in July 1988, between Tyson and
Cayton, reducing Cayton's percentage as manager from the standard
33% to 20%, at the instigation of Donald Trump.

APPENDIX: DOCUMENTS

PROMOTION AGREEMENT between MICHAEL TYSON ("Tyson"), 110 Ravine Lake Road, Bernardsville, New Jersey 09724, and DON KING PRODUCTIONS, INC. ("DKP"), a New York corporation with offices at 32 East 69th Street, New York, New York 10021.

WHEREAS, Tyson wishes to grant to DKP the sole and exclusive right to secure, arrange and promote all professional boxing bouts ("Bouts") requiring Tyson's services as a professional boxer and DKP wishes to secure, arrange and promote such Bouts.

1. Tyson hereby grants to DKP the sole and exclusive right to secure, arrange and promote all Bouts requiring Tyson's services as a professional boxer during the term hereof, and DKP undertakes to secure, arrange and promote such Bouts, all upon and subject to the terms and conditions hereinafter set forth.

2. This Agreement shall be for a term of four (4) years commencing on the date hereof.

Dated: Chicago, Illinois
          October 21, 1988

MICHAEL TYSON

By: _____
    Michael Tyson

By: _____
    William D. Cayton, Manager

DON KING PRODUCTIONS, INC.

By: _____
    Don King, President

A portion of the four year exclusive promotional agreement signed between Don King and Mike Tyson. Cayton has refused to sign, causing Tyson to file a lawsuit to break his contract with him. Cayton, in turn, has instituted a lawsuit against King for interfering with his contract with Tyson.